NSZERO

9 DON'T SHED A TEAR

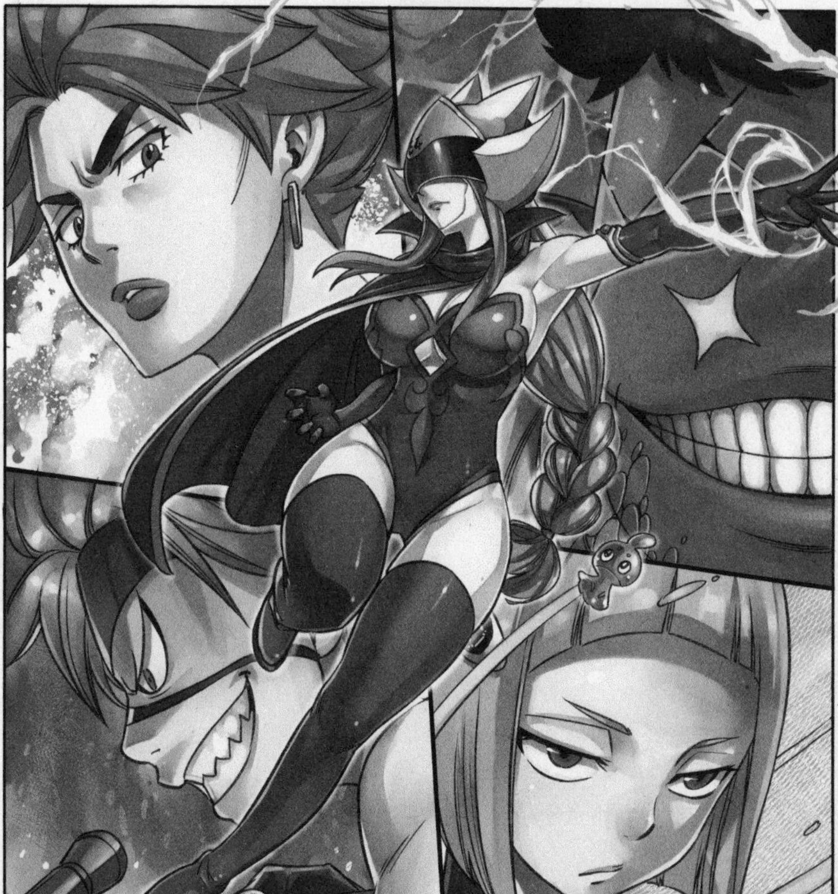

HIRO MASHIMA

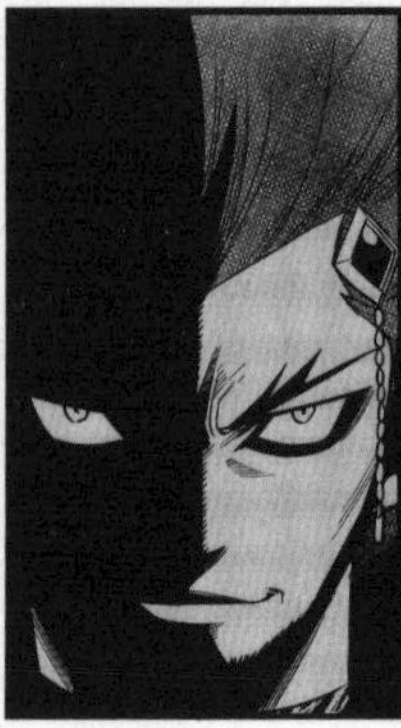

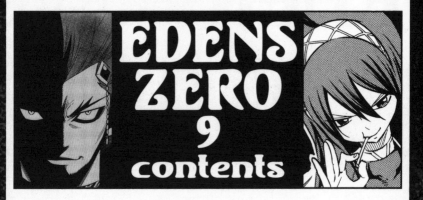

EDENS ZERO 9 contents

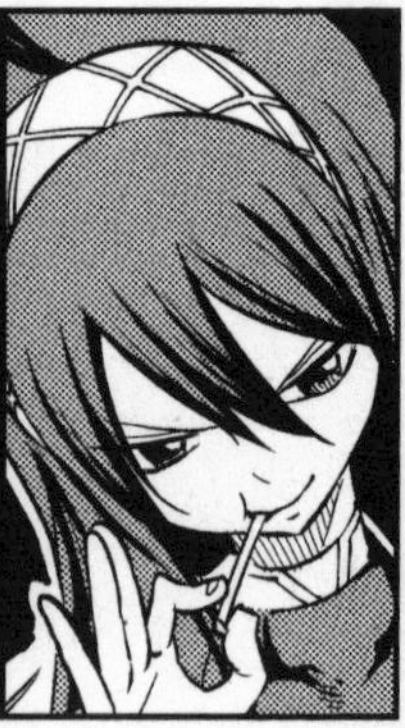

EDENS ZERO

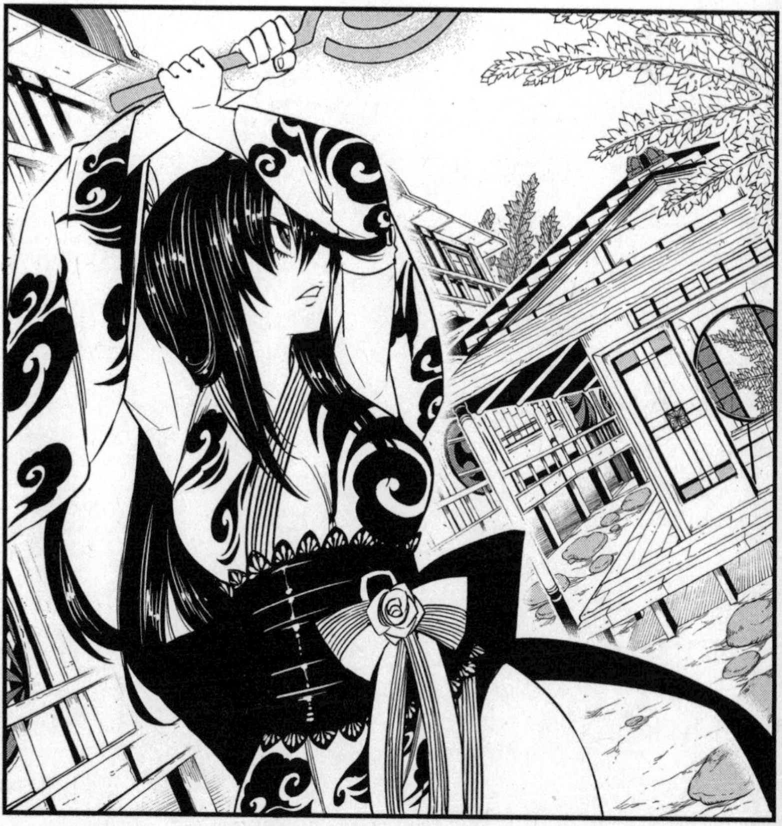

CHAPTER 69: REBECCA'S NIGHTMARE

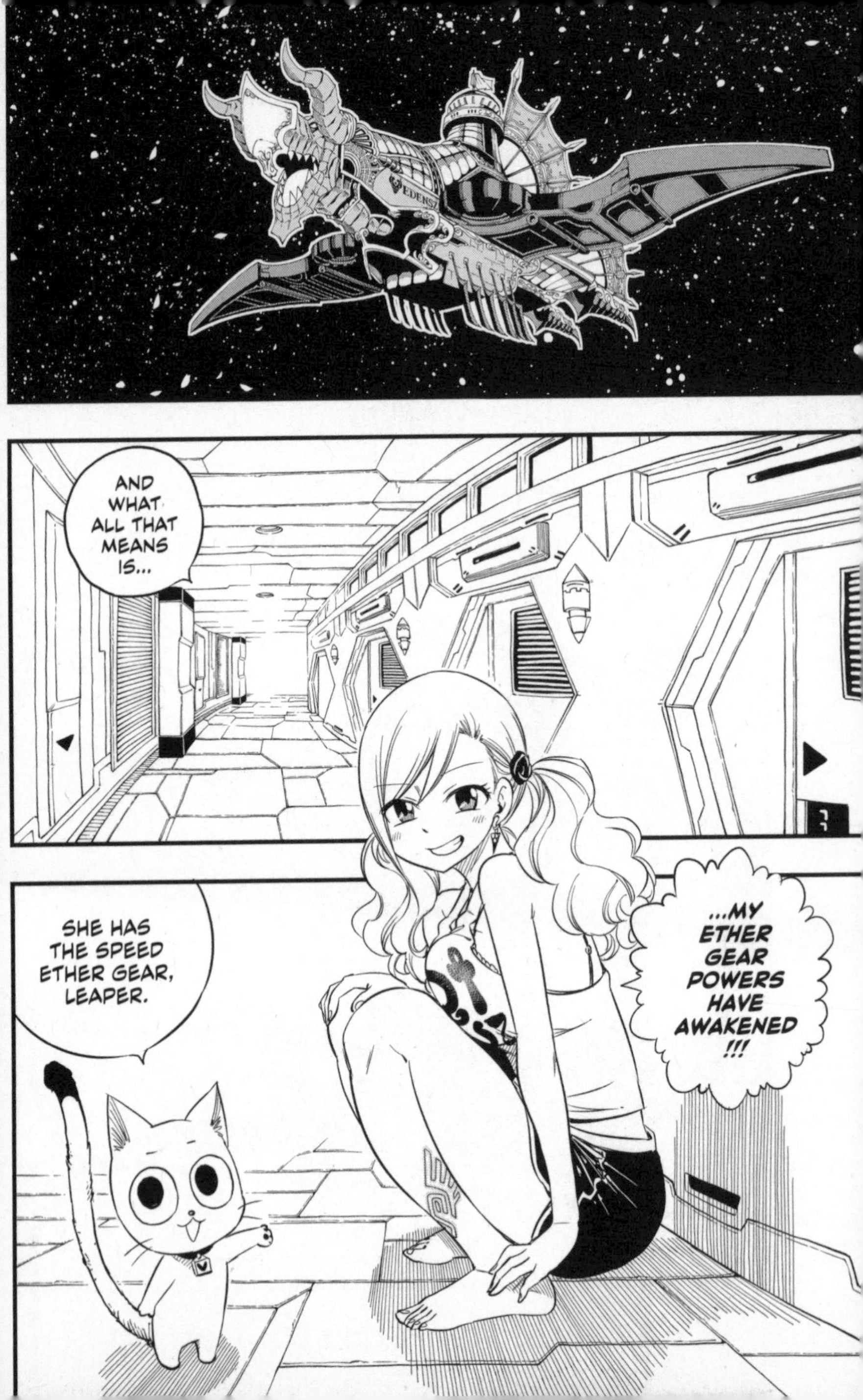
AND WHAT ALL THAT MEANS IS...
...MY ETHER GEAR POWERS HAVE AWAKENED!!!
SHE HAS THE SPEED ETHER GEAR, LEAPER.

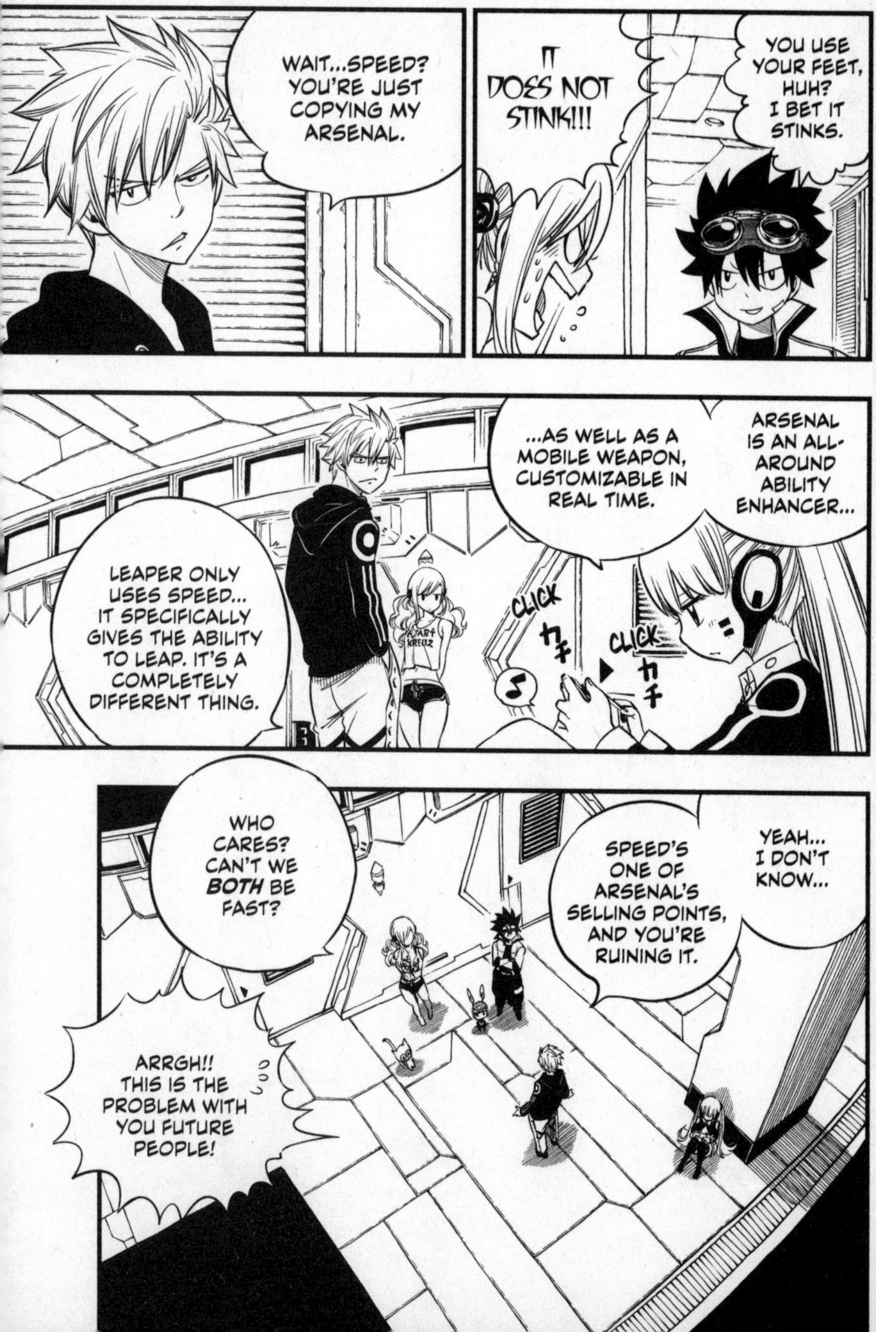
YOU USE YOUR FEET, HUH? I BET IT STINKS.
IT DOES NOT STINK!!!
WAIT...SPEED? YOU'RE JUST COPYING MY ARSENAL.
ARSENAL IS AN ALL-AROUND ABILITY ENHANCER...
...AS WELL AS A MOBILE WEAPON, CUSTOMIZABLE IN REAL TIME.
CLICK
カチ
CLICK
カチ
LEAPER ONLY USES SPEED... IT SPECIFICALLY GIVES THE ABILITY TO LEAP. IT'S A COMPLETELY DIFFERENT THING.
YEAH... I DON'T KNOW...
SPEED'S ONE OF ARSENAL'S SELLING POINTS, AND YOU'RE RUINING IT.
WHO CARES? CAN'T WE *BOTH* BE FAST?
ARRGH!! THIS IS THE PROBLEM WITH YOU FUTURE PEOPLE!

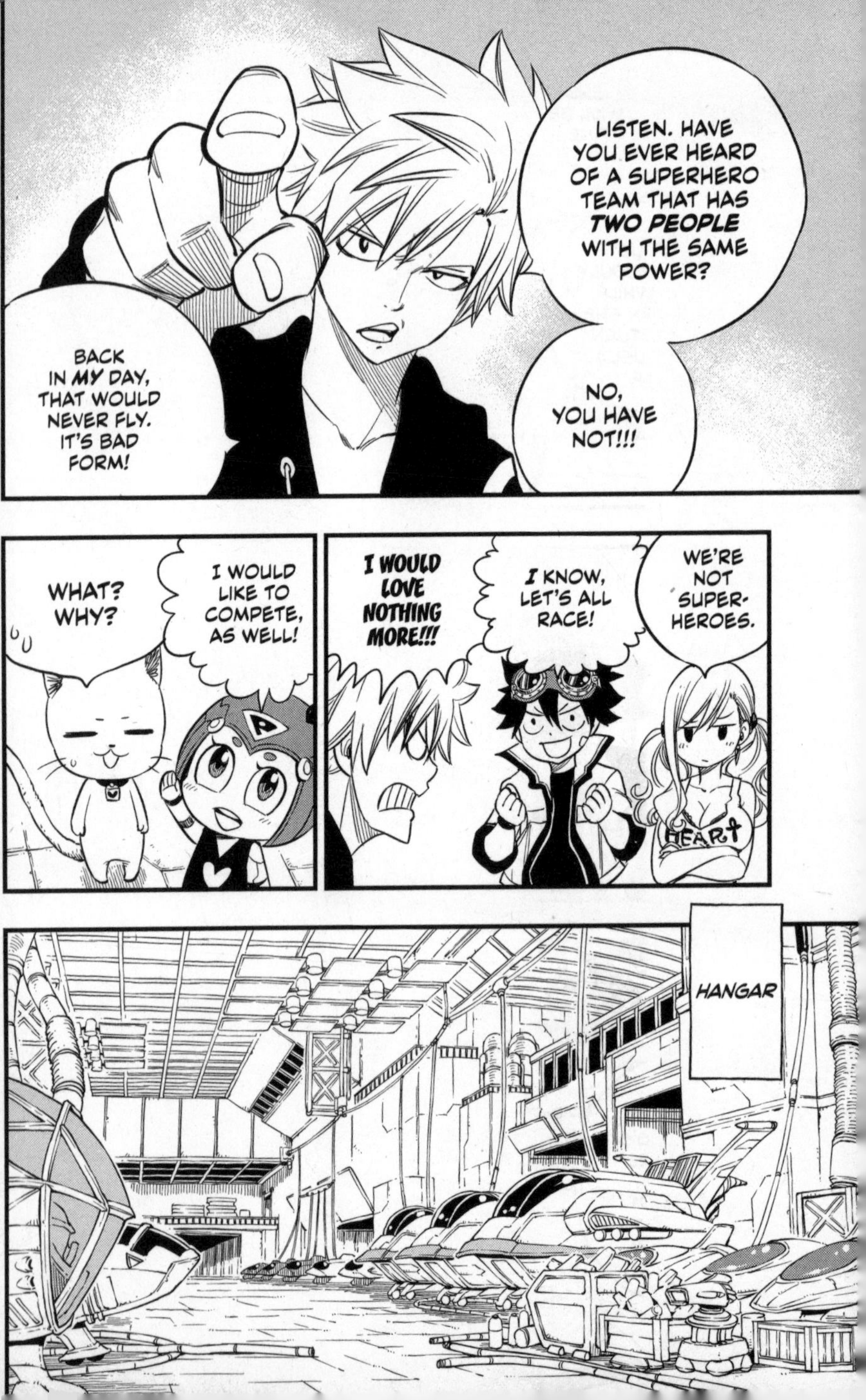
LISTEN. HAVE YOU EVER HEARD OF A SUPERHERO TEAM THAT HAS ***TWO PEOPLE*** WITH THE SAME POWER?
NO, YOU HAVE NOT!!!
BACK IN ***MY*** DAY, THAT WOULD NEVER FLY. IT'S BAD FORM!
WE'RE NOT SUPER-HEROES.
HEART
I KNOW, LET'S ALL RACE!
I WOULD LOVE NOTHING MORE!!!
I WOULD LIKE TO COMPETE, AS WELL!
WHAT? WHY?
HANGAR

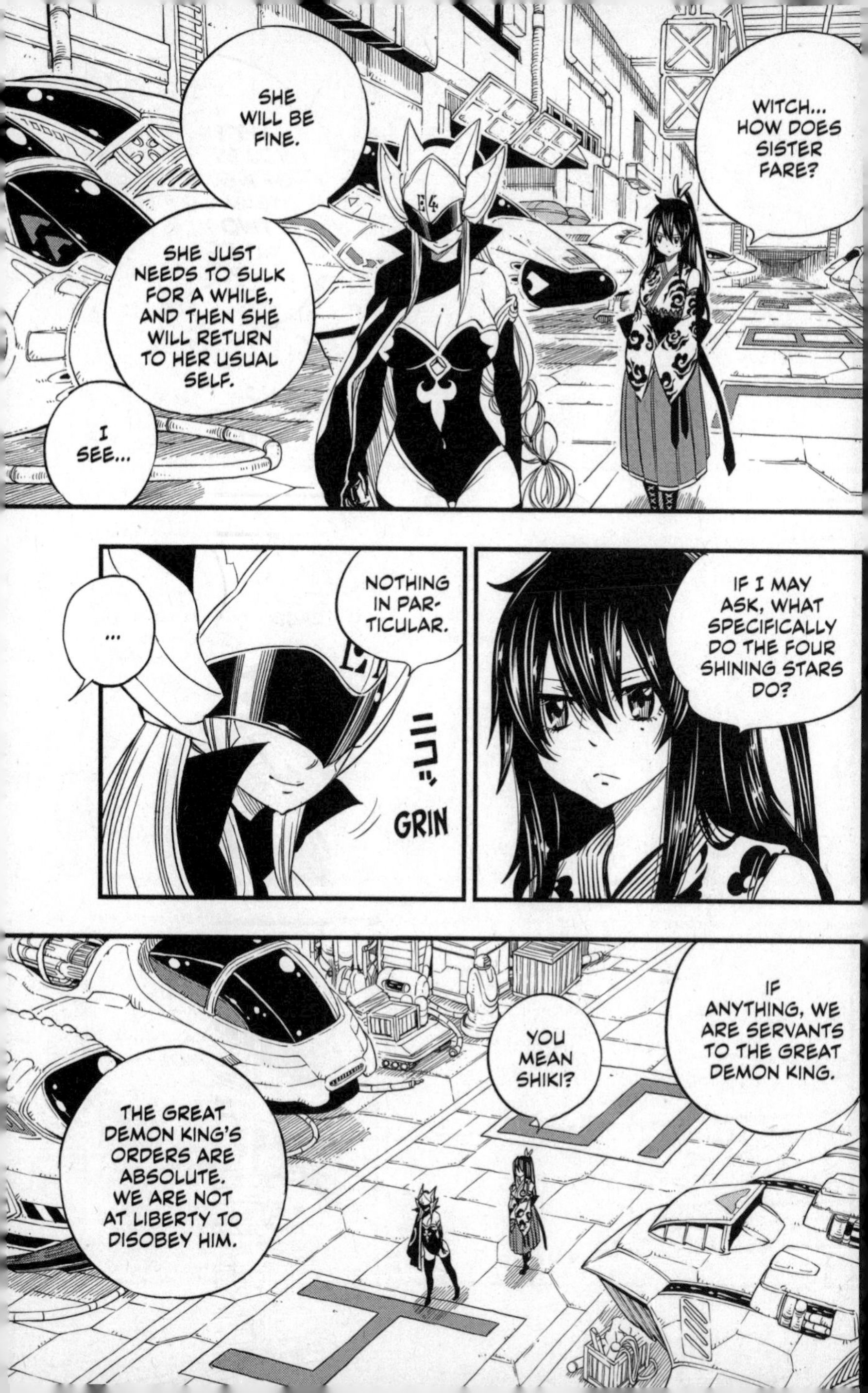
WITCH... HOW DOES SISTER FARE?
SHE WILL BE FINE.
SHE JUST NEEDS TO SULK FOR A WHILE, AND THEN SHE WILL RETURN TO HER USUAL SELF.
I SEE...
IF I MAY ASK, WHAT SPECIFICALLY DO THE FOUR SHINING STARS DO?
NOTHING IN PARTICULAR.
...
ニコッ
GRIN
IF ANYTHING, WE ARE SERVANTS TO THE GREAT DEMON KING.
YOU MEAN SHIKI?
THE GREAT DEMON KING'S ORDERS ARE ABSOLUTE. WE ARE NOT AT LIBERTY TO DISOBEY HIM.

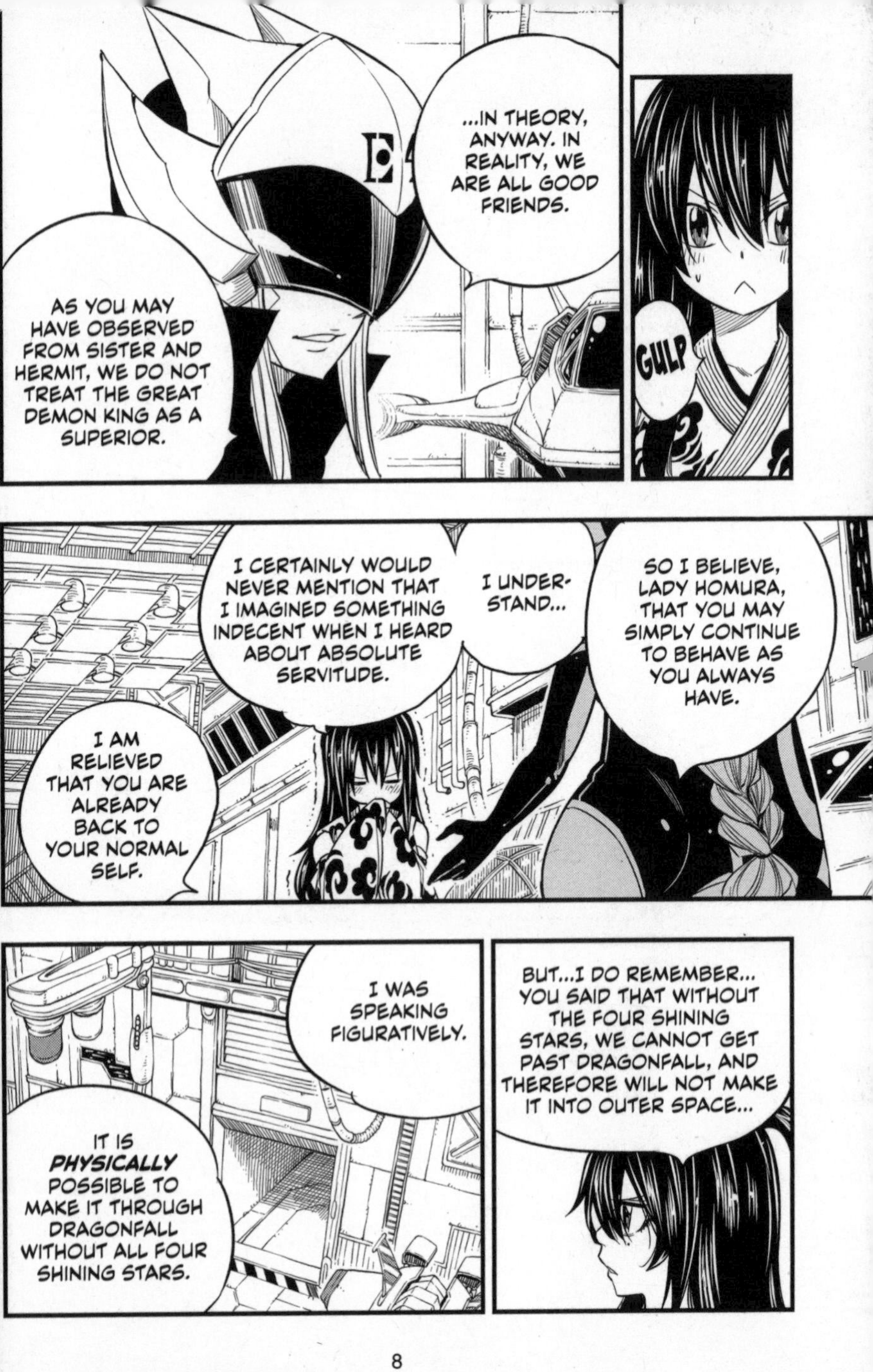
GULP
...IN THEORY, ANYWAY. IN REALITY, WE ARE ALL GOOD FRIENDS.
AS YOU MAY HAVE OBSERVED FROM SISTER AND HERMIT, WE DO NOT TREAT THE GREAT DEMON KING AS A SUPERIOR.
SO I BELIEVE, LADY HOMURA, THAT YOU MAY SIMPLY CONTINUE TO BEHAVE AS YOU ALWAYS HAVE.
I UNDER-STAND...
I CERTAINLY WOULD NEVER MENTION THAT I IMAGINED SOMETHING INDECENT WHEN I HEARD ABOUT ABSOLUTE SERVITUDE.
I AM RELIEVED THAT YOU ARE ALREADY BACK TO YOUR NORMAL SELF.
BUT...I DO REMEMBER... YOU SAID THAT WITHOUT THE FOUR SHINING STARS, WE CANNOT GET PAST DRAGONFALL, AND THEREFORE WILL NOT MAKE IT INTO OUTER SPACE...
I WAS SPEAKING FIGURATIVELY.
IT IS *PHYSICALLY* POSSIBLE TO MAKE IT THROUGH DRAGONFALL WITHOUT ALL FOUR SHINING STARS.

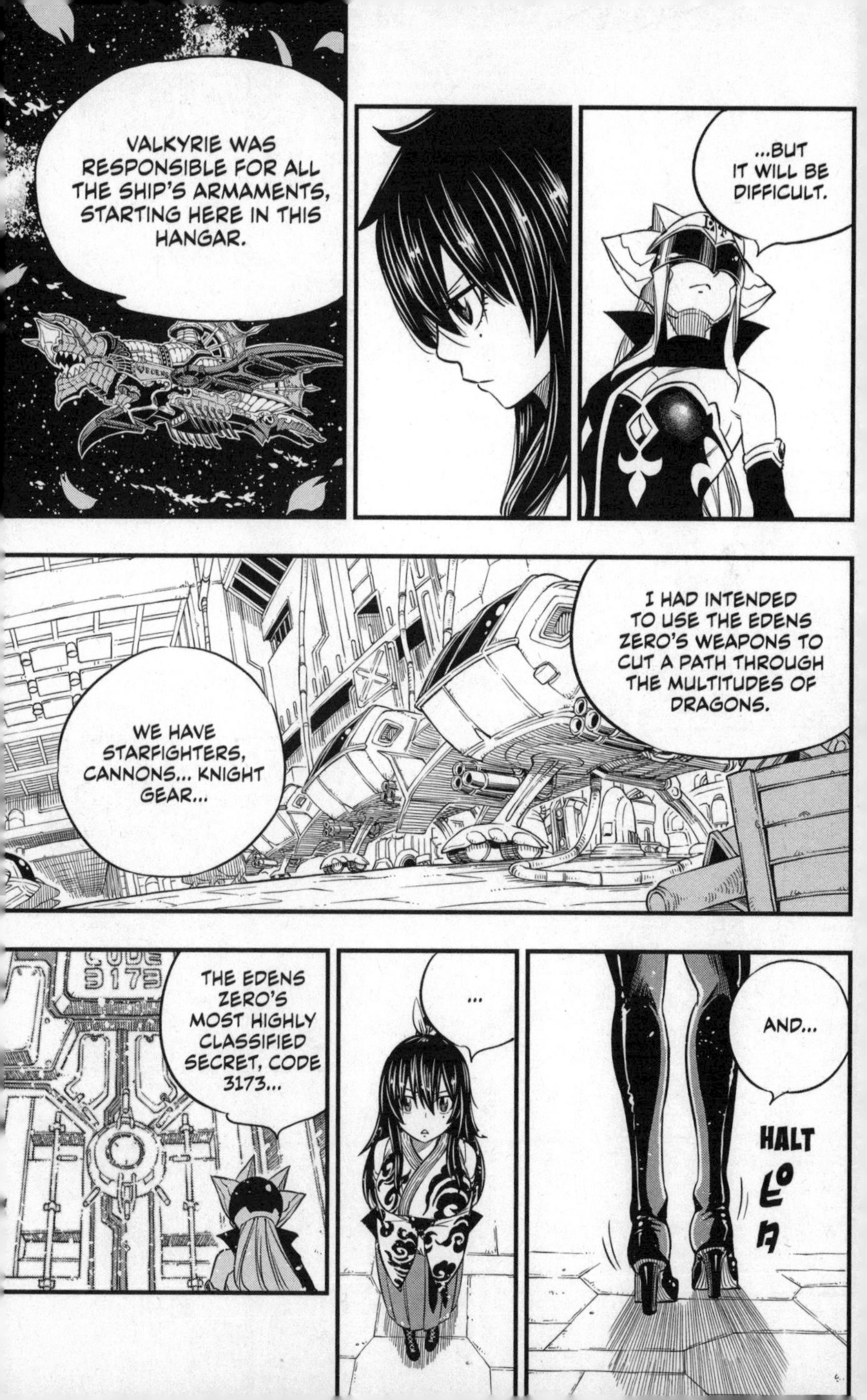
...BUT IT WILL BE DIFFICULT.
VALKYRIE WAS RESPONSIBLE FOR ALL THE SHIP'S ARMAMENTS, STARTING HERE IN THIS HANGAR.
I HAD INTENDED TO USE THE EDENS ZERO'S WEAPONS TO CUT A PATH THROUGH THE MULTITUDES OF DRAGONS.
WE HAVE STARFIGHTERS, CANNONS... KNIGHT GEAR...
AND...
HALT
ピタ
...
CODE 3173
THE EDENS ZERO'S MOST HIGHLY CLASSIFIED SECRET, CODE 3173...

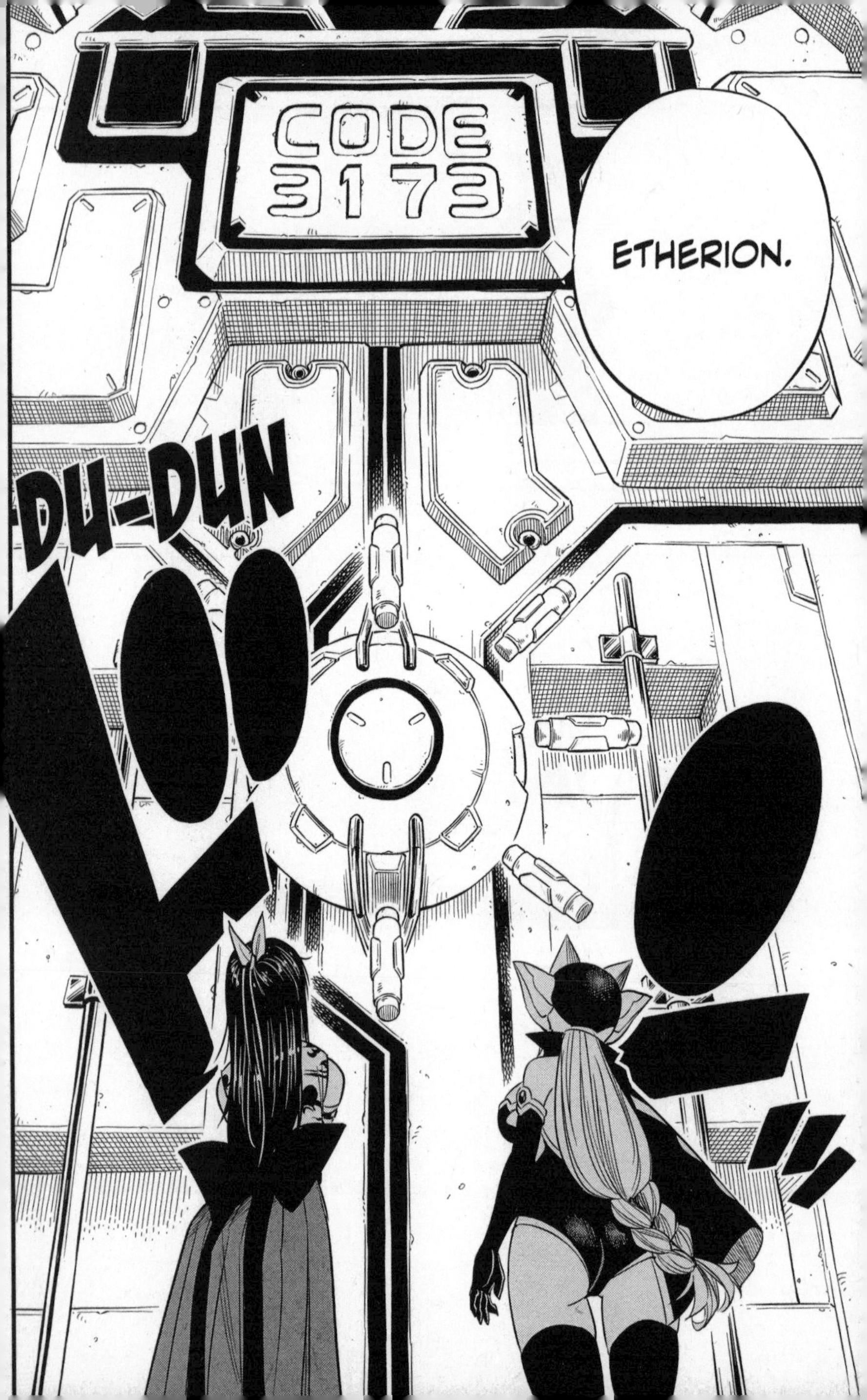
CODE 3173
ETHERION.
DU-DUN

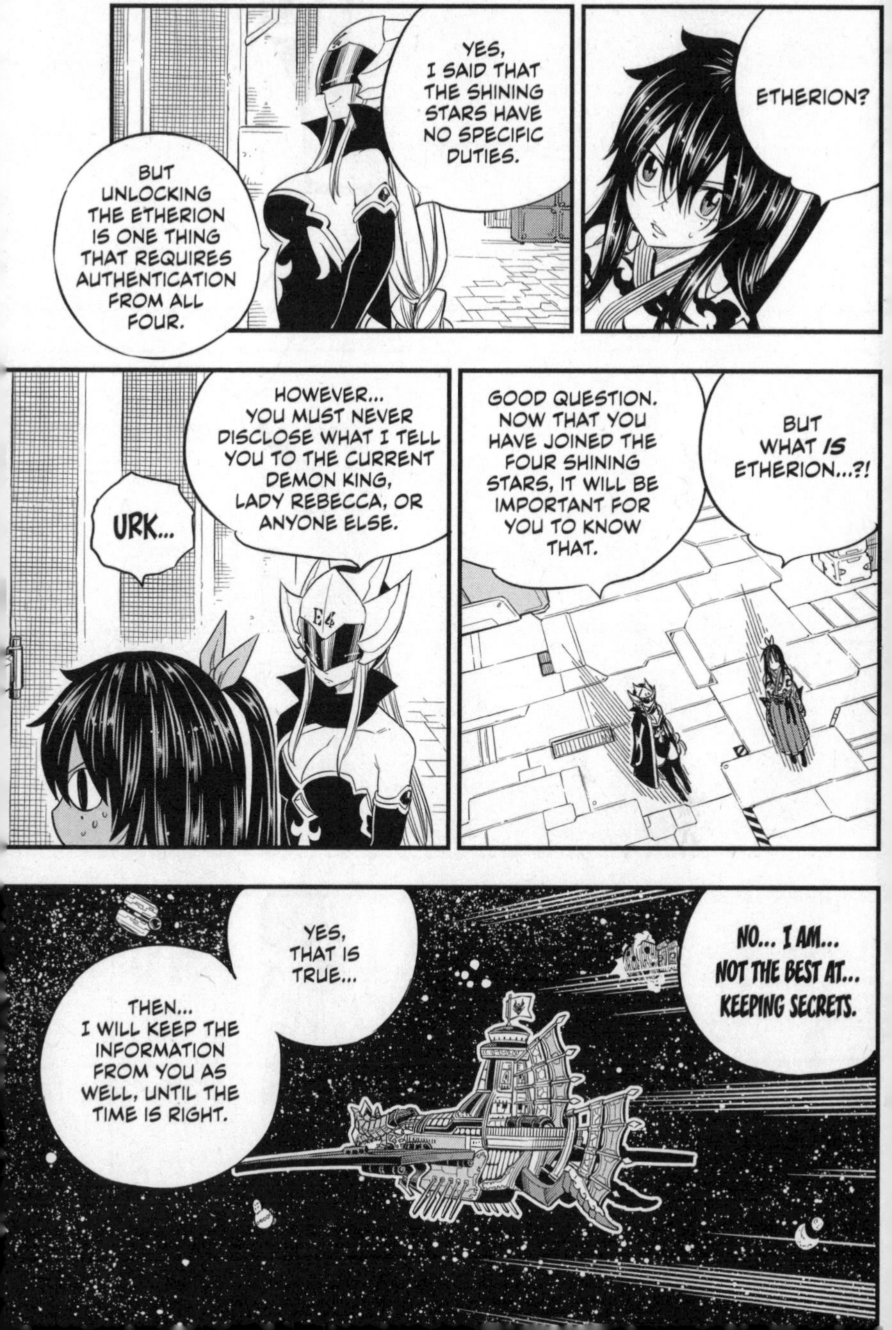
ETHERION?
YES, I SAID THAT THE SHINING STARS HAVE NO SPECIFIC DUTIES.
BUT UNLOCKING THE ETHERION IS ONE THING THAT REQUIRES AUTHENTICATION FROM ALL FOUR.
BUT WHAT *IS* ETHERION...?!
GOOD QUESTION. NOW THAT YOU HAVE JOINED THE FOUR SHINING STARS, IT WILL BE IMPORTANT FOR YOU TO KNOW THAT.
HOWEVER... YOU MUST NEVER DISCLOSE WHAT I TELL YOU TO THE CURRENT DEMON KING, LADY REBECCA, OR ANYONE ELSE.
URK...
NO... I AM... NOT THE BEST AT... KEEPING SECRETS.
YES, THAT IS TRUE...
THEN... I WILL KEEP THE INFORMATION FROM YOU AS WELL, UNTIL THE TIME IS RIGHT.

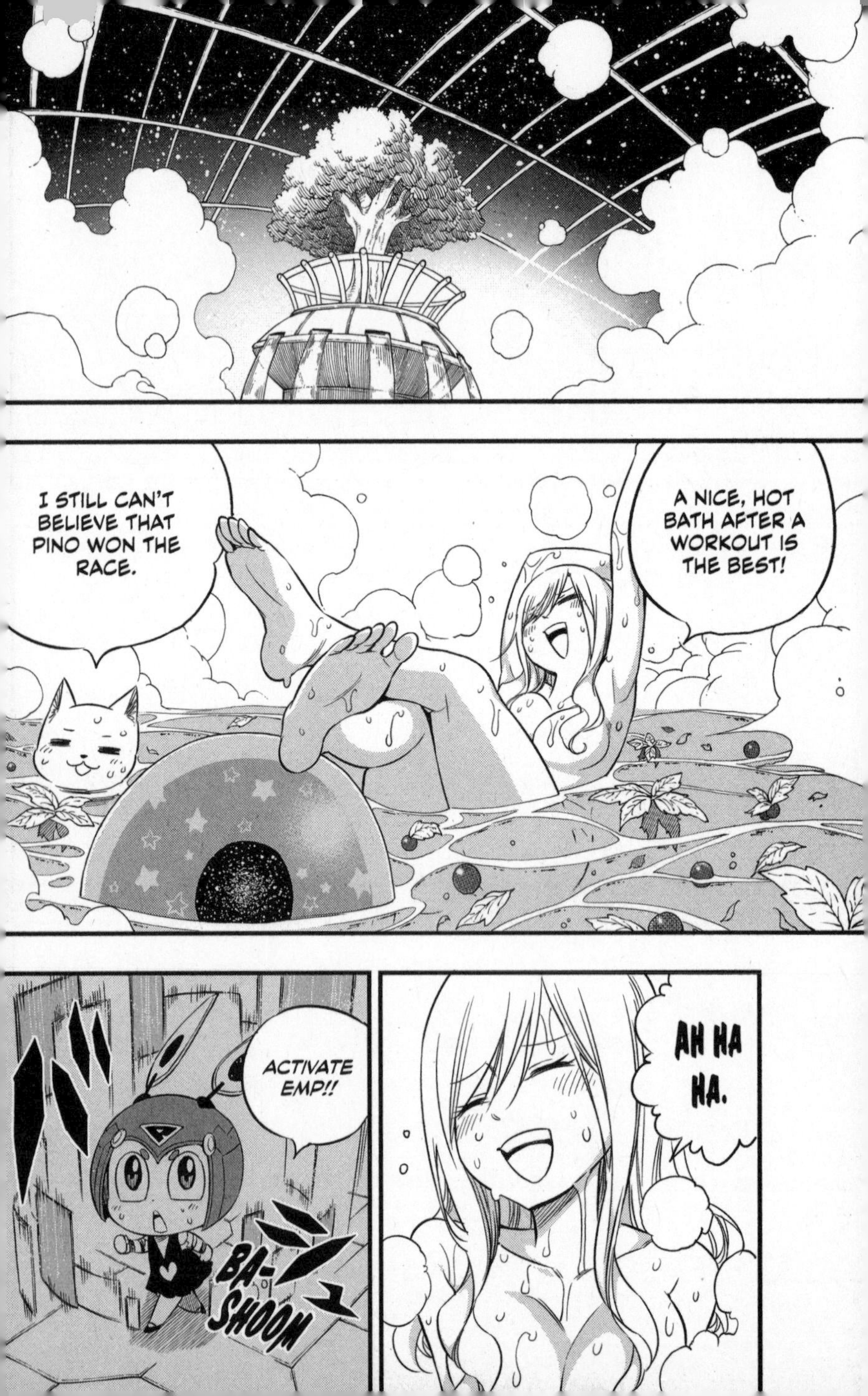
A NICE, HOT BATH AFTER A WORKOUT IS THE BEST!
I STILL CAN'T BELIEVE THAT PINO WON THE RACE.
AH HA HA.
ACTIVATE EMP!!
BA-SHOOM

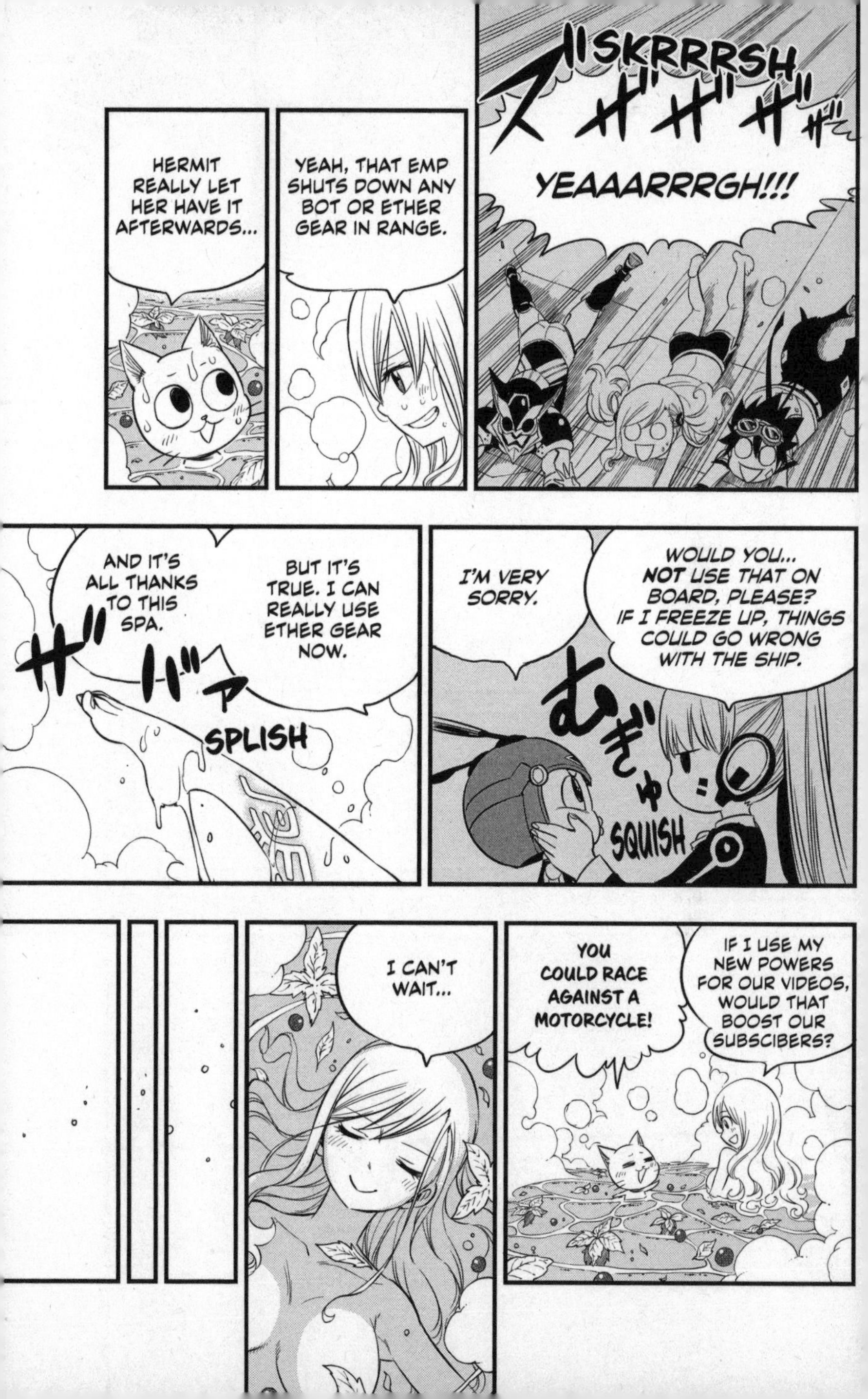
SKRRRSH
YEAAARRRGH!!!
YEAH, THAT EMP SHUTS DOWN ANY BOT OR ETHER GEAR IN RANGE.
HERMIT REALLY LET HER HAVE IT AFTERWARDS...
WOULD YOU... NOT USE THAT ON BOARD, PLEASE? IF I FREEZE UP, THINGS COULD GO WRONG WITH THE SHIP.
I'M VERY SORRY.
SQUISH
BUT IT'S TRUE. I CAN REALLY USE ETHER GEAR NOW.
AND IT'S ALL THANKS TO THIS SPA.
SPLISH
IF I USE MY NEW POWERS FOR OUR VIDEOS, WOULD THAT BOOST OUR SUBSCIBERS?
YOU COULD RACE AGAINST A MOTORCYCLE!
I CAN'T WAIT...

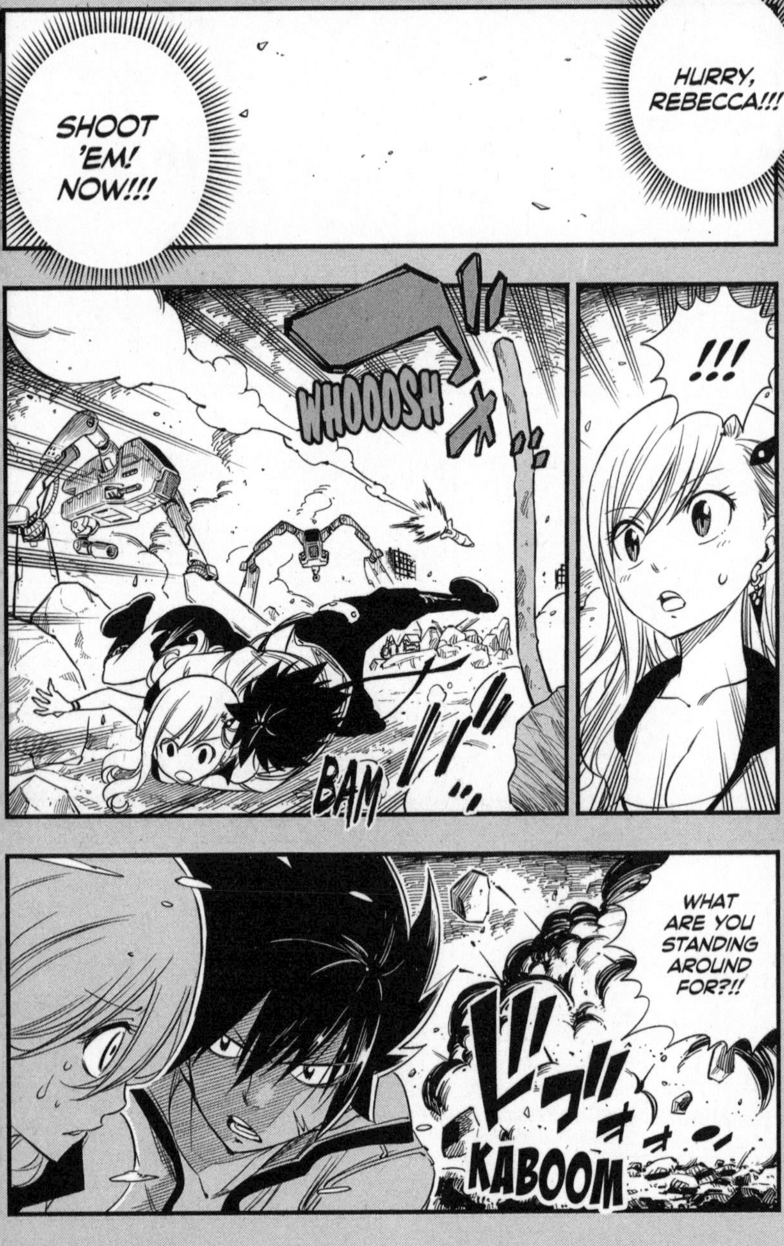
HURRY, REBECCA!!!
SHOOT 'EM! NOW!!!
!!!
WHOOOSH
BAM
WHAT ARE YOU STANDING AROUND FOR?!!
KABOOM

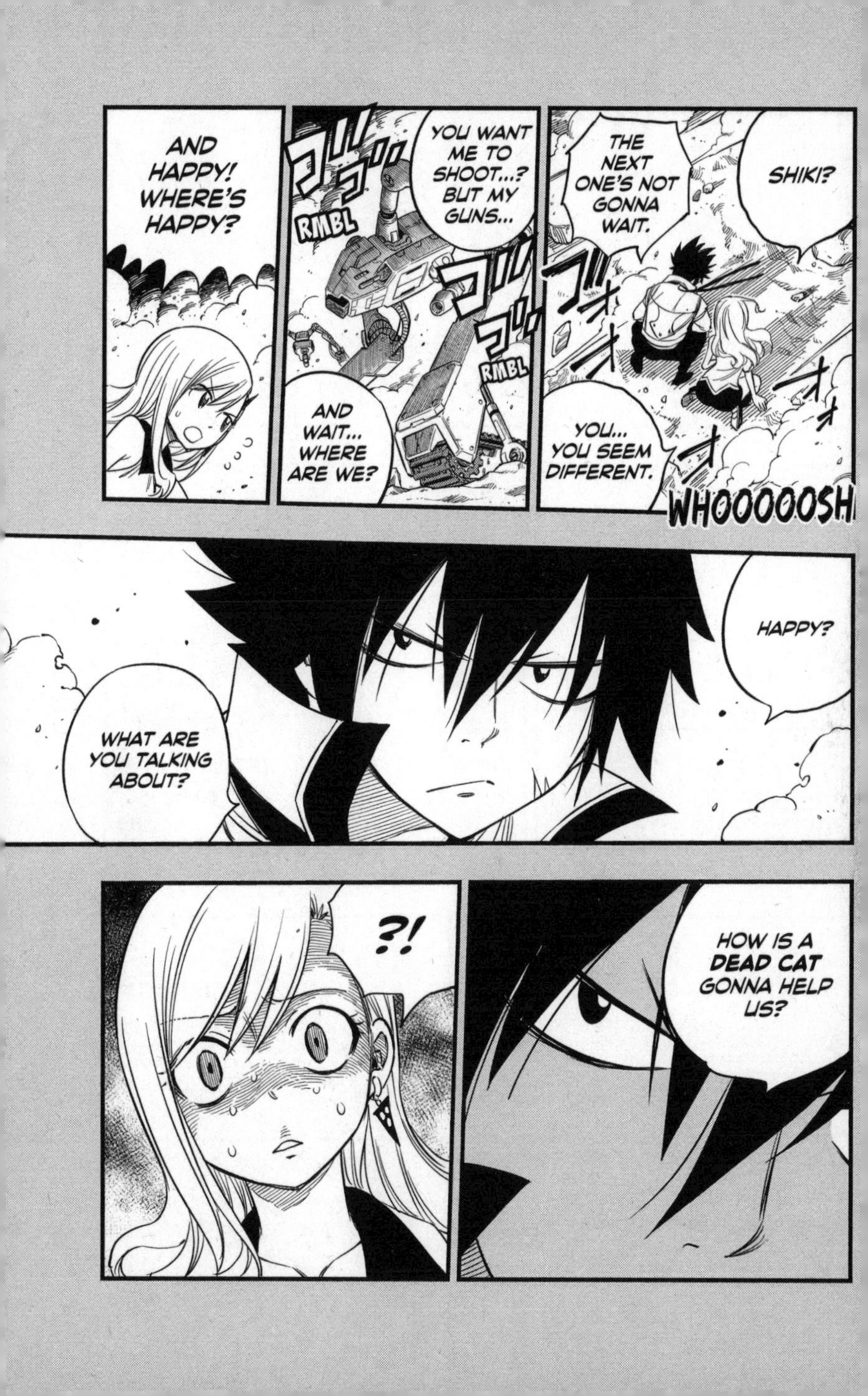
SHIKI?
THE NEXT ONE'S NOT GONNA WAIT.
YOU... YOU SEEM DIFFERENT.
WHOOOOOSH
YOU WANT ME TO SHOOT...? BUT MY GUNS...
RMBL
RMBL
AND WAIT... WHERE ARE WE?
AND HAPPY! WHERE'S HAPPY?
HAPPY?
WHAT ARE YOU TALKING ABOUT?
HOW IS A DEAD CAT GONNA HELP US?
?!

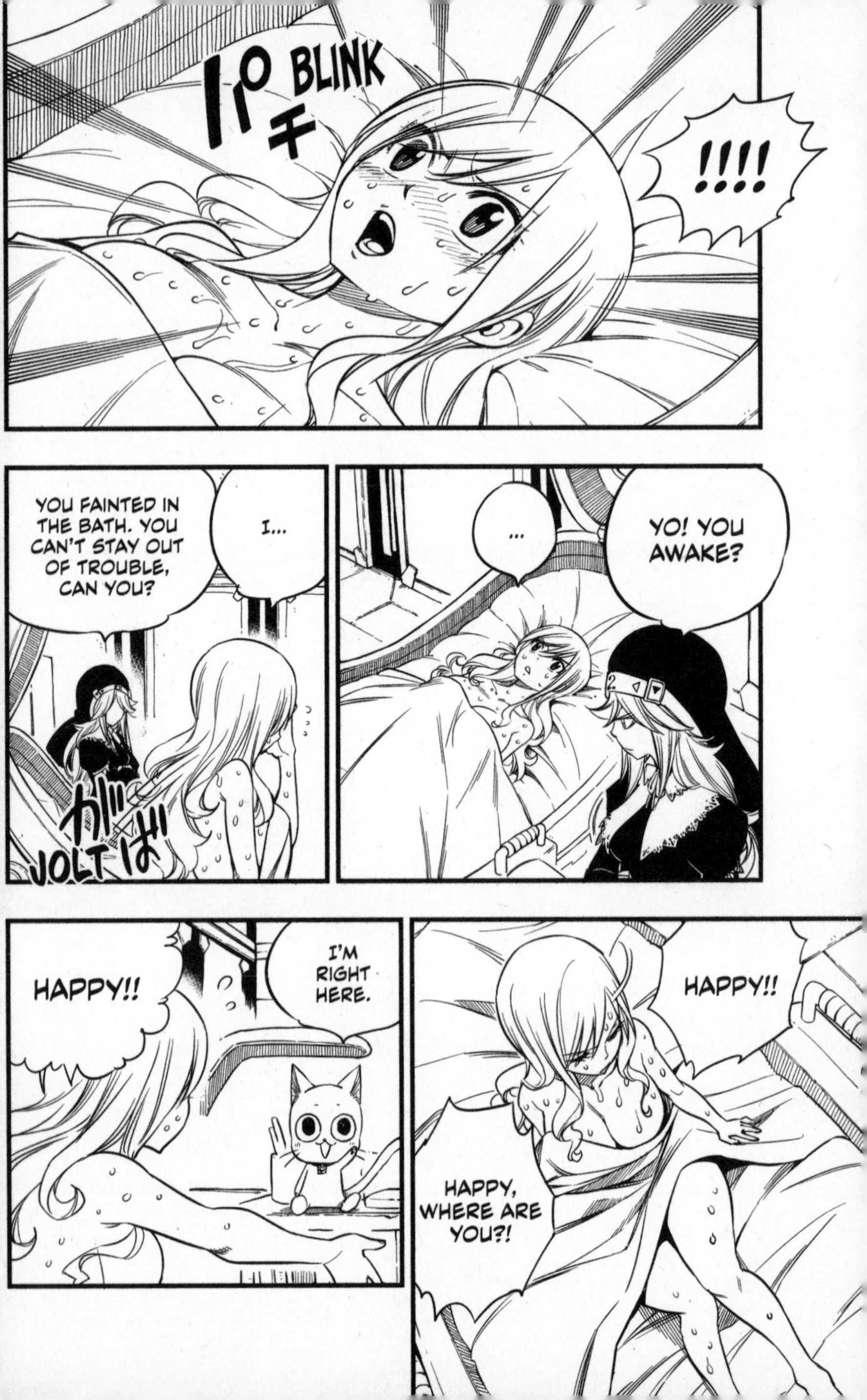

パチ BLINK
!!!!
YO! YOU AWAKE?
...
I...
YOU FAINTED IN THE BATH. YOU CAN'T STAY OUT OF TROUBLE, CAN YOU?
がばっ JOLT
HAPPY!!
HAPPY, WHERE ARE YOU?!
HAPPY!!
I'M RIGHT HERE.

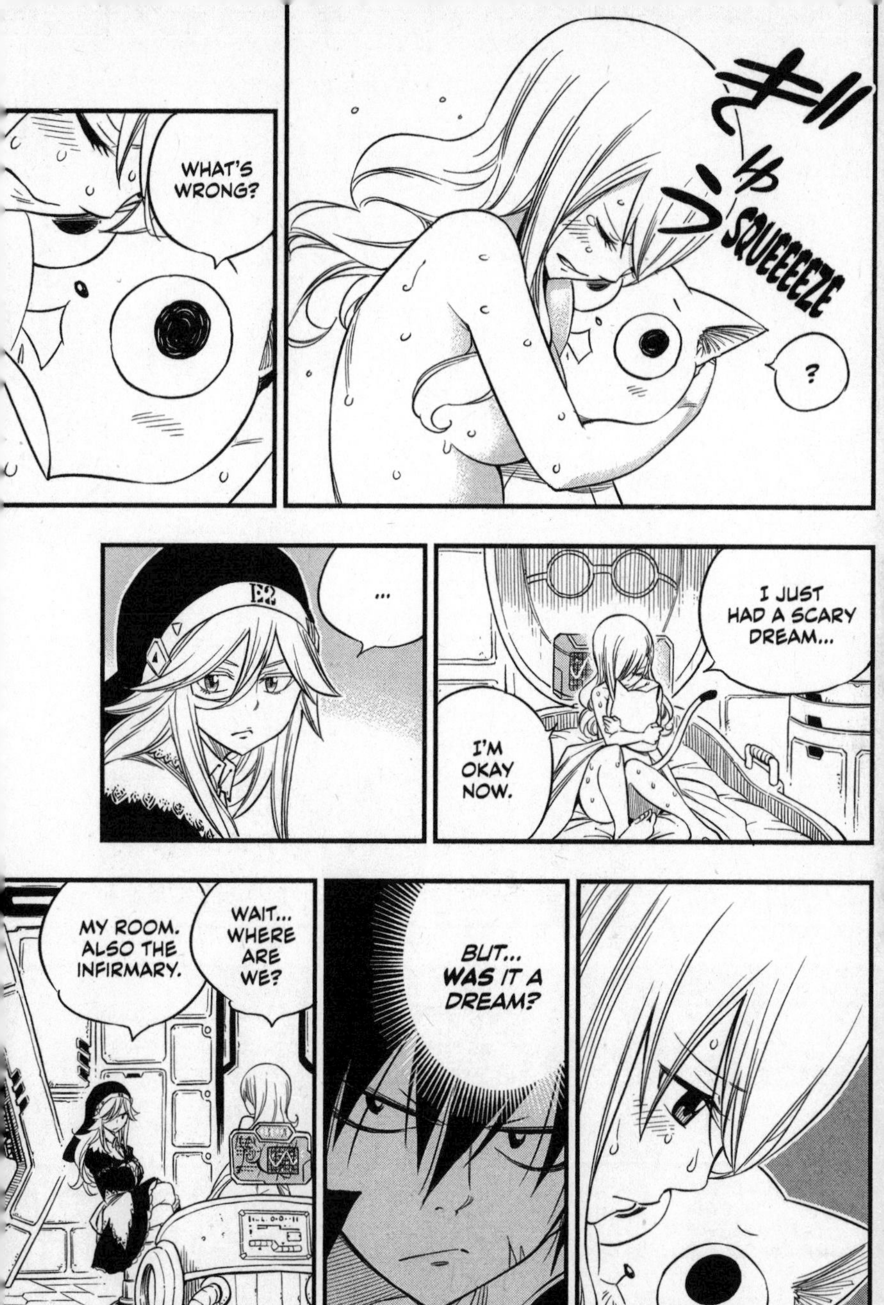
SQUEEEEZE
?
WHAT'S WRONG?
I JUST HAD A SCARY DREAM...
I'M OKAY NOW.
...
BUT... WAS IT A DREAM?
WAIT... WHERE ARE WE?
MY ROOM. ALSO THE INFIRMARY.

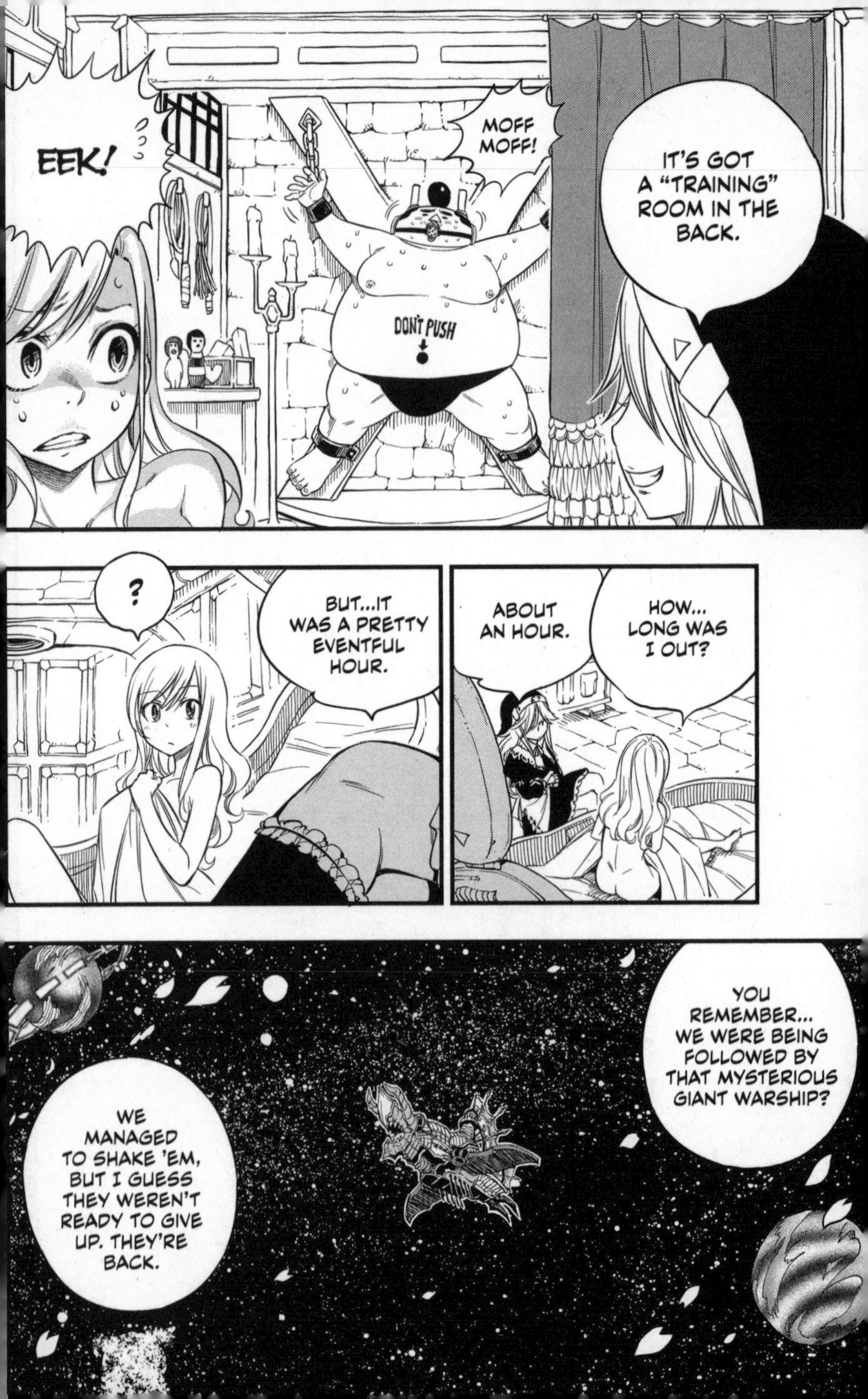
IT'S GOT A "TRAINING" ROOM IN THE BACK.
MOFF MOFF!
DON'T PUSH
EEK!
HOW... LONG WAS I OUT?
ABOUT AN HOUR.
BUT...IT WAS A PRETTY EVENTFUL HOUR.
?
YOU REMEMBER... WE WERE BEING FOLLOWED BY THAT MYSTERIOUS GIANT WARSHIP?
WE MANAGED TO SHAKE 'EM, BUT I GUESS THEY WEREN'T READY TO GIVE UP. THEY'RE BACK.

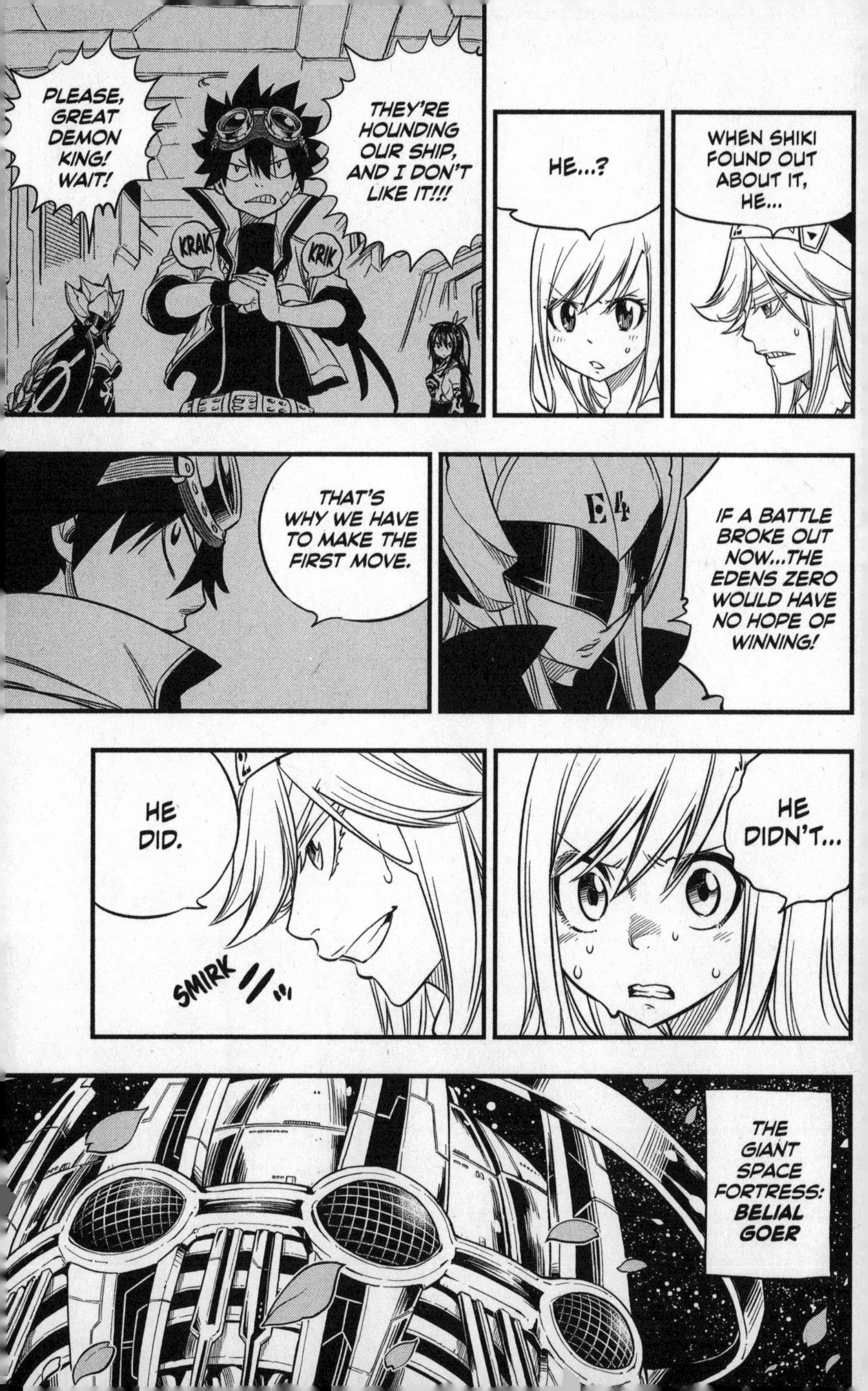
WHEN SHIKI FOUND OUT ABOUT IT, HE...
HE...?
THEY'RE HOUNDING OUR SHIP, AND I DON'T LIKE IT!!!
PLEASE, GREAT DEMON KING! WAIT!
KRIK
KRAK
IF A BATTLE BROKE OUT NOW...THE EDENS ZERO WOULD HAVE NO HOPE OF WINNING!
E4
THAT'S WHY WE HAVE TO MAKE THE FIRST MOVE.
HE DIDN'T...
HE DID.
SMIRK
THE GIANT SPACE FORTRESS: BELIAL GOER

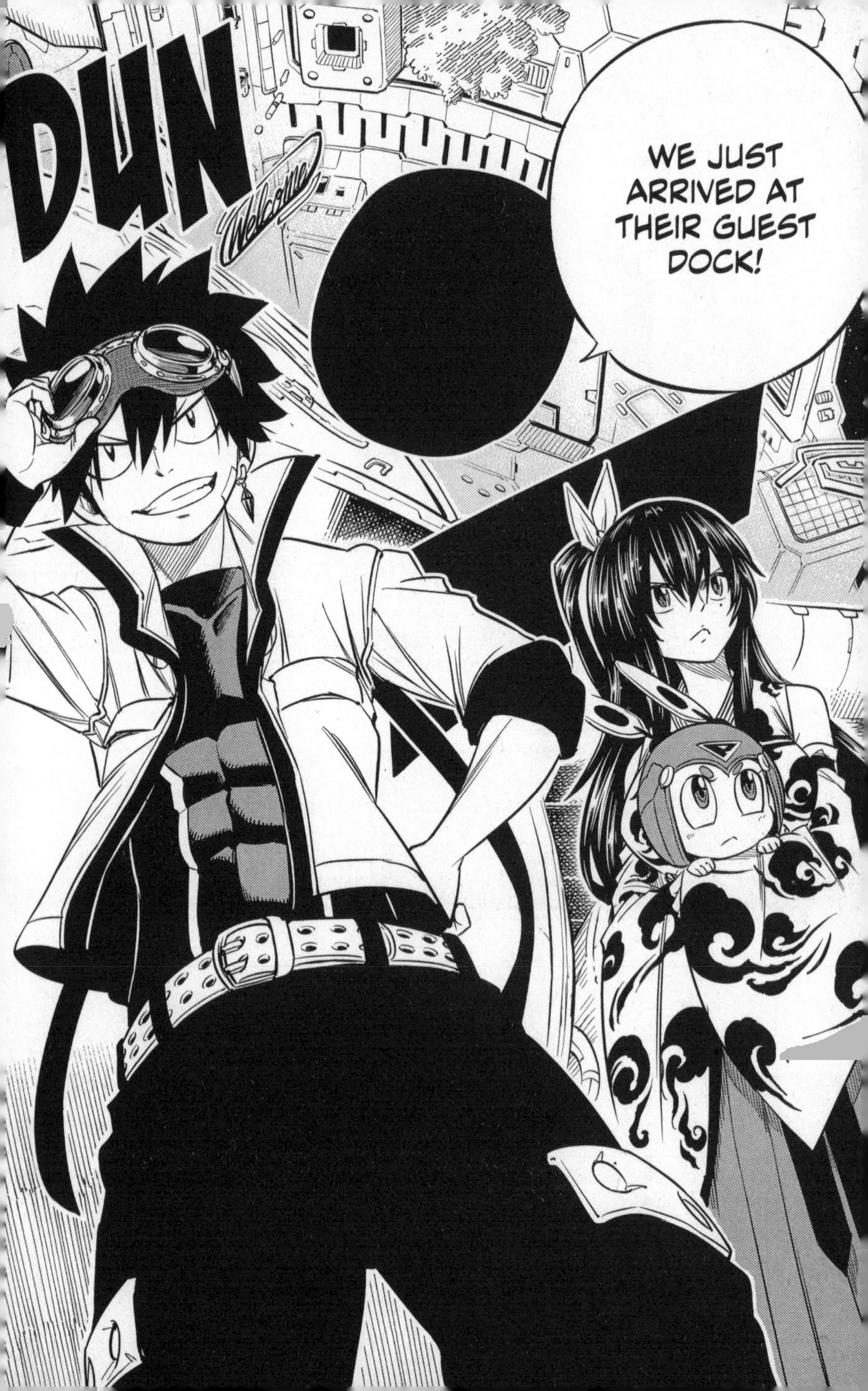
WE JUST ARRIVED AT THEIR GUEST DOCK!
Welcome
DUN

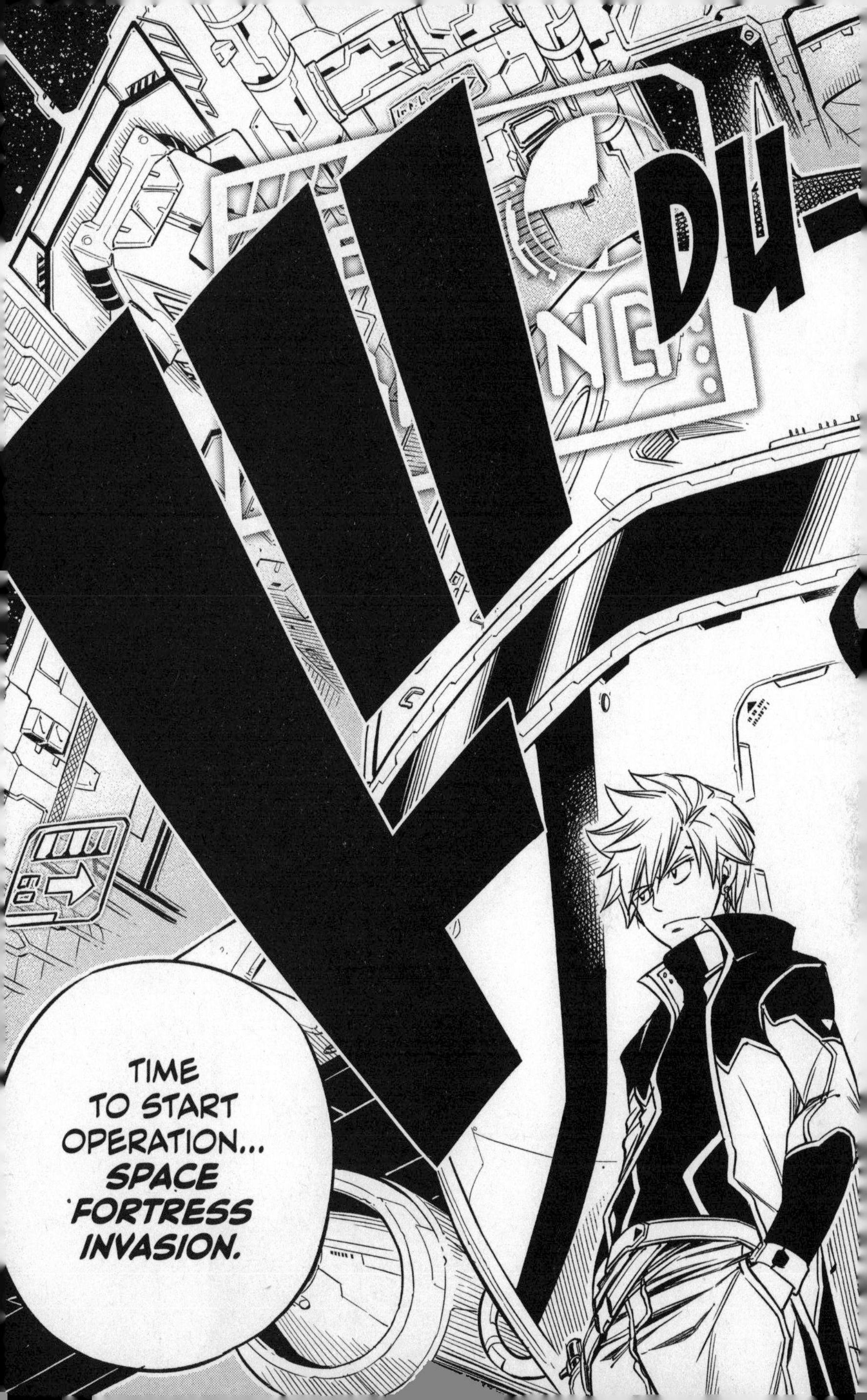
DU-
TIME TO START OPERATION... SPACE FORTRESS INVASION.

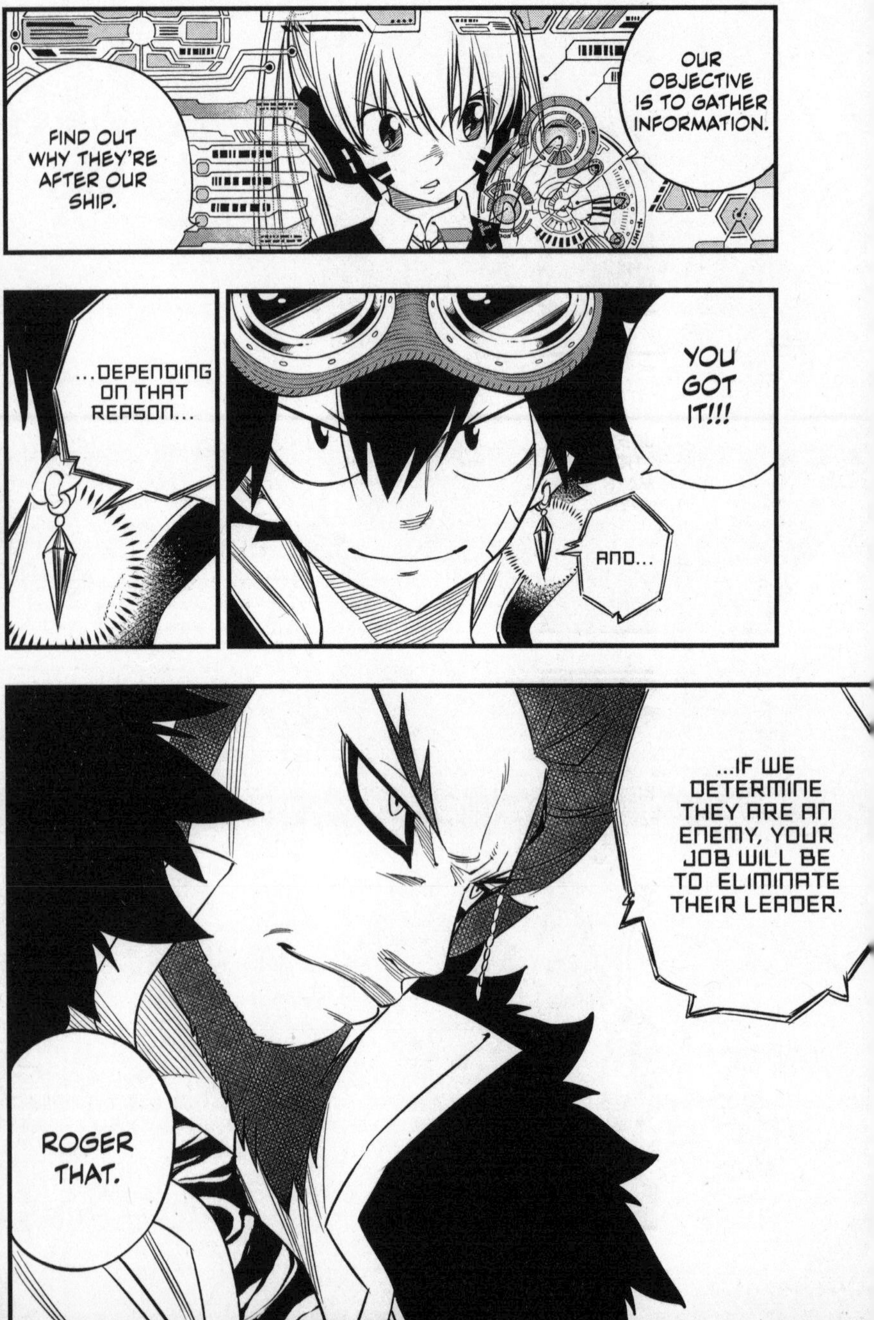
OUR OBJECTIVE IS TO GATHER INFORMATION.
FIND OUT WHY THEY'RE AFTER OUR SHIP.
YOU GOT IT!!!
AND...
...DEPENDING ON THAT REASON...
...IF WE DETERMINE THEY ARE AN ENEMY, YOUR JOB WILL BE TO ELIMINATE THEIR LEADER.
ROGER THAT.

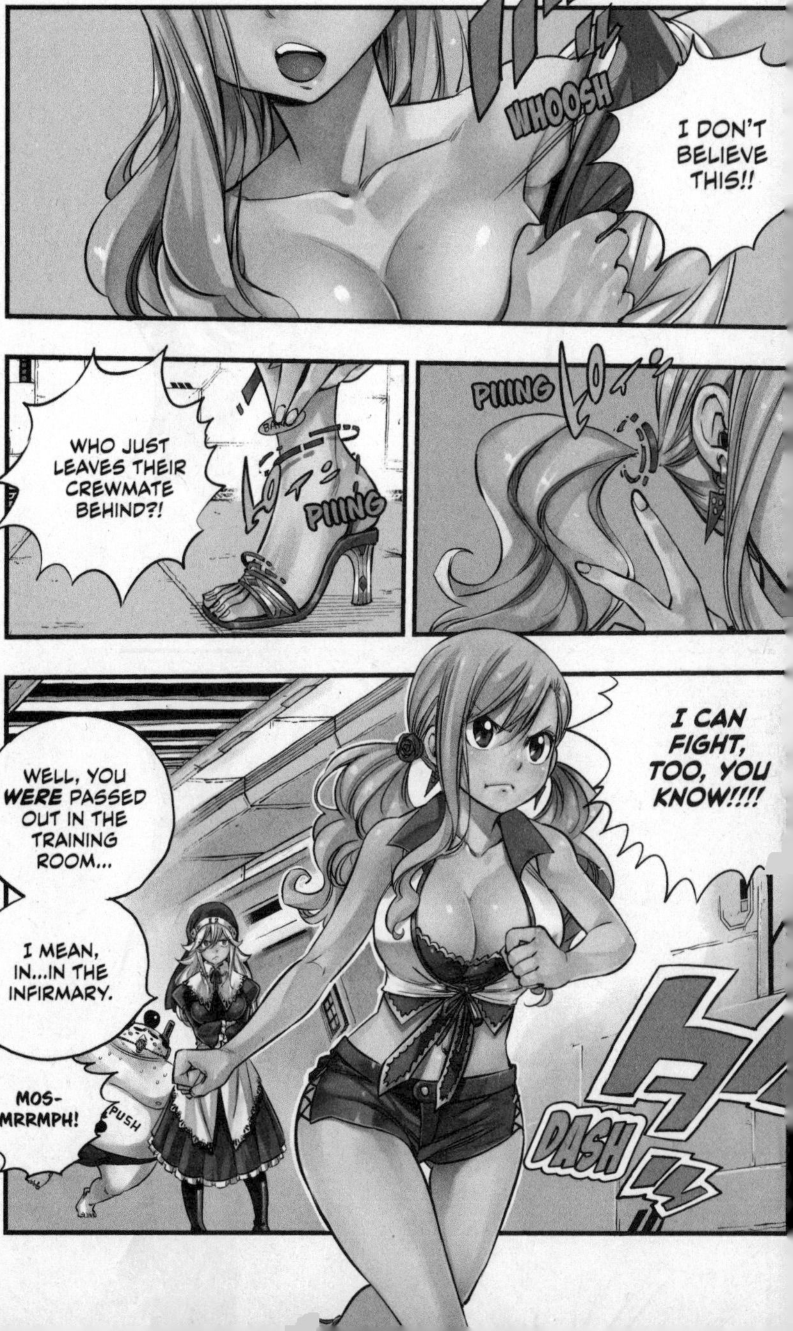
WHOOSH
I DON'T BELIEVE THIS!!
PIIING
WHO JUST LEAVES THEIR CREWMATE BEHIND?!
PIIING
I CAN FIGHT, TOO, YOU KNOW!!!!
DASH
WELL, YOU *WERE* PASSED OUT IN THE TRAINING ROOM...
I MEAN, IN...IN THE INFIRMARY.
PUSH
MOS-MRRMPH!

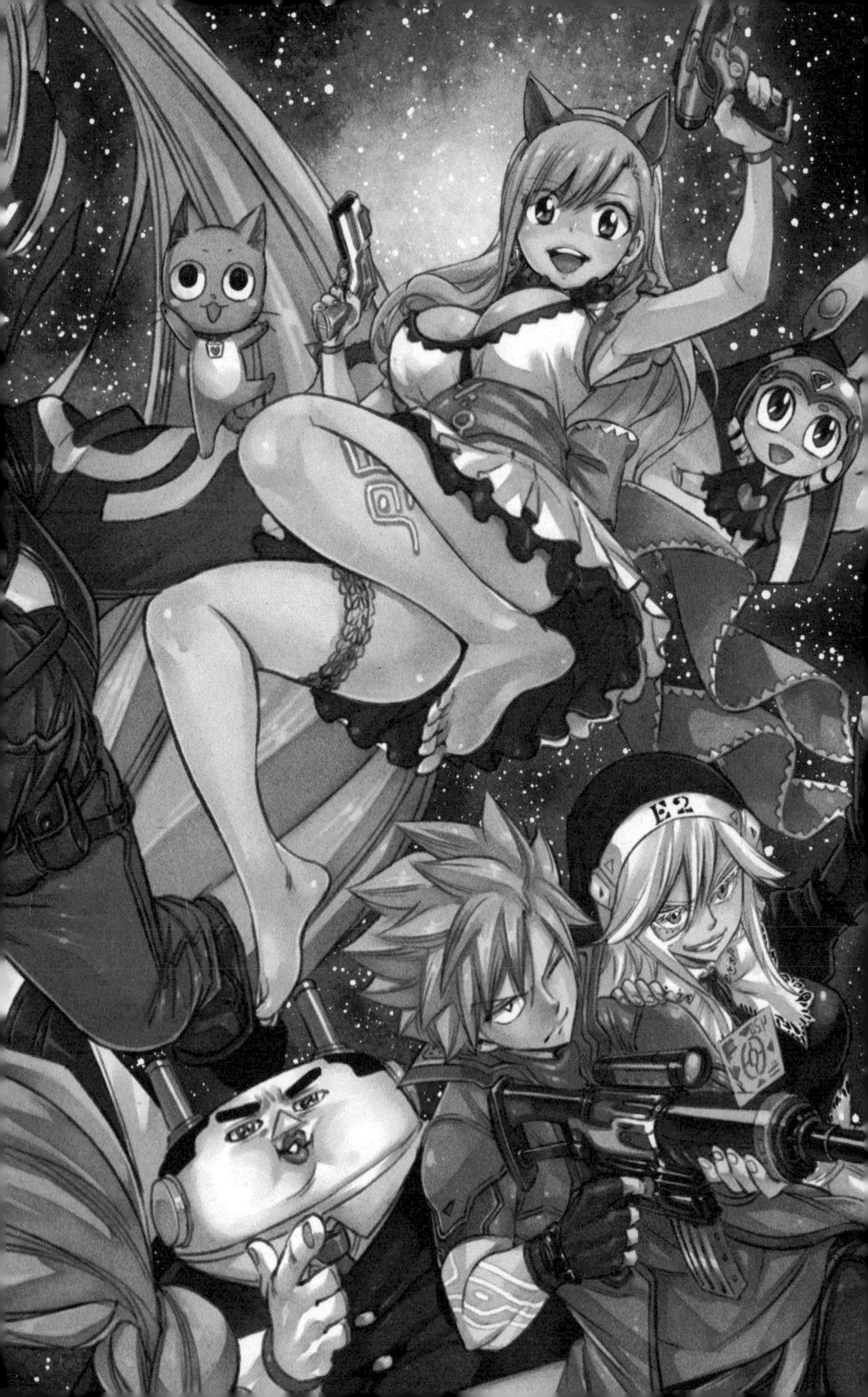
E2

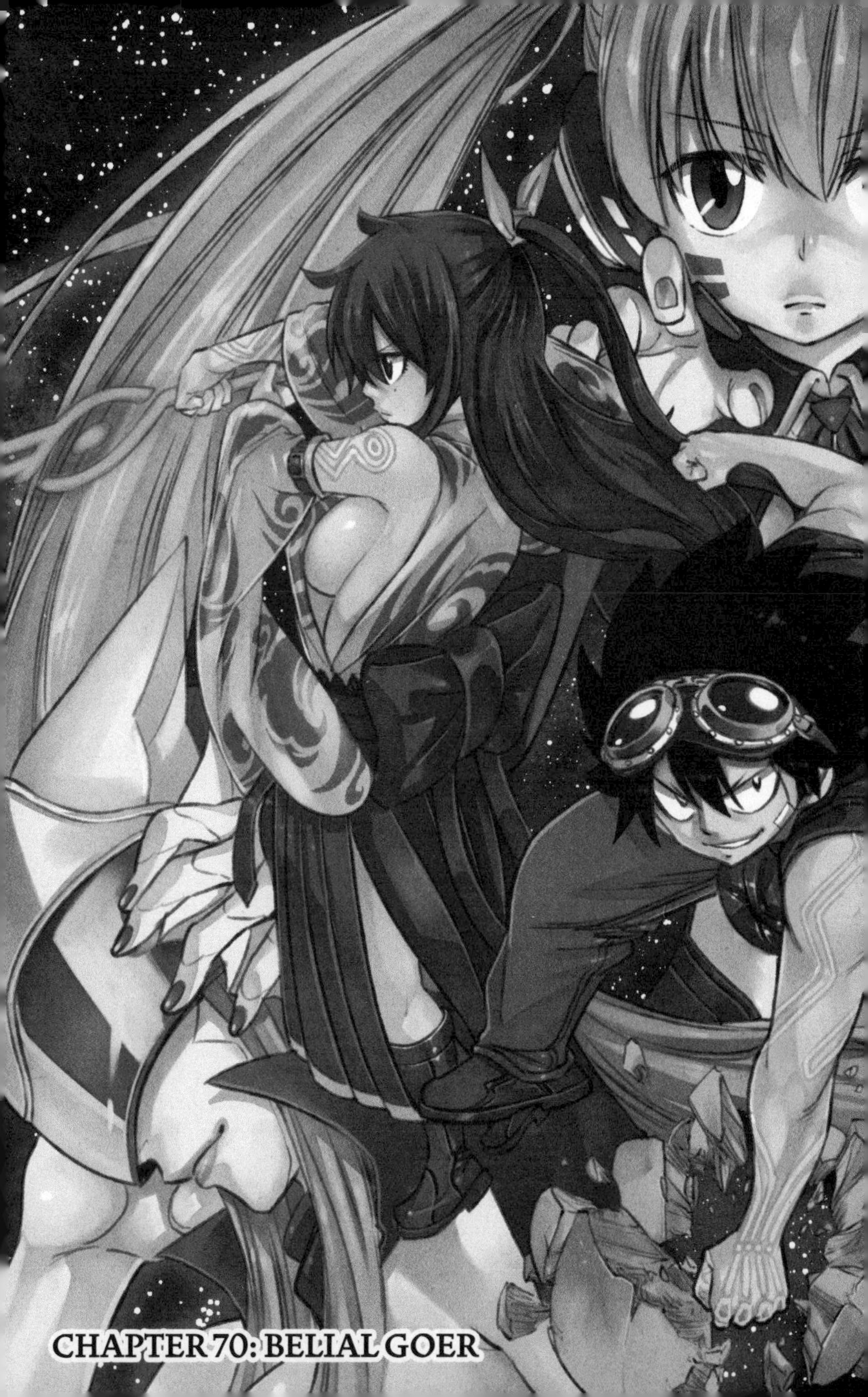
CHAPTER 70: BELIAL GOER

EDENSZERO

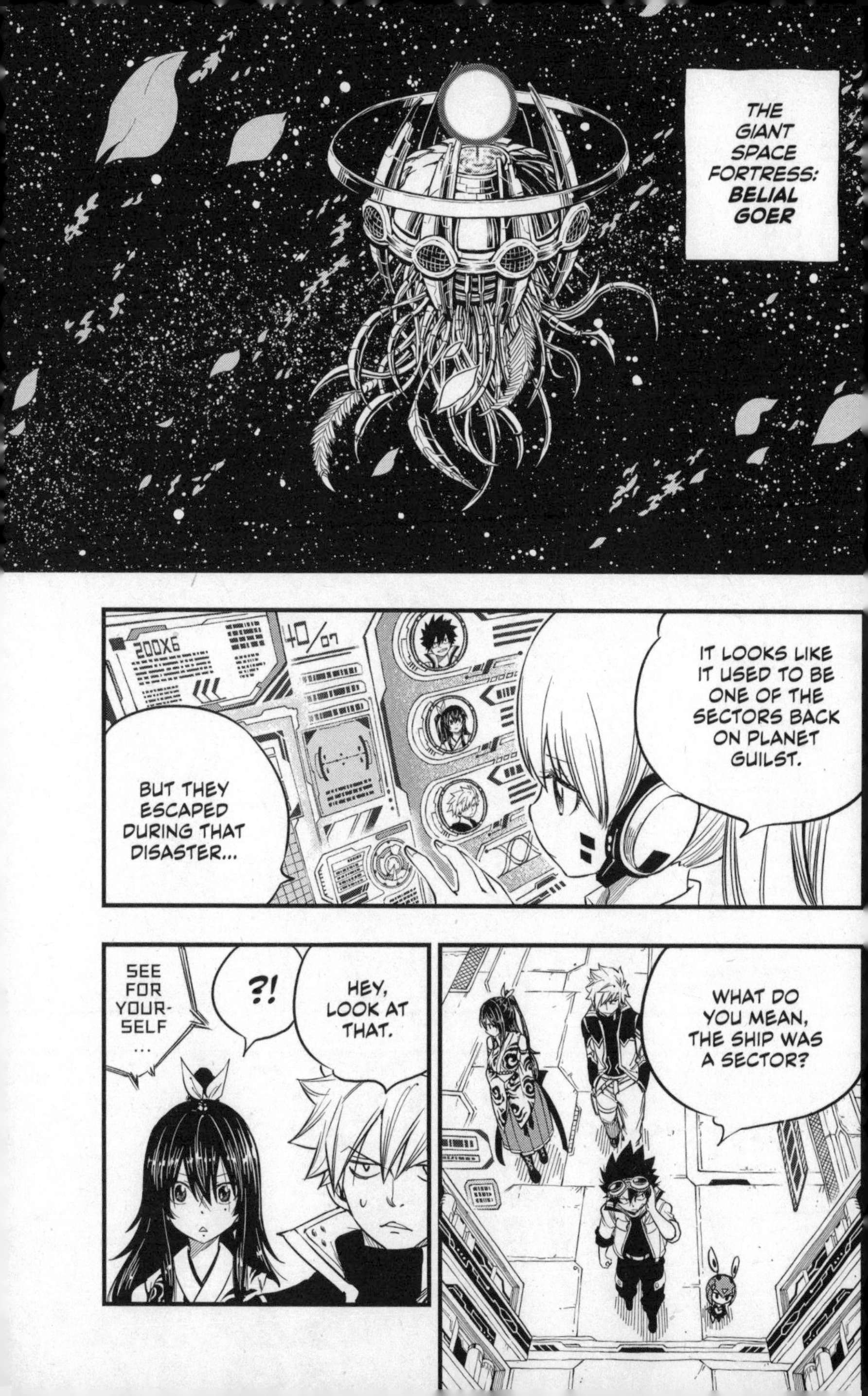
THE GIANT SPACE FORTRESS: BELIAL GOER
IT LOOKS LIKE IT USED TO BE ONE OF THE SECTORS BACK ON PLANET GUILST.
BUT THEY ESCAPED DURING THAT DISASTER...
WHAT DO YOU MEAN, THE SHIP WAS A SECTOR?
HEY, LOOK AT THAT.
?!
SEE FOR YOUR-SELF...

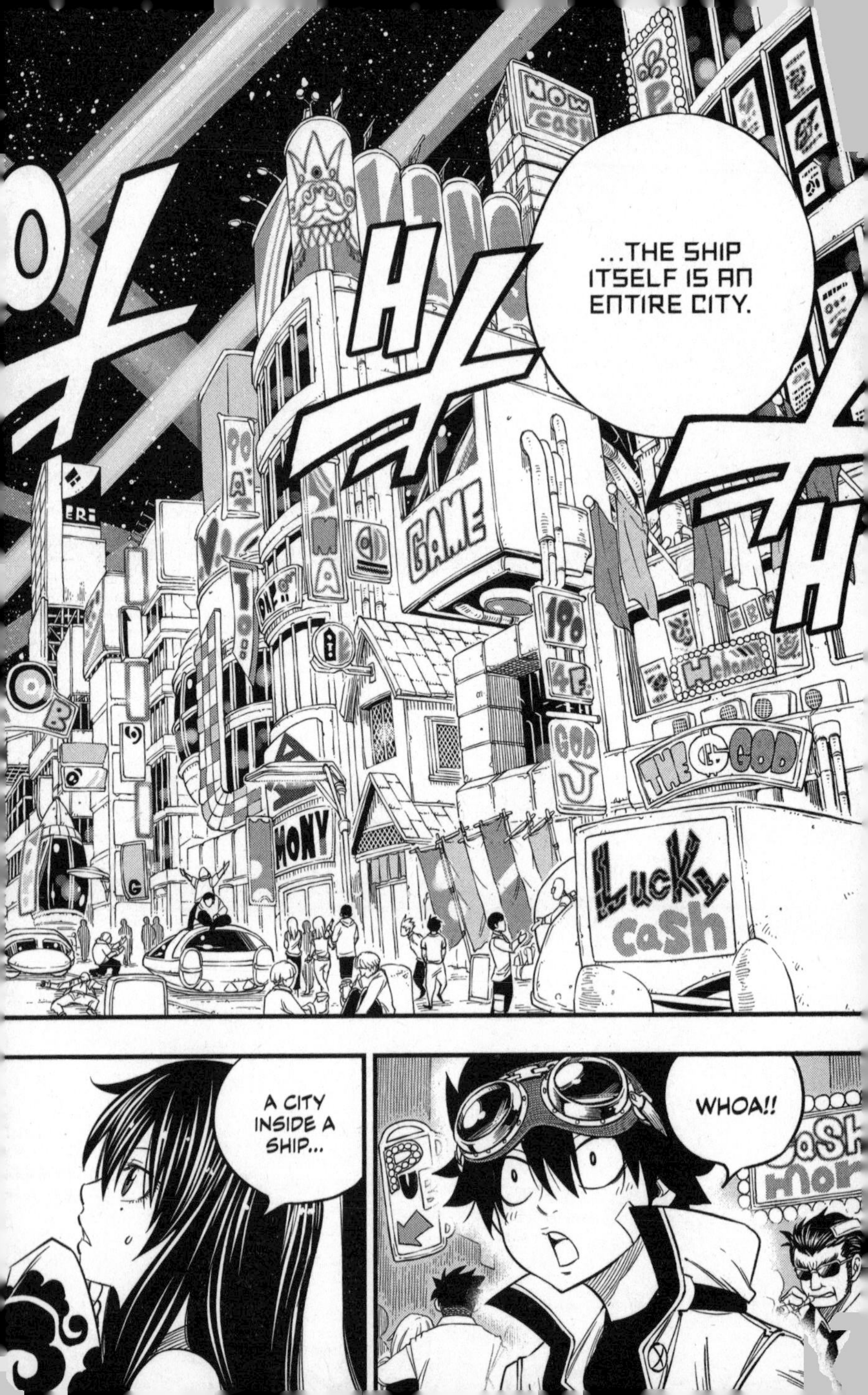
...THE SHIP ITSELF IS AN ENTIRE CITY.
NOW CASH
GAME
MONY
THE G GOD
Lucky cash
WHOA!!
A CITY INSIDE A SHIP...

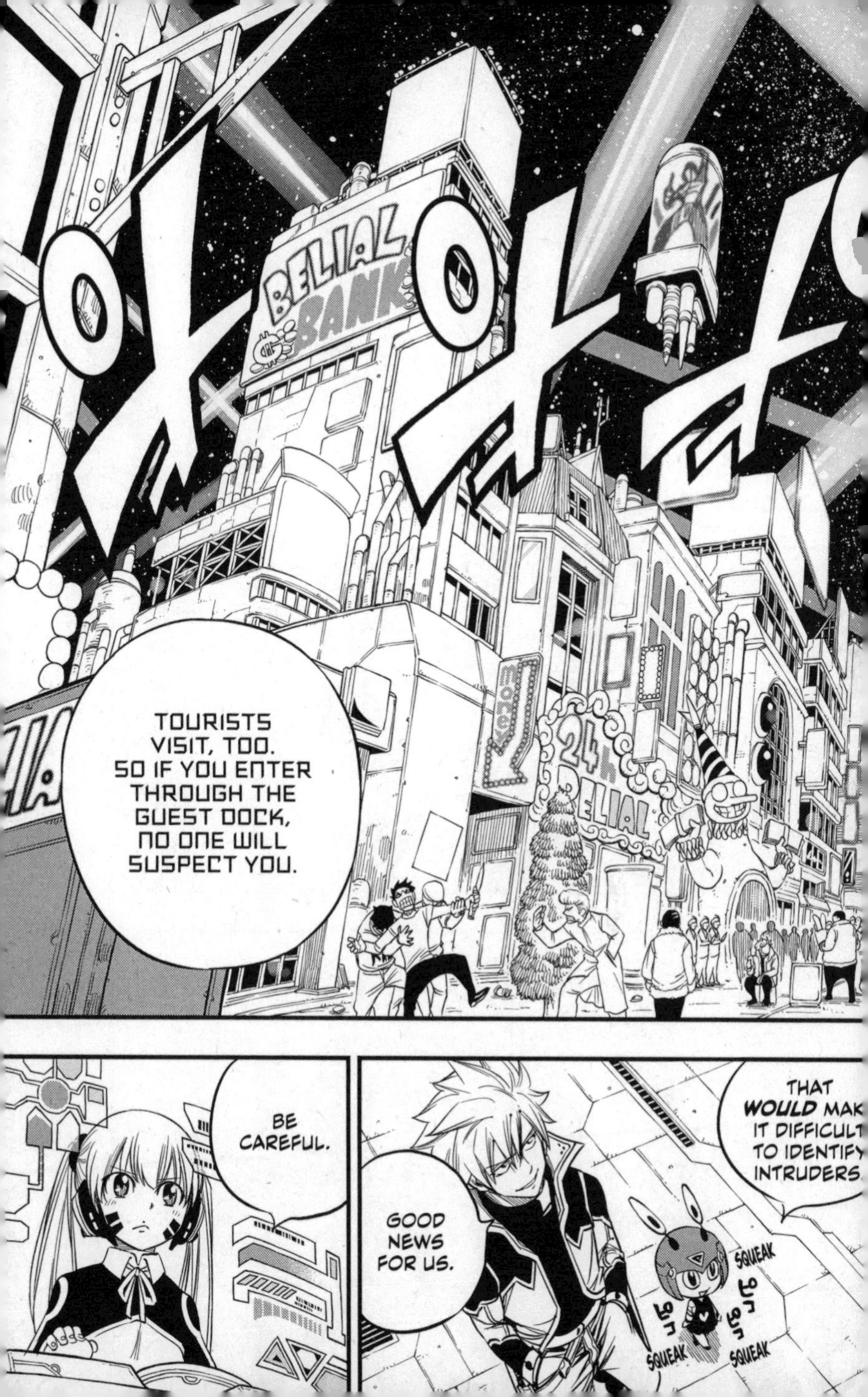
BELIAL BANK
money
24h BELIAL
TOURISTS VISIT, TOO. SO IF YOU ENTER THROUGH THE GUEST DOCK, NO ONE WILL SUSPECT YOU.
THAT ***WOULD*** MAK IT DIFFICULT TO IDENTIFY INTRUDERS
GOOD NEWS FOR US.
SQUEAK
SQUEAK
SQUEAK
SQUEAK
BE CAREFUL.

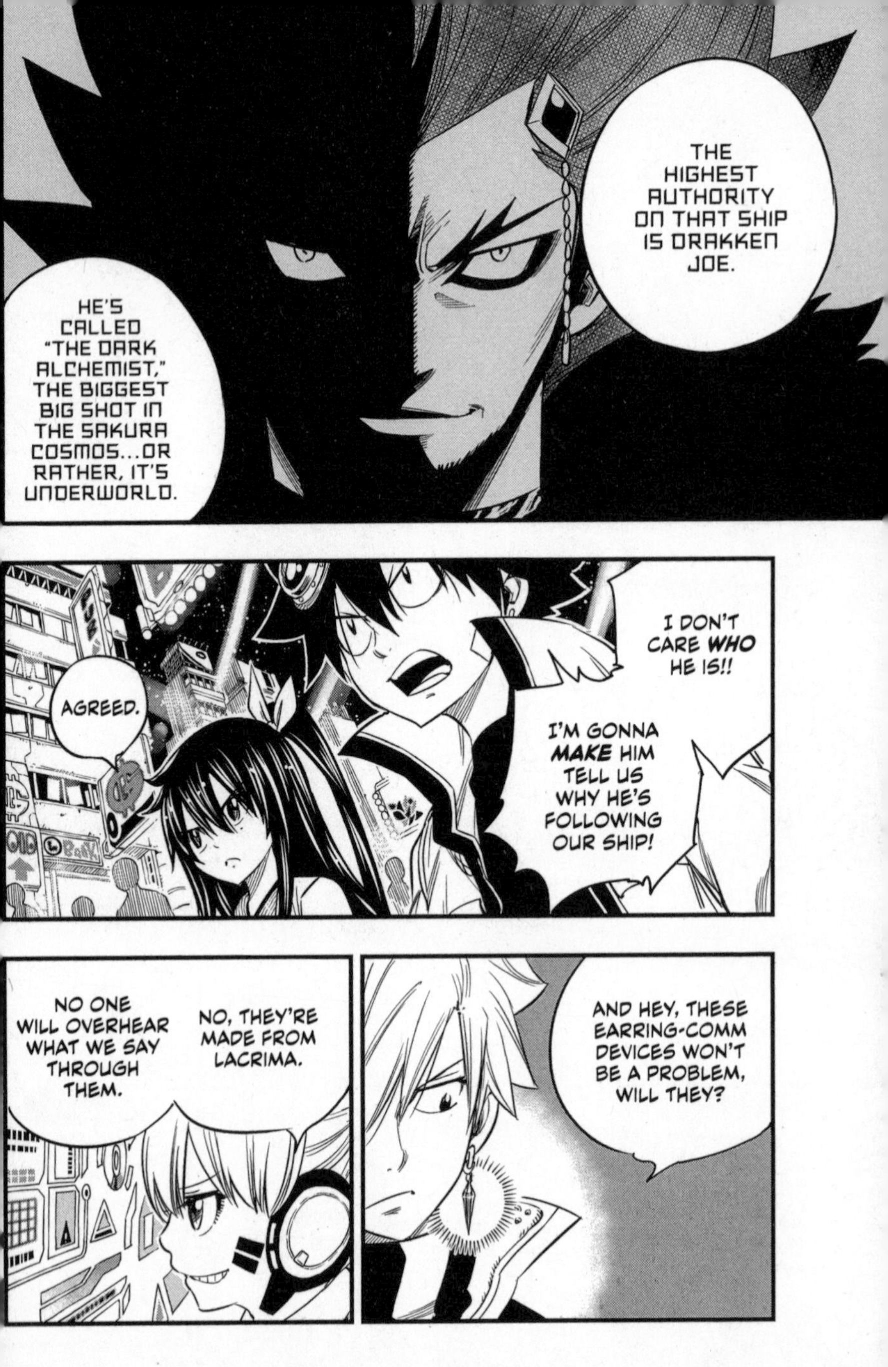
THE HIGHEST AUTHORITY ON THAT SHIP IS DRAKKEN JOE.
HE'S CALLED "THE DARK ALCHEMIST," THE BIGGEST BIG SHOT IN THE SAKURA COSMOS...OR RATHER, IT'S UNDERWORLD.
I DON'T CARE ***WHO*** HE IS!!
I'M GONNA ***MAKE*** HIM TELL US WHY HE'S FOLLOWING OUR SHIP!
AGREED.
AND HEY, THESE EARRING-COMM DEVICES WON'T BE A PROBLEM, WILL THEY?
NO, THEY'RE MADE FROM LACRIMA.
NO ONE WILL OVERHEAR WHAT WE SAY THROUGH THEM.

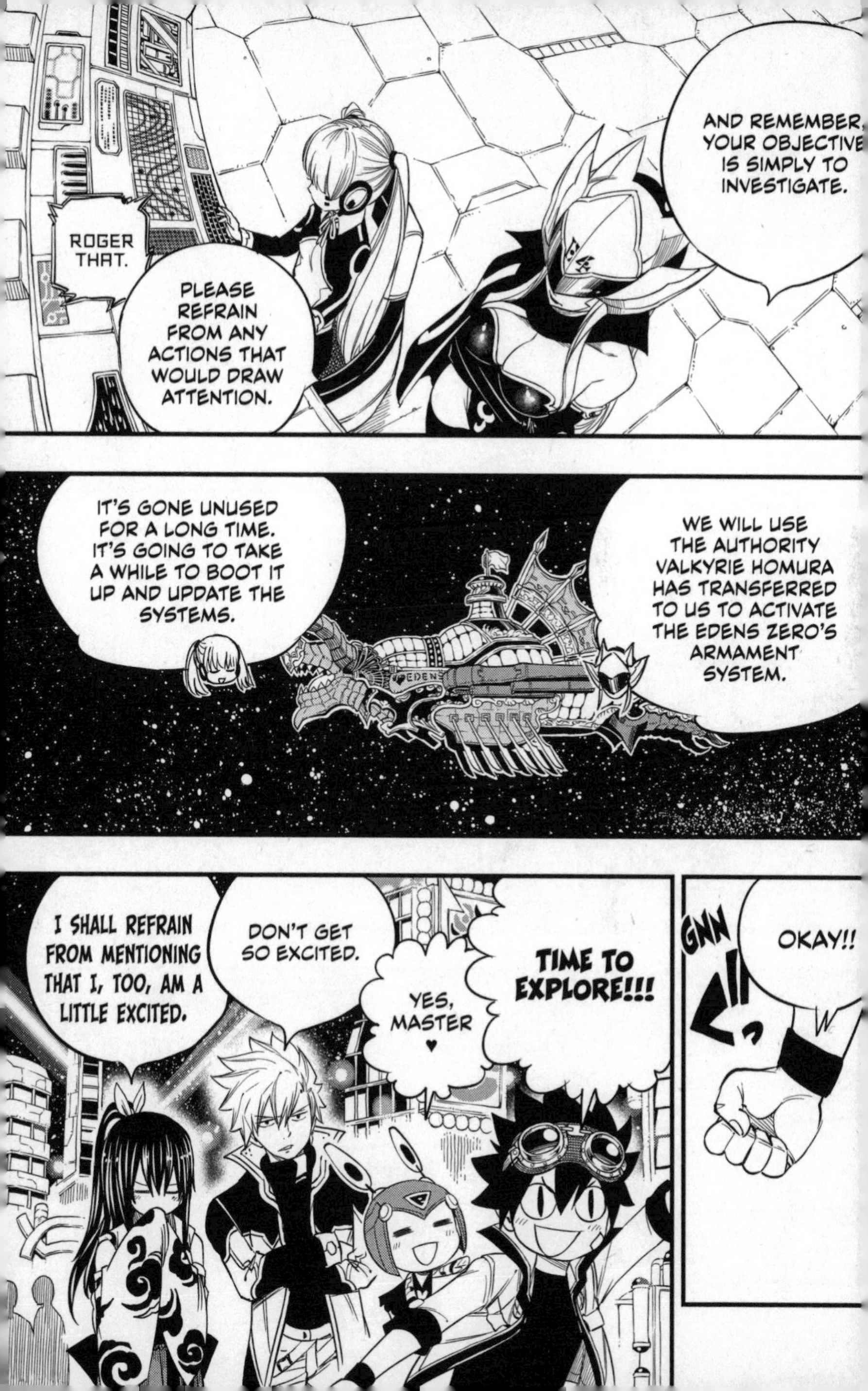
AND REMEMBER, YOUR OBJECTIVE IS SIMPLY TO INVESTIGATE.
PLEASE REFRAIN FROM ANY ACTIONS THAT WOULD DRAW ATTENTION.
ROGER THAT.
WE WILL USE THE AUTHORITY VALKYRIE HOMURA HAS TRANSFERRED TO US TO ACTIVATE THE EDENS ZERO'S ARMAMENT SYSTEM.
IT'S GONE UNUSED FOR A LONG TIME. IT'S GOING TO TAKE A WHILE TO BOOT IT UP AND UPDATE THE SYSTEMS.
EDENS
GNN
OKAY!!
TIME TO EXPLORE!!!
YES, MASTER ♥
DON'T GET SO EXCITED.
I SHALL REFRAIN FROM MENTIONING THAT I, TOO, AM A LITTLE EXCITED.

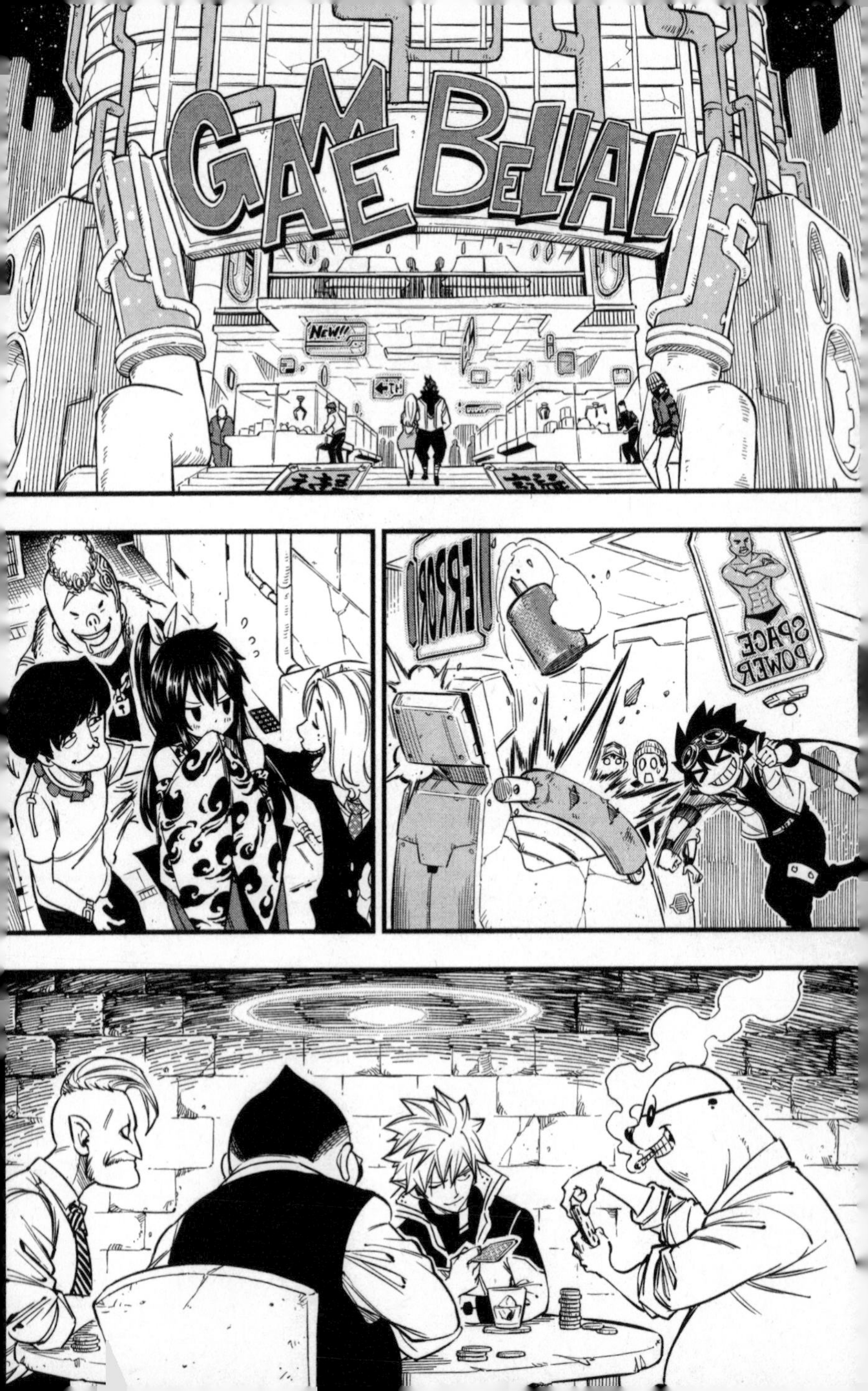
GAME BELIAL
NEW!!
SPACE POWER

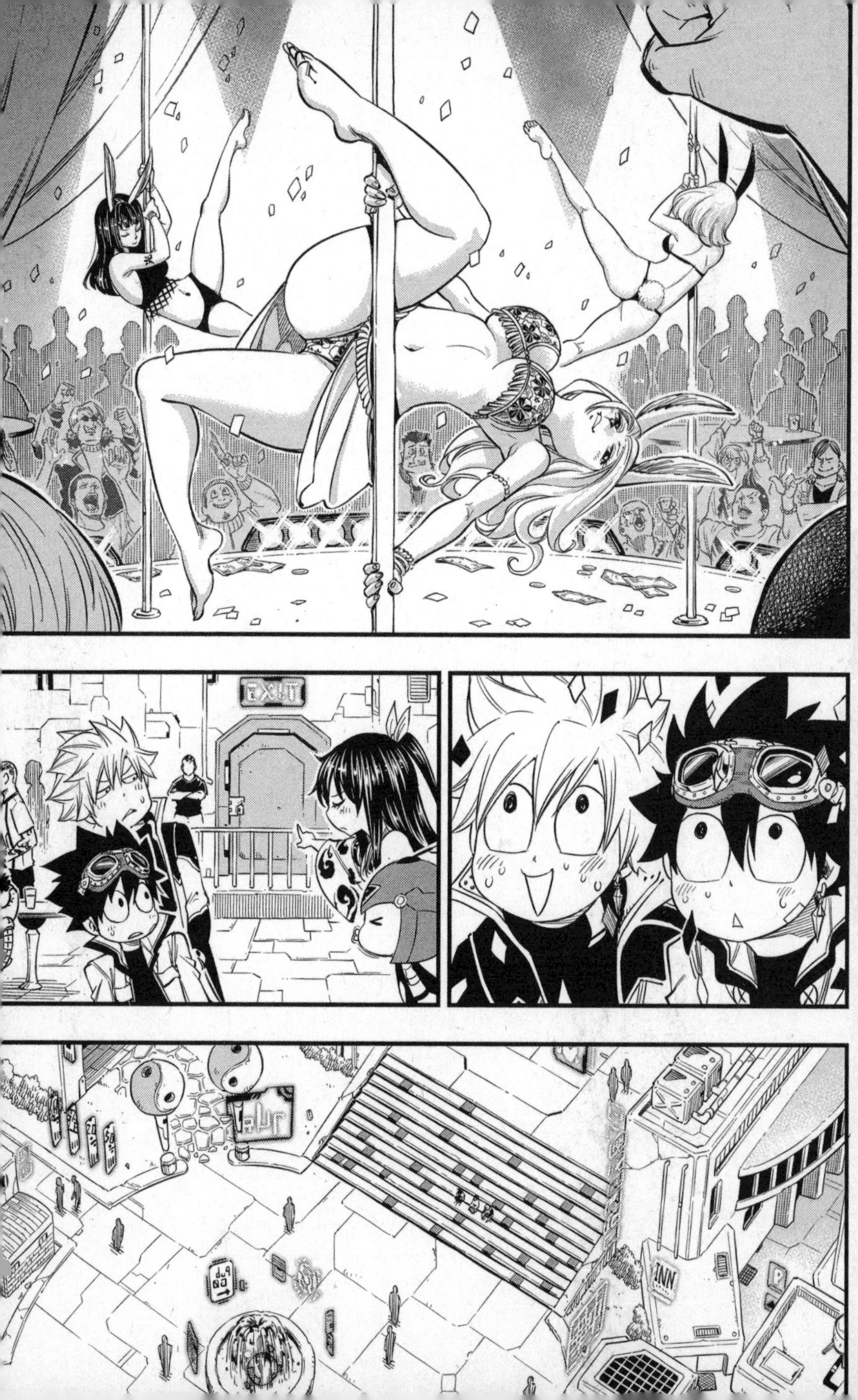
EXIT
INN

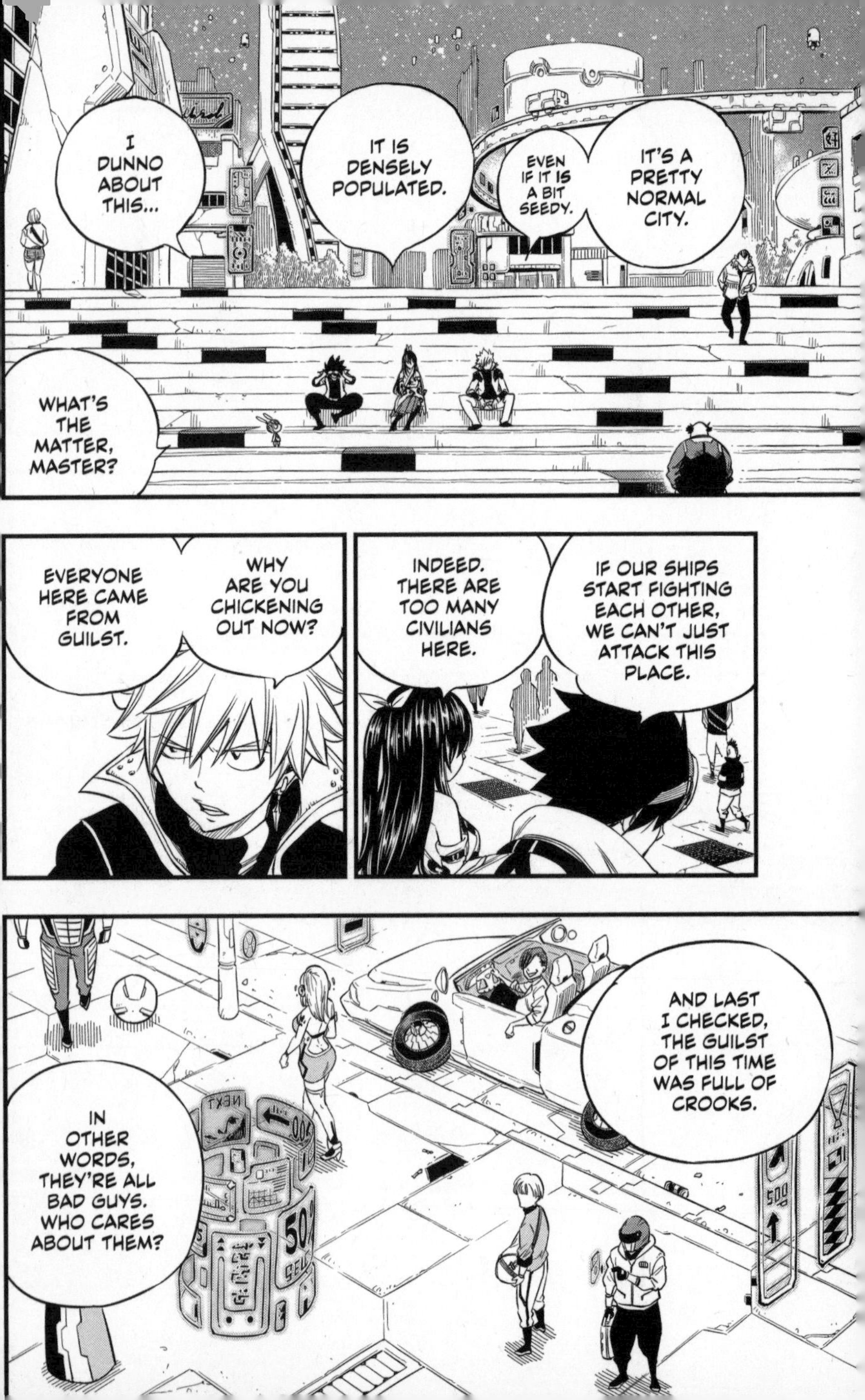
IT'S A PRETTY NORMAL CITY.
EVEN IF IT IS A BIT SEEDY.
IT IS DENSELY POPULATED.
I DUNNO ABOUT THIS...
WHAT'S THE MATTER, MASTER?
IF OUR SHIPS START FIGHTING EACH OTHER, WE CAN'T JUST ATTACK THIS PLACE.
INDEED. THERE ARE TOO MANY CIVILIANS HERE.
WHY ARE YOU CHICKENING OUT NOW?
EVERYONE HERE CAME FROM GUILST.
AND LAST I CHECKED, THE GUILST OF THIS TIME WAS FULL OF CROOKS.
IN OTHER WORDS, THEY'RE ALL BAD GUYS. WHO CARES ABOUT THEM?

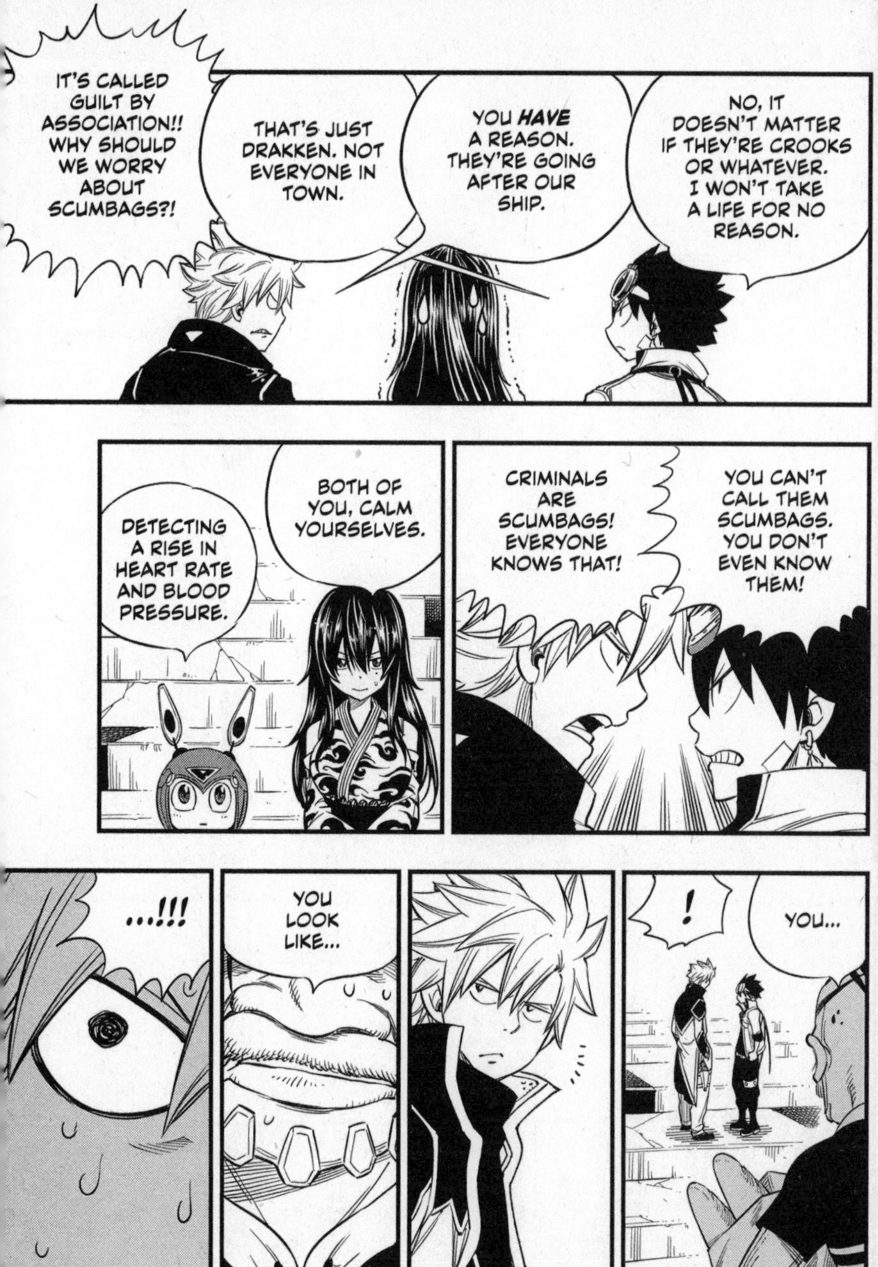
NO, IT DOESN'T MATTER IF THEY'RE CROOKS OR WHATEVER. I WON'T TAKE A LIFE FOR NO REASON.
YOU **HAVE** A REASON. THEY'RE GOING AFTER OUR SHIP.
THAT'S JUST DRAKKEN. NOT EVERYONE IN TOWN.
IT'S CALLED GUILT BY ASSOCIATION!! WHY SHOULD WE WORRY ABOUT SCUMBAGS?!
YOU CAN'T CALL THEM SCUMBAGS. YOU DON'T EVEN KNOW THEM!
CRIMINALS ARE SCUMBAGS! EVERYONE KNOWS THAT!
BOTH OF YOU, CALM YOURSELVES.
DETECTING A RISE IN HEART RATE AND BLOOD PRESSURE.
!
YOU...
YOU LOOK LIKE...
...!!!

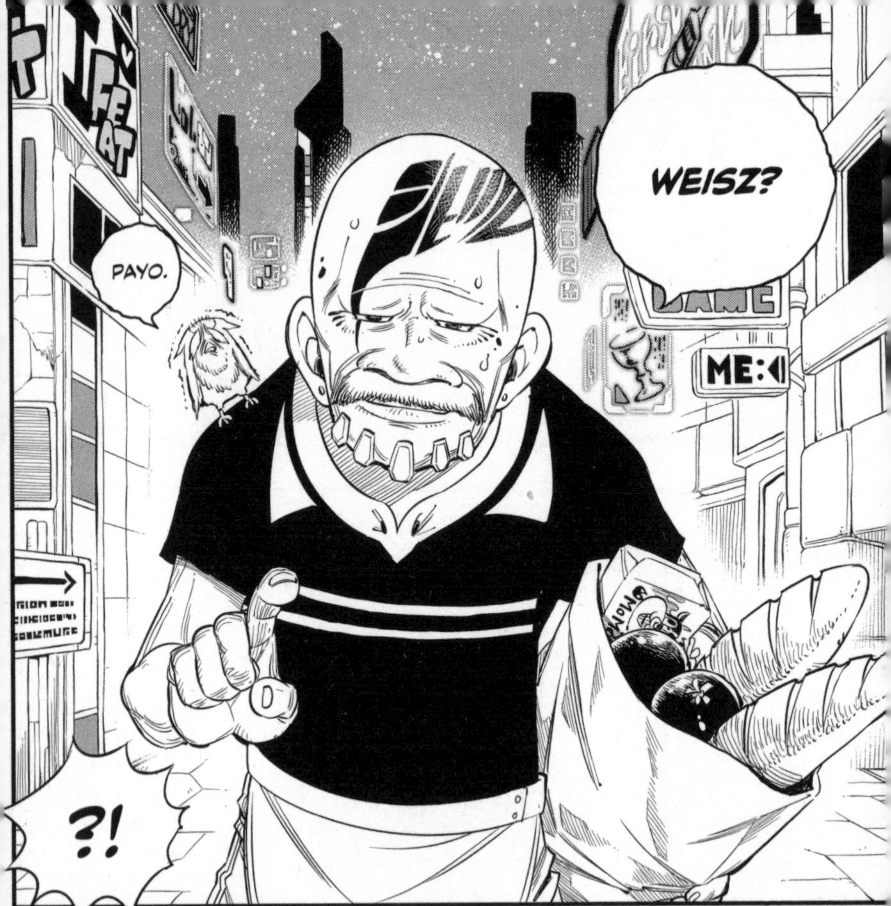
WEISZ?
PAYO.
?!

Tattoo: Sibir

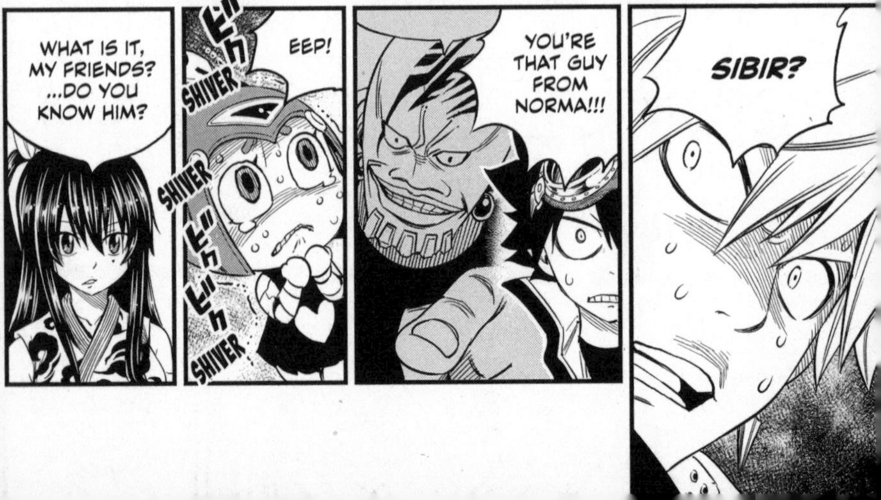
SIBIR?
YOU'RE THAT GUY FROM NORMA!!!
EEP!
SHIVER
SHIVER
SHIVER
WHAT IS IT, MY FRIENDS? ...DO YOU KNOW HIM?

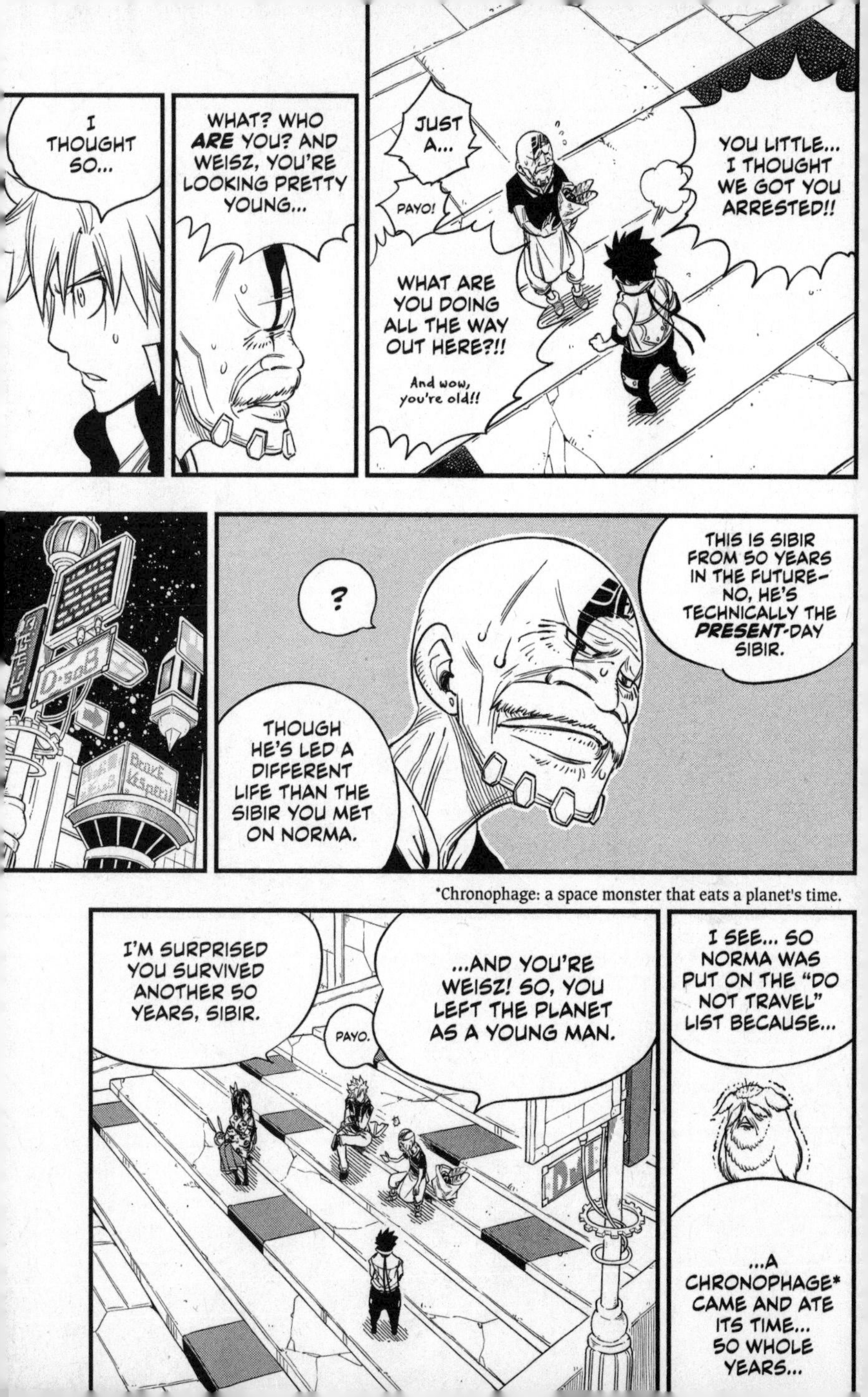
YOU LITTLE... I THOUGHT WE GOT YOU ARRESTED!!
JUST A...
PAYO!
WHAT ARE YOU DOING ALL THE WAY OUT HERE?!!
And wow, you're old!!
WHAT? WHO **ARE** YOU? AND WEISZ, YOU'RE LOOKING PRETTY YOUNG...
I THOUGHT SO...
THIS IS SIBIR FROM 50 YEARS IN THE FUTURE— NO, HE'S TECHNICALLY THE ***PRESENT***-DAY SIBIR.
?
THOUGH HE'S LED A DIFFERENT LIFE THAN THE SIBIR YOU MET ON NORMA.
I SEE... SO NORMA WAS PUT ON THE "DO NOT TRAVEL" LIST BECAUSE...
...A CHRONOPHAGE* CAME AND ATE ITS TIME... 50 WHOLE YEARS...
...AND YOU'RE WEISZ! SO, YOU LEFT THE PLANET AS A YOUNG MAN.
PAYO.
I'M SURPRISED YOU SURVIVED ANOTHER 50 YEARS, SIBIR.

*Chronophage: a space monster that eats a planet's time.

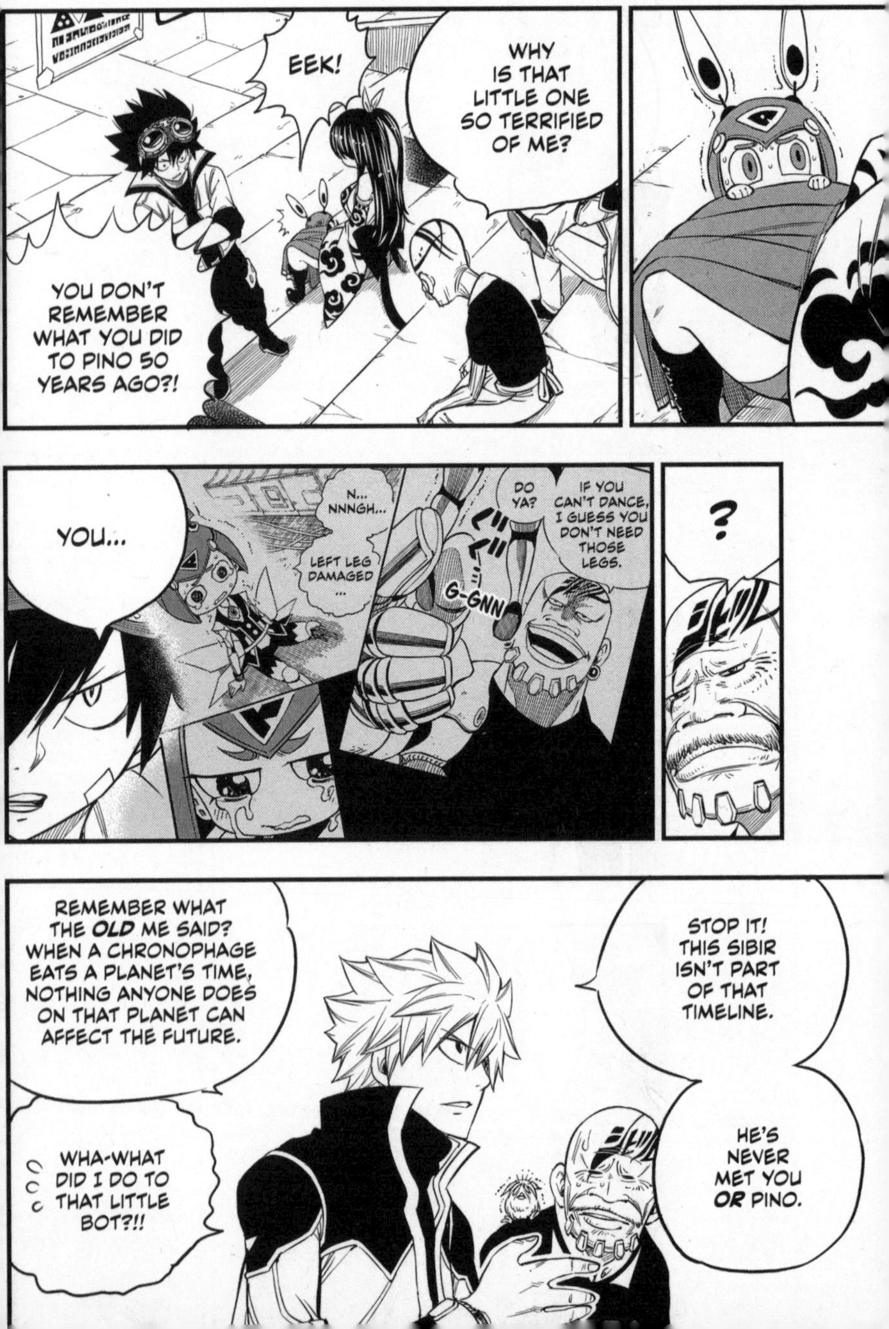
WHY IS THAT LITTLE ONE SO TERRIFIED OF ME?
EEK!
YOU DON'T REMEMBER WHAT YOU DID TO PINO 50 YEARS AGO?!
?
IF YOU CAN'T DANCE, I GUESS YOU DON'T NEED THOSE LEGS.
DO YA?
G-GNN
N... NNNGH...
LEFT LEG DAMAGED ...
YOU...
STOP IT! THIS SIBIR ISN'T PART OF THAT TIMELINE.
HE'S NEVER MET YOU OR PINO.
REMEMBER WHAT THE OLD ME SAID? WHEN A CHRONOPHAGE EATS A PLANET'S TIME, NOTHING ANYONE DOES ON THAT PLANET CAN AFFECT THE FUTURE.
WHA-WHAT DID I DO TO THAT LITTLE BOT?!!

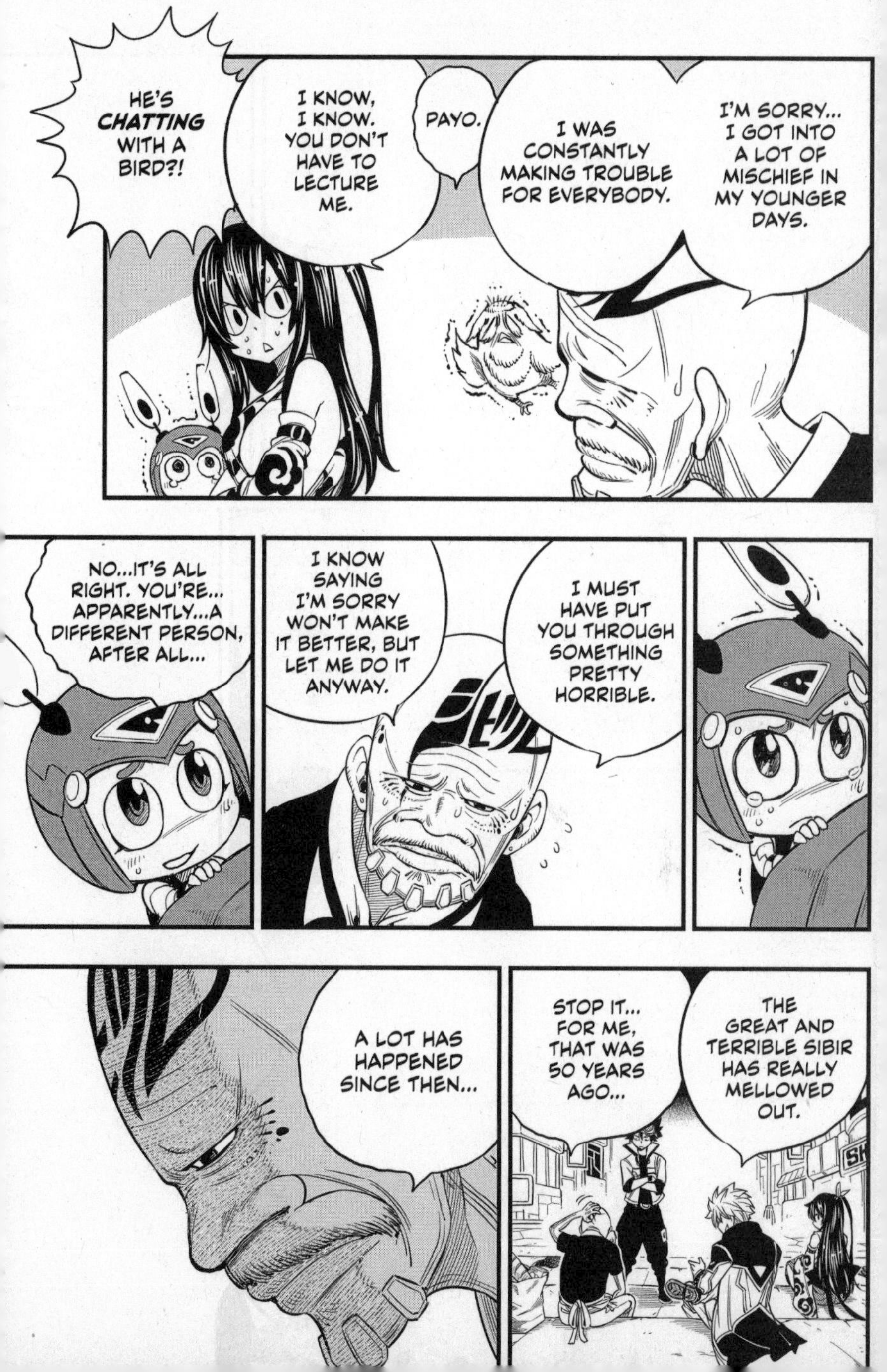
I'M SORRY... I GOT INTO A LOT OF MISCHIEF IN MY YOUNGER DAYS.
I WAS CONSTANTLY MAKING TROUBLE FOR EVERYBODY.
PAYO.
I KNOW, I KNOW. YOU DON'T HAVE TO LECTURE ME.
HE'S ***CHATTING*** WITH A BIRD?!
I MUST HAVE PUT YOU THROUGH SOMETHING PRETTY HORRIBLE.
I KNOW SAYING I'M SORRY WON'T MAKE IT BETTER, BUT LET ME DO IT ANYWAY.
NO...IT'S ALL RIGHT. YOU'RE... APPARENTLY...A DIFFERENT PERSON, AFTER ALL...
THE GREAT AND TERRIBLE SIBIR HAS REALLY MELLOWED OUT.
STOP IT... FOR ME, THAT WAS 50 YEARS AGO...
A LOT HAS HAPPENED SINCE THEN...

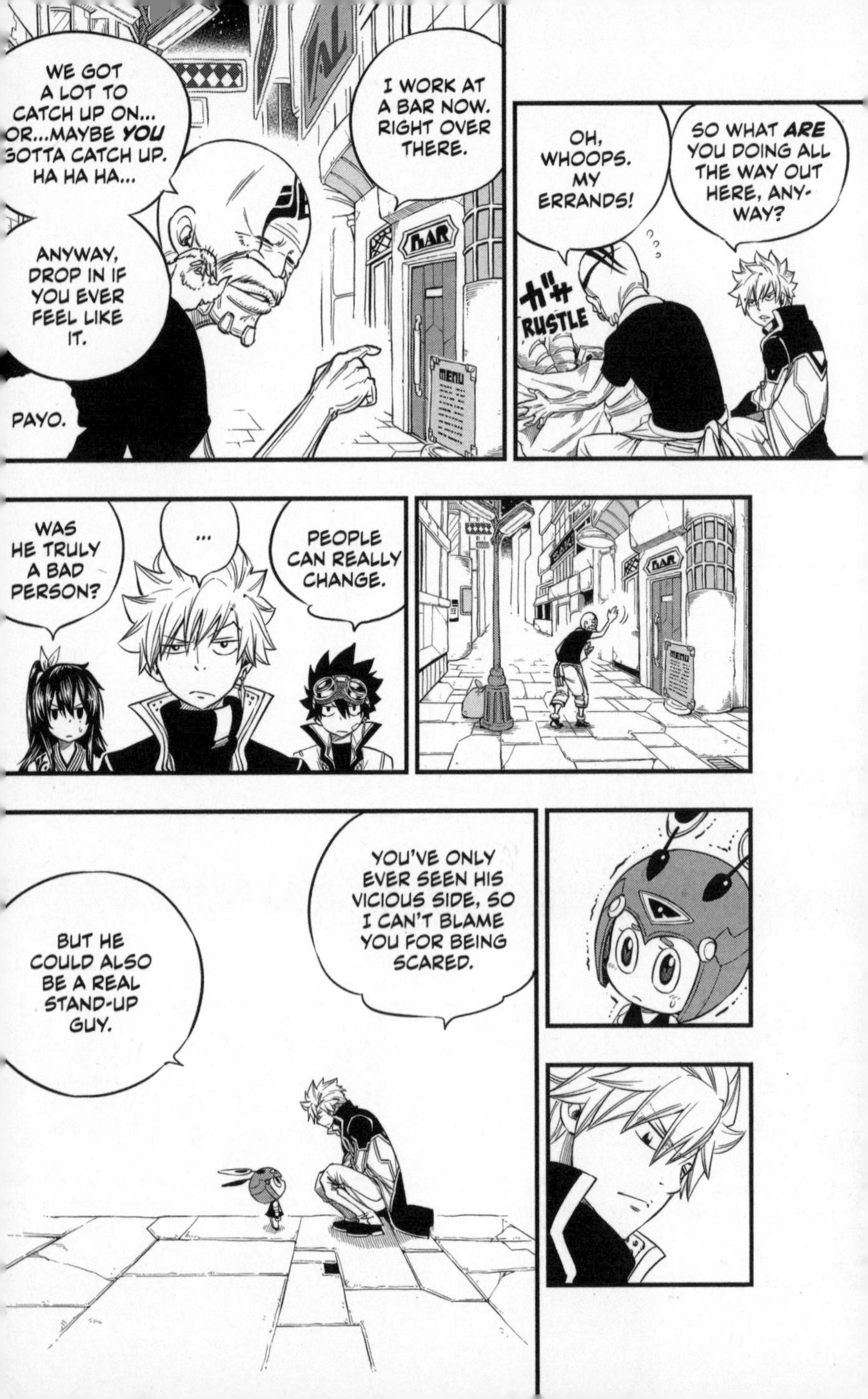
SO WHAT **ARE** YOU DOING ALL THE WAY OUT HERE, ANY-WAY?
OH, WHOOPS. MY ERRANDS!
ガサ
RUSTLE
WE GOT A LOT TO CATCH UP ON... OR...MAYBE ***YOU*** GOTTA CATCH UP. HA HA HA...
I WORK AT A BAR NOW. RIGHT OVER THERE.
BAR
MENU
ANYWAY, DROP IN IF YOU EVER FEEL LIKE IT.
PAYO.
BAR
MENU
PEOPLE CAN REALLY CHANGE.
...
WAS HE TRULY A BAD PERSON?
YOU'VE ONLY EVER SEEN HIS VICIOUS SIDE, SO I CAN'T BLAME YOU FOR BEING SCARED.
BUT HE COULD ALSO BE A REAL STAND-UP GUY.

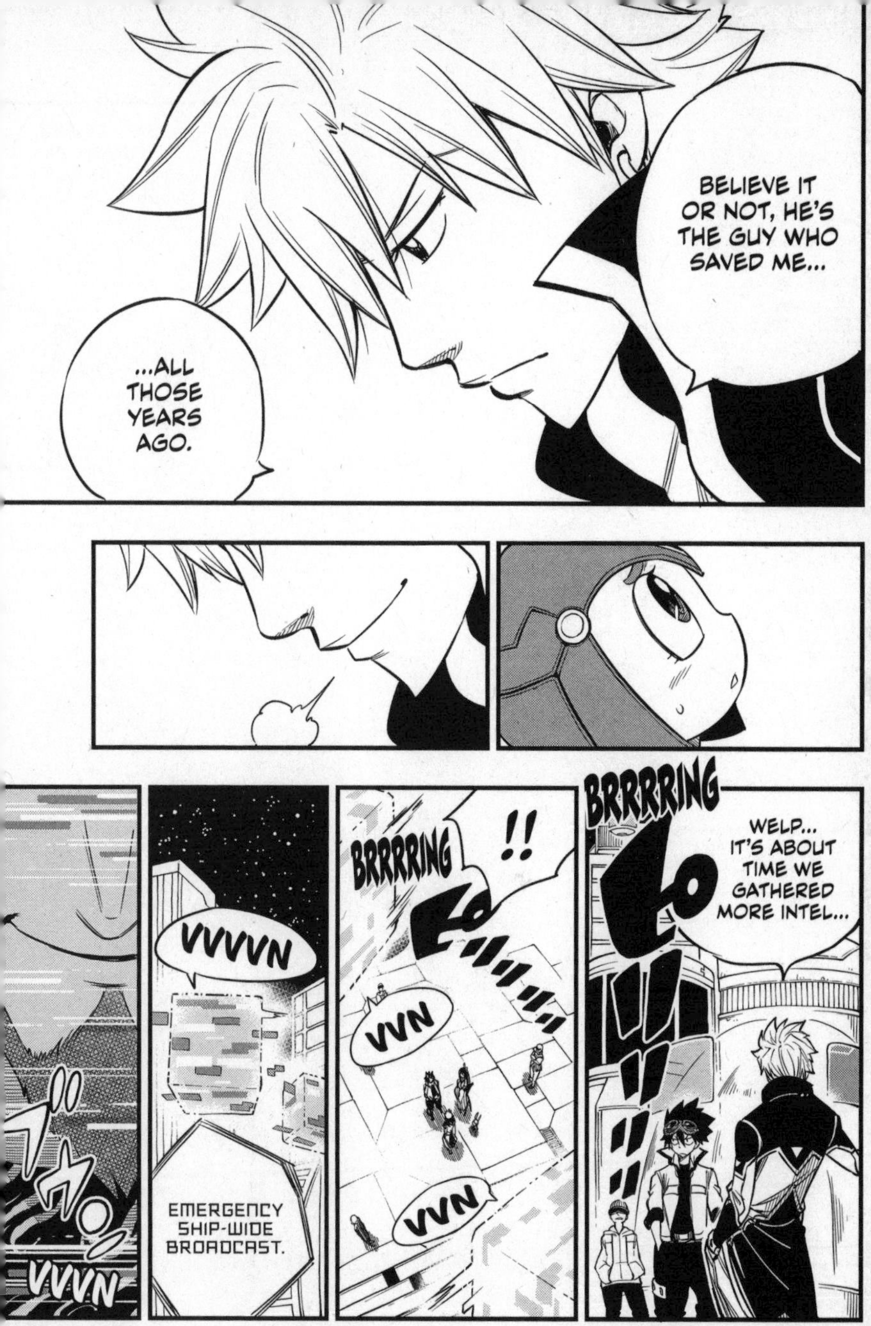
BELIEVE IT OR NOT, HE'S THE GUY WHO SAVED ME...
...ALL THOSE YEARS AGO.
BRRRRING
WELP... IT'S ABOUT TIME WE GATHERED MORE INTEL...
BRRRRING
!!
VVN
VVN
VVVVN
EMERGENCY SHIP-WIDE BROADCAST.
VVVN

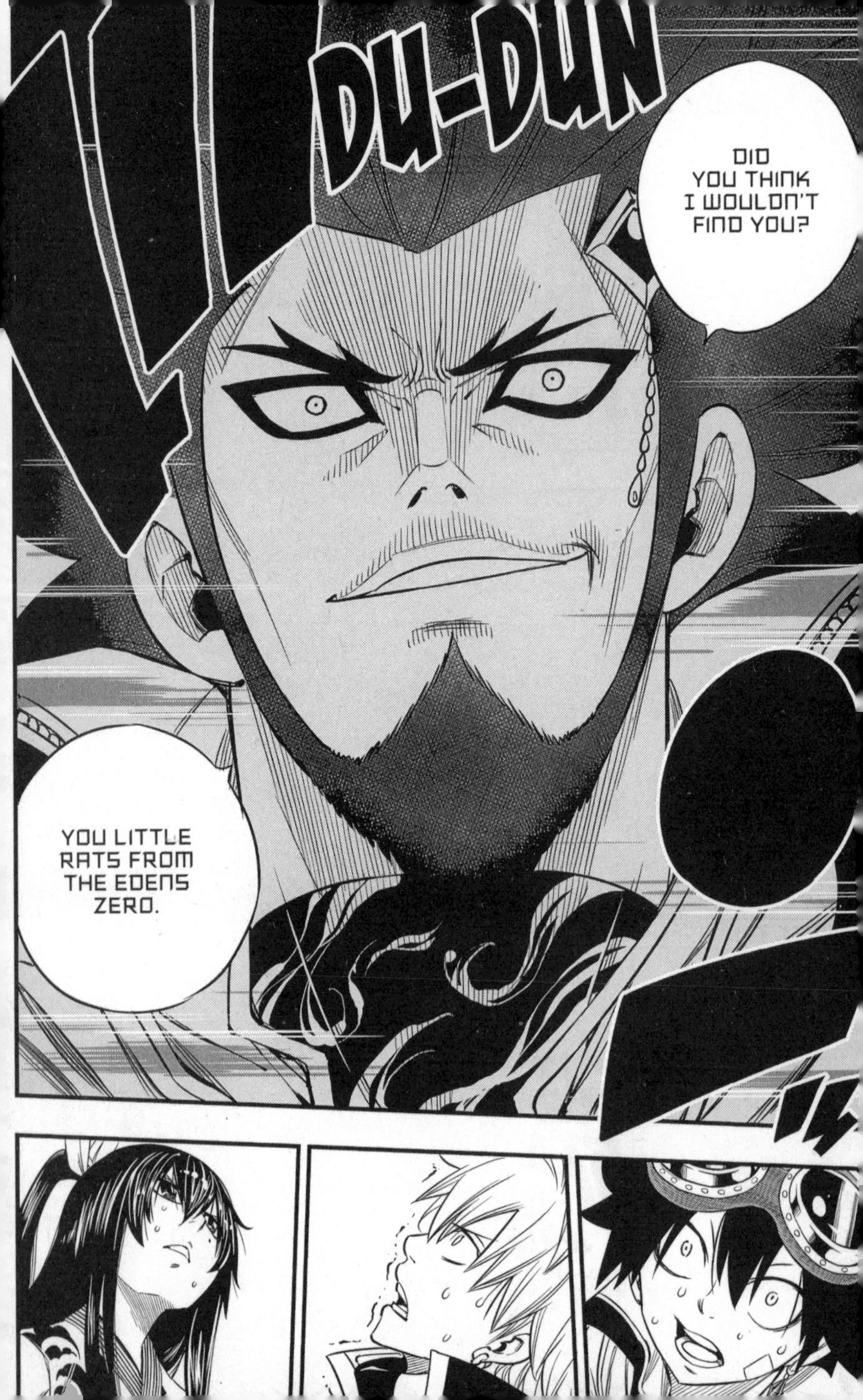
DU-DUN
DID YOU THINK I WOULDN'T FIND YOU?
YOU LITTLE RATS FROM THE EDENS ZERO.

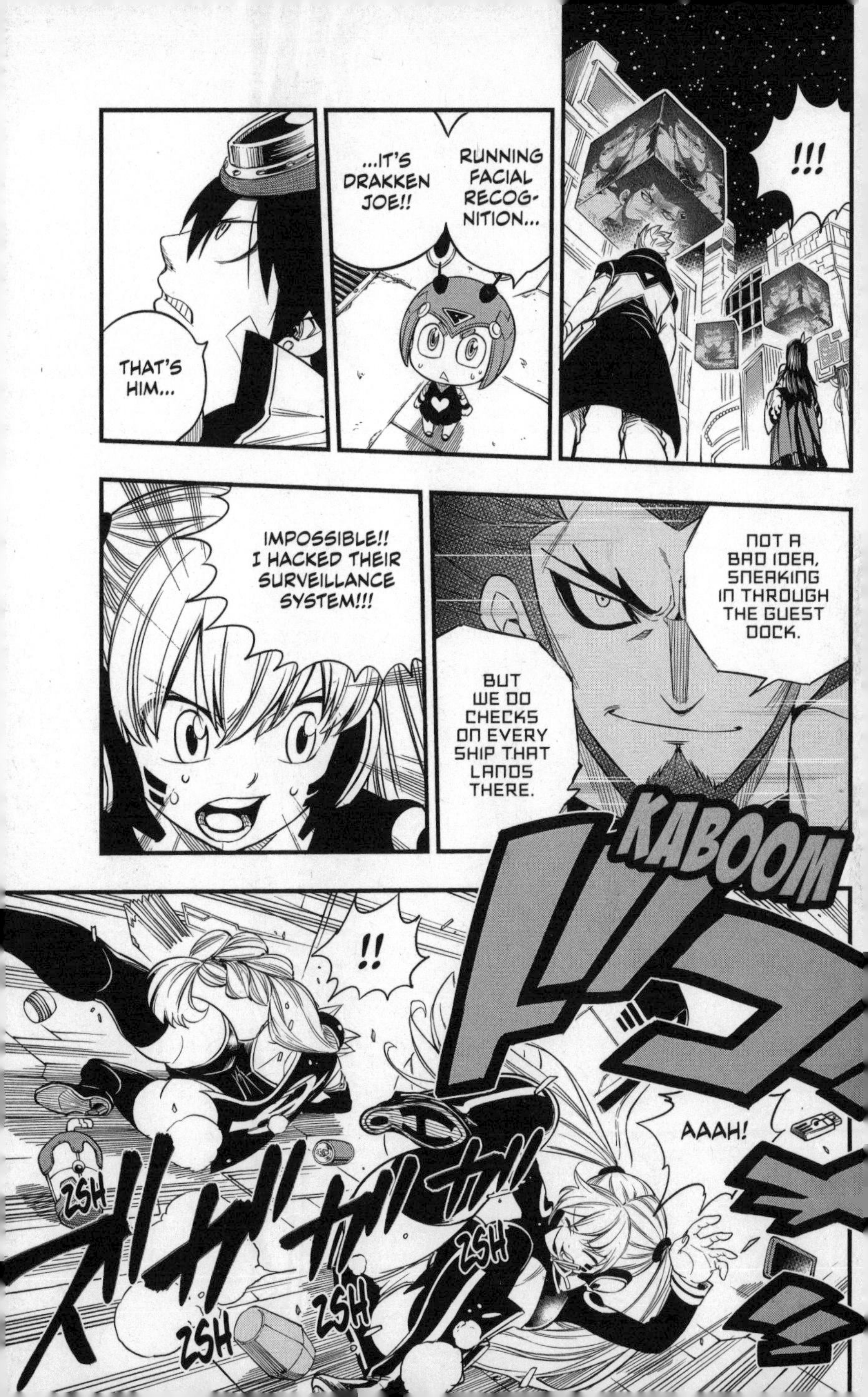
!!!
RUNNING FACIAL RECOG-NITION...
...IT'S DRAKKEN JOE!!
THAT'S HIM...
NOT A BAD IDEA, SNEAKING IN THROUGH THE GUEST DOCK.
BUT WE DO CHECKS ON EVERY SHIP THAT LANDS THERE.
IMPOSSIBLE!! I HACKED THEIR SURVEILLANCE SYSTEM!!!
KABOOM
AAAH!
!!
ZSH
ZSH
ZSH
ZSH

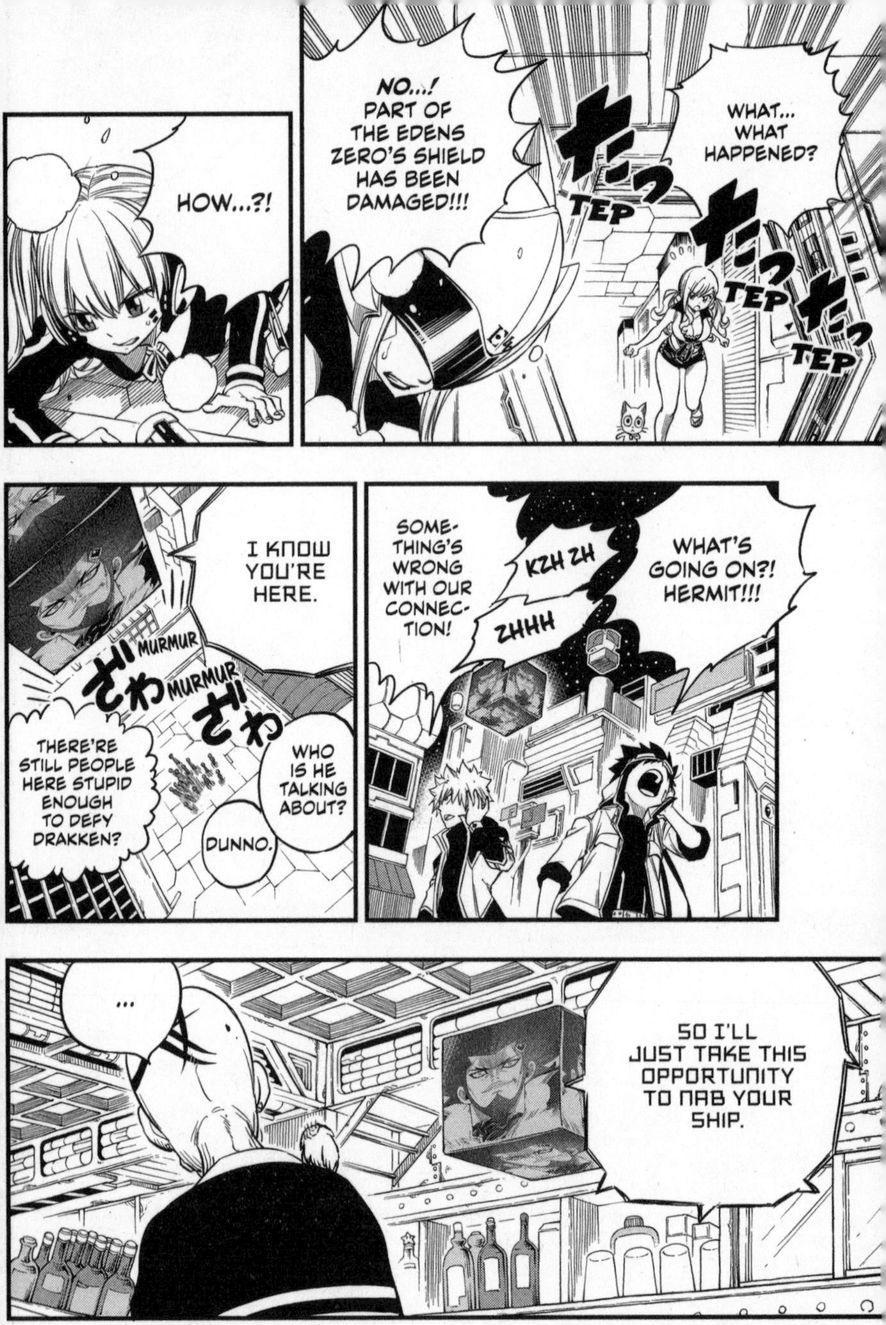
WHAT... WHAT HAPPENED?
たっ TEP
たっ TEP
たっ TEP
NO...! PART OF THE EDENS ZERO'S SHIELD HAS BEEN DAMAGED!!!
HOW...?!
WHAT'S GOING ON?! HERMIT!!!
KZH ZH
ZHHH
SOME-THING'S WRONG WITH OUR CONNEC-TION!
I KNOW YOU'RE HERE.
ざわ MURMUR
ざわ MURMUR
WHO IS HE TALKING ABOUT?
THERE'RE STILL PEOPLE HERE STUPID ENOUGH TO DEFY DRAKKEN?
DUNNO.
SO I'LL JUST TAKE THIS OPPORTUNITY TO NAB YOUR SHIP.
...

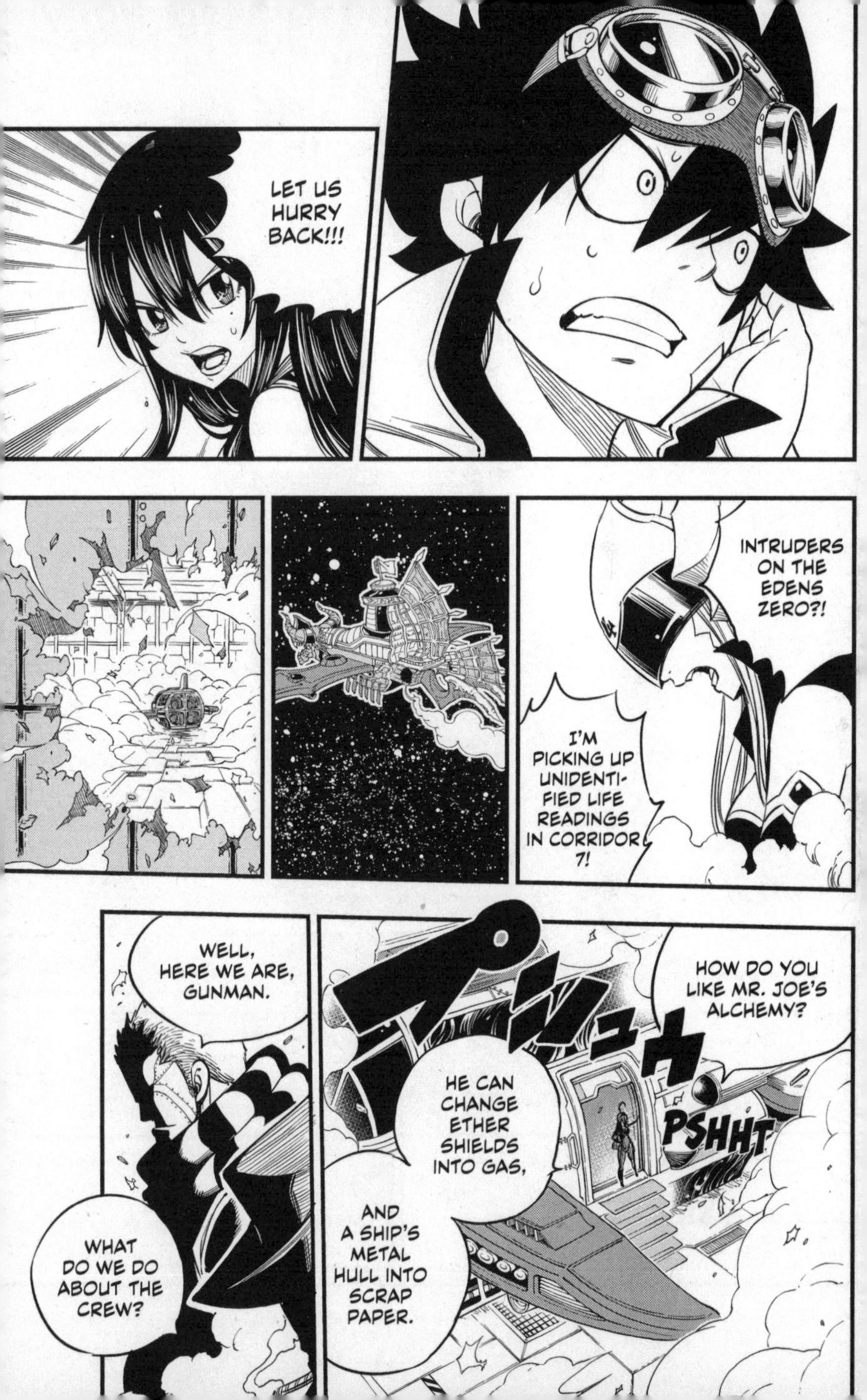
LET US HURRY BACK!!!
INTRUDERS ON THE EDENS ZERO?!
I'M PICKING UP UNIDENTI-FIED LIFE READINGS IN CORRIDOR 7!
HOW DO YOU LIKE MR. JOE'S ALCHEMY?
PSHHT
HE CAN CHANGE ETHER SHIELDS INTO GAS,
AND A SHIP'S METAL HULL INTO SCRAP PAPER.
WELL, HERE WE ARE, GUNMAN.
WHAT DO WE DO ABOUT THE CREW?

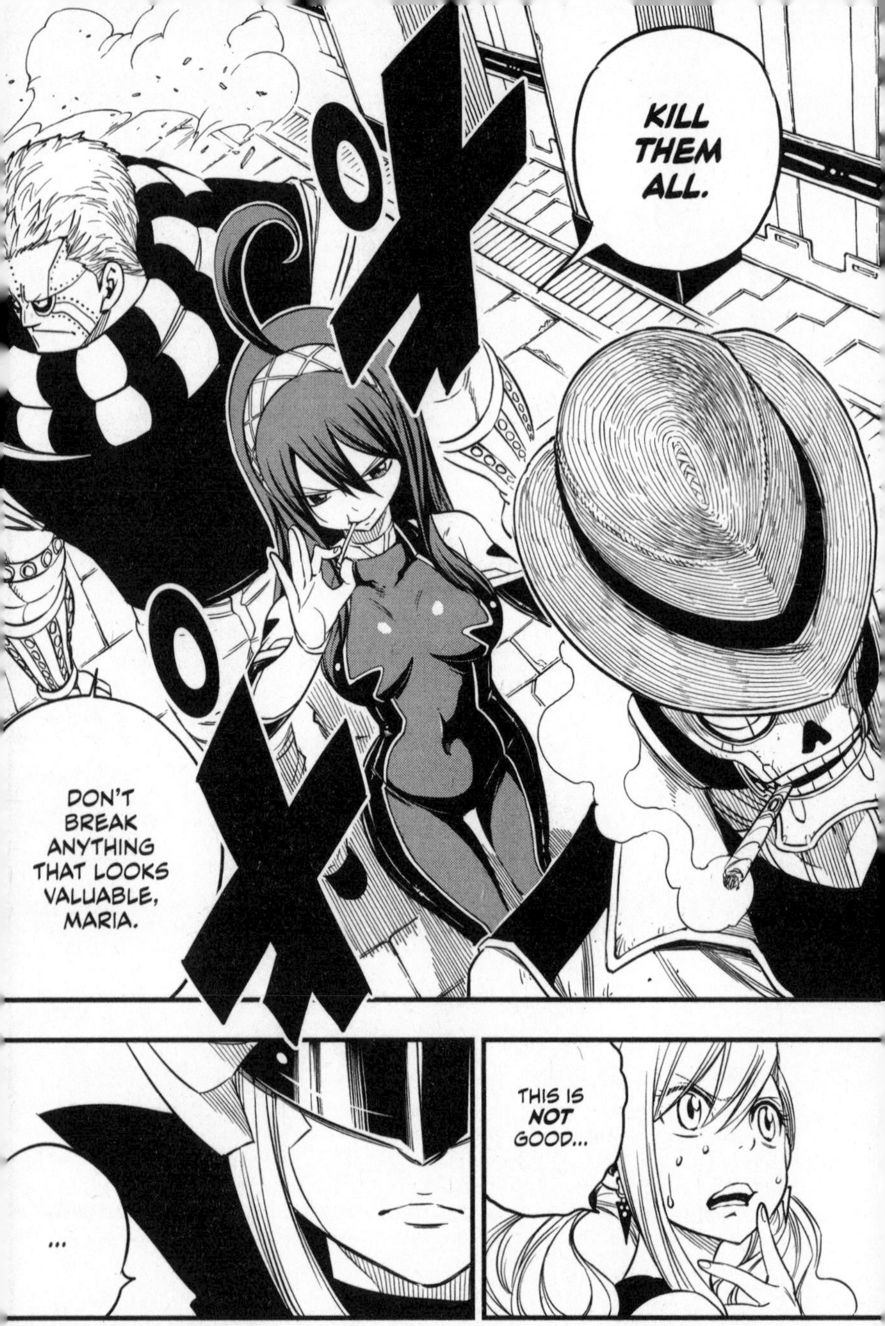
KILL THEM ALL.
DON'T BREAK ANYTHING THAT LOOKS VALUABLE, MARIA.
THIS IS *NOT* GOOD...
...

EDENS ZERO

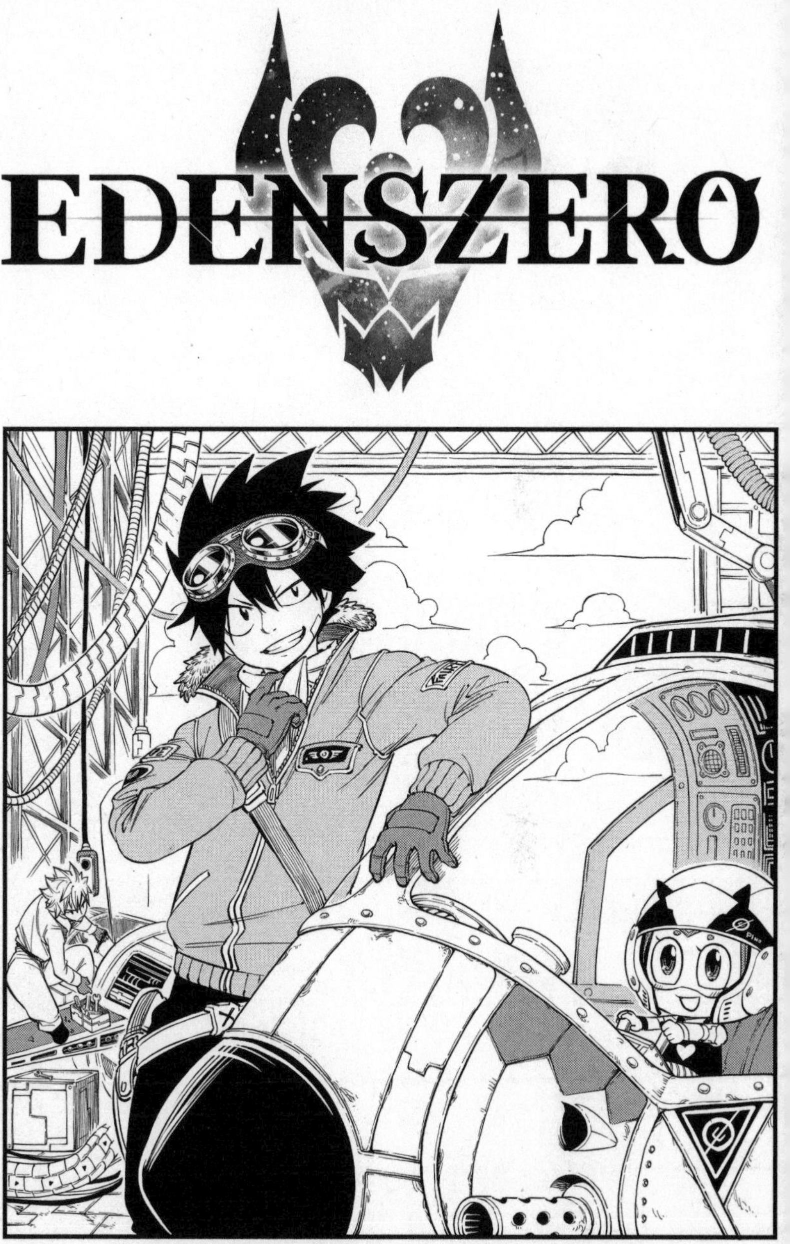

CHAPTER 71: THE STEEL SORCERESS

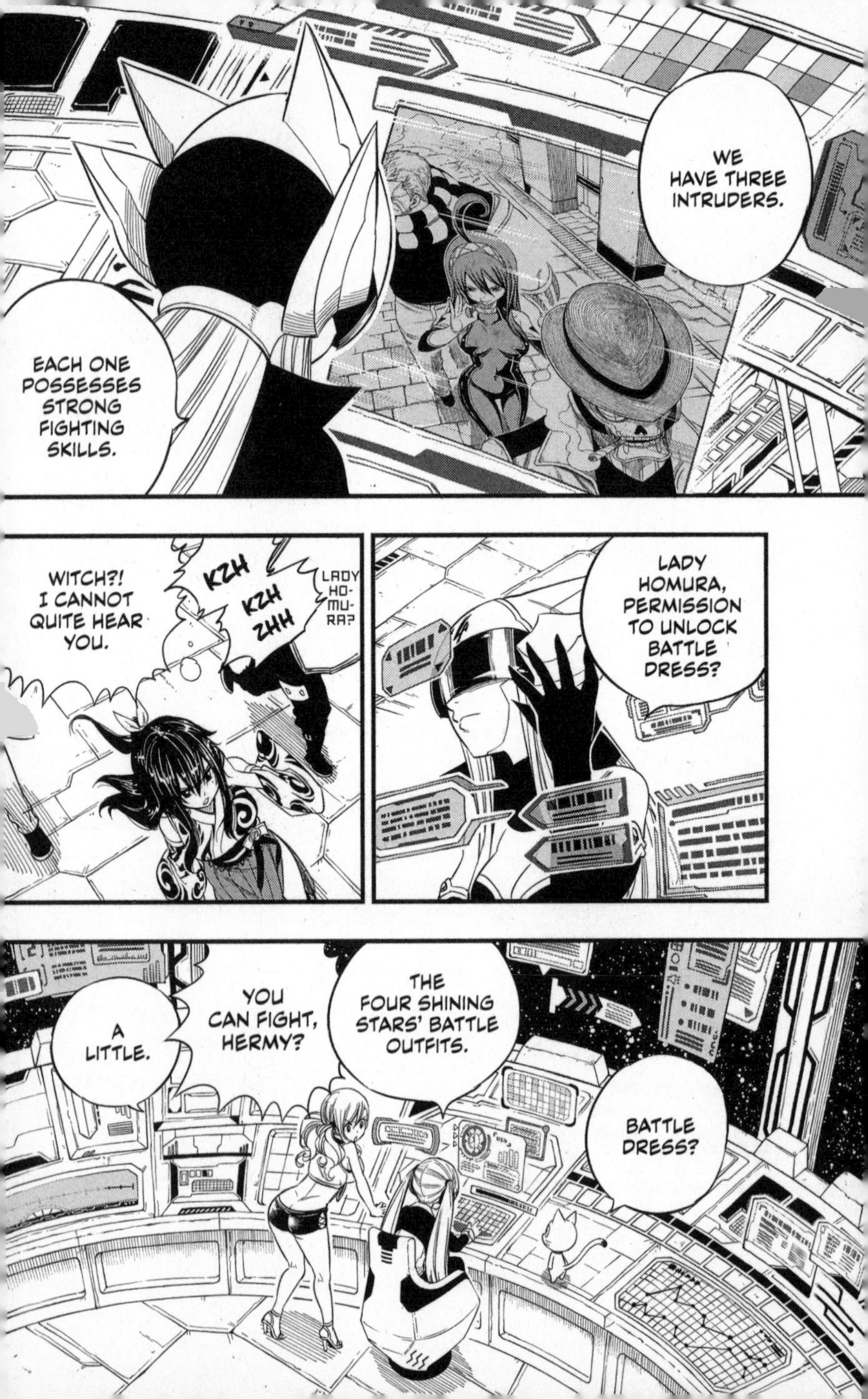
WE HAVE THREE INTRUDERS.
EACH ONE POSSESSES STRONG FIGHTING SKILLS.
LADY HOMURA, PERMISSION TO UNLOCK BATTLE DRESS?
LADY HO-MU-RA?
KZH
KZH ZHH
WITCH?! I CANNOT QUITE HEAR YOU.
BATTLE DRESS?
THE FOUR SHINING STARS' BATTLE OUTFITS.
YOU CAN FIGHT, HERMY?
A LITTLE.

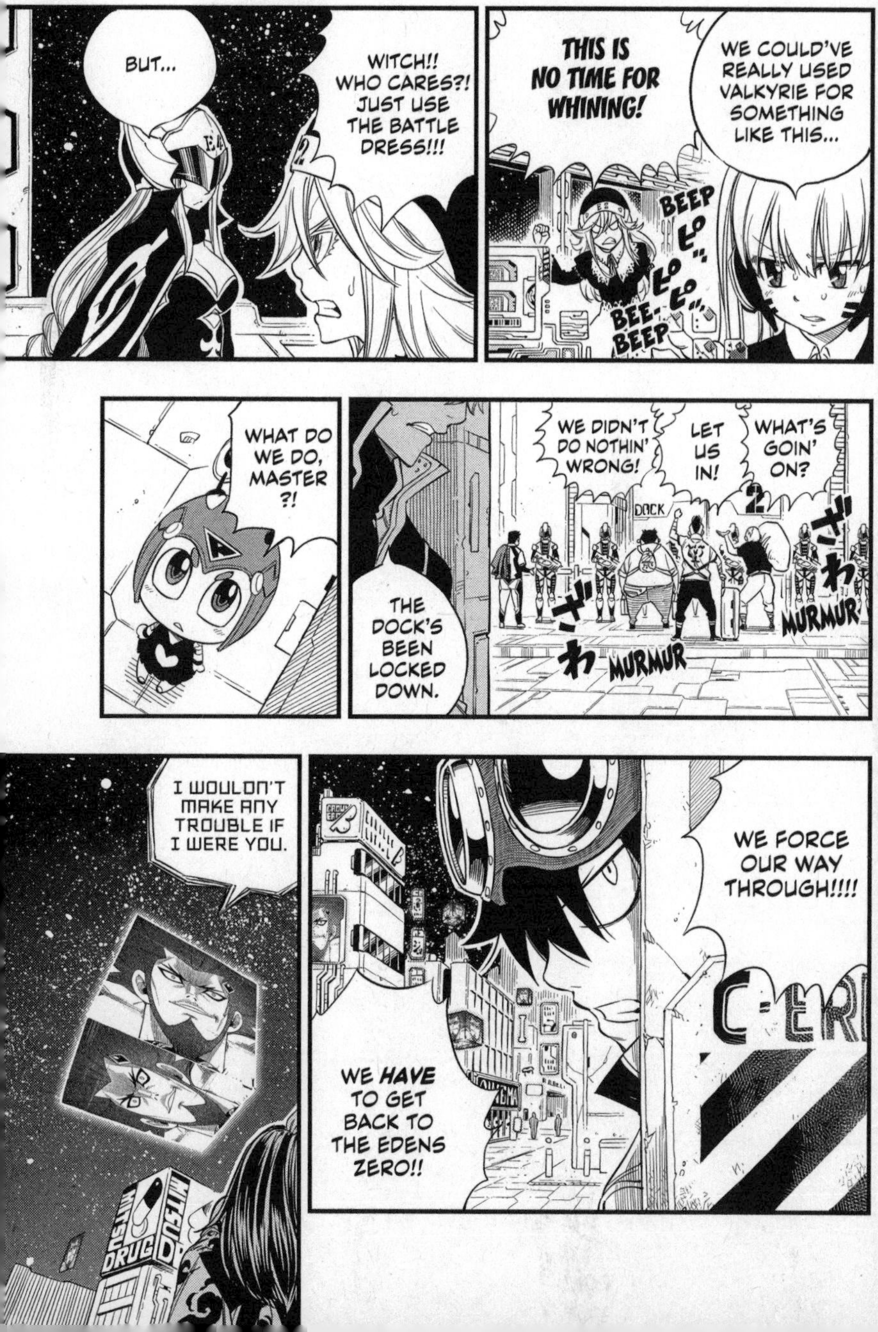

WE COULD'VE REALLY USED VALKYRIE FOR SOMETHING LIKE THIS...
THIS IS NO TIME FOR WHINING!
BEEP
BEE-BEEP
WITCH!! WHO CARES?! JUST USE THE BATTLE DRESS!!!
BUT...
WHAT'S GOIN' ON?
LET US IN!
WE DIDN'T DO NOTHIN' WRONG!
DOCK
MURMUR
MURMUR
THE DOCK'S BEEN LOCKED DOWN.
WHAT DO WE DO, MASTER?!
WE FORCE OUR WAY THROUGH!!!!
WE HAVE TO GET BACK TO THE EDENS ZERO!!
I WOULDN'T MAKE ANY TROUBLE IF I WERE YOU.
MITSUDRUG

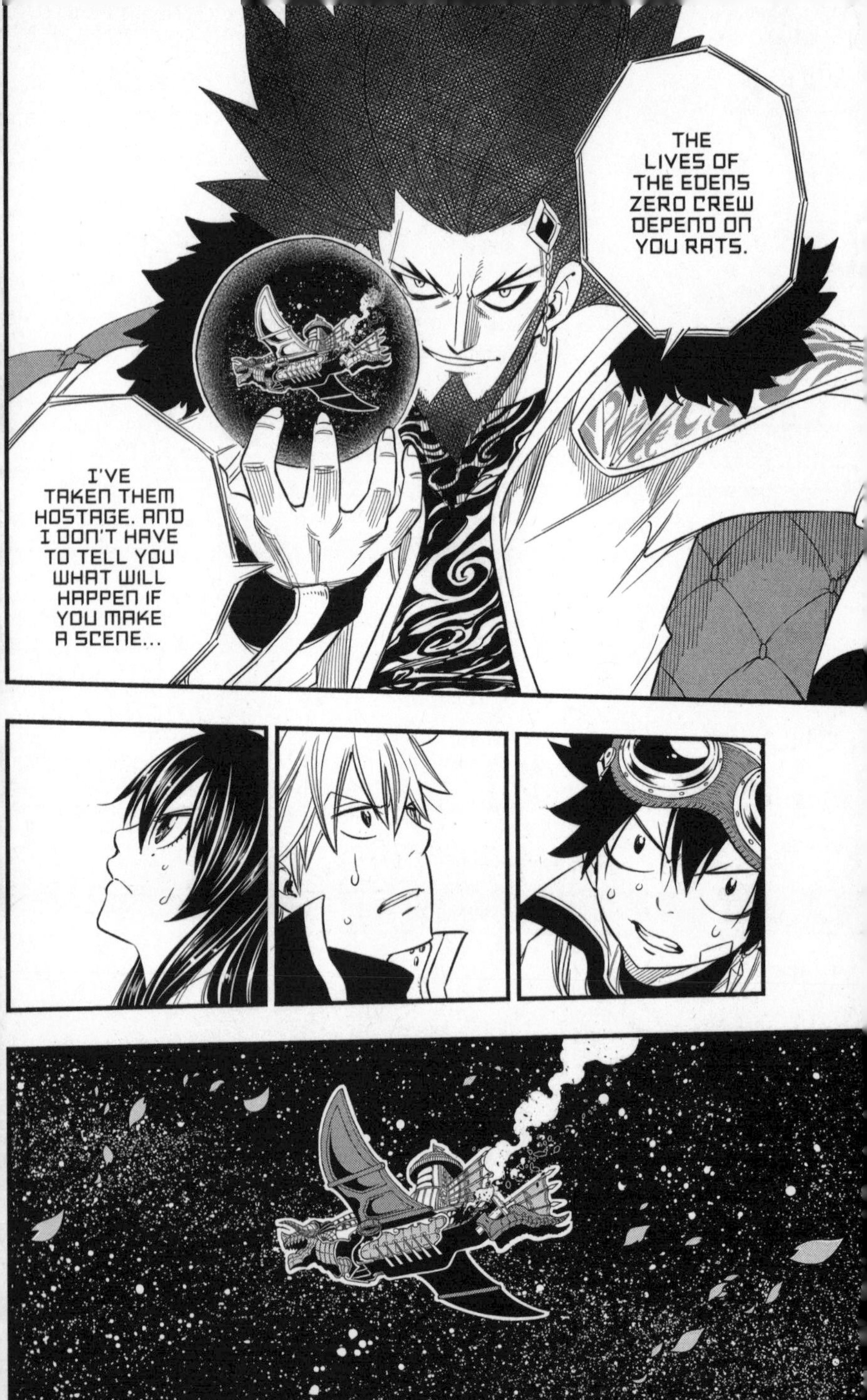
THE LIVES OF THE EDENS ZERO CREW DEPEND ON YOU RATS.
I'VE TAKEN THEM HOSTAGE. AND I DON'T HAVE TO TELL YOU WHAT WILL HAPPEN IF YOU MAKE A SCENE...

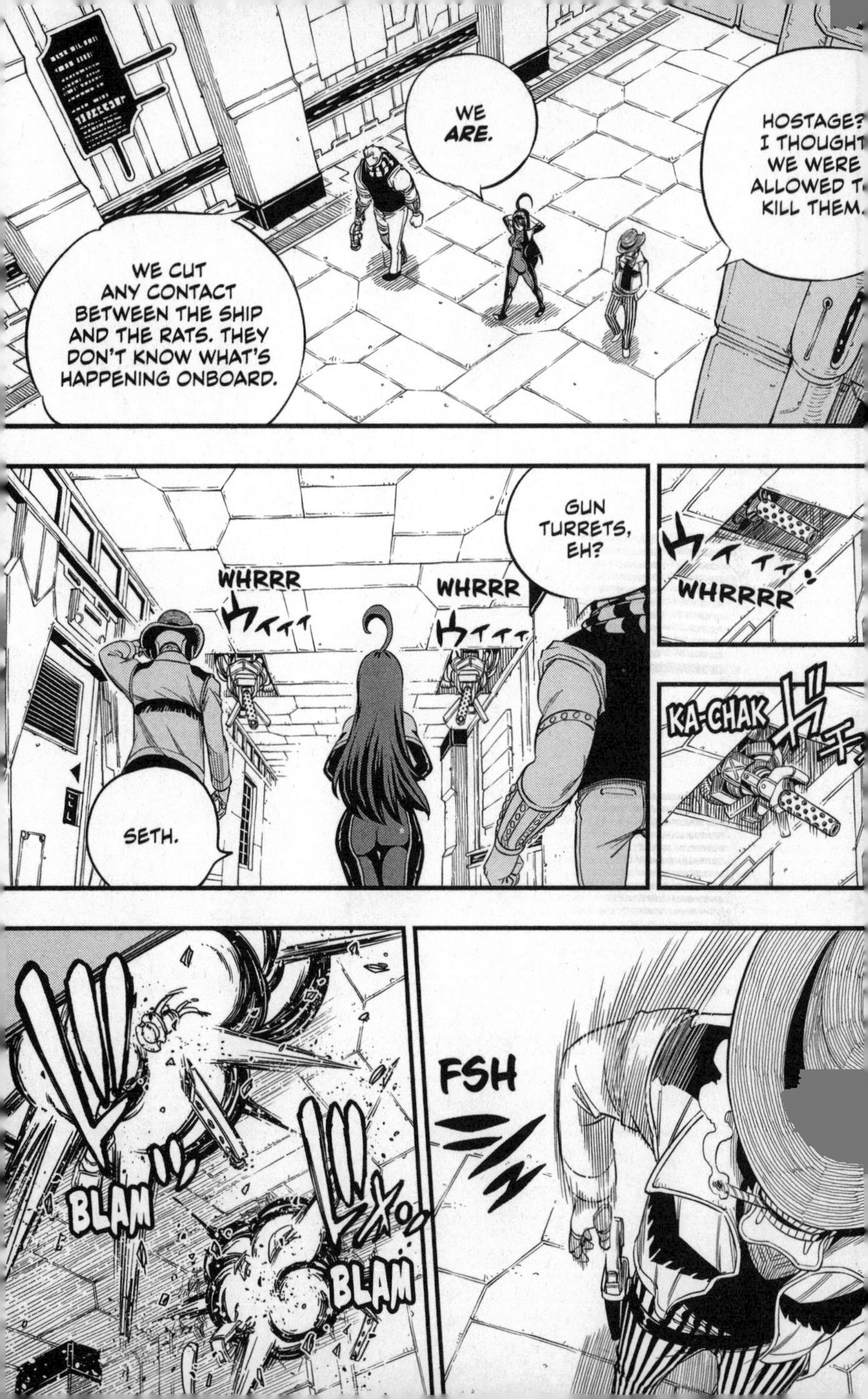
HOSTAGE? I THOUGHT WE WERE ALLOWED T KILL THEM.
WE ARE.
WE CUT ANY CONTACT BETWEEN THE SHIP AND THE RATS. THEY DON'T KNOW WHAT'S HAPPENING ONBOARD.
WHRRRR
KA-CHAK
GUN TURRETS, EH?
WHRRR
WHRRR
SETH.
FSH
BLAM
BLAM

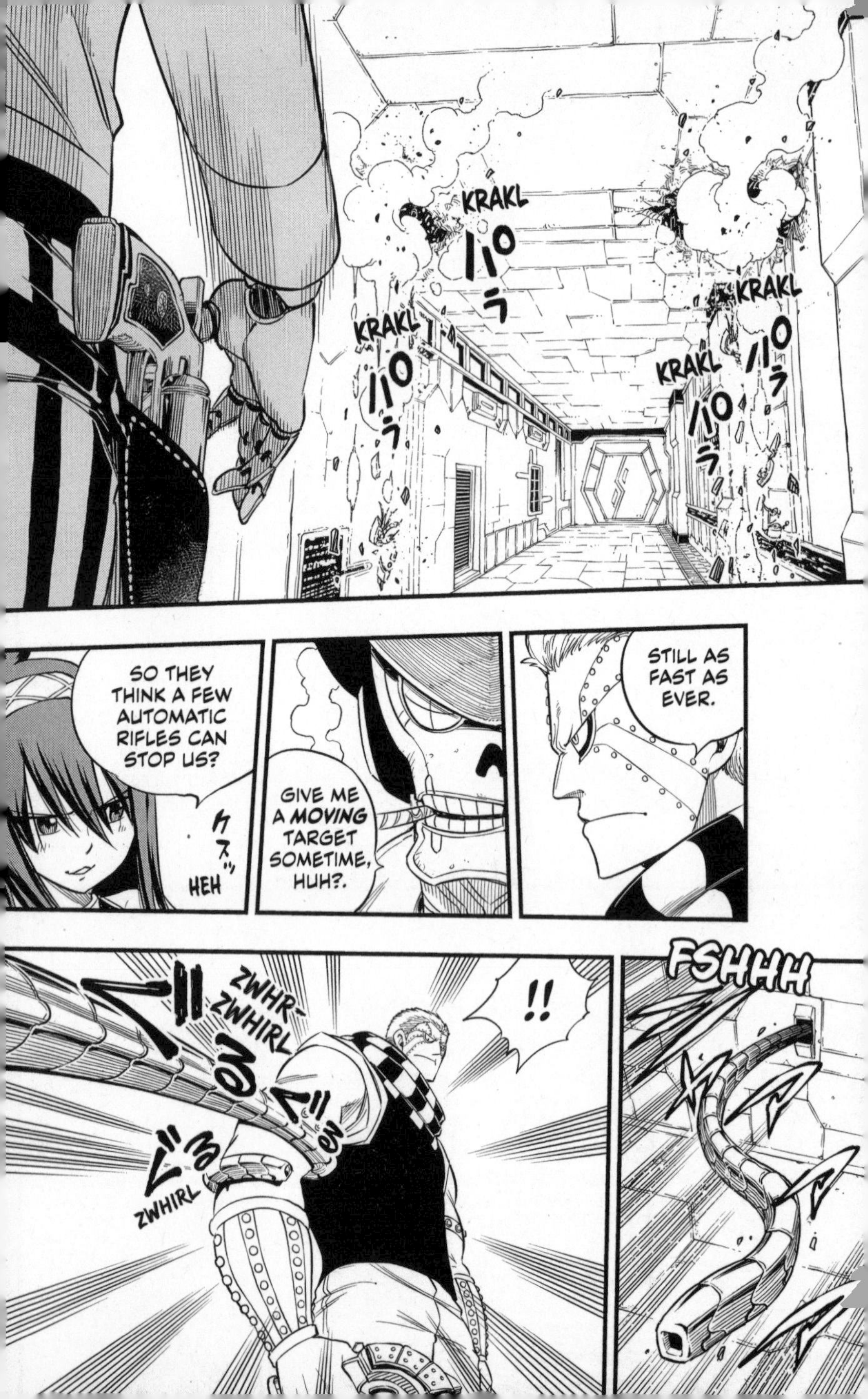
KRAKL
パラ
KRAKL
パラ
KRAKL
パラ
KRAKL
パラ
STILL AS FAST AS EVER.
GIVE ME A *MOVING* TARGET SOMETIME, HUH?.
SO THEY THINK A FEW AUTOMATIC RIFLES CAN STOP US?
クスッ
HEH
FSHHH
!!
ZWHR-ZWHIRL
ZWHIRL

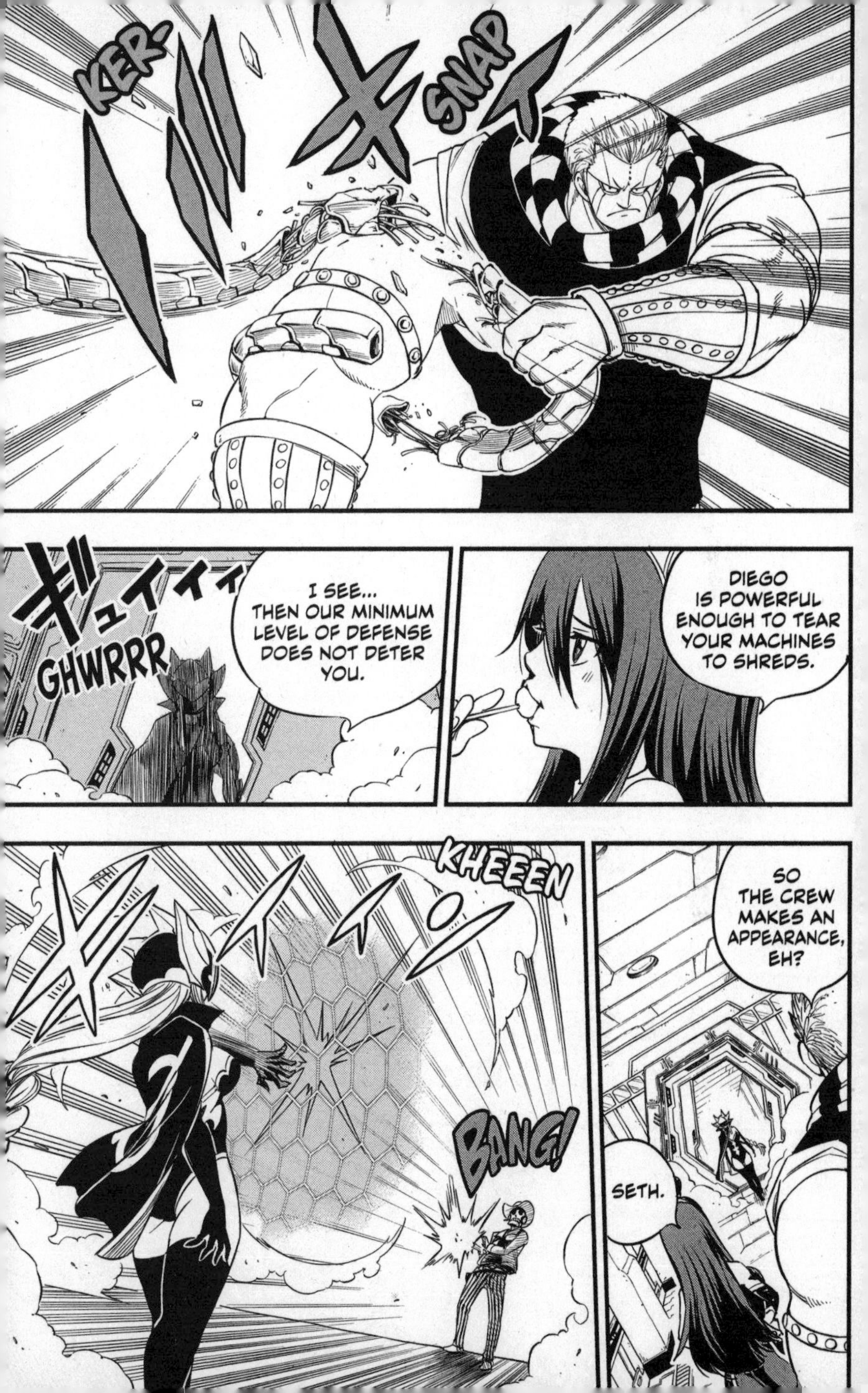
KER-
SNAP
DIEGO IS POWERFUL ENOUGH TO TEAR YOUR MACHINES TO SHREDS.
I SEE... THEN OUR MINIMUM LEVEL OF DEFENSE DOES NOT DETER YOU.
ギュイイイ
GHWRRR
SO THE CREW MAKES AN APPEARANCE, EH?
SETH.
KHEEEN
BANG!

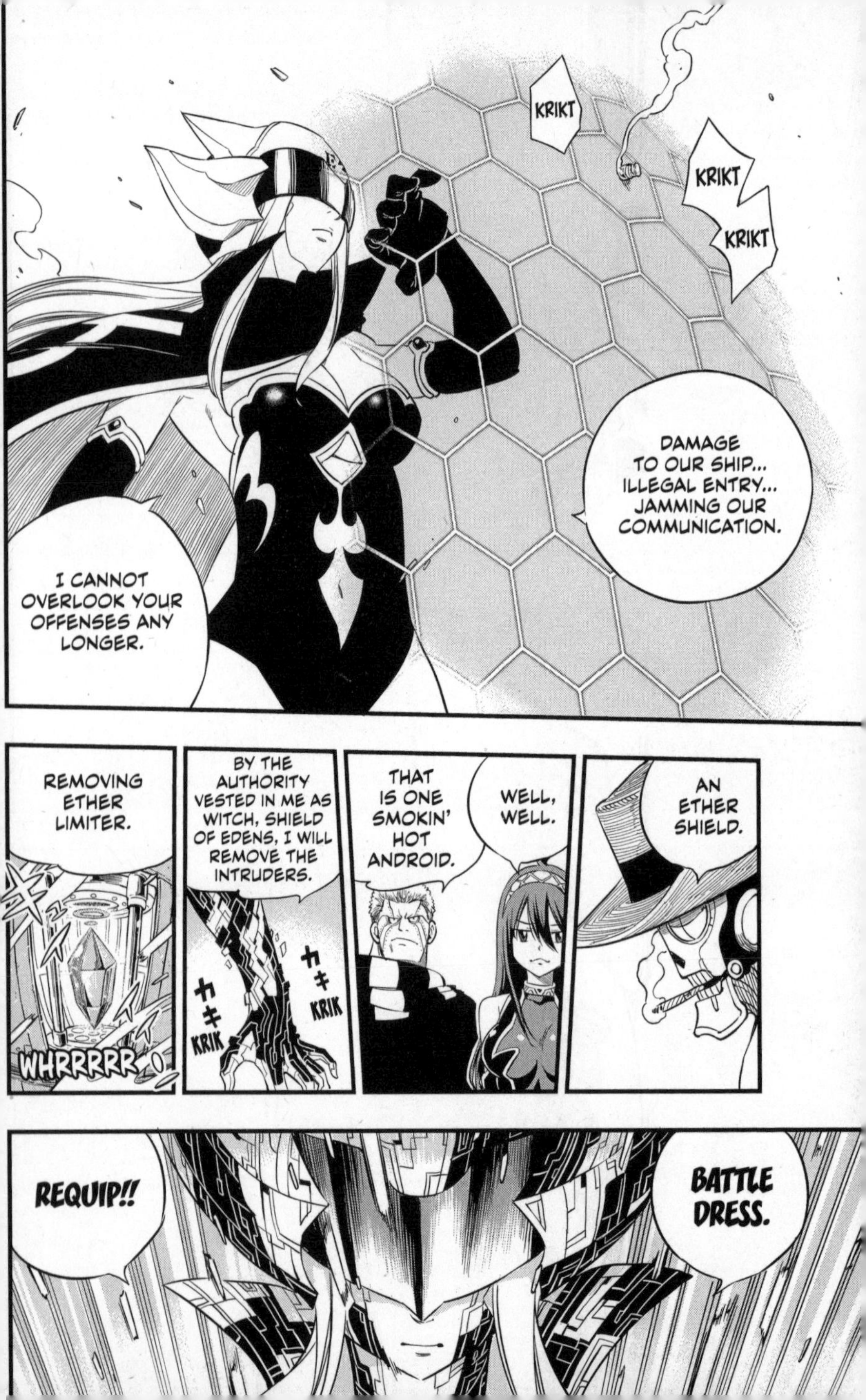
KRIKT
KRIKT
KRIKT
DAMAGE TO OUR SHIP... ILLEGAL ENTRY... JAMMING OUR COMMUNICATION.
I CANNOT OVERLOOK YOUR OFFENSES ANY LONGER.
AN ETHER SHIELD.
WELL, WELL.
THAT IS ONE SMOKIN' HOT ANDROID.
BY THE AUTHORITY VESTED IN ME AS WITCH, SHIELD OF EDENS, I WILL REMOVE THE INTRUDERS.
カキ
KRIK
カキ
KRIK
REMOVING ETHER LIMITER.
WHRRRRR
BATTLE DRESS.
REQUIP!!

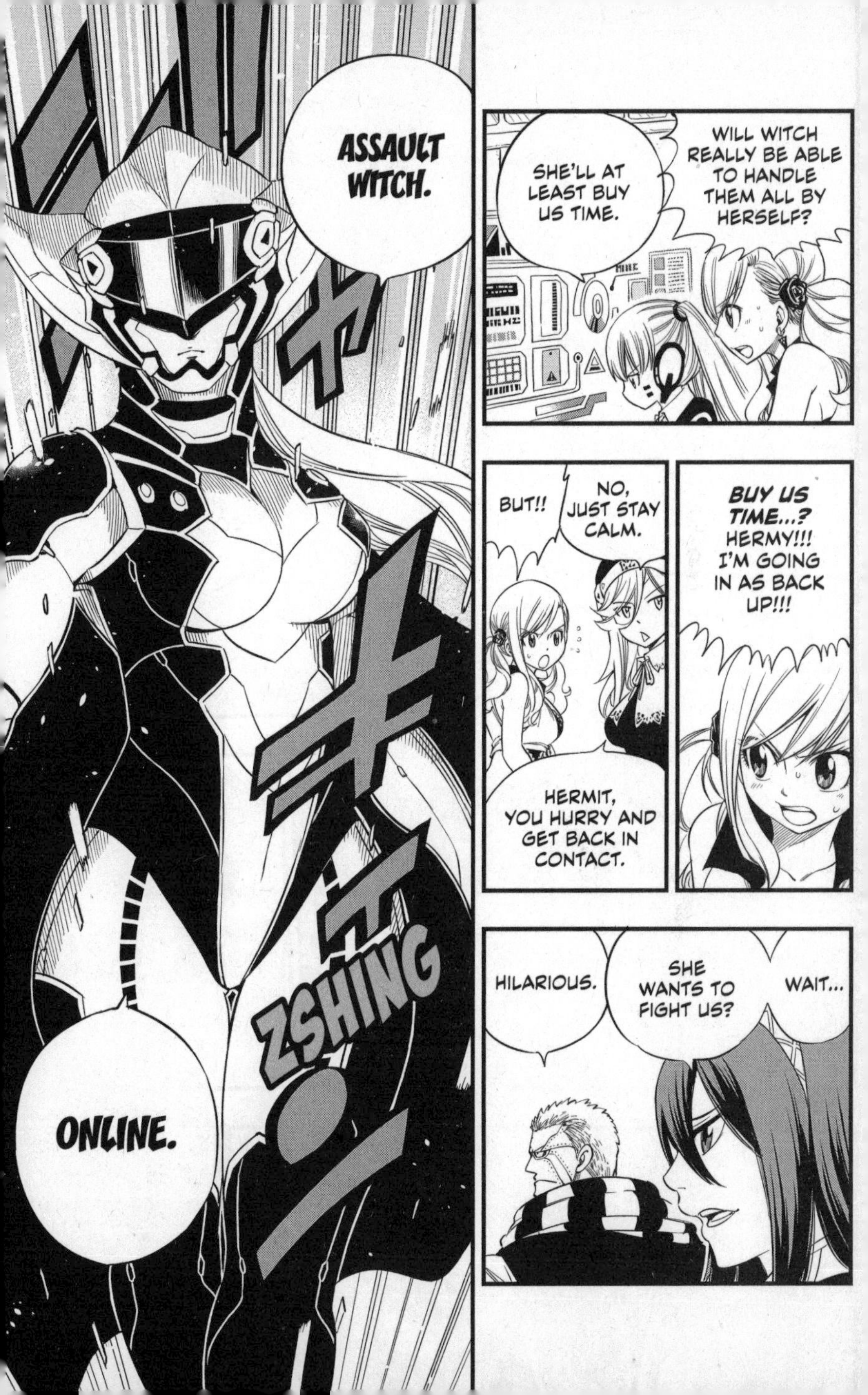
WILL WITCH REALLY BE ABLE TO HANDLE THEM ALL BY HERSELF?
SHE'LL AT LEAST BUY US TIME.
BUY US TIME...? HERMY!!! I'M GOING IN AS BACK UP!!!
NO, JUST STAY CALM.
BUT!!
HERMIT, YOU HURRY AND GET BACK IN CONTACT.
WAIT...
SHE WANTS TO FIGHT US?
HILARIOUS.
ASSAULT WITCH.
ZSHING
ONLINE.

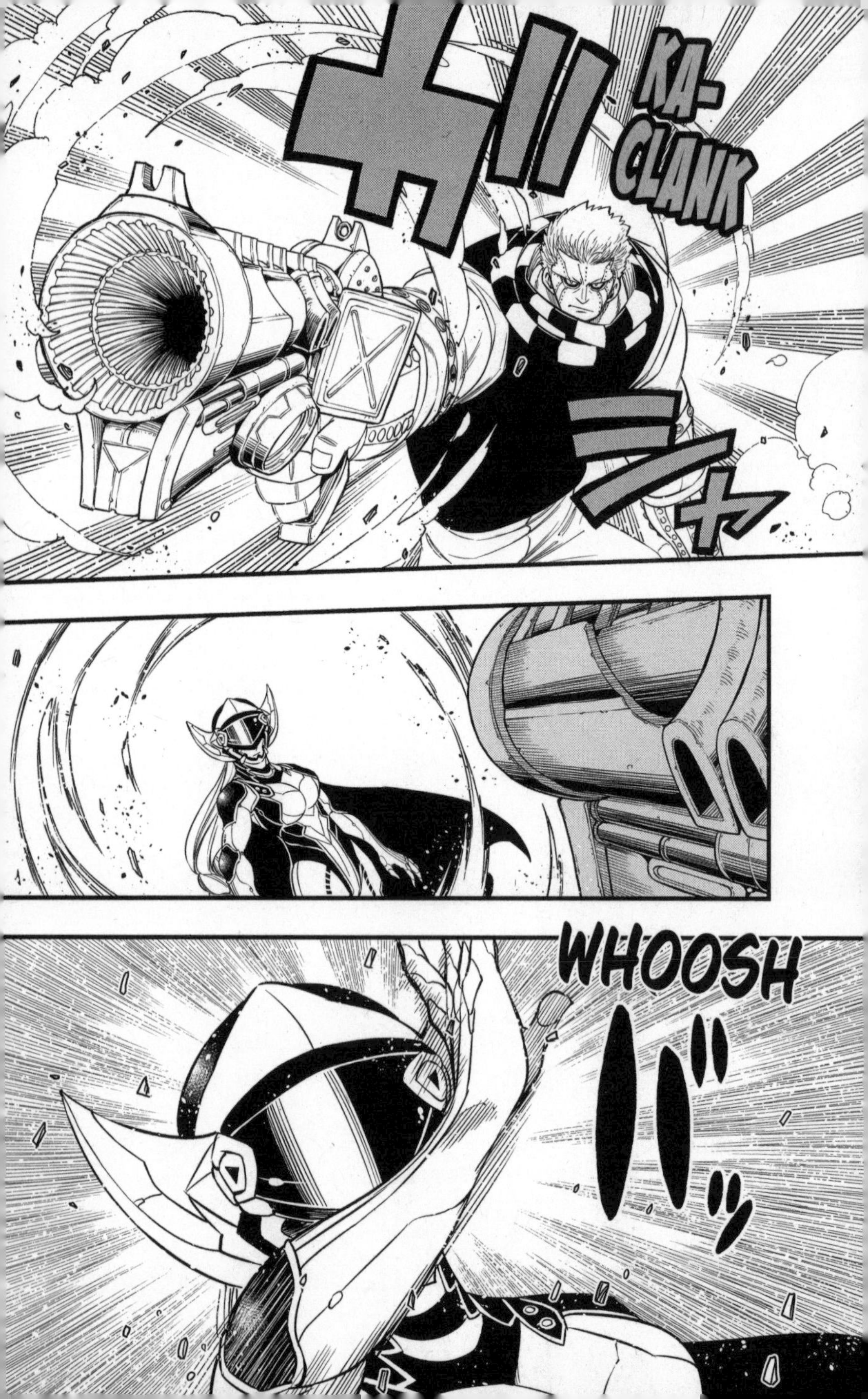
KA-CLANK
WHOOSH

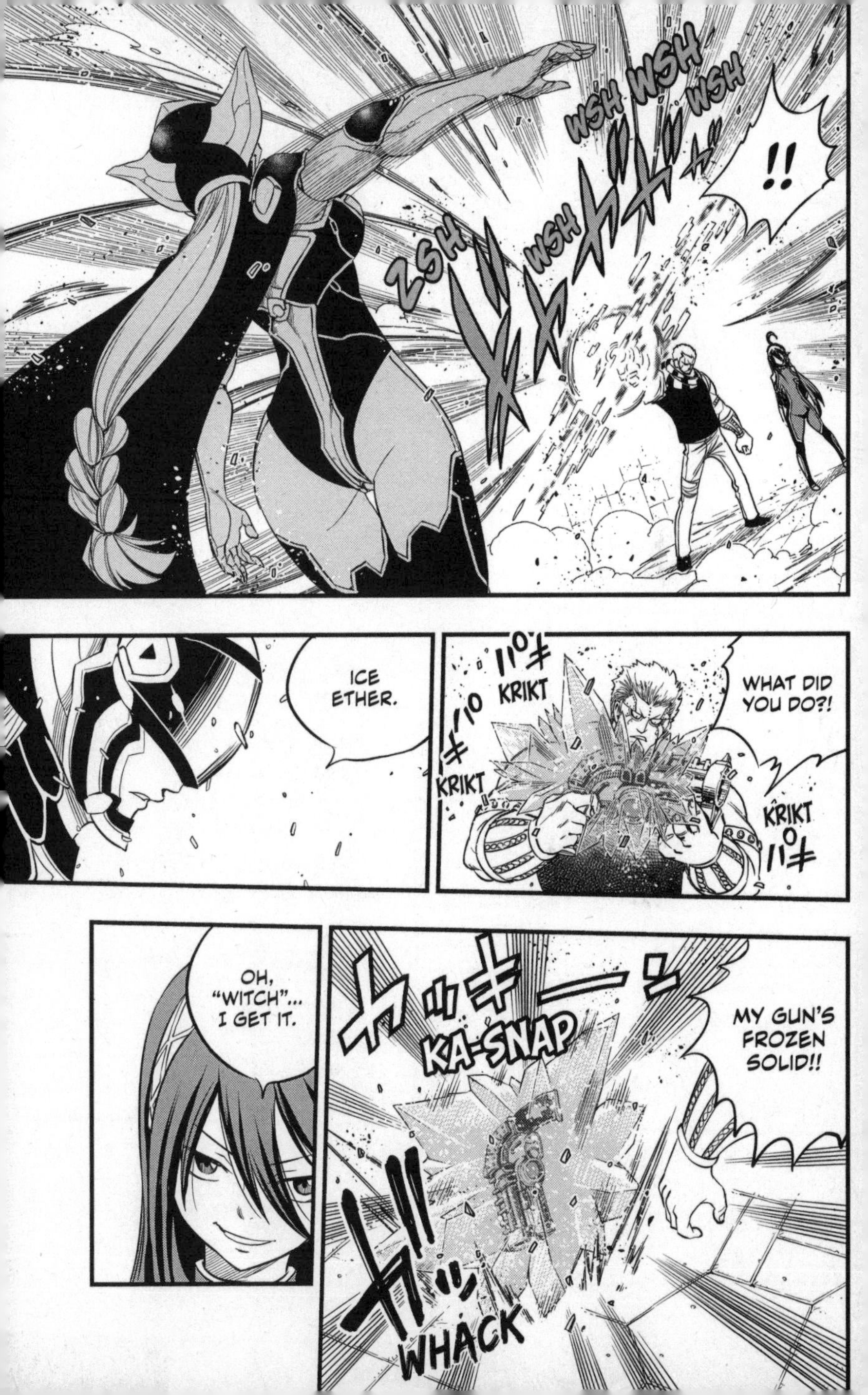
!!
WSH WSH
WSH
WSH
ZSH
WHAT DID YOU DO?!
KRIKT
KRIKT
KRIKT
ICE ETHER.
MY GUN'S FROZEN SOLID!!
KA-SNAP
WHACK
OH, "WITCH"... I GET IT.

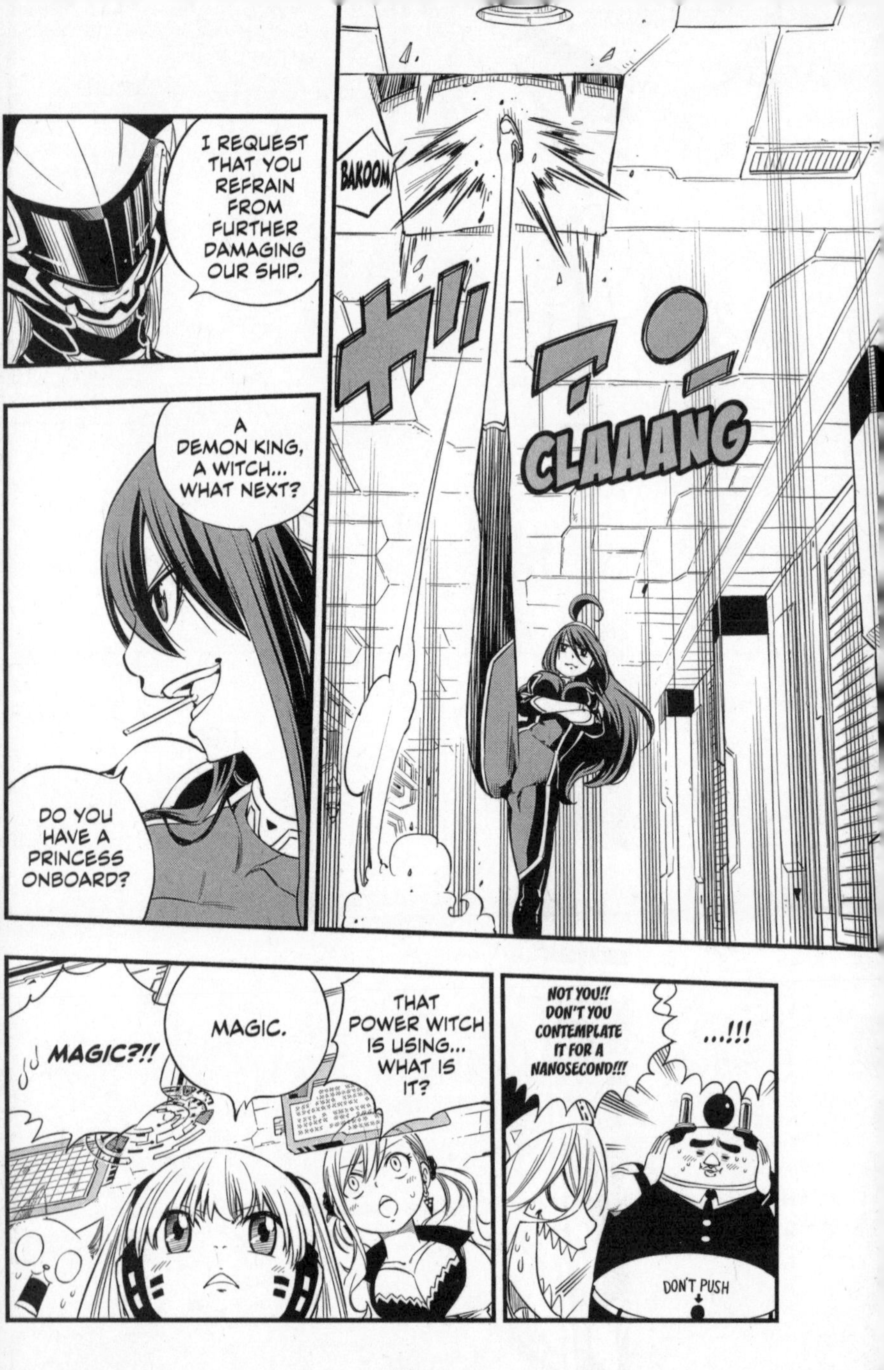
BAKOOM
CLAAANG
I REQUEST THAT YOU REFRAIN FROM FURTHER DAMAGING OUR SHIP.
A DEMON KING, A WITCH... WHAT NEXT?
DO YOU HAVE A PRINCESS ONBOARD?
NOT YOU!! DON'T YOU CONTEMPLATE IT FOR A NANOSECOND!!!
...!!!
DON'T PUSH
THAT POWER WITCH IS USING... WHAT IS IT?
MAGIC.
MAGIC?!!

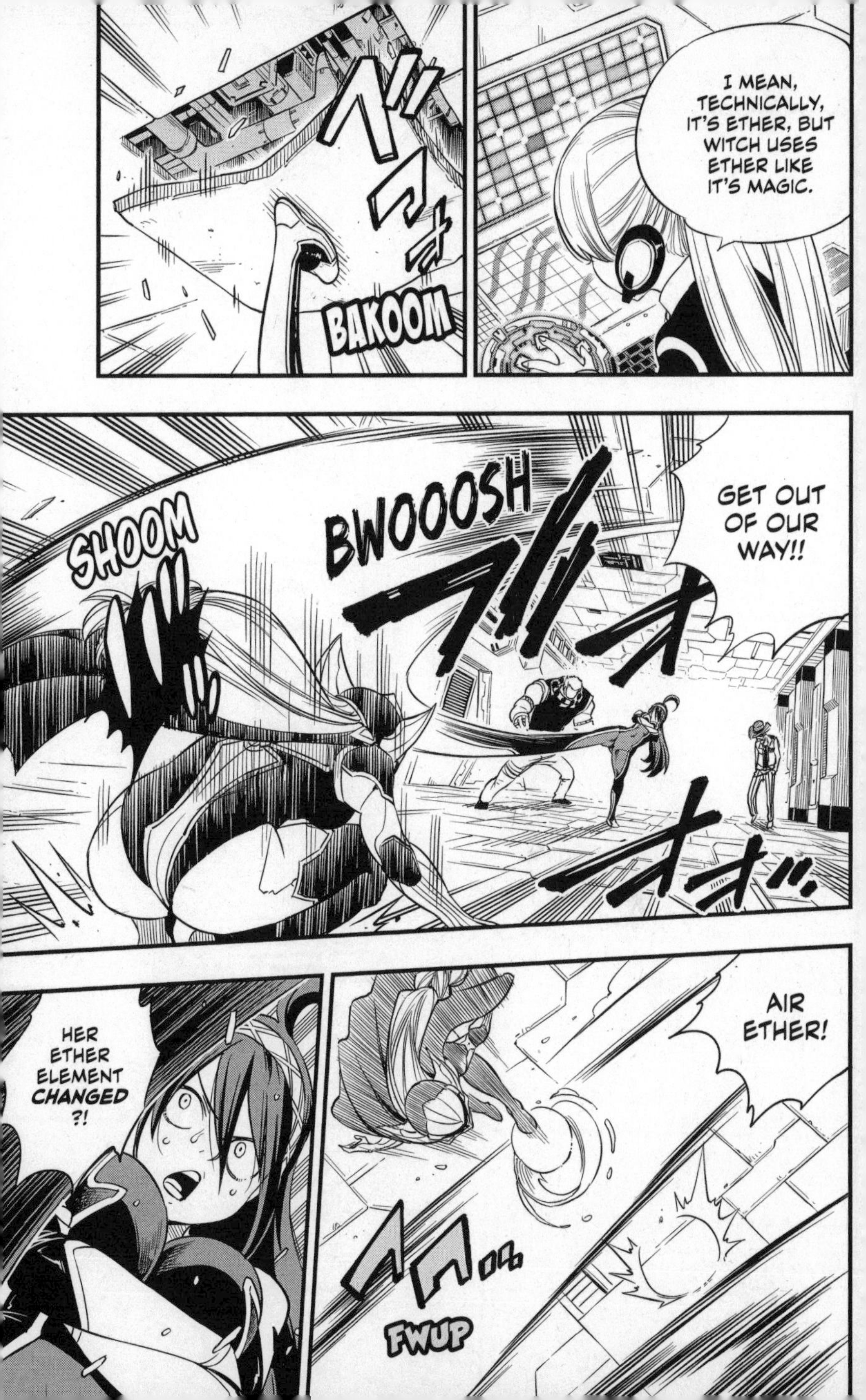
I MEAN, TECHNICALLY, IT'S ETHER, BUT WITCH USES ETHER LIKE IT'S MAGIC.
BAKOOM
GET OUT OF OUR WAY!!
BWOOOSH
SHOOM
AIR ETHER!
FWUP
HER ETHER ELEMENT CHANGED?!

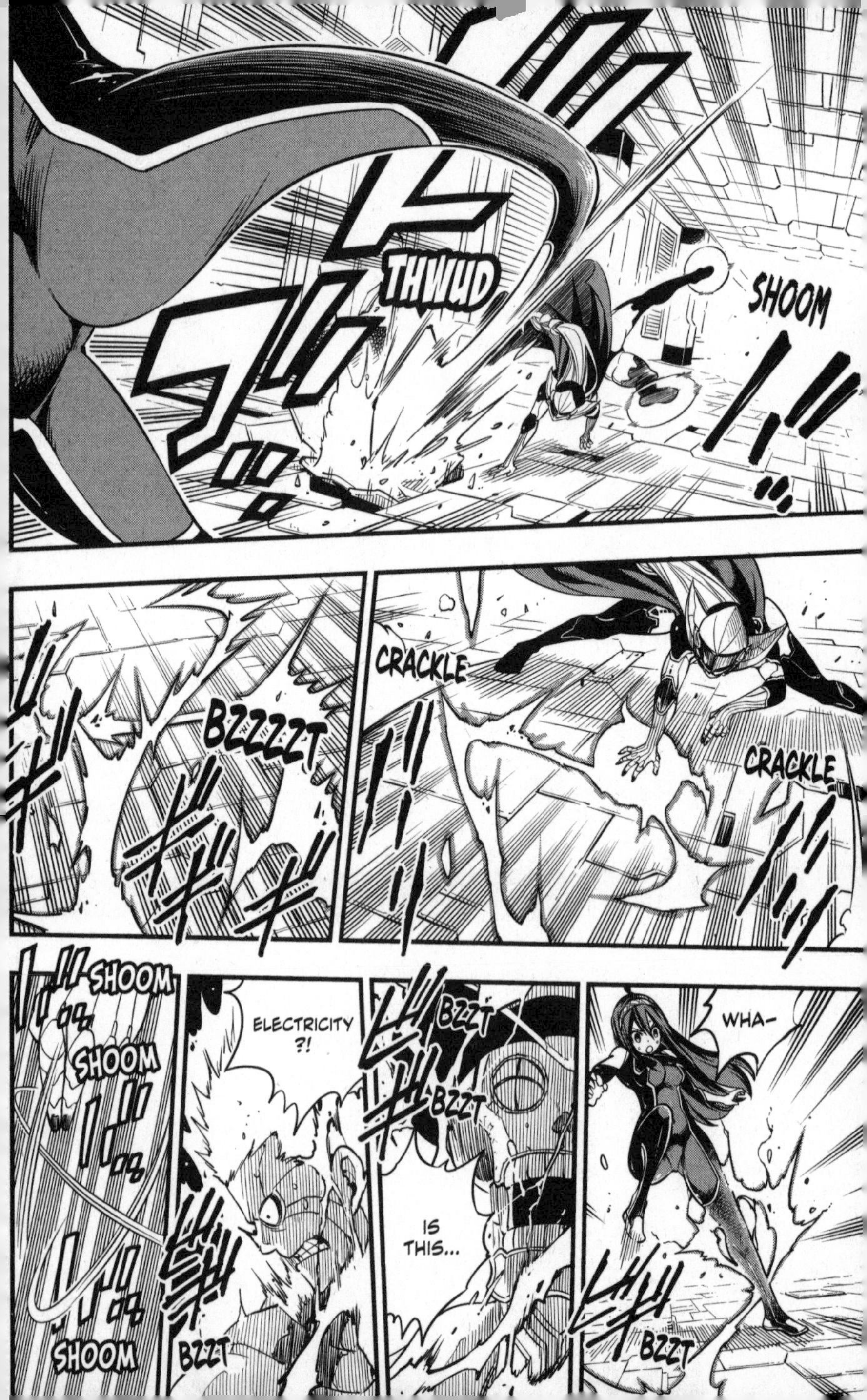
SHOOM
THWUD
CRACKLE
CRACKLE
BZZZZZT
WHA-
BZZT
BZZT
BZZT
IS THIS...
ELECTRICITY ?!
BZZT
SHOOM
SHOOM
SHOOM

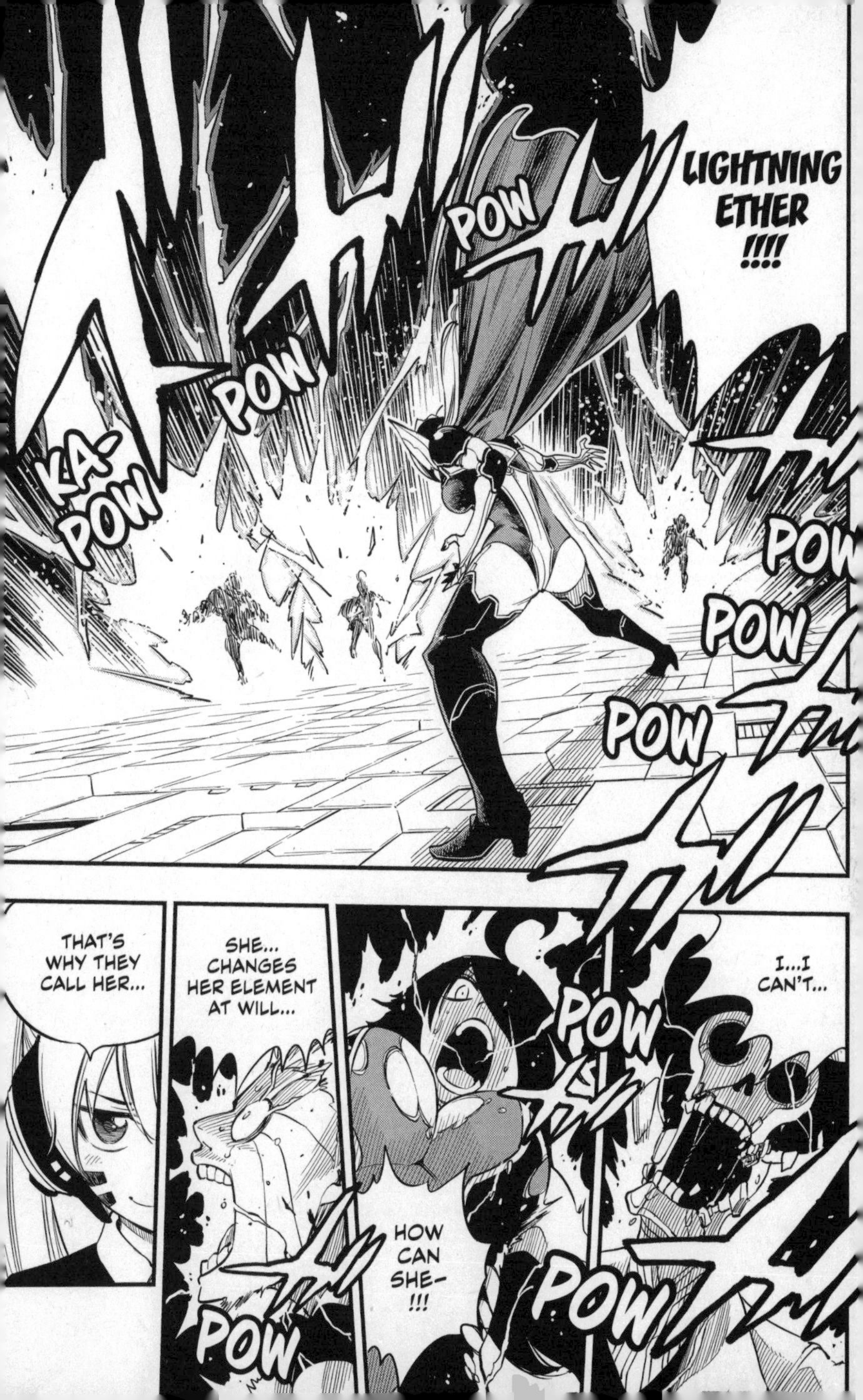
LIGHTNING ETHER !!!!
POW
POW
POW
POW
POW
KA-POW
I...I CAN'T...
POW
POW
HOW CAN SHE-!!!
POW
SHE... CHANGES HER ELEMENT AT WILL...
THAT'S WHY THEY CALL HER...

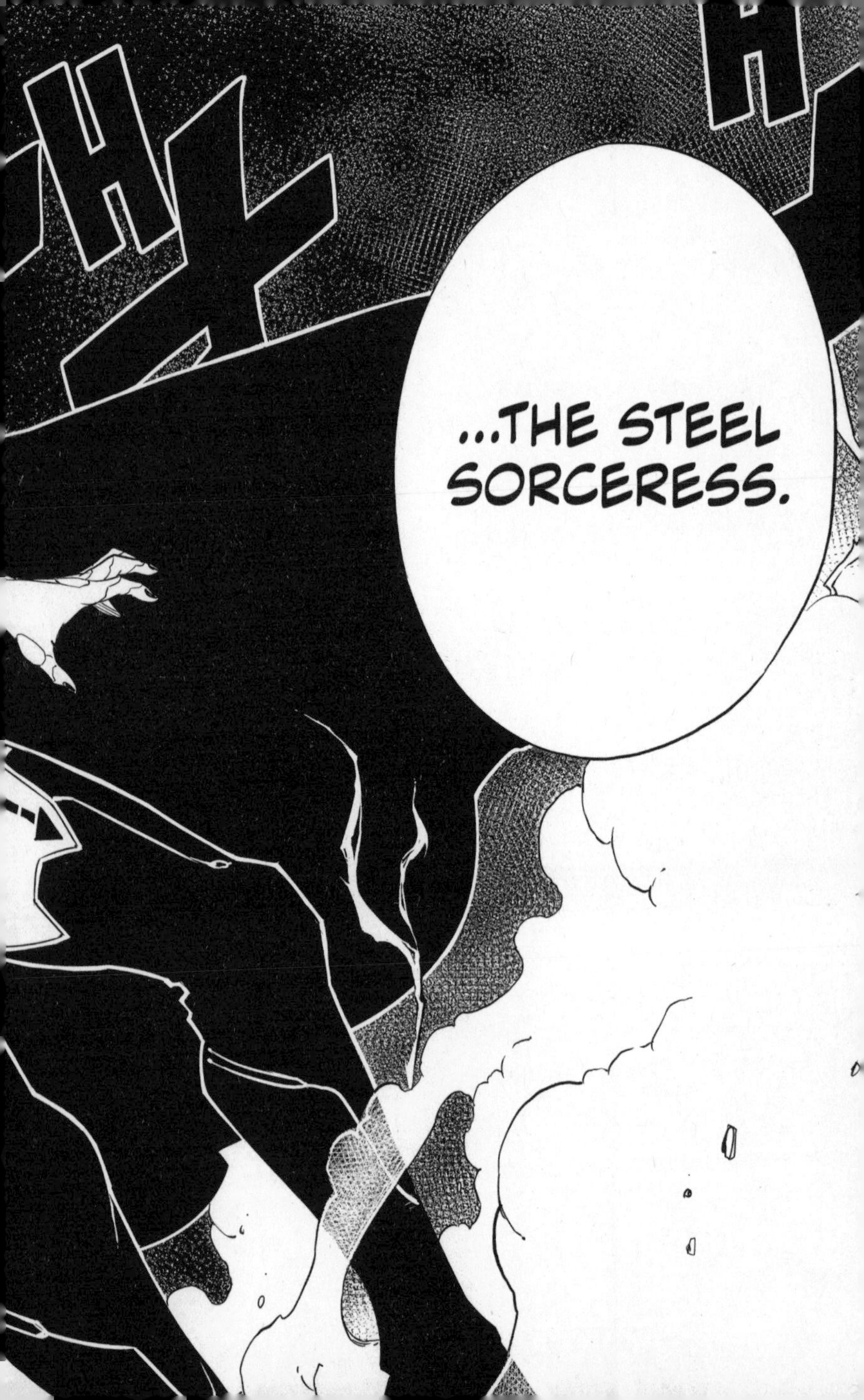
...THE STEEL SORCERESS.

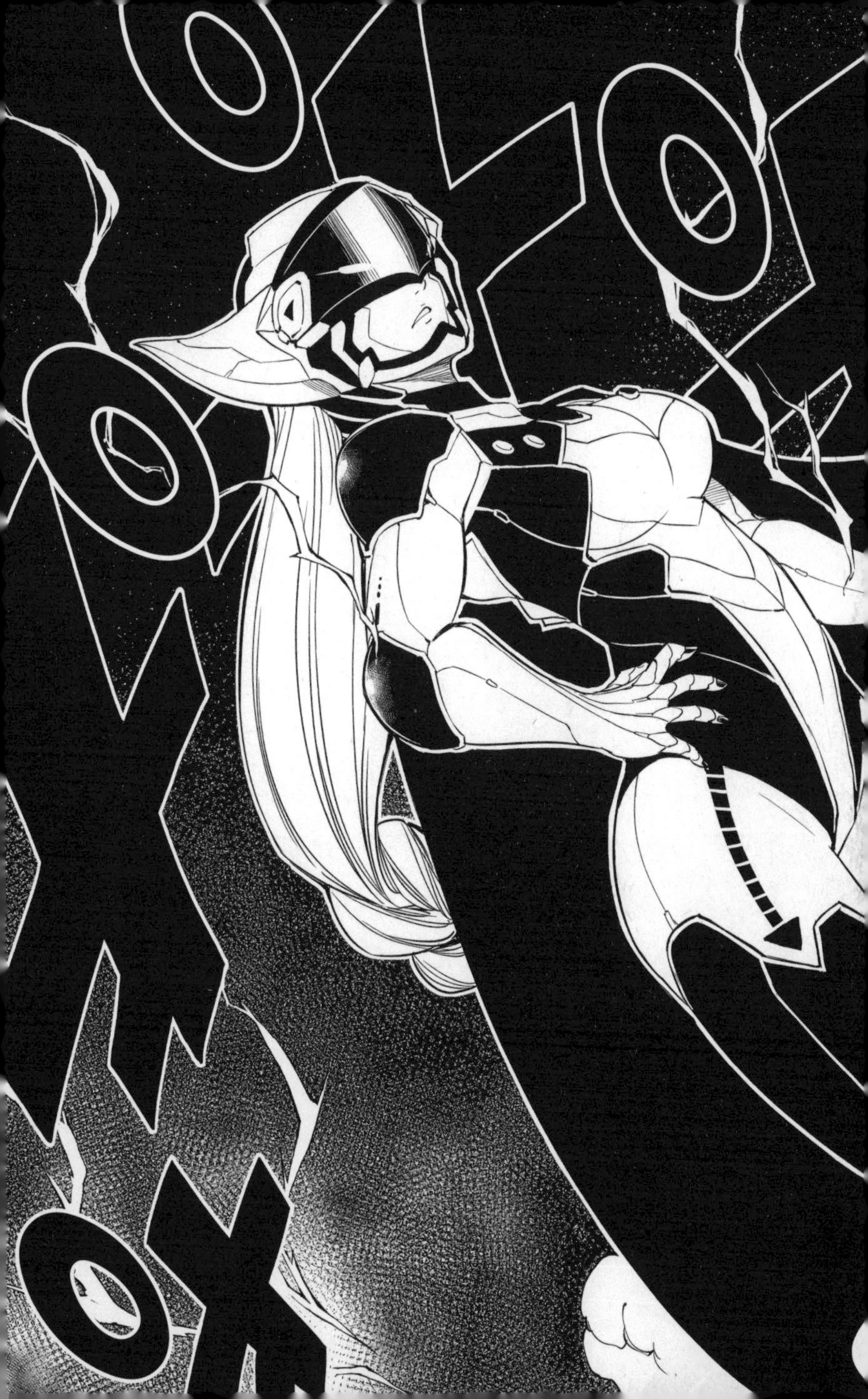

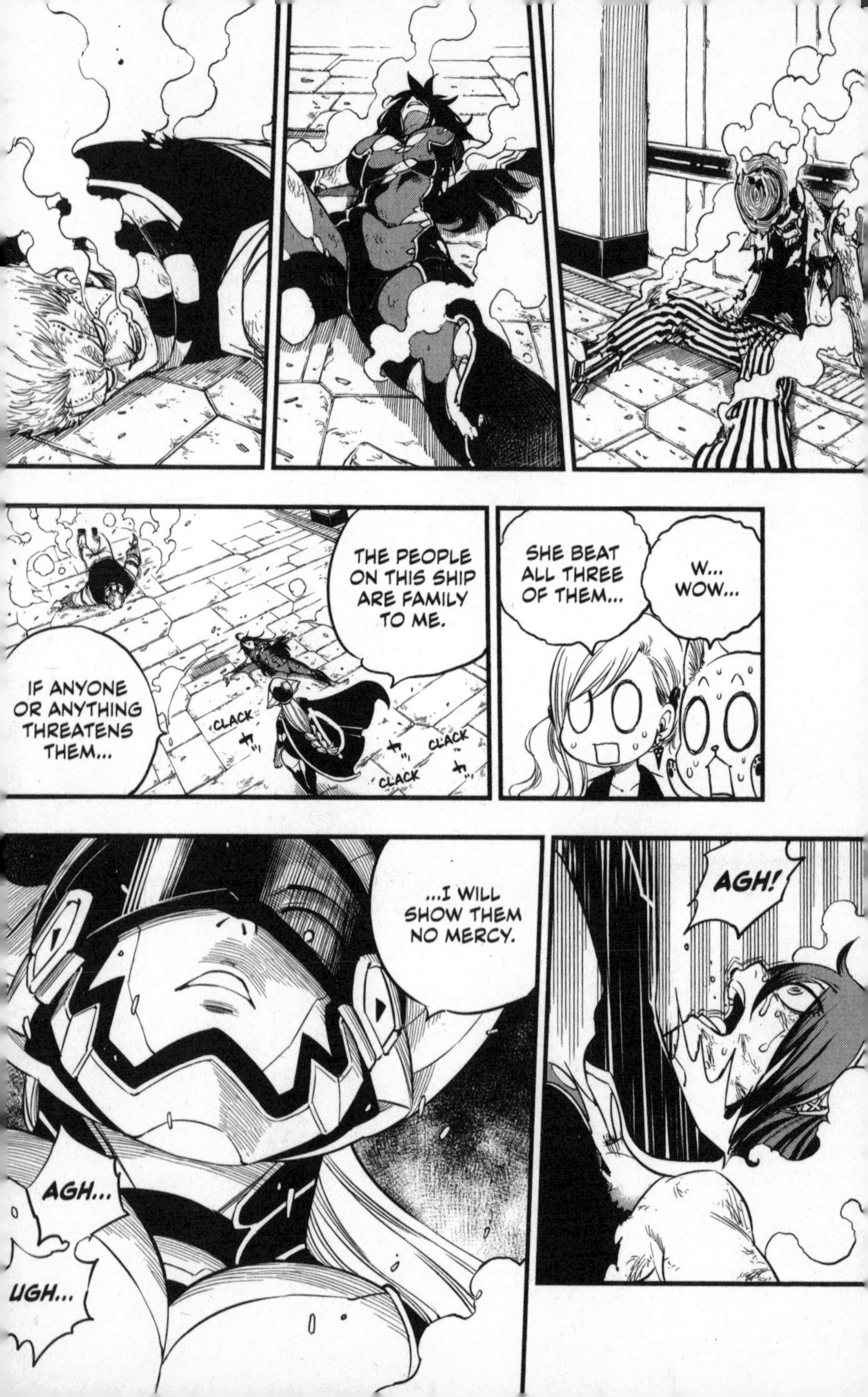
W... WOW...
SHE BEAT ALL THREE OF THEM...
THE PEOPLE ON THIS SHIP ARE FAMILY TO ME.
CLACK
CLACK
CLACK
IF ANYONE OR ANYTHING THREATENS THEM...
AGH!
...I WILL SHOW THEM NO MERCY.
AGH...
UGH...

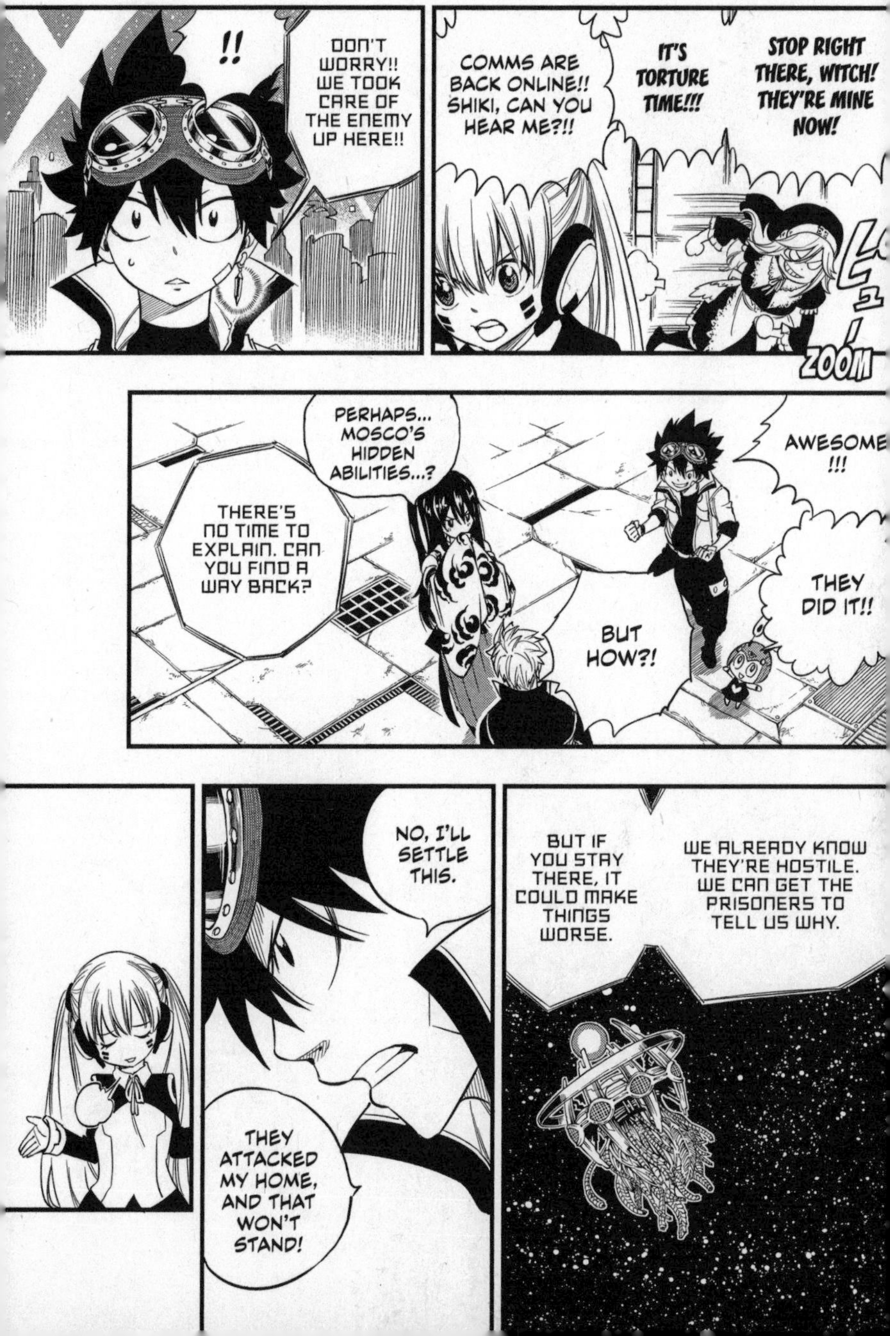
STOP RIGHT THERE, WITCH! THEY'RE MINE NOW!
IT'S TORTURE TIME!!!
COMMS ARE BACK ONLINE!! SHIKI, CAN YOU HEAR ME?!!
ZOOM
DON'T WORRY!! WE TOOK CARE OF THE ENEMY UP HERE!!
!!
AWESOME!!!
PERHAPS... MOSCO'S HIDDEN ABILITIES...?
THEY DID IT!!
THERE'S NO TIME TO EXPLAIN. CAN YOU FIND A WAY BACK?
BUT HOW?!
WE ALREADY KNOW THEY'RE HOSTILE. WE CAN GET THE PRISONERS TO TELL US WHY.
BUT IF YOU STAY THERE, IT COULD MAKE THINGS WORSE.
NO, I'LL SETTLE THIS.
THEY ATTACKED MY HOME, AND THAT WON'T STAND!

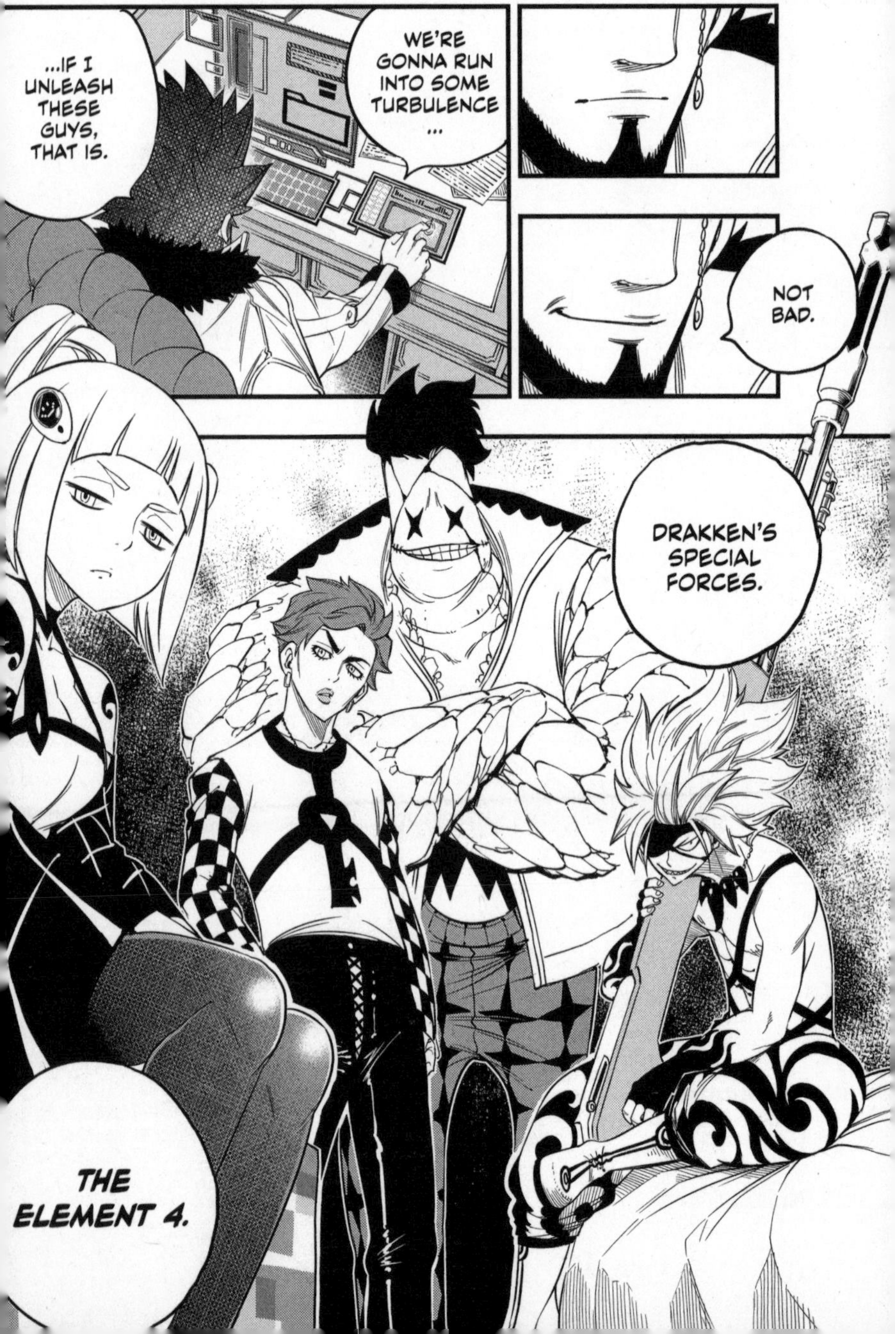
NOT BAD.
WE'RE GONNA RUN INTO SOME TURBULENCE...
...IF I UNLEASH THESE GUYS, THAT IS.
DRAKKEN'S SPECIAL FORCES.
THE ELEMENT 4.

EDENS ZERO

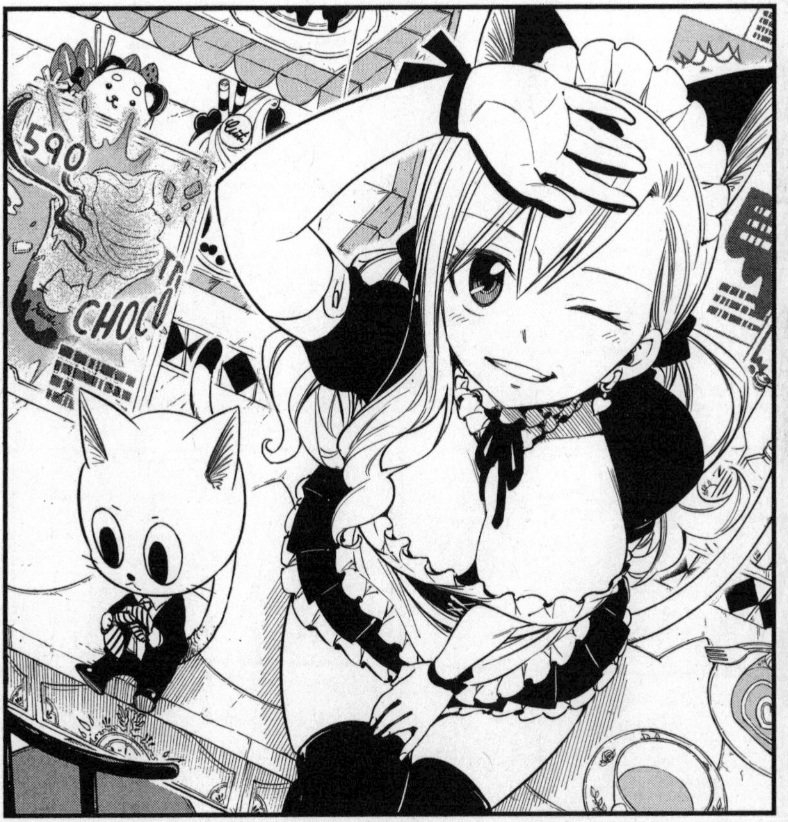
590
CHOCO

CHAPTER 72: THE ELEMENT 4

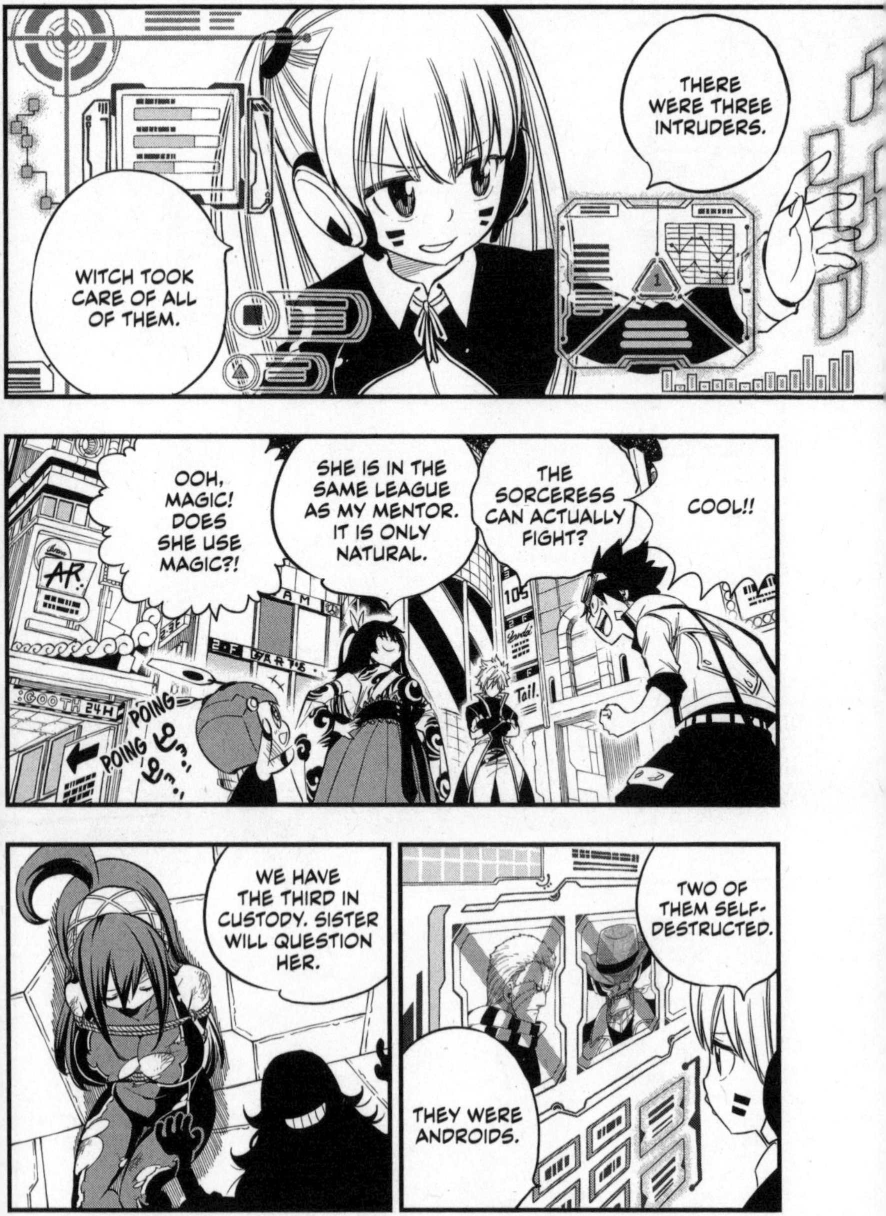
THERE WERE THREE INTRUDERS.
WITCH TOOK CARE OF ALL OF THEM.
COOL!!
THE SORCERESS CAN ACTUALLY FIGHT?
SHE IS IN THE SAME LEAGUE AS MY MENTOR. IT IS ONLY NATURAL.
OOH, MAGIC! DOES SHE USE MAGIC?!
POING
POING
TWO OF THEM SELF-DESTRUCTED.
THEY WERE ANDROIDS.
WE HAVE THE THIRD IN CUSTODY. SISTER WILL QUESTION HER.

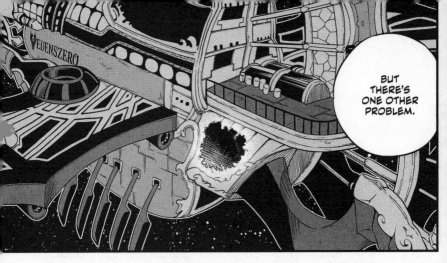

BUT THERE'S ONE OTHER PROBLEM.

THE EDGES OF THE HOLE ARE FLUTTERING AROUND LIKE PAPER...

HOW DID THEY DO THAT TO IT?

THE EDENS ZERO'S ARMOR IS MADE OF A SPECIAL MATERIAL CALLED GUARNANIUM.

YOUR AVERAGE WEAPON COULD NOT EVEN SCRATCH IT.

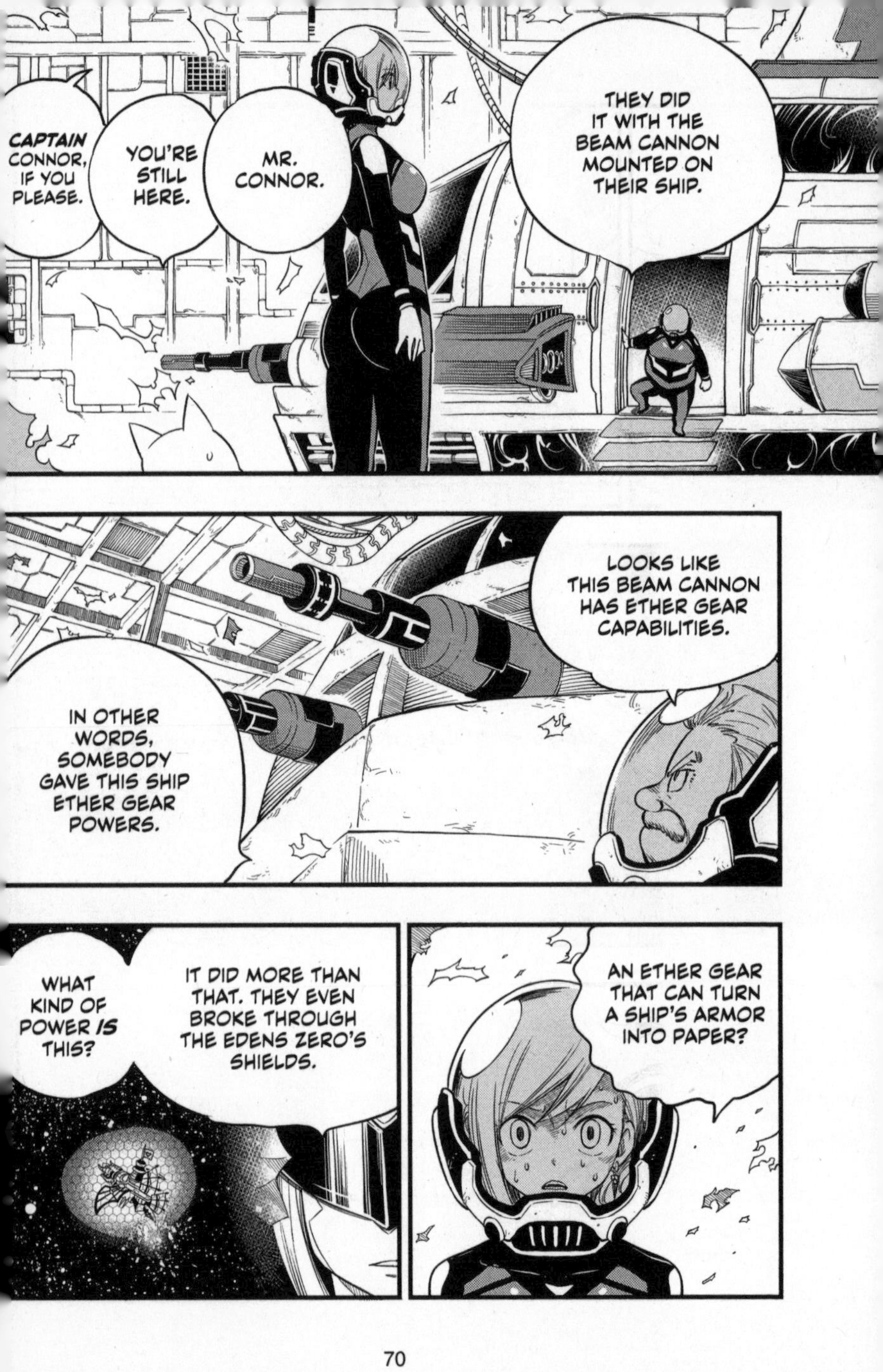
THEY DID IT WITH THE BEAM CANNON MOUNTED ON THEIR SHIP.
MR. CONNOR.
YOU'RE STILL HERE.
CAPTAIN CONNOR, IF YOU PLEASE.
LOOKS LIKE THIS BEAM CANNON HAS ETHER GEAR CAPABILITIES.
IN OTHER WORDS, SOMEBODY GAVE THIS SHIP ETHER GEAR POWERS.
AN ETHER GEAR THAT CAN TURN A SHIP'S ARMOR INTO PAPER?
IT DID MORE THAN THAT. THEY EVEN BROKE THROUGH THE EDENS ZERO'S SHIELDS.
WHAT KIND OF POWER *IS* THIS?

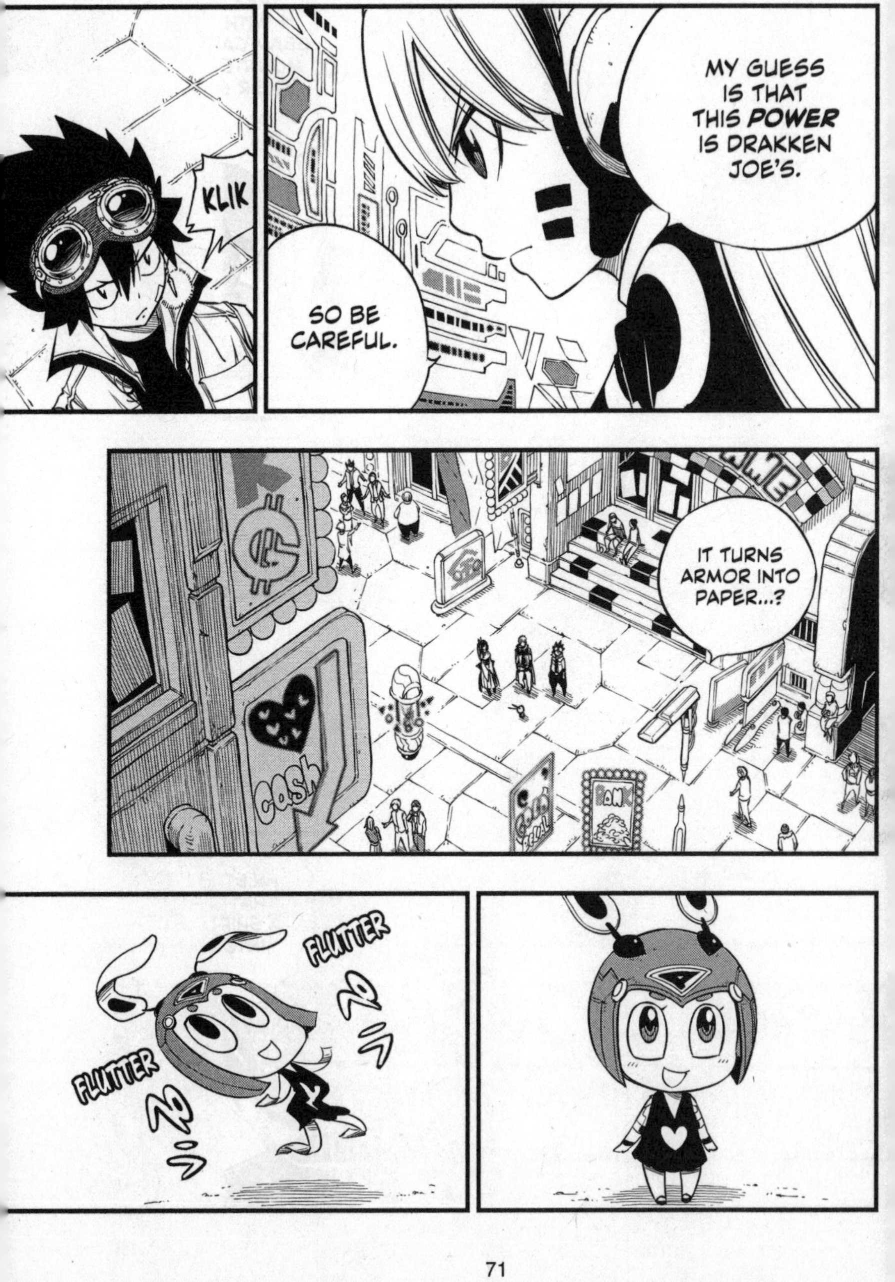
MY GUESS IS THAT THIS ***POWER*** IS DRAKKEN JOE'S.
SO BE CAREFUL.
KLIK
IT TURNS ARMOR INTO PAPER...?
FLUTTER
FLUTTER

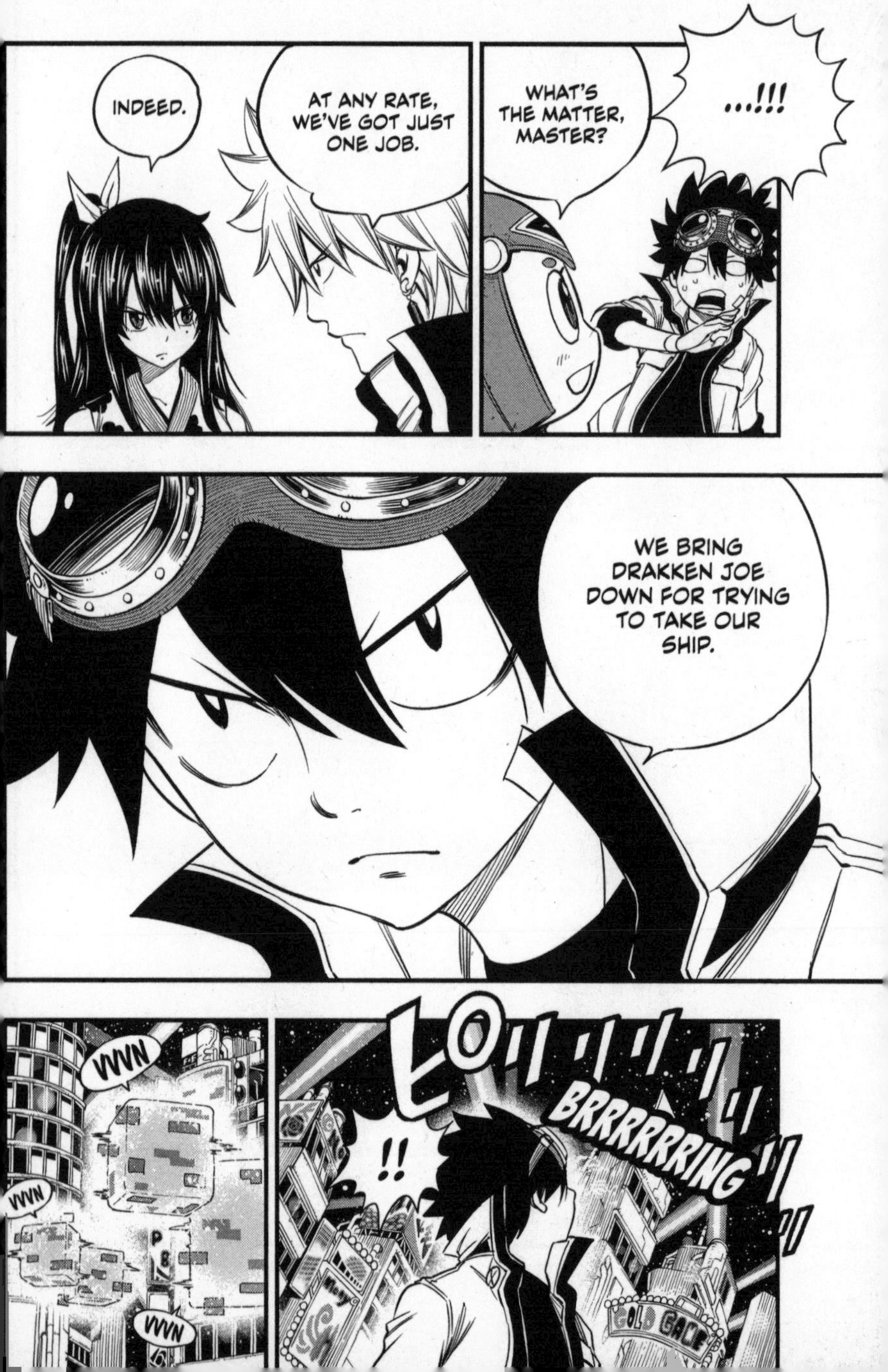
...!!!
WHAT'S THE MATTER, MASTER?
AT ANY RATE, WE'VE GOT JUST ONE JOB.
INDEED.
WE BRING DRAKKEN JOE DOWN FOR TRYING TO TAKE OUR SHIP.
BRRRRRRRING
!!
VVVN
VVVN
VVVN

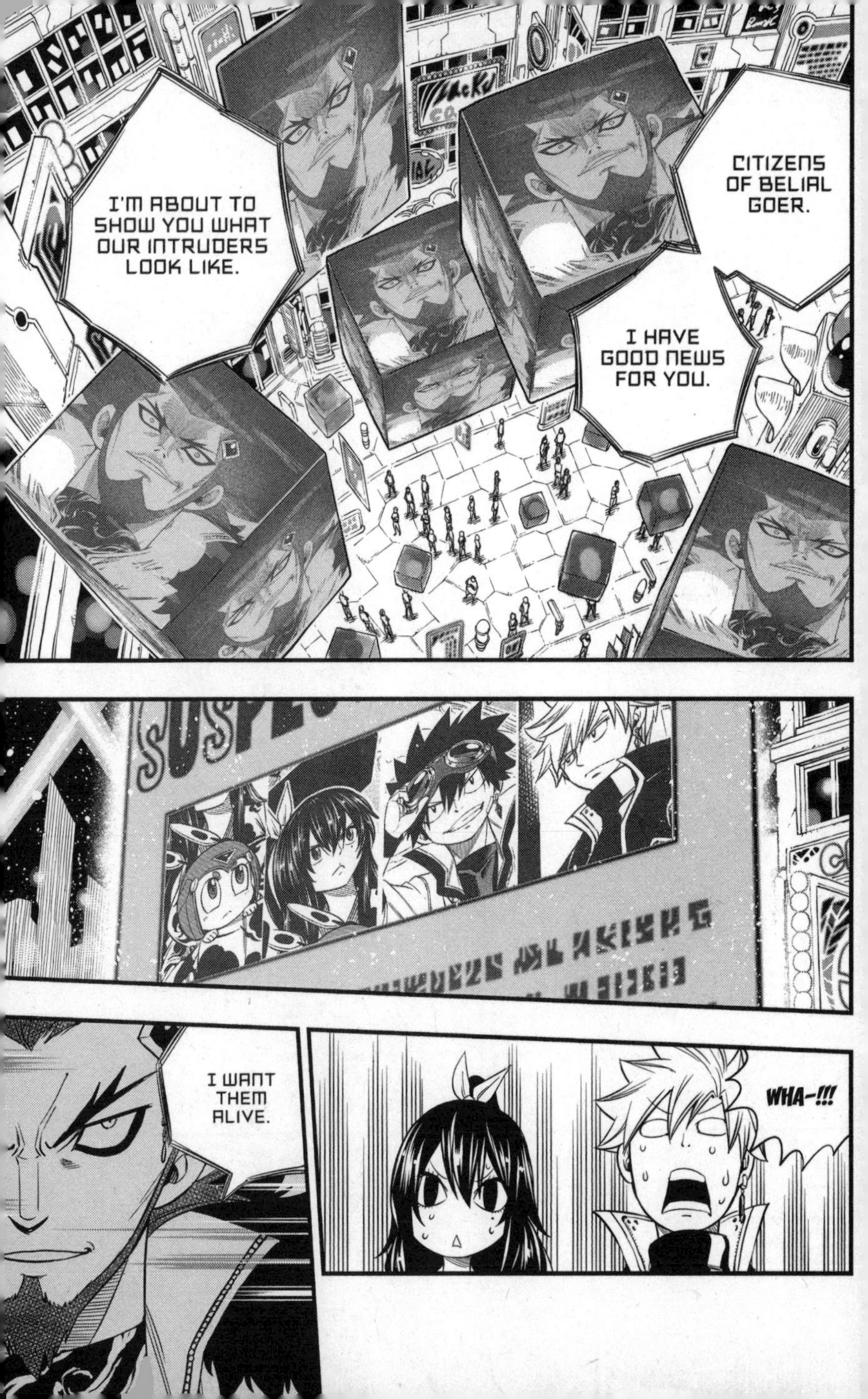
CITIZENS OF BELIAL GOER.
I HAVE GOOD NEWS FOR YOU.
I'M ABOUT TO SHOW YOU WHAT OUR INTRUDERS LOOK LIKE.
WHA-!!!
I WANT THEM ALIVE.

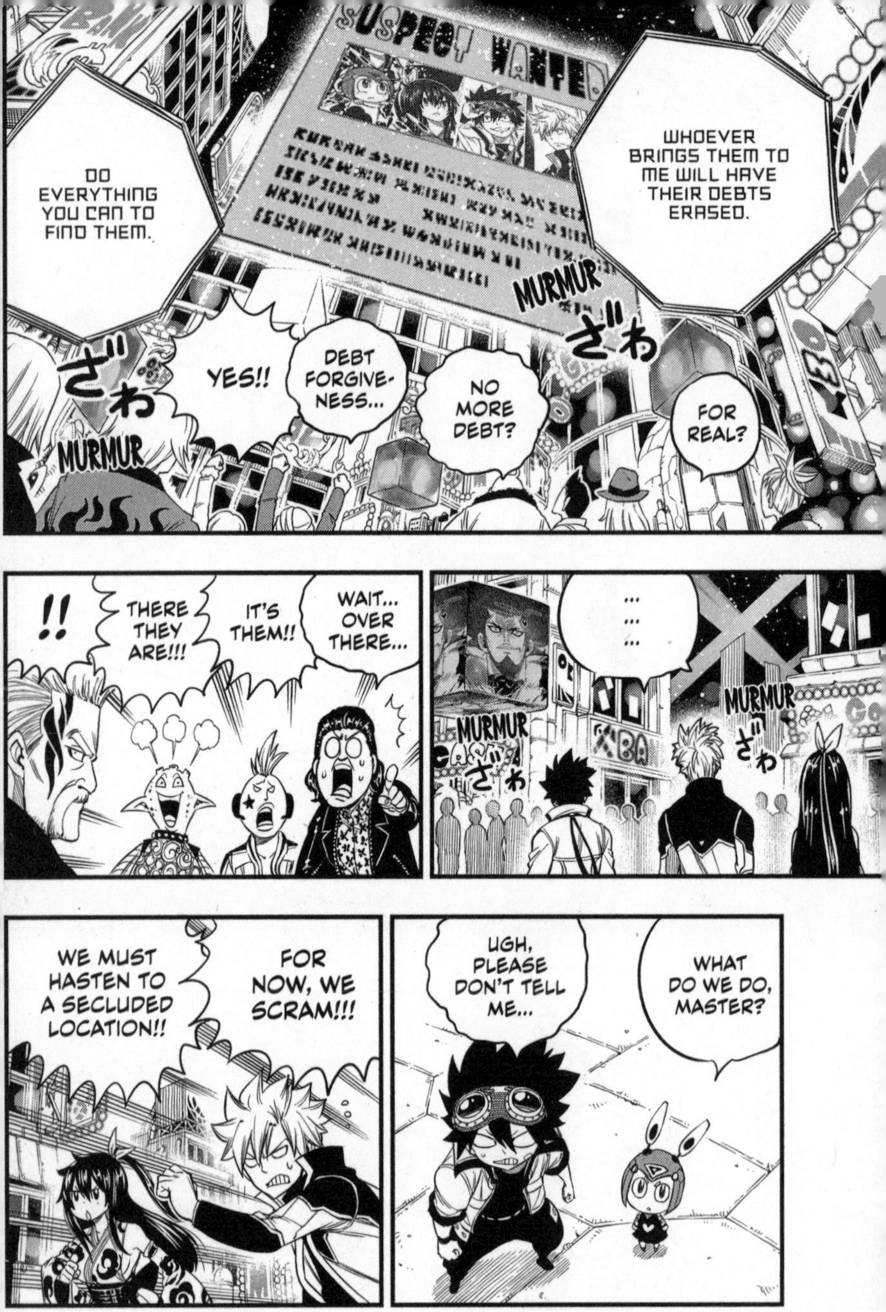
SUSPECT WANTED
WHOEVER BRINGS THEM TO ME WILL HAVE THEIR DEBTS ERASED.
DO EVERYTHING YOU CAN TO FIND THEM.
MURMUR
ざわ
FOR REAL?
NO MORE DEBT?
DEBT FORGIVE-NESS...
YES!!
ざわ
MURMUR
...
...
...
MURMUR
ざわ
MURMUR
ざわ
WAIT... OVER THERE...
IT'S THEM!!
THERE THEY ARE!!!
!!
WHAT DO WE DO, MASTER?
UGH, PLEASE DON'T TELL ME...
FOR NOW, WE SCRAM!!!
WE MUST HASTEN TO A SECLUDED LOCATION!!

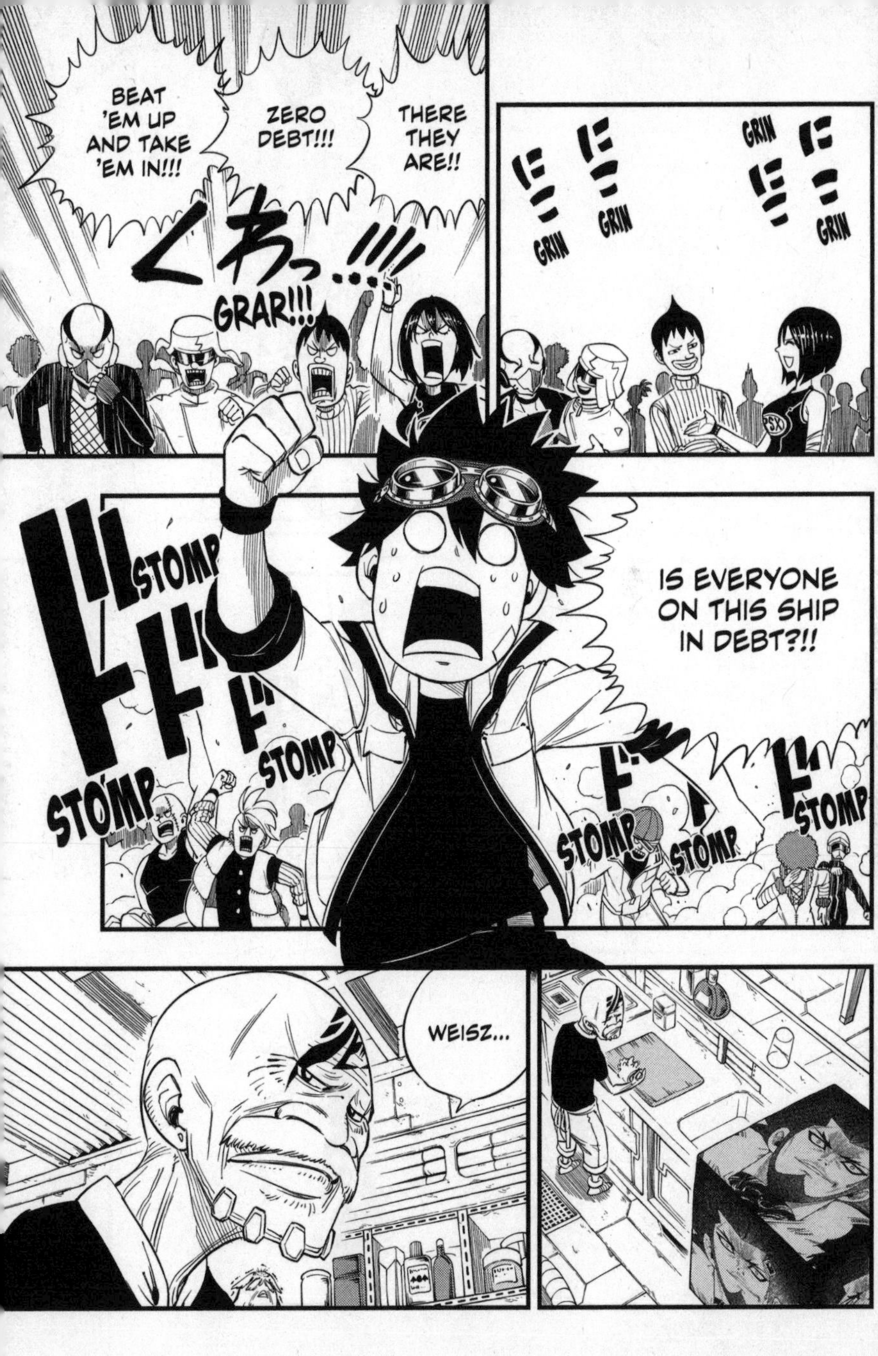
にこ GRIN
にこ GRIN
にこ GRIN
にこ GRIN
THERE THEY ARE!!
ZERO DEBT!!!
BEAT 'EM UP AND TAKE 'EM IN!!!
くわっ..!!!!
GRAR!!!
IS EVERYONE ON THIS SHIP IN DEBT?!!
ド STOMP
ド STOMP
ド STOMP
ド STOMP
ド STOMP
ド STOMP
ド STOMP
WEISZ...

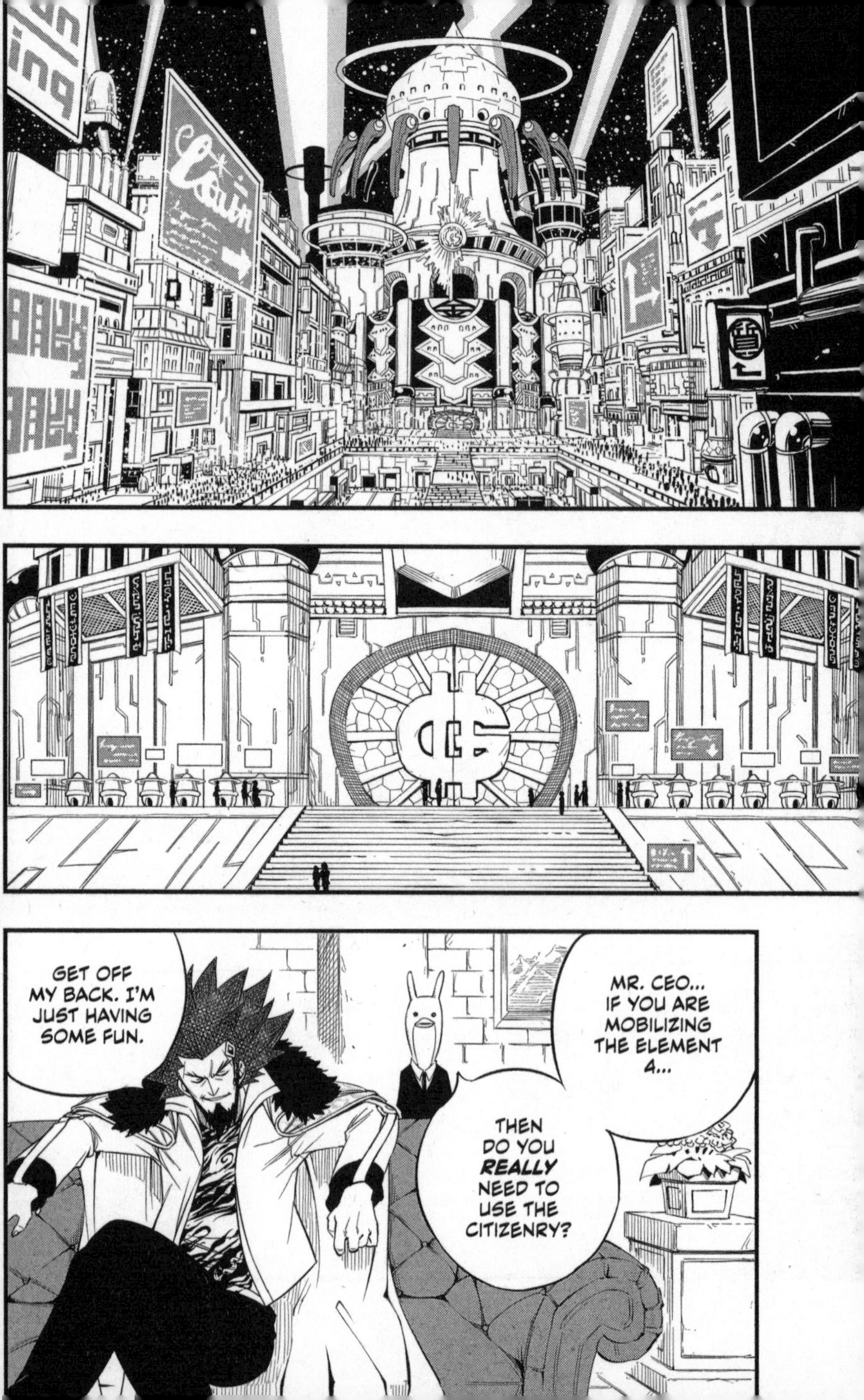
MR. CEO... IF YOU ARE MOBILIZING THE ELEMENT 4...
THEN DO YOU ***REALLY*** NEED TO USE THE CITIZENRY?
GET OFF MY BACK. I'M JUST HAVING SOME FUN.

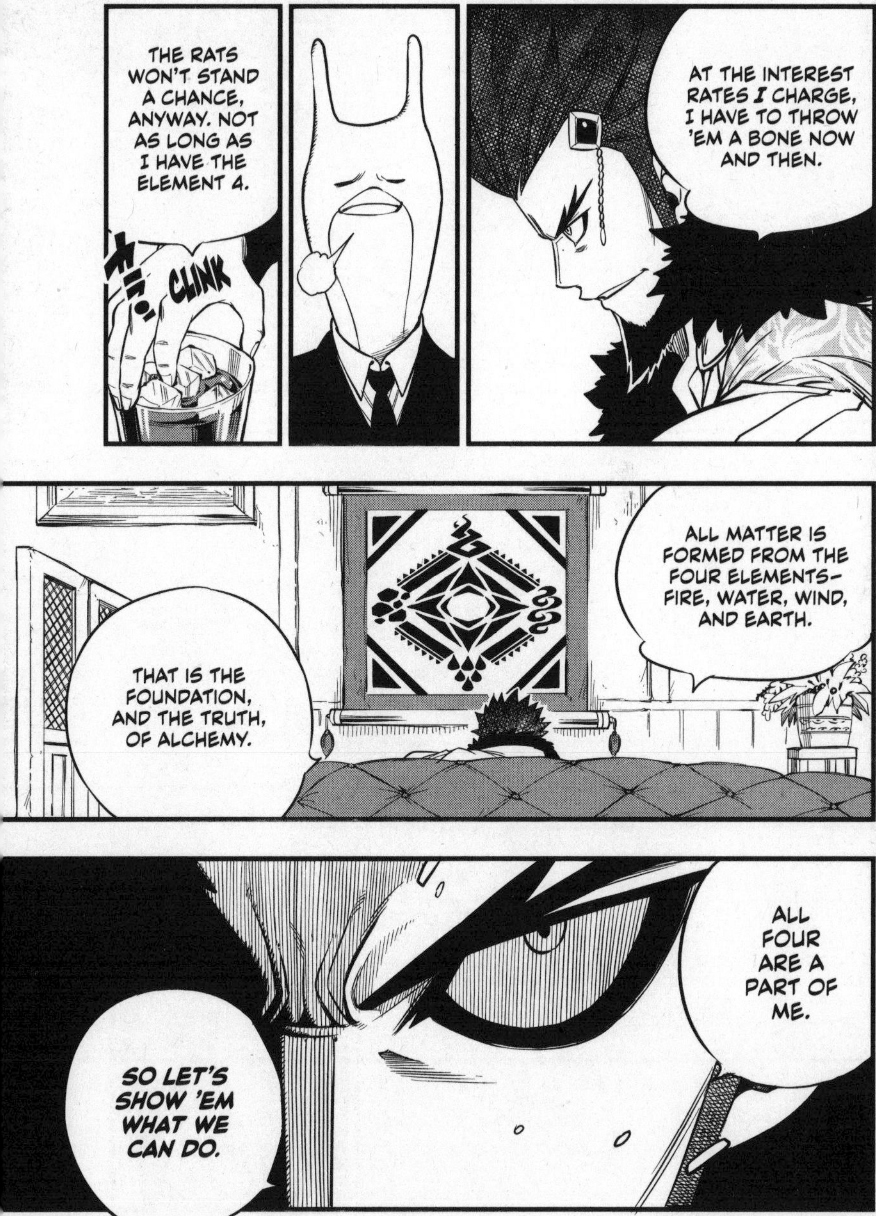
AT THE INTEREST RATES *I* CHARGE, I HAVE TO THROW 'EM A BONE NOW AND THEN.
THE RATS WON'T STAND A CHANCE, ANYWAY. NOT AS LONG AS I HAVE THE ELEMENT 4.
CLINK
ALL MATTER IS FORMED FROM THE FOUR ELEMENTS—FIRE, WATER, WIND, AND EARTH.
THAT IS THE FOUNDATION, AND THE TRUTH, OF ALCHEMY.
ALL FOUR ARE A PART OF ME.
SO LET'S SHOW 'EM WHAT WE CAN DO.

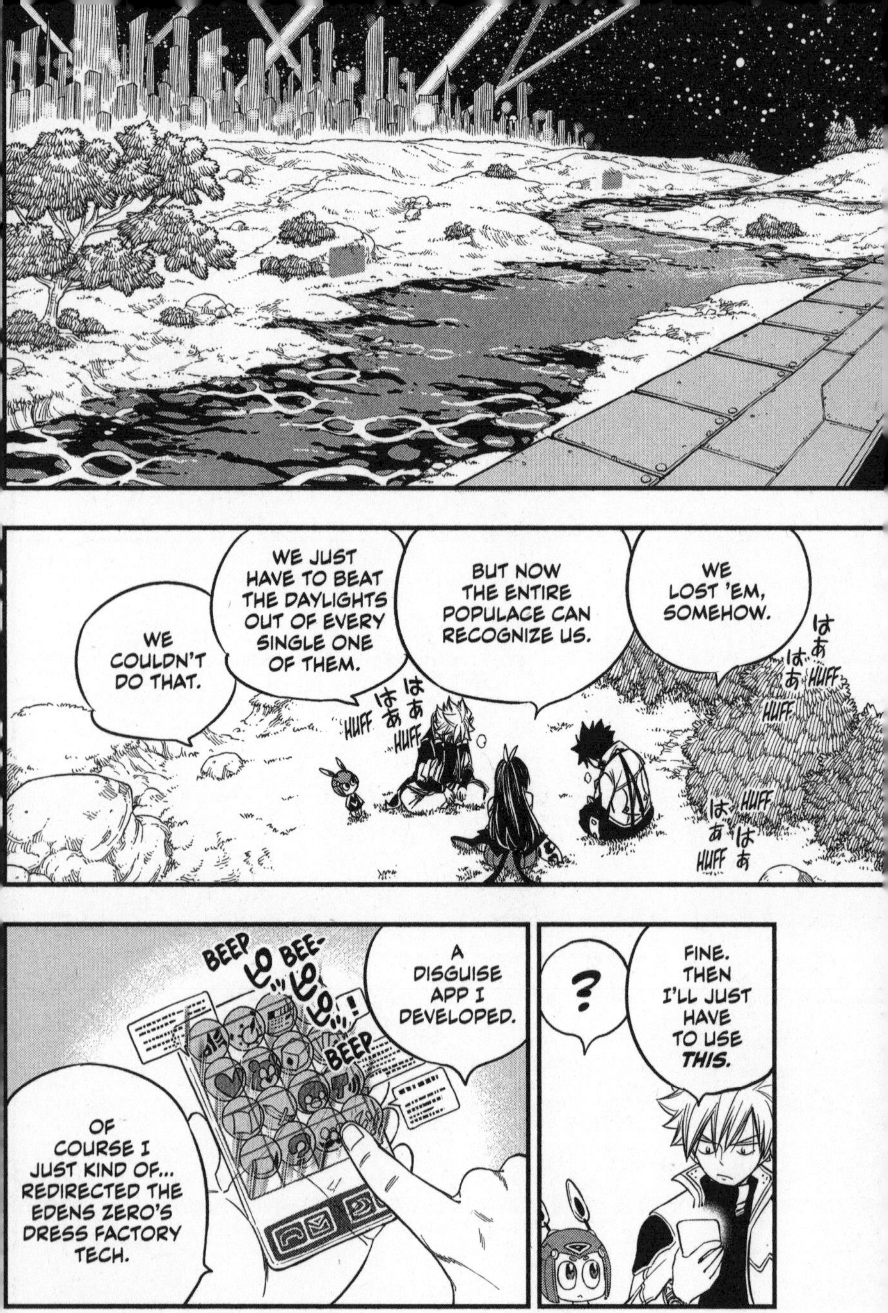

WE LOST 'EM, SOMEHOW.
はあ はあ HUFF HUFF
BUT NOW THE ENTIRE POPULACE CAN RECOGNIZE US.
WE JUST HAVE TO BEAT THE DAYLIGHTS OUT OF EVERY SINGLE ONE OF THEM.
はあ はあ HUFF HUFF
WE COULDN'T DO THAT.
HUFF はあ HUFF はあ
FINE. THEN I'LL JUST HAVE TO USE ***THIS.***
?
A DISGUISE APP I DEVELOPED.
BEEP ピ BEE- ピピピ BEEP
OF COURSE I JUST KIND OF... REDIRECTED THE EDENS ZERO'S DRESS FACTORY TECH.

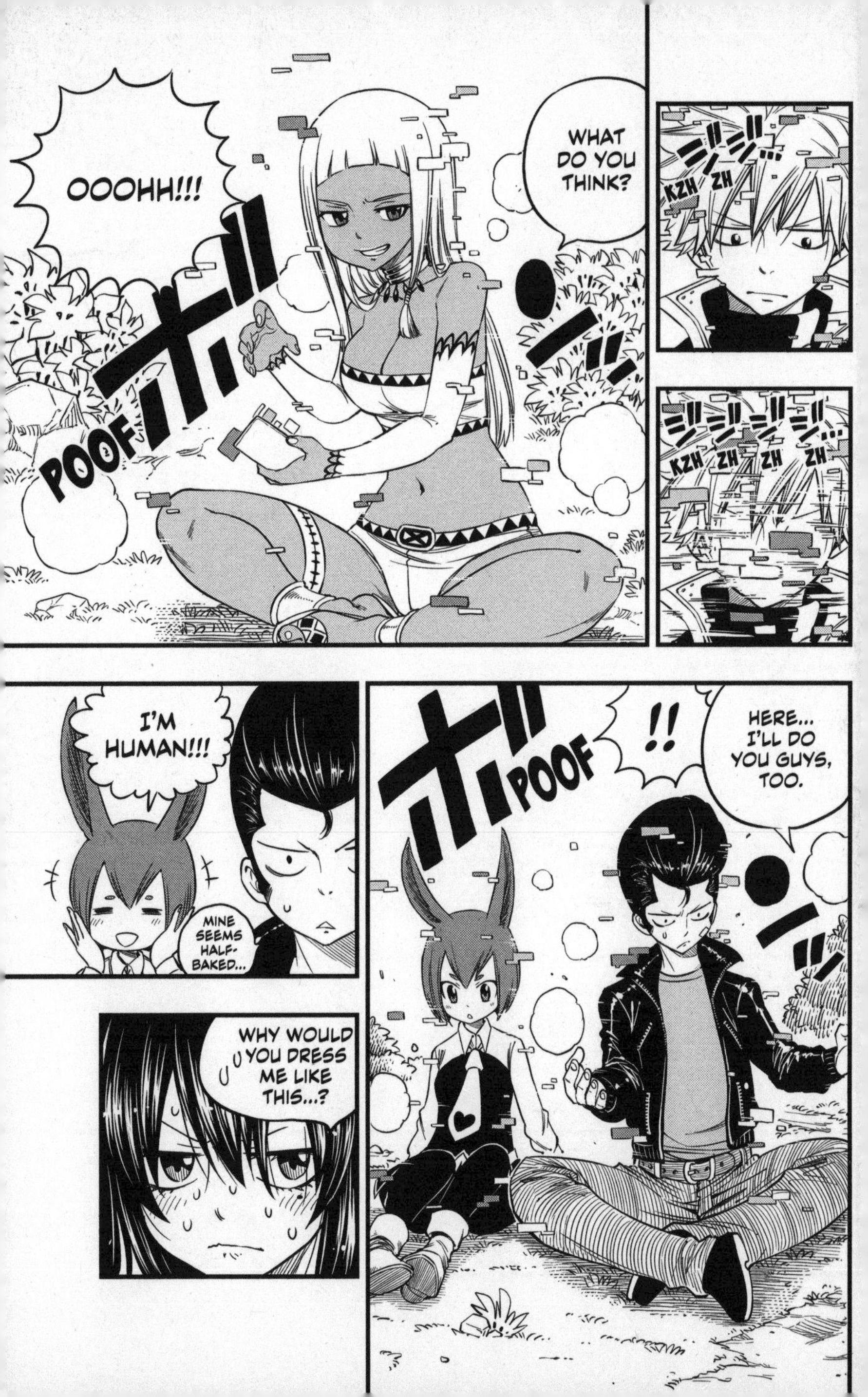
KZH ZH
KZH ZH ZH ZH
WHAT DO YOU THINK?
POOF
OOOHH!!!
HERE... I'LL DO YOU GUYS, TOO.
!!
POOF
I'M HUMAN!!!
MINE SEEMS HALF-BAKED...
WHY WOULD YOU DRESS ME LIKE THIS...?

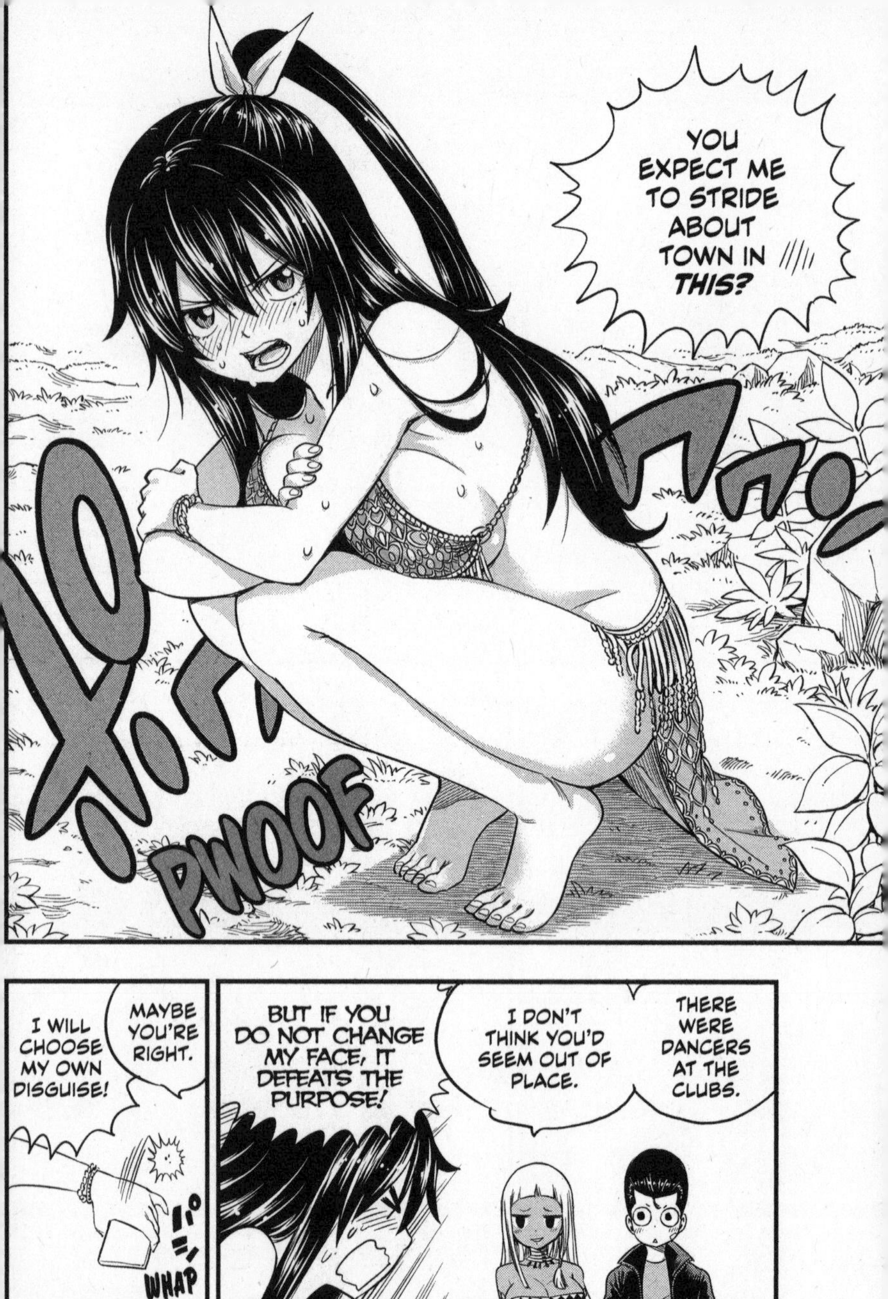
YOU EXPECT ME TO STRIDE ABOUT TOWN IN THIS?
PWOOF
THERE WERE DANCERS AT THE CLUBS.
I DON'T THINK YOU'D SEEM OUT OF PLACE.
BUT IF YOU DO NOT CHANGE MY FACE, IT DEFEATS THE PURPOSE!
MAYBE YOU'RE RIGHT.
I WILL CHOOSE MY OWN DISGUISE!
WHAP

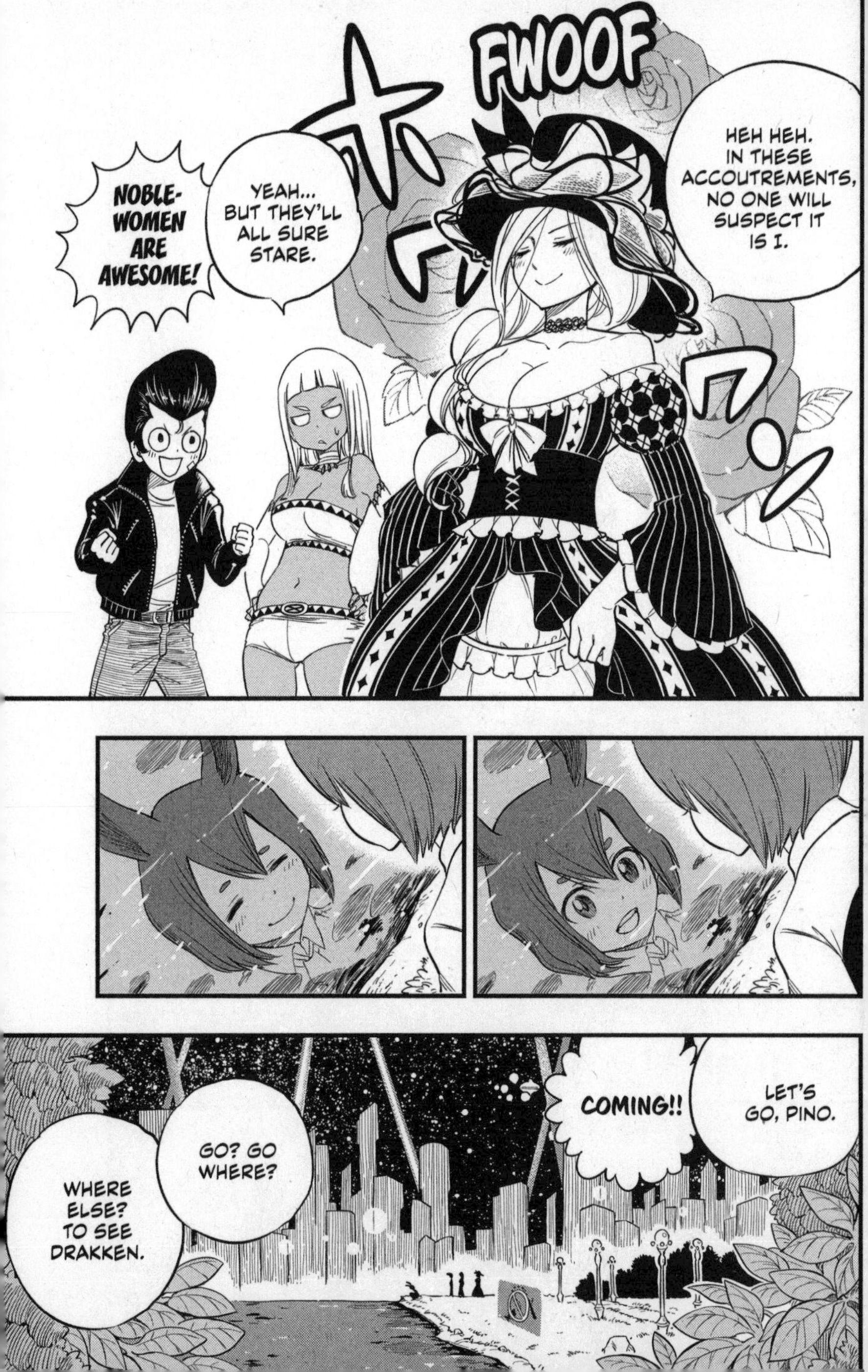
FWOOF
HEH HEH. IN THESE ACCOUTREMENTS, NO ONE WILL SUSPECT IT IS I.
YEAH... BUT THEY'LL ALL SURE STARE.
NOBLE-WOMEN ARE AWESOME!
LET'S GO, PINO.
COMING!!
GO? GO WHERE?
WHERE ELSE? TO SEE DRAKKEN.

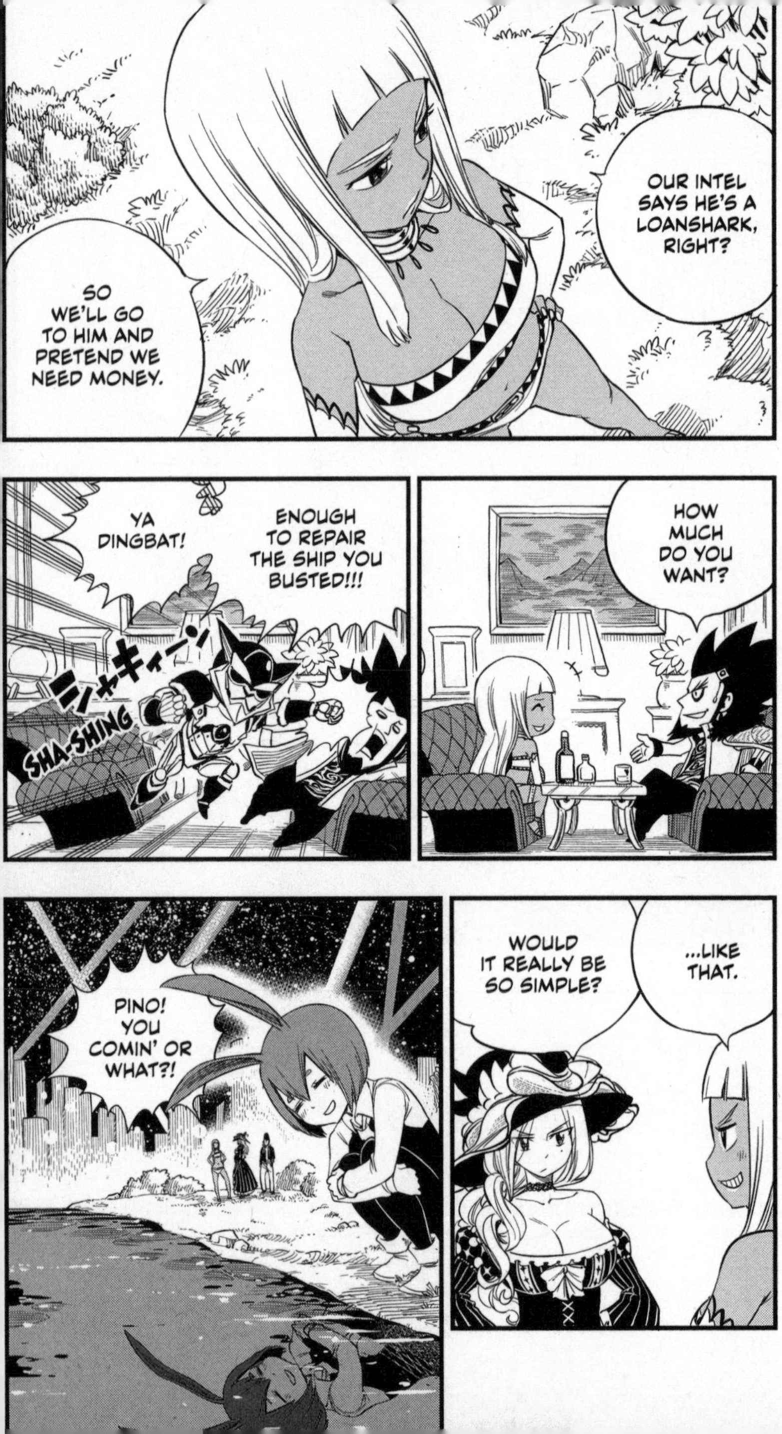
OUR INTEL SAYS HE'S A LOANSHARK, RIGHT?
SO WE'LL GO TO HIM AND PRETEND WE NEED MONEY.
HOW MUCH DO YOU WANT?
ENOUGH TO REPAIR THE SHIP YOU BUSTED!!!
YA DINGBAT!
SHA-SHING
...LIKE THAT.
WOULD IT REALLY BE SO SIMPLE?
PINO! YOU COMIN' OR WHAT?!

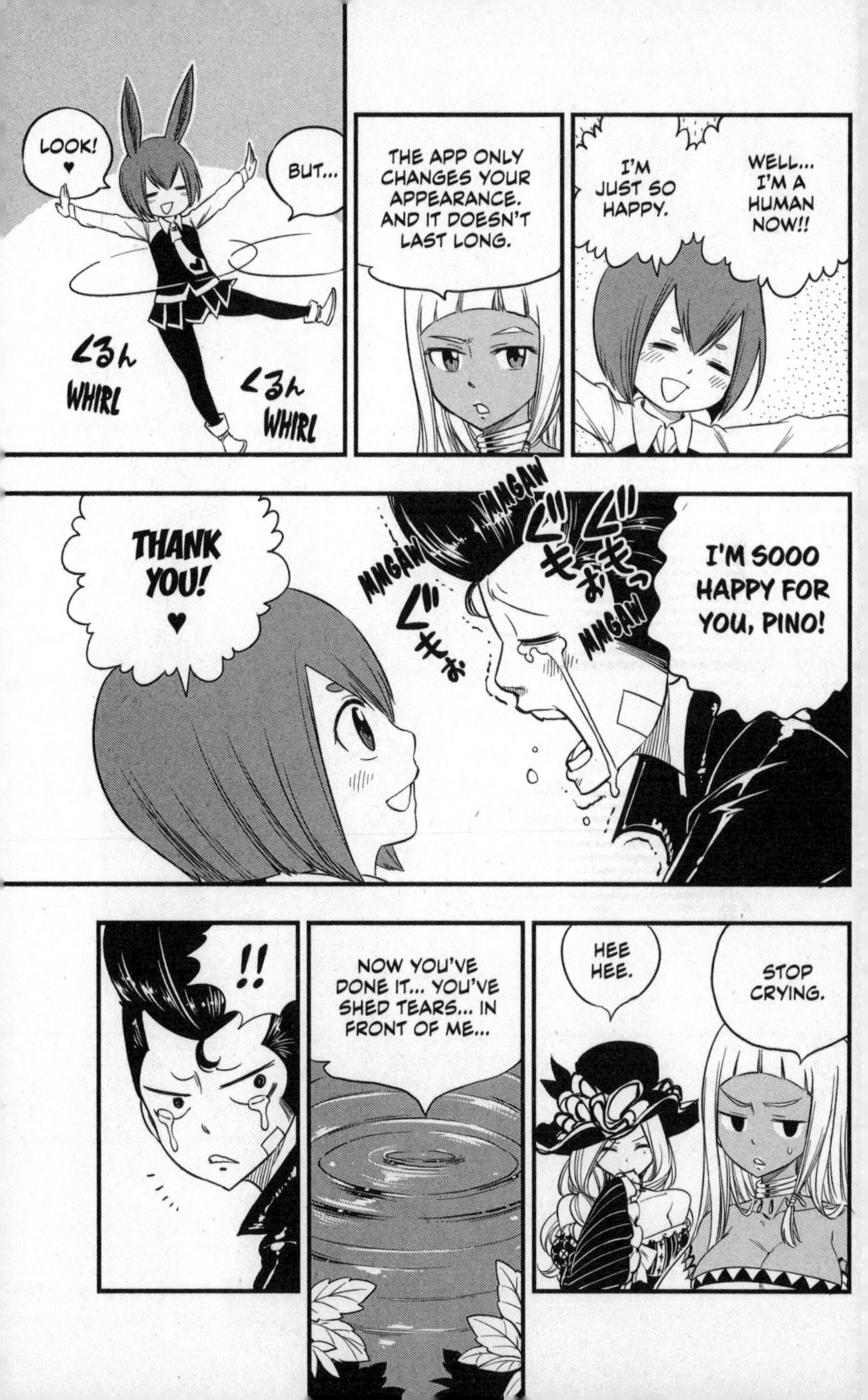
WELL... I'M A HUMAN NOW!!
I'M JUST SO HAPPY.
THE APP ONLY CHANGES YOUR APPEARANCE. AND IT DOESN'T LAST LONG.
BUT...
LOOK! ♥
くるん
WHIRL
くるん
WHIRL
I'M SOOO HAPPY FOR YOU, PINO!
MMGAW
MMGAW
MMGAW
ぐぎぉ
THANK YOU! ♥
STOP CRYING.
HEE HEE.
NOW YOU'VE DONE IT... YOU'VE SHED TEARS... IN FRONT OF ME...
!!

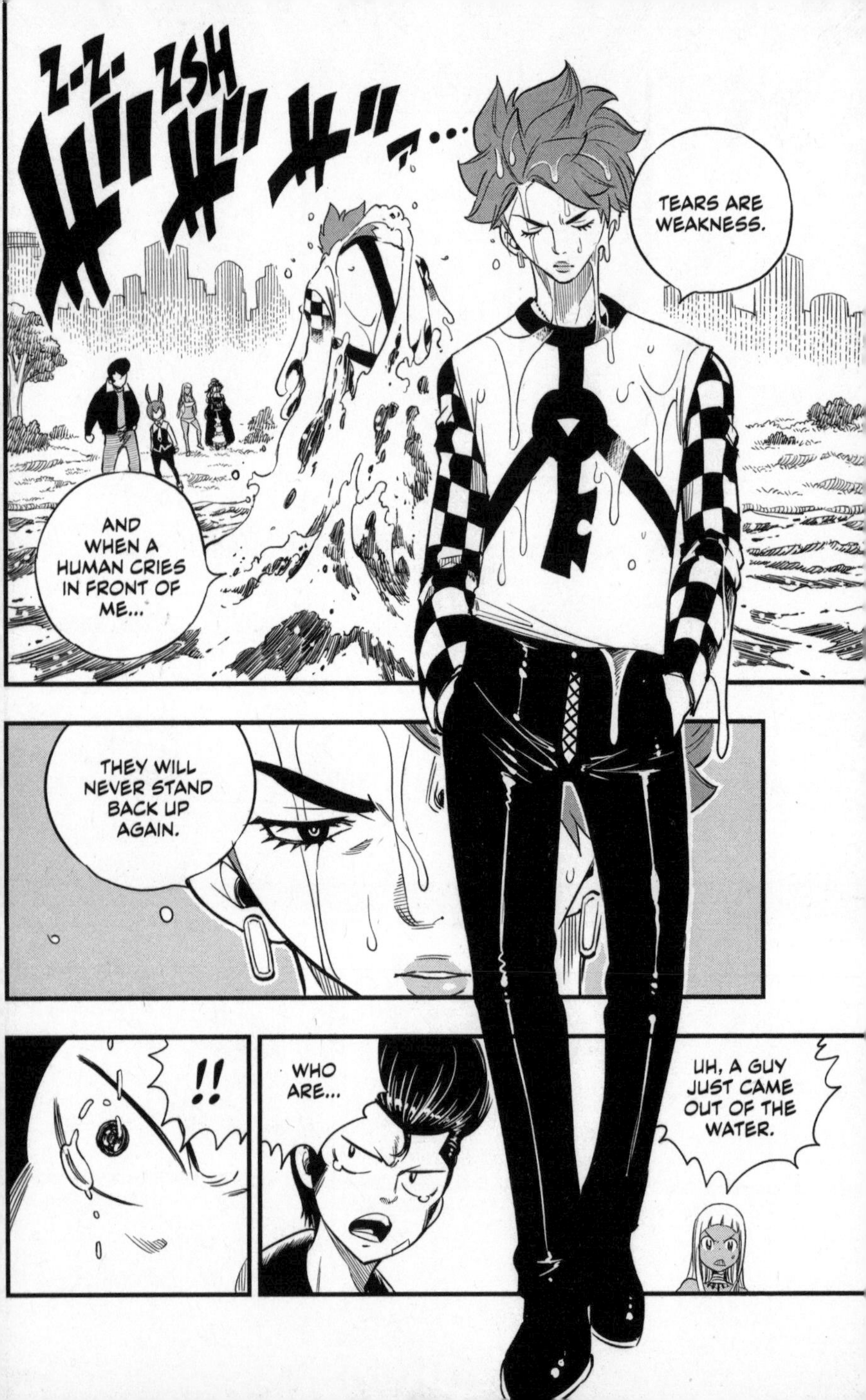

Z-Z-ZSH
ア...
TEARS ARE WEAKNESS.
AND WHEN A HUMAN CRIES IN FRONT OF ME...
THEY WILL NEVER STAND BACK UP AGAIN.
UH, A GUY JUST CAME OUT OF THE WATER.
WHO ARE...
!!

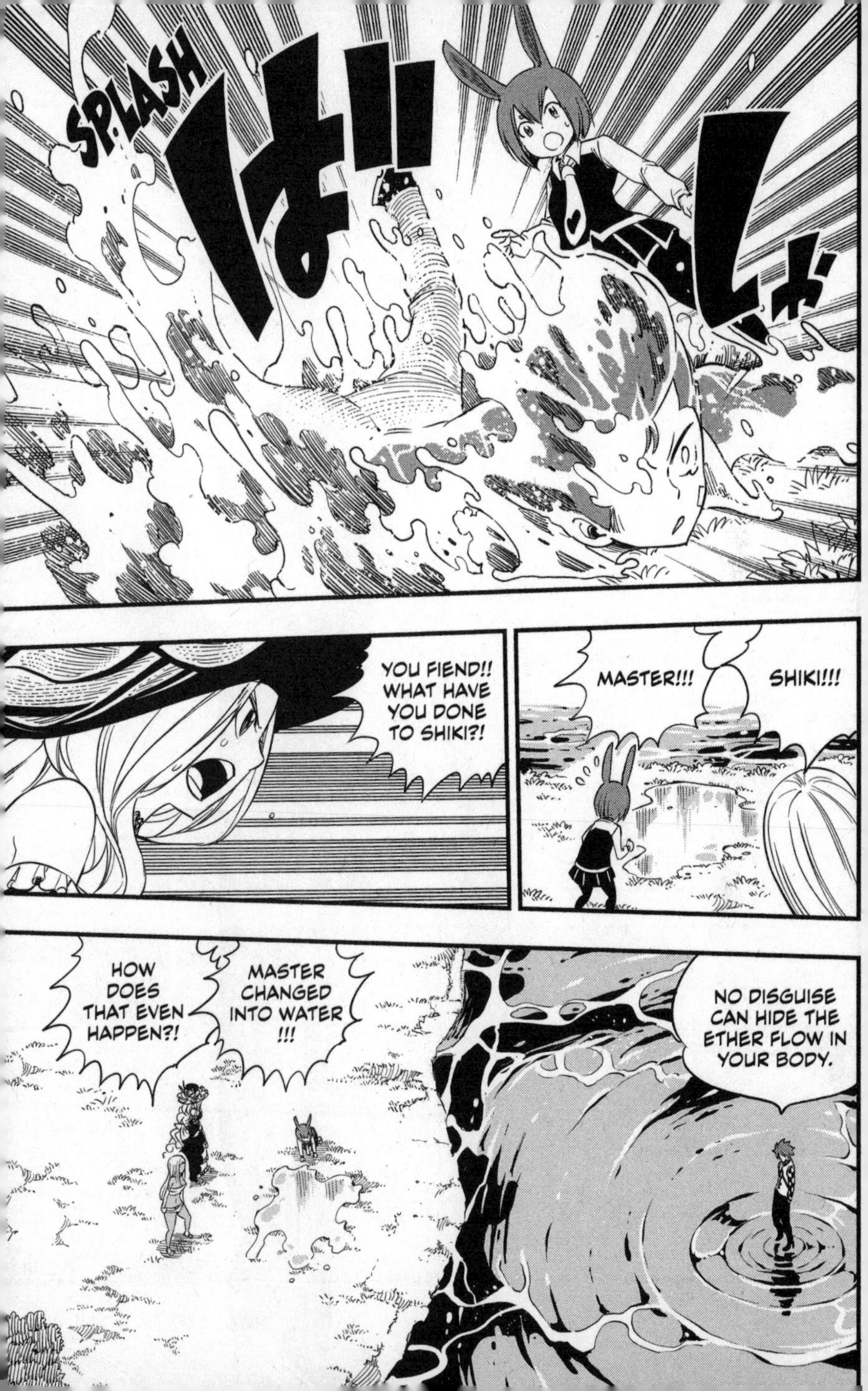
SPLASH
SHIKI!!!
MASTER!!!
YOU FIEND!! WHAT HAVE YOU DONE TO SHIKI?!
NO DISGUISE CAN HIDE THE ETHER FLOW IN YOUR BODY.
MASTER CHANGED INTO WATER !!!
HOW DOES THAT EVEN HAPPEN?!

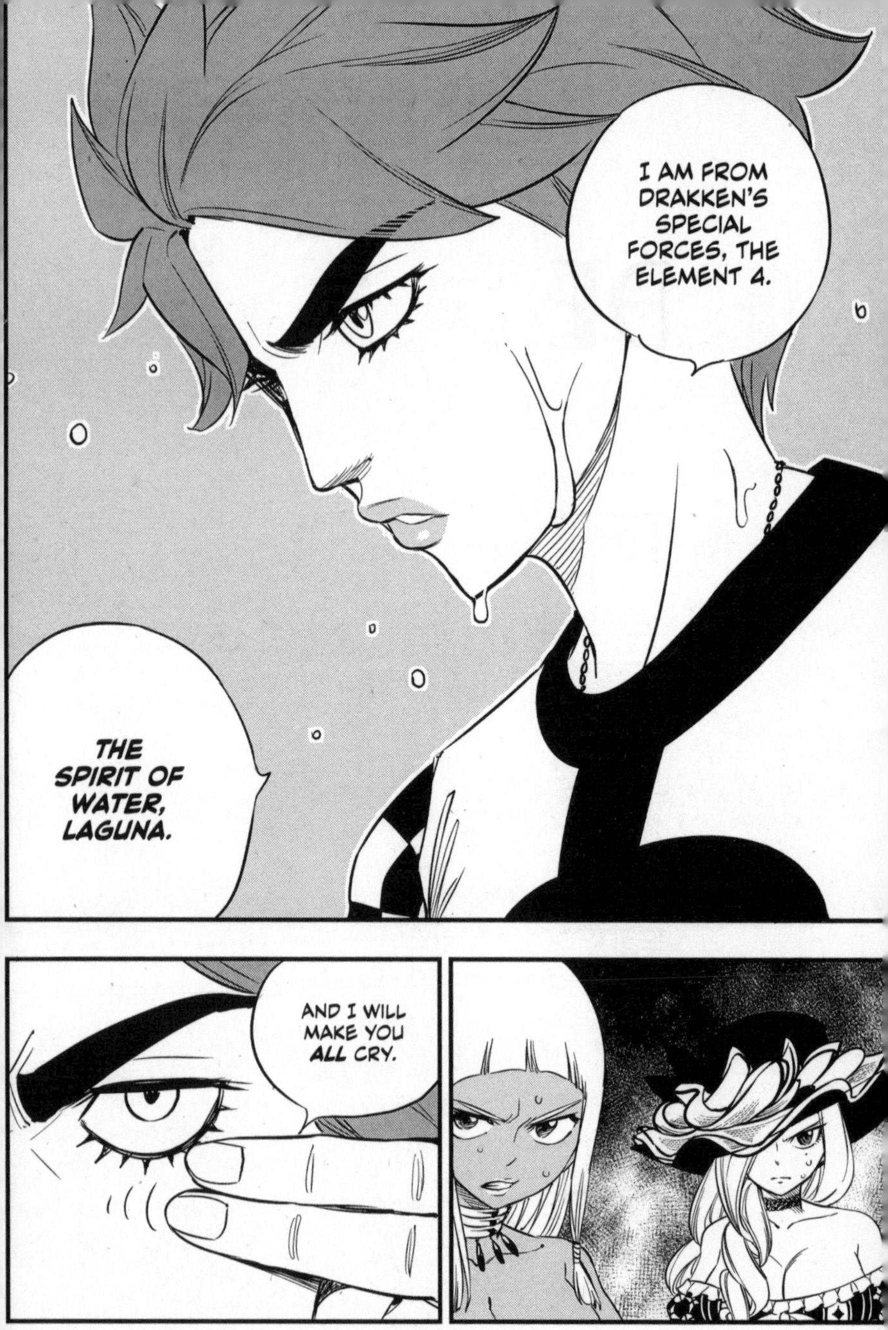
I AM FROM DRAKKEN'S SPECIAL FORCES, THE ELEMENT 4.
THE SPIRIT OF WATER, LAGUNA.
AND I WILL MAKE YOU ALL CRY.

EDENS ZERO

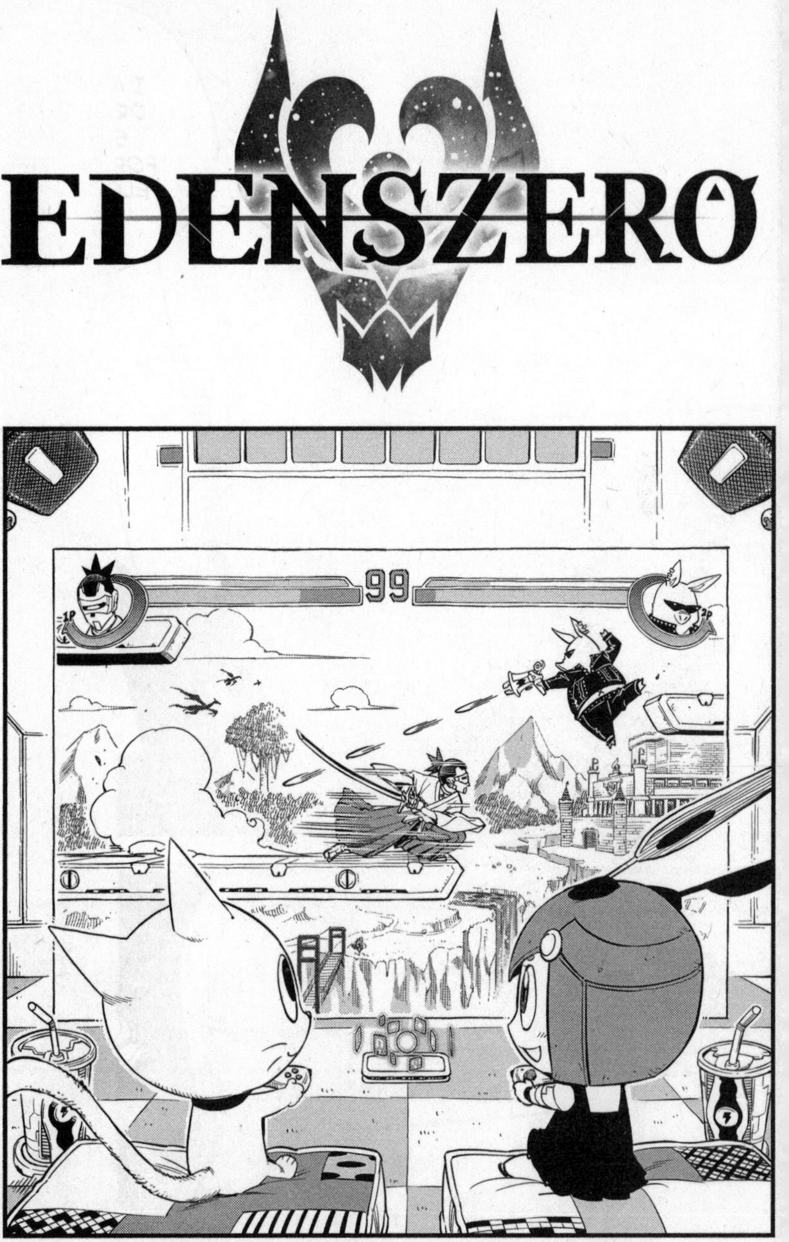
99
1P
2P

CHAPTER 73: DON'T SHED A TEAR

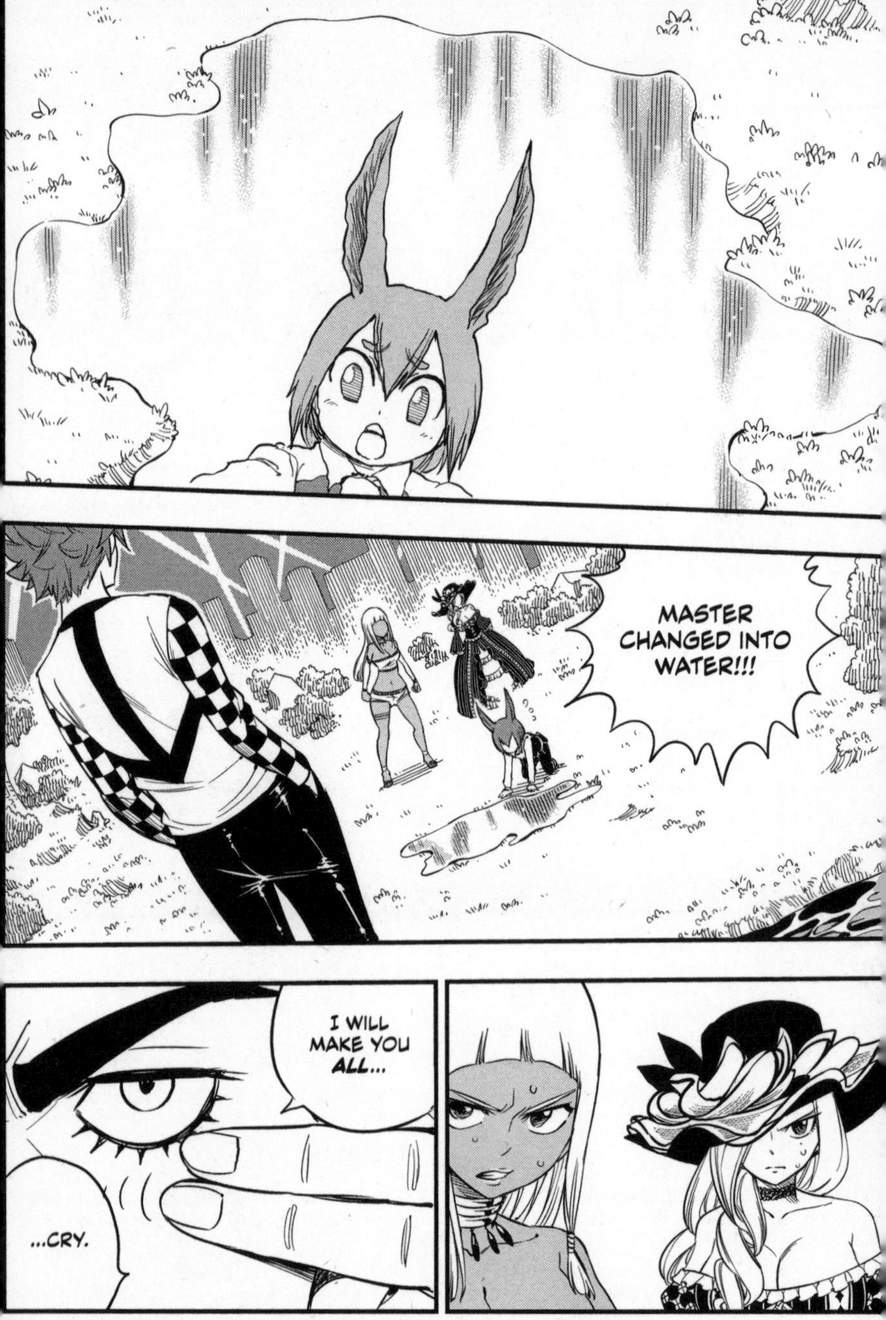
MASTER CHANGED INTO WATER!!!
I WILL MAKE YOU ALL...
...CRY.

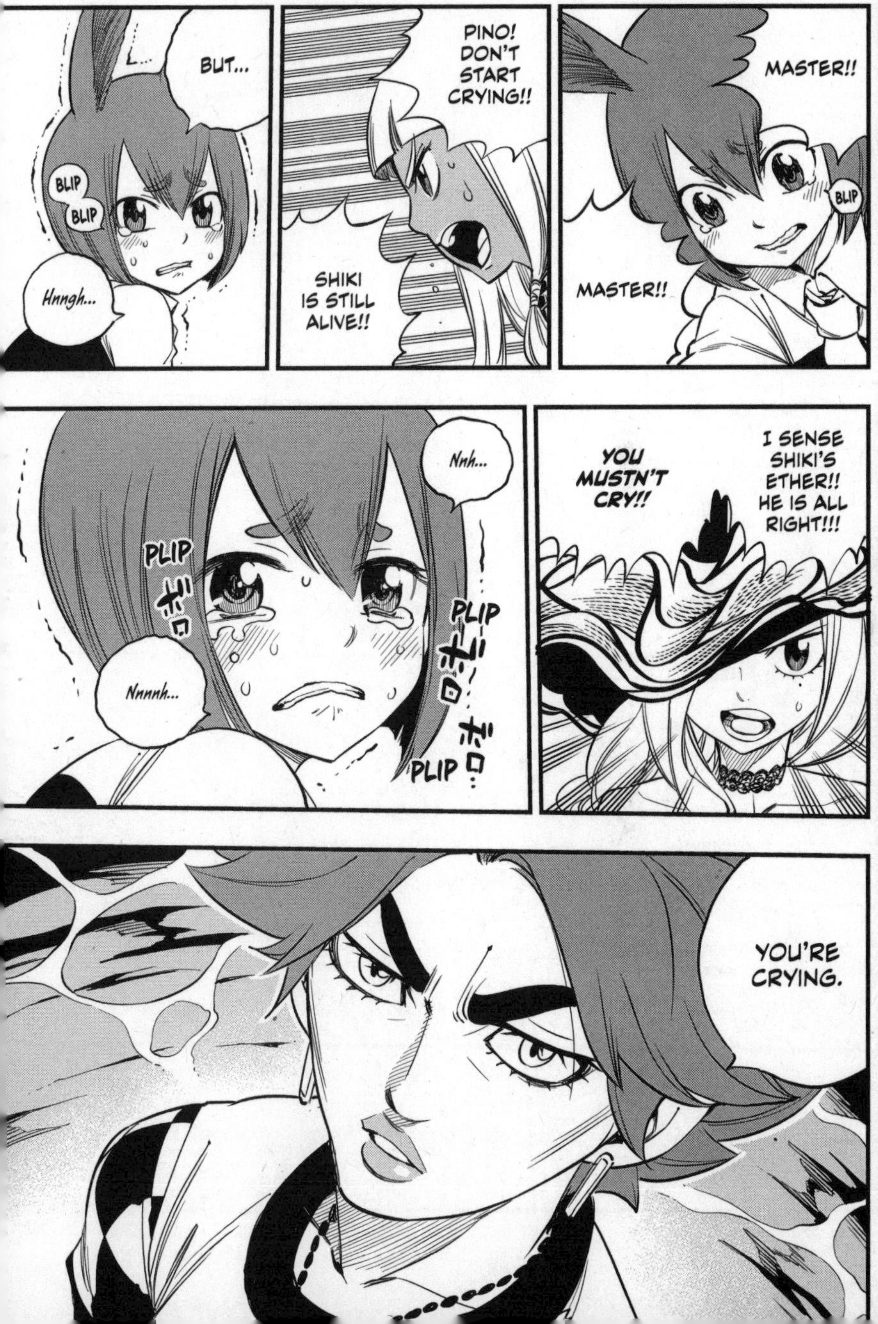
MASTER!!
BLIP
MASTER!!
PINO! DON'T START CRYING!!
SHIKI IS STILL ALIVE!!
L...
BUT...
BLIP
BLIP
Hnngh...
I SENSE SHIKI'S ETHER!! HE IS ALL RIGHT!!!
YOU MUSTN'T CRY!!
Nnh...
PLIP
ボロ
PLIP
ボロ
ボロ
Nnnnh...
PLIP
YOU'RE CRYING.

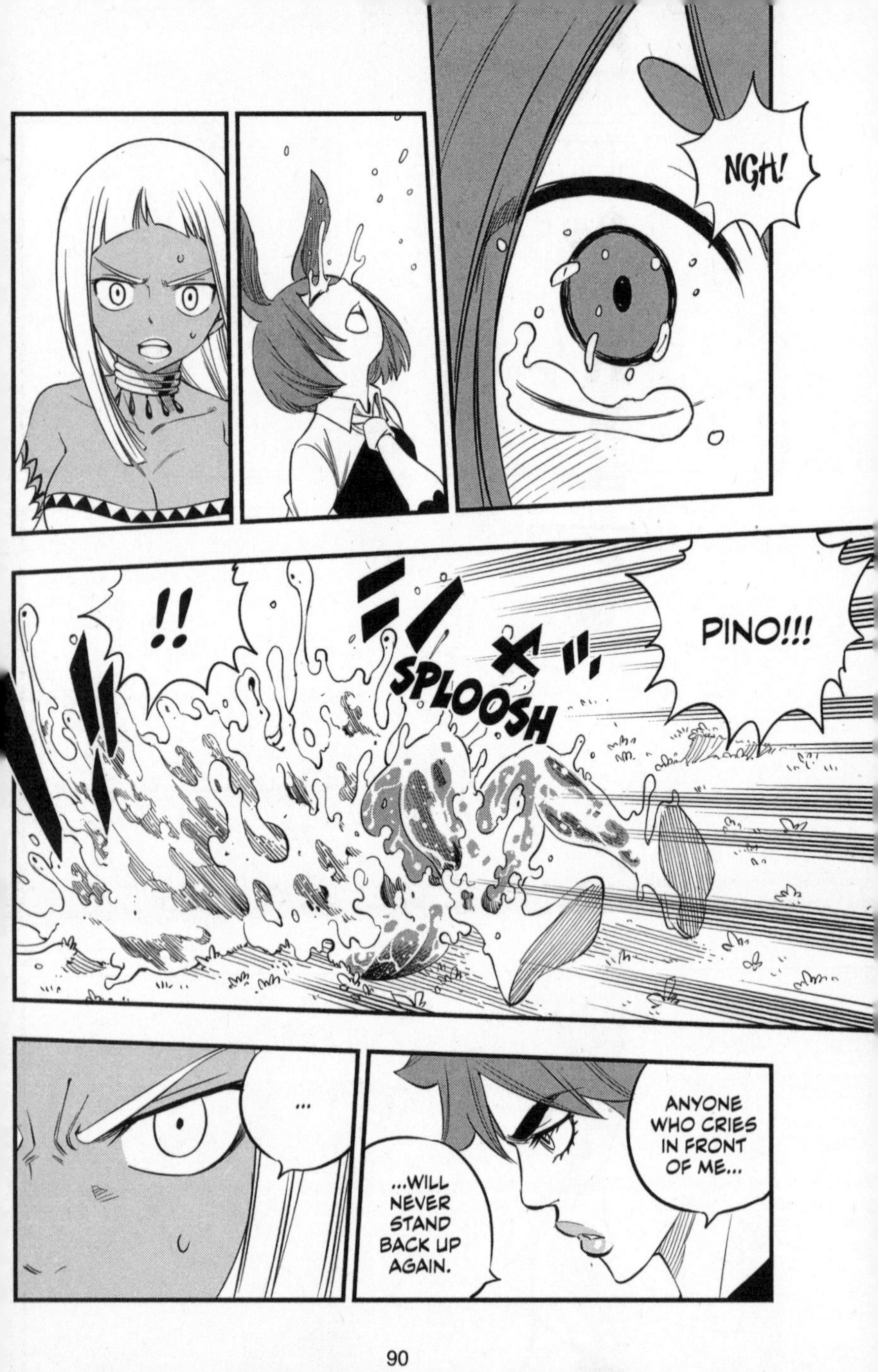
NGH!
PINO!!!
SPLOOSH
!!
ANYONE WHO CRIES IN FRONT OF ME...
...WILL NEVER STAND BACK UP AGAIN.
...

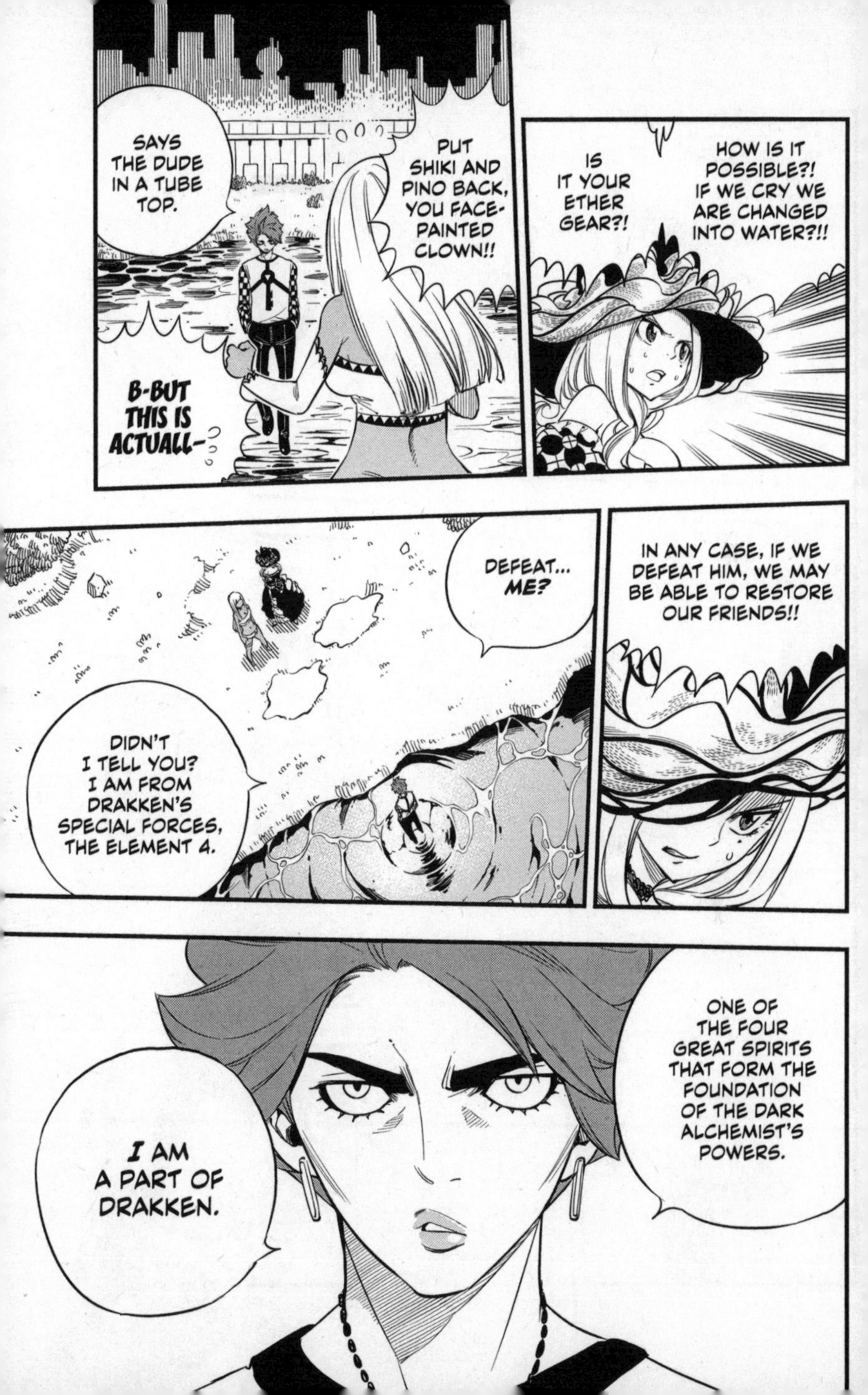
HOW IS IT POSSIBLE?! IF WE CRY WE ARE CHANGED INTO WATER?!!
IS IT YOUR ETHER GEAR?!
PUT SHIKI AND PINO BACK, YOU FACE-PAINTED CLOWN!!
SAYS THE DUDE IN A TUBE TOP.
B-BUT THIS IS ACTUALL-
IN ANY CASE, IF WE DEFEAT HIM, WE MAY BE ABLE TO RESTORE OUR FRIENDS!!
DEFEAT... *ME?*
DIDN'T I TELL YOU? I AM FROM DRAKKEN'S SPECIAL FORCES, THE ELEMENT 4.
ONE OF THE FOUR GREAT SPIRITS THAT FORM THE FOUNDATION OF THE DARK ALCHEMIST'S POWERS.
I AM A PART OF DRAKKEN.

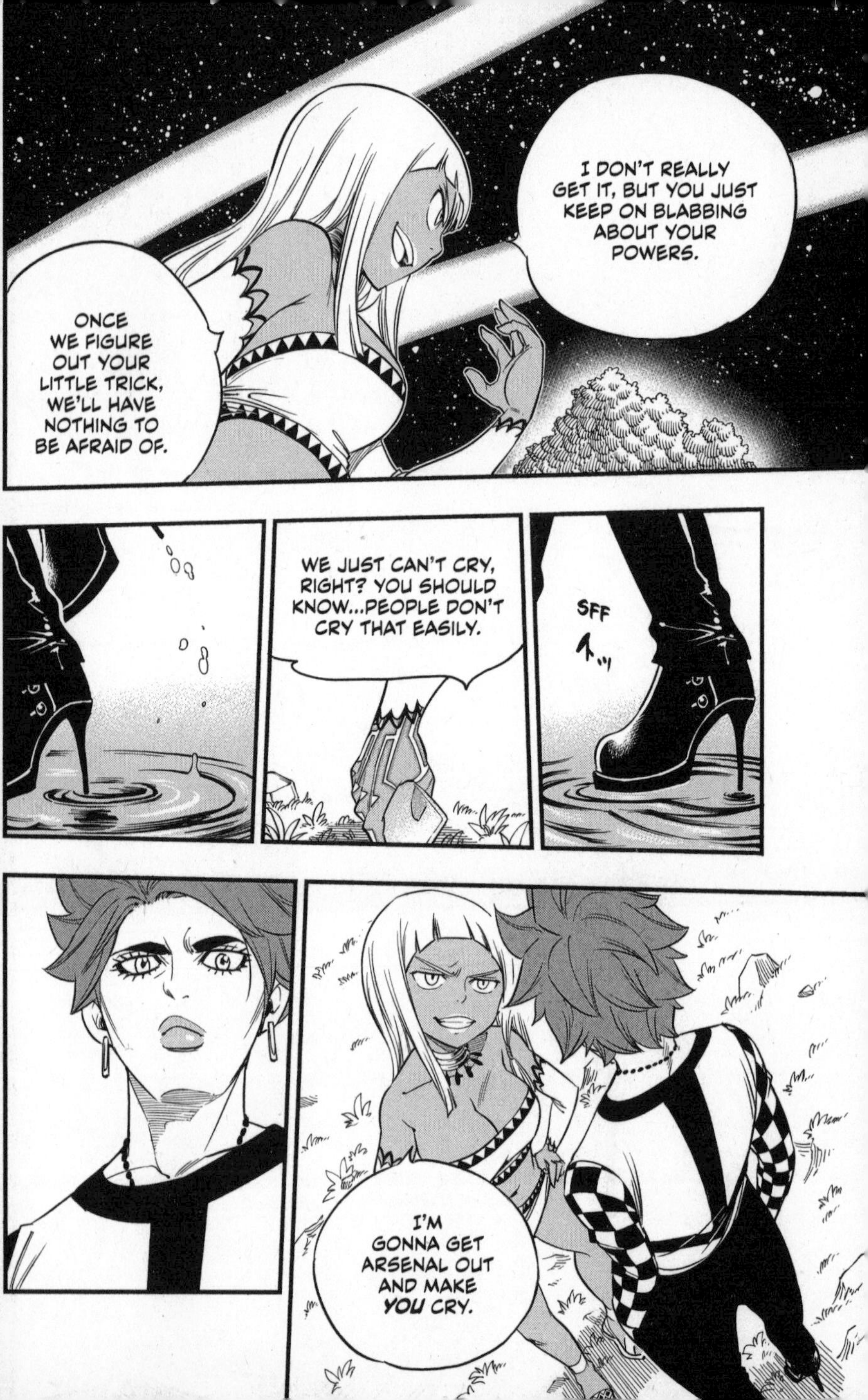
I DON'T REALLY GET IT, BUT YOU JUST KEEP ON BLABBING ABOUT YOUR POWERS.
ONCE WE FIGURE OUT YOUR LITTLE TRICK, WE'LL HAVE NOTHING TO BE AFRAID OF.
SFF
WE JUST CAN'T CRY, RIGHT? YOU SHOULD KNOW...PEOPLE DON'T CRY THAT EASILY.
I'M GONNA GET ARSENAL OUT AND MAKE *YOU* CRY.

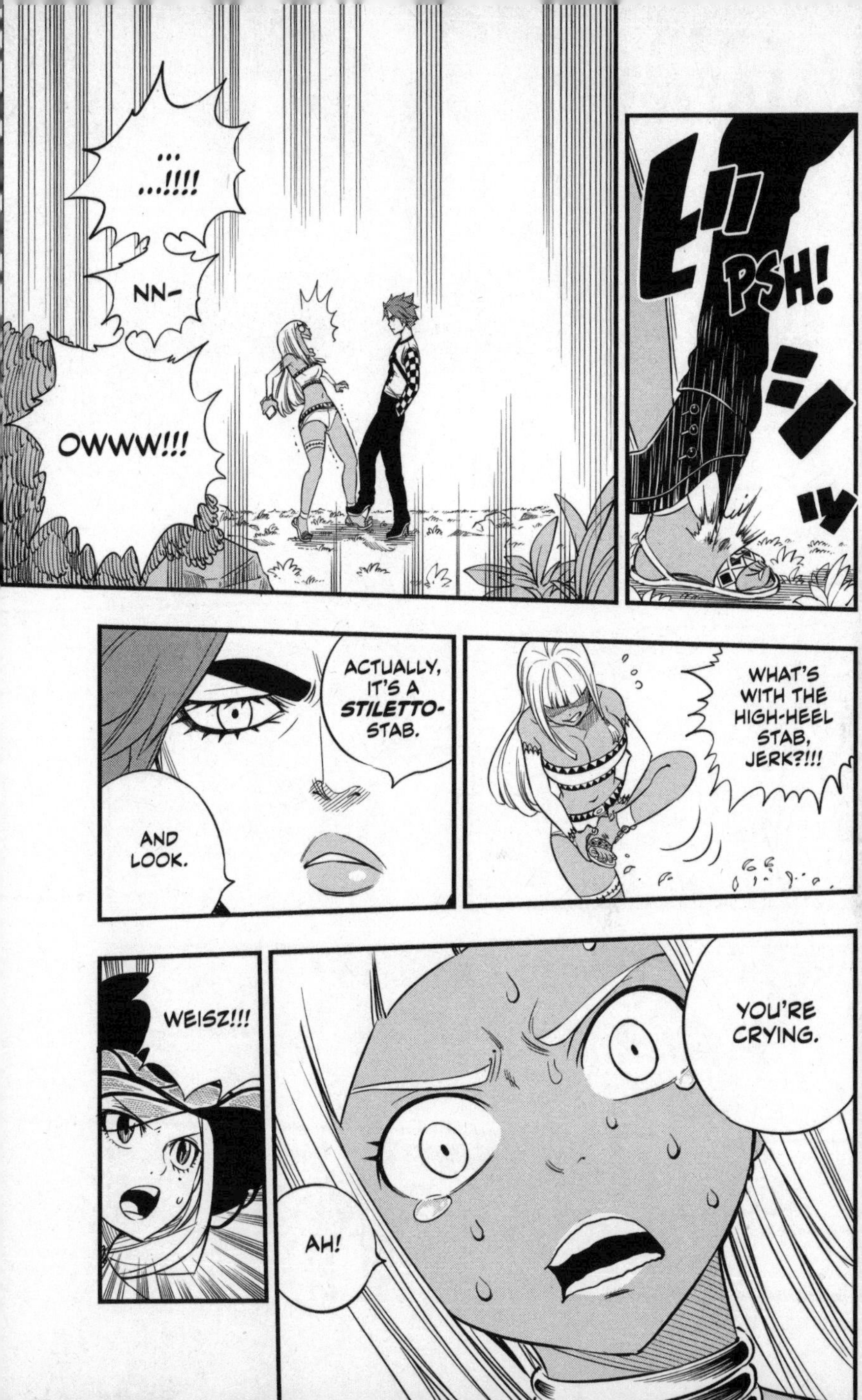
PSH!
...
...!!!!
NN-
OWWW!!!
WHAT'S WITH THE HIGH-HEEL STAB, JERK?!!!
ACTUALLY, IT'S A *STILETTO*-STAB.
AND LOOK.
YOU'RE CRYING.
AH!
WEISZ!!!

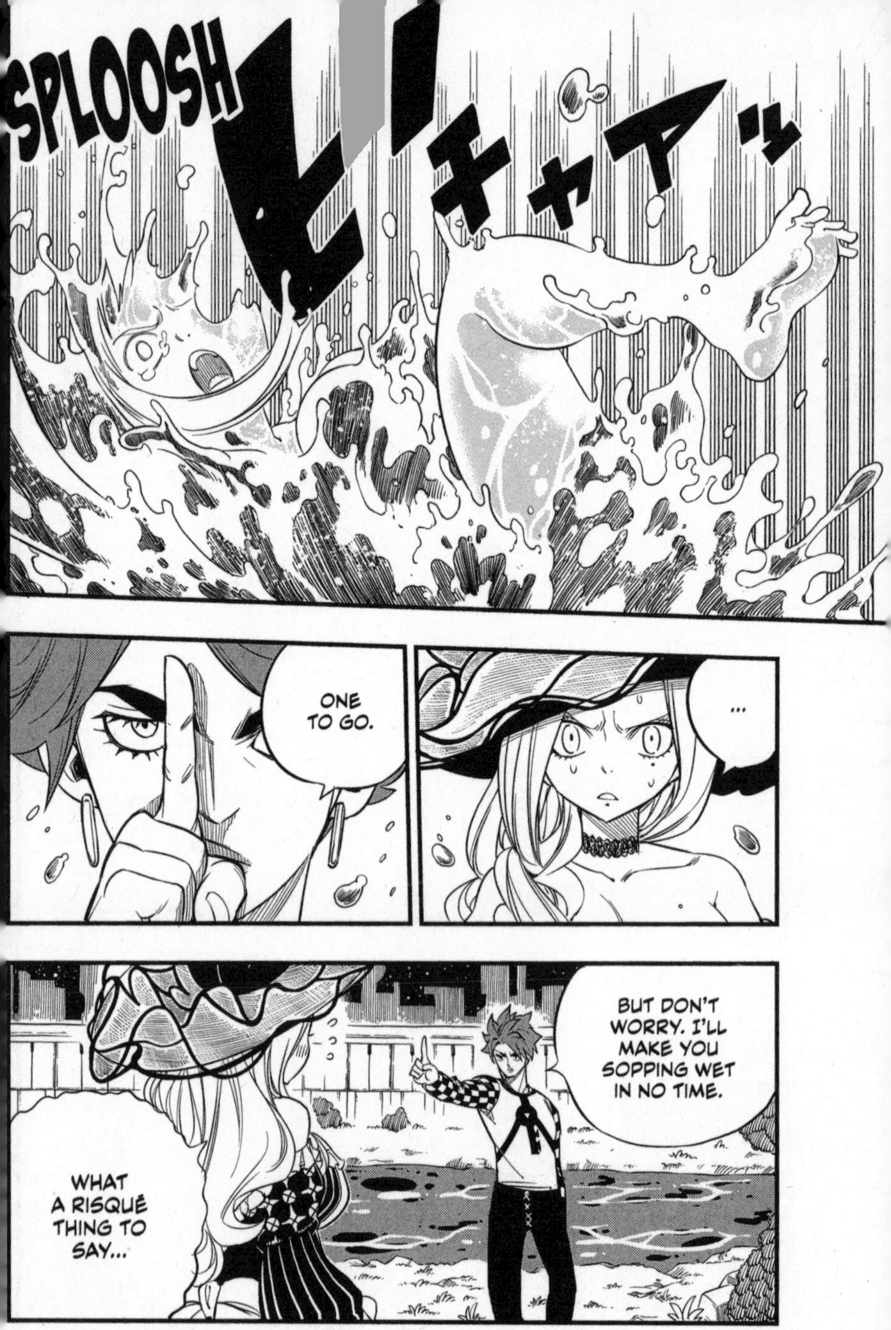
SPLOOSH
ビシャアッ
...
ONE TO GO.
BUT DON'T WORRY. I'LL MAKE YOU SOPPING WET IN NO TIME.
WHAT A RISQUÉ THING TO SAY...

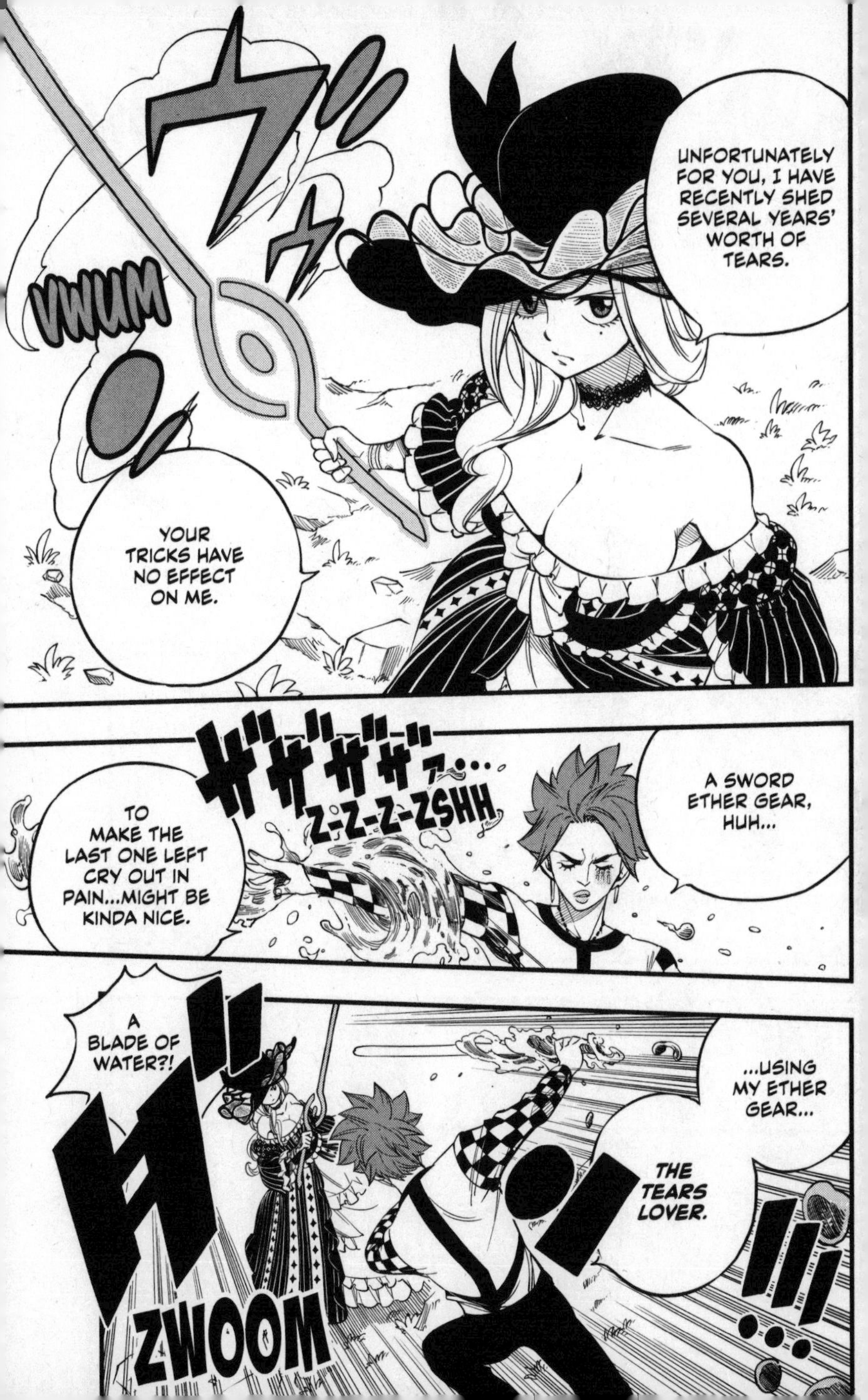
UNFORTUNATELY FOR YOU, I HAVE RECENTLY SHED SEVERAL YEARS' WORTH OF TEARS.
VWUM
YOUR TRICKS HAVE NO EFFECT ON ME.
A SWORD ETHER GEAR, HUH...
Z-Z-Z-ZSHH
TO MAKE THE LAST ONE LEFT CRY OUT IN PAIN...MIGHT BE KINDA NICE.
...USING MY ETHER GEAR...
THE TEARS LOVER.
A BLADE OF WATER?!
ZWOOM

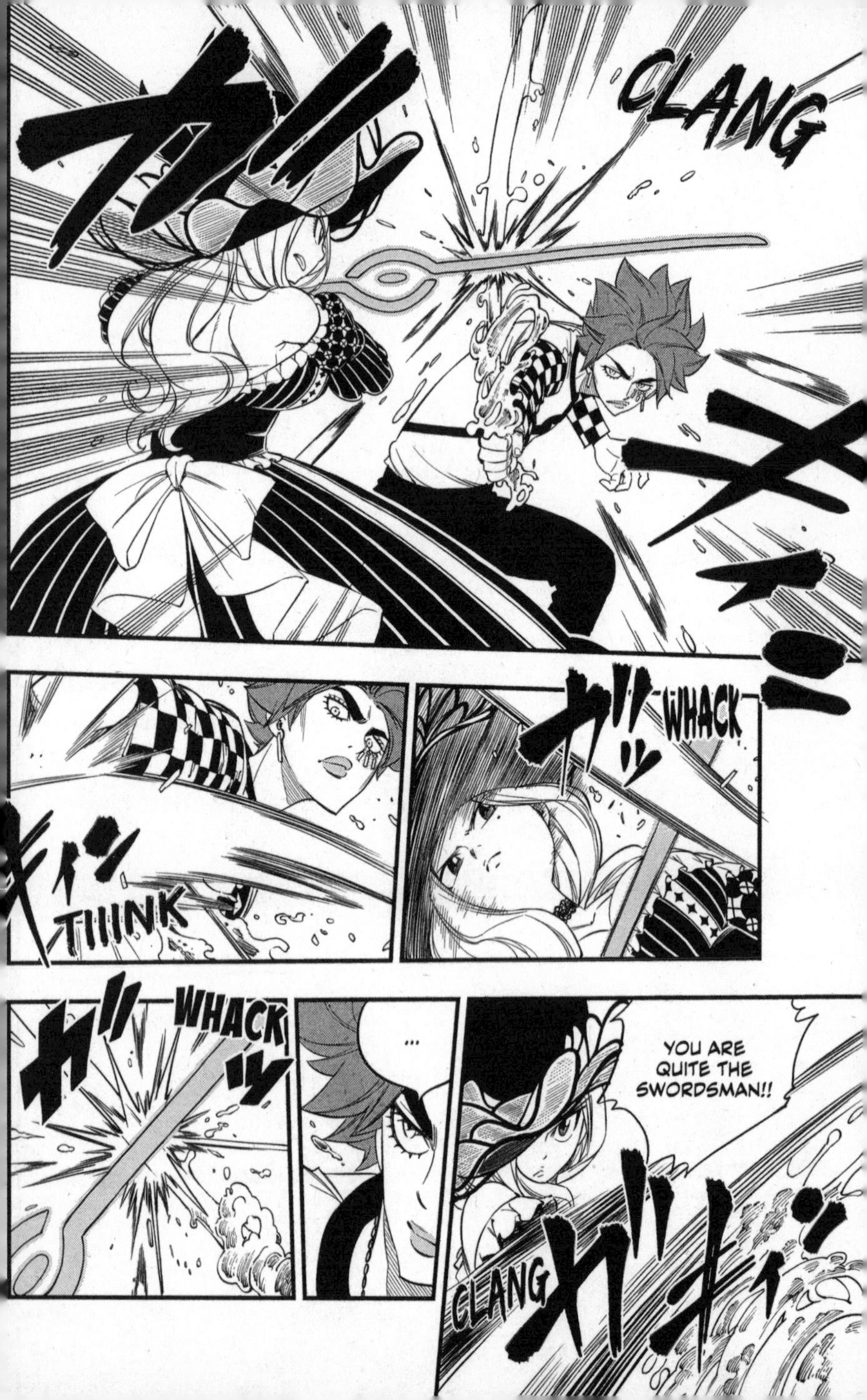
CLANG
WHACK
TIIINK
YOU ARE QUITE THE SWORDSMAN!!
CLANG
...
WHACK

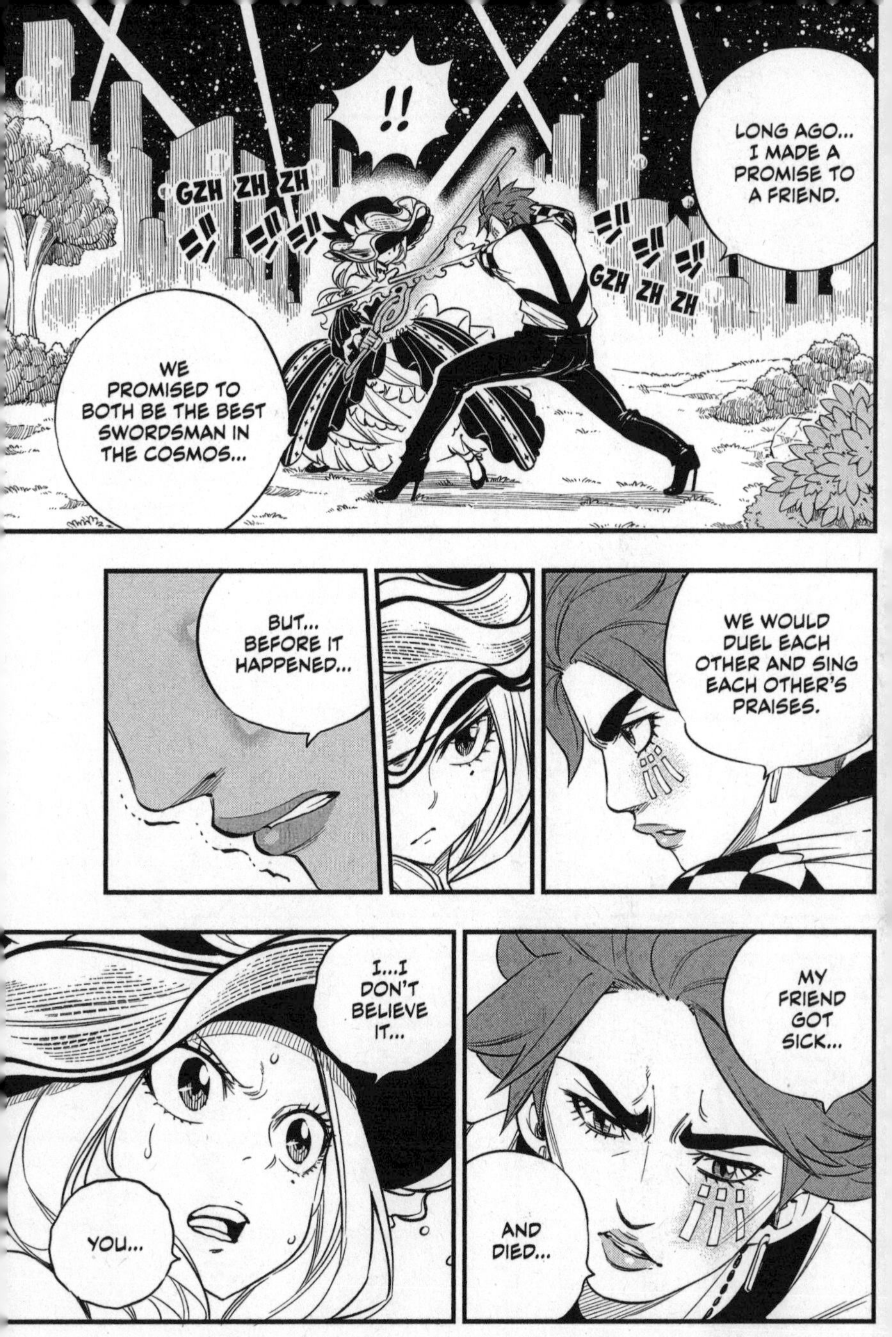
LONG AGO... I MADE A PROMISE TO A FRIEND.
!!
GZH ZH ZH
GZH ZH ZH
WE PROMISED TO BOTH BE THE BEST SWORDSMAN IN THE COSMOS...
WE WOULD DUEL EACH OTHER AND SING EACH OTHER'S PRAISES.
BUT... BEFORE IT HAPPENED...
MY FRIEND GOT SICK...
AND DIED...
I...I DON'T BELIEVE IT...
YOU...

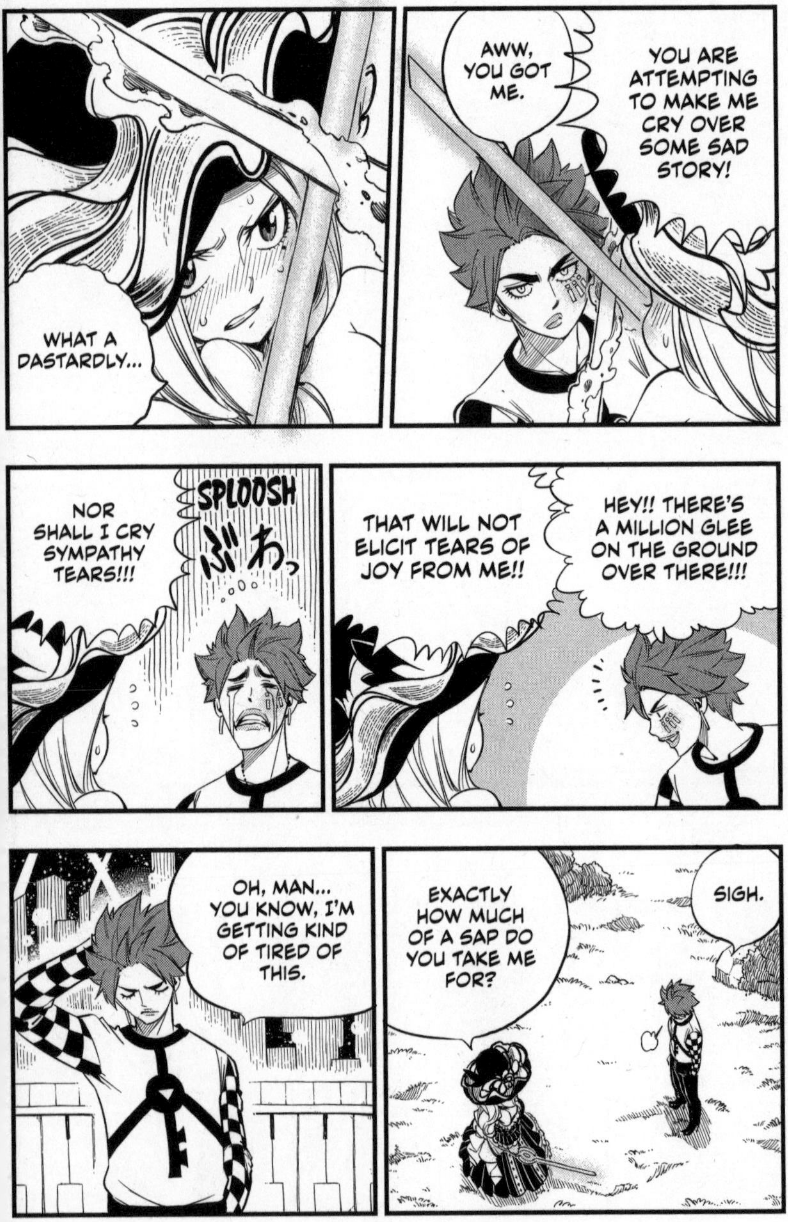
YOU ARE ATTEMPTING TO MAKE ME CRY OVER SOME SAD STORY!
AWW, YOU GOT ME.
WHAT A DASTARDLY...
HEY!! THERE'S A MILLION GLEE ON THE GROUND OVER THERE!!!
THAT WILL NOT ELICIT TEARS OF JOY FROM ME!!
SPLOOSH
ぶわっ
NOR SHALL I CRY SYMPATHY TEARS!!!
SIGH.
EXACTLY HOW MUCH OF A SAP DO YOU TAKE ME FOR?
OH, MAN... YOU KNOW, I'M GETTING KIND OF TIRED OF THIS.

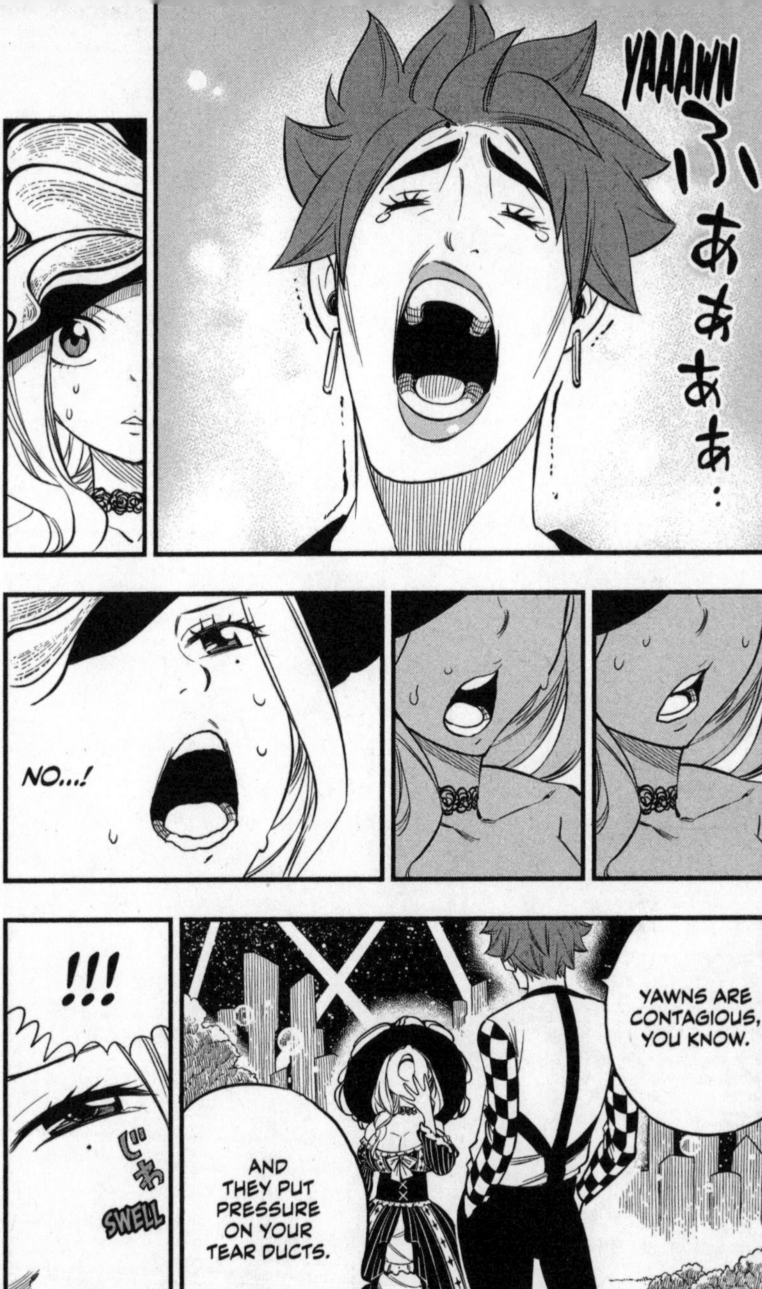

YAAAWN
ふああああ…
NO...!
YAWNS ARE CONTAGIOUS, YOU KNOW.
AND THEY PUT PRESSURE ON YOUR TEAR DUCTS.
!!!
じわ
SWELL

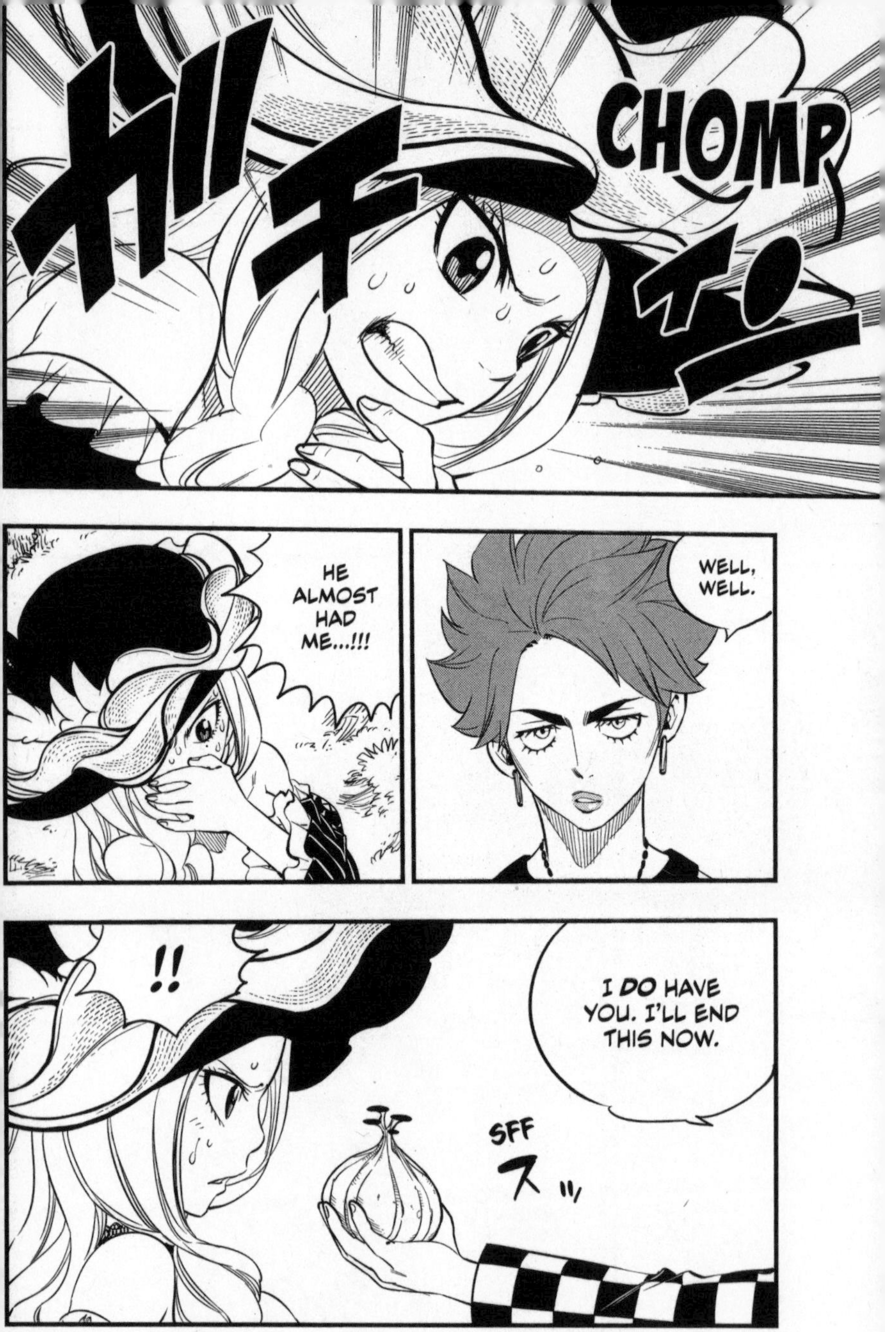
CHOMP
WELL, WELL.
HE ALMOST HAD ME...!!!
I DO HAVE YOU. I'LL END THIS NOW.
!!
SFF

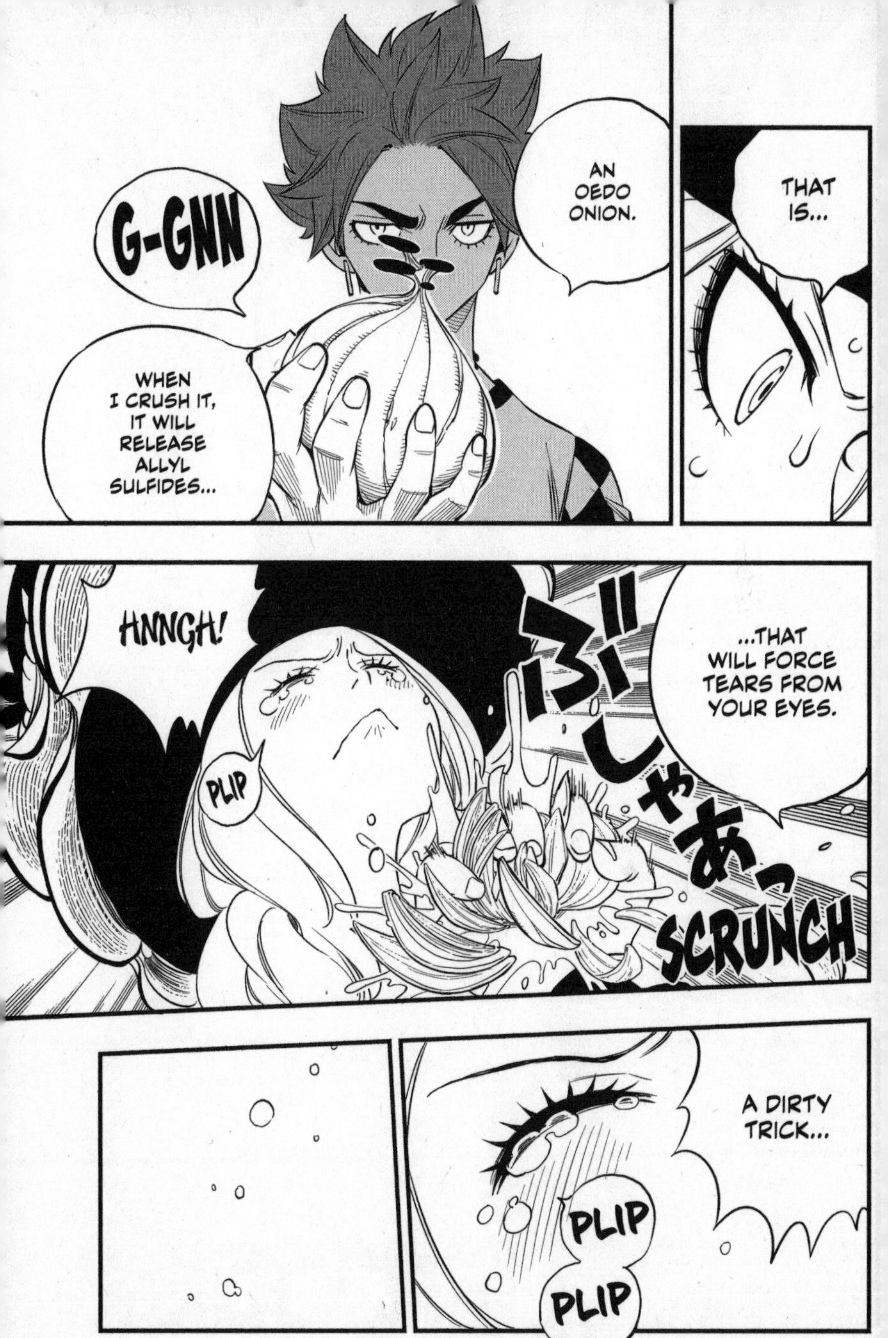
THAT IS...
AN OEDO ONION.
G-GNN
WHEN I CRUSH IT, IT WILL RELEASE ALLYL SULFIDES...
...THAT WILL FORCE TEARS FROM YOUR EYES.
ぶじゃあっ
SCRUNCH
HNNGH!
PLIP
A DIRTY TRICK...
PLIP
PLIP

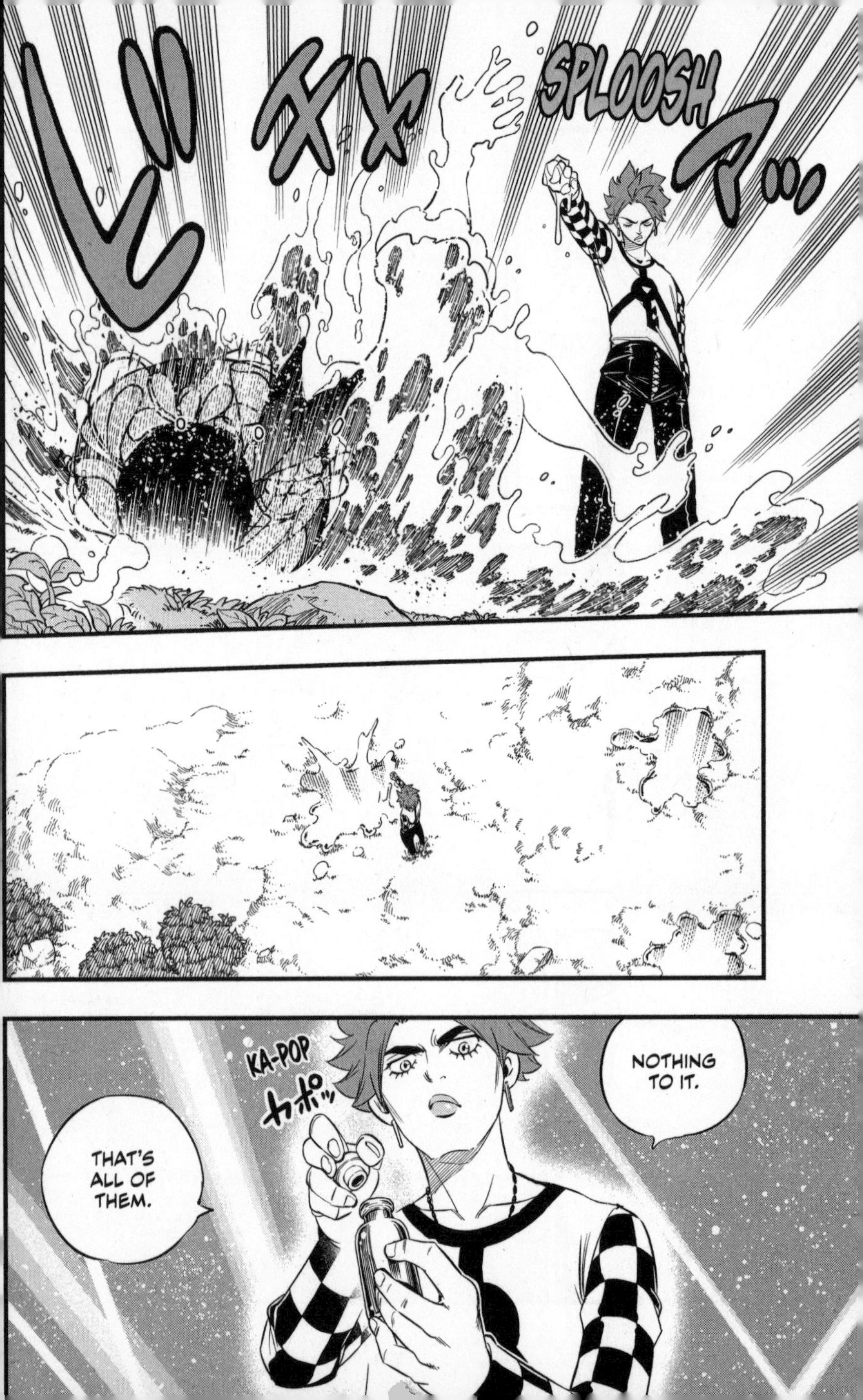
SPLOOSH
NOTHING TO IT.
KA-POP
カポッ
THAT'S ALL OF THEM.

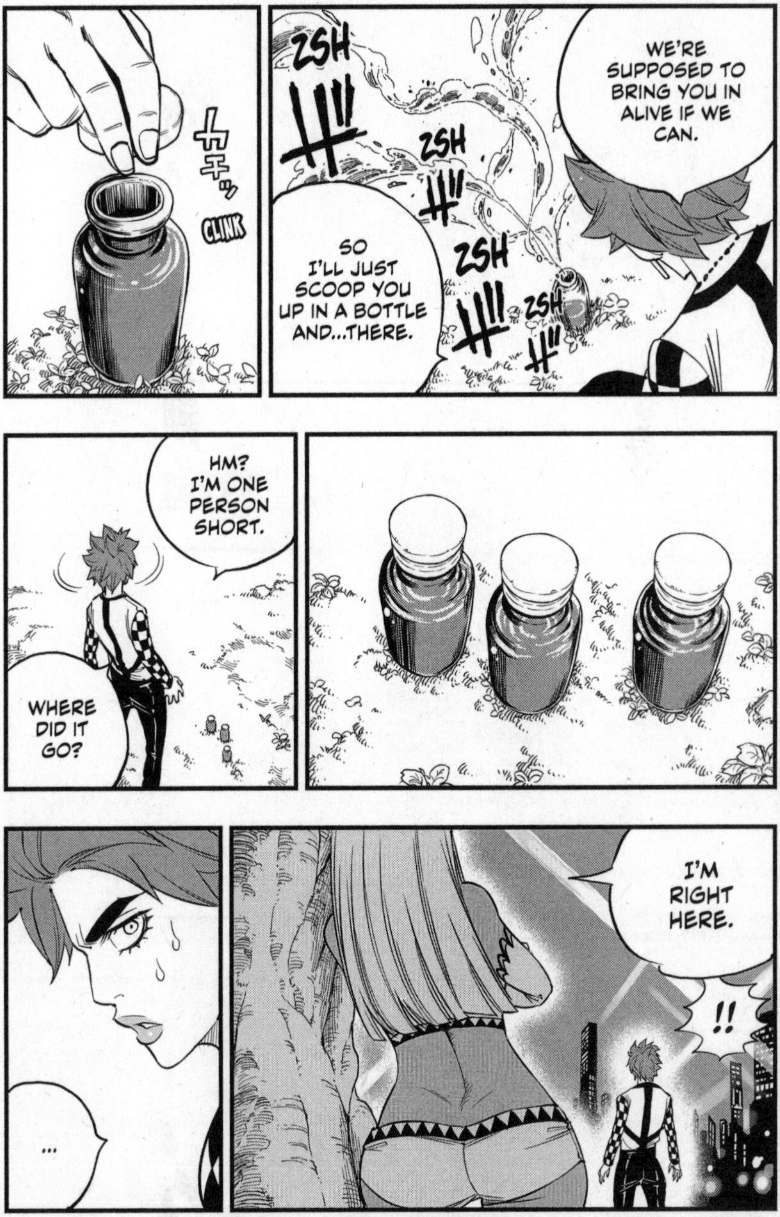
WE'RE SUPPOSED TO BRING YOU IN ALIVE IF WE CAN.
ZSH
ZSH
SO I'LL JUST SCOOP YOU UP IN A BOTTLE AND...THERE.
ZSH
ZSH
カチッ
CLINK
HM? I'M ONE PERSON SHORT.
WHERE DID IT GO?
I'M RIGHT HERE.
!!
...

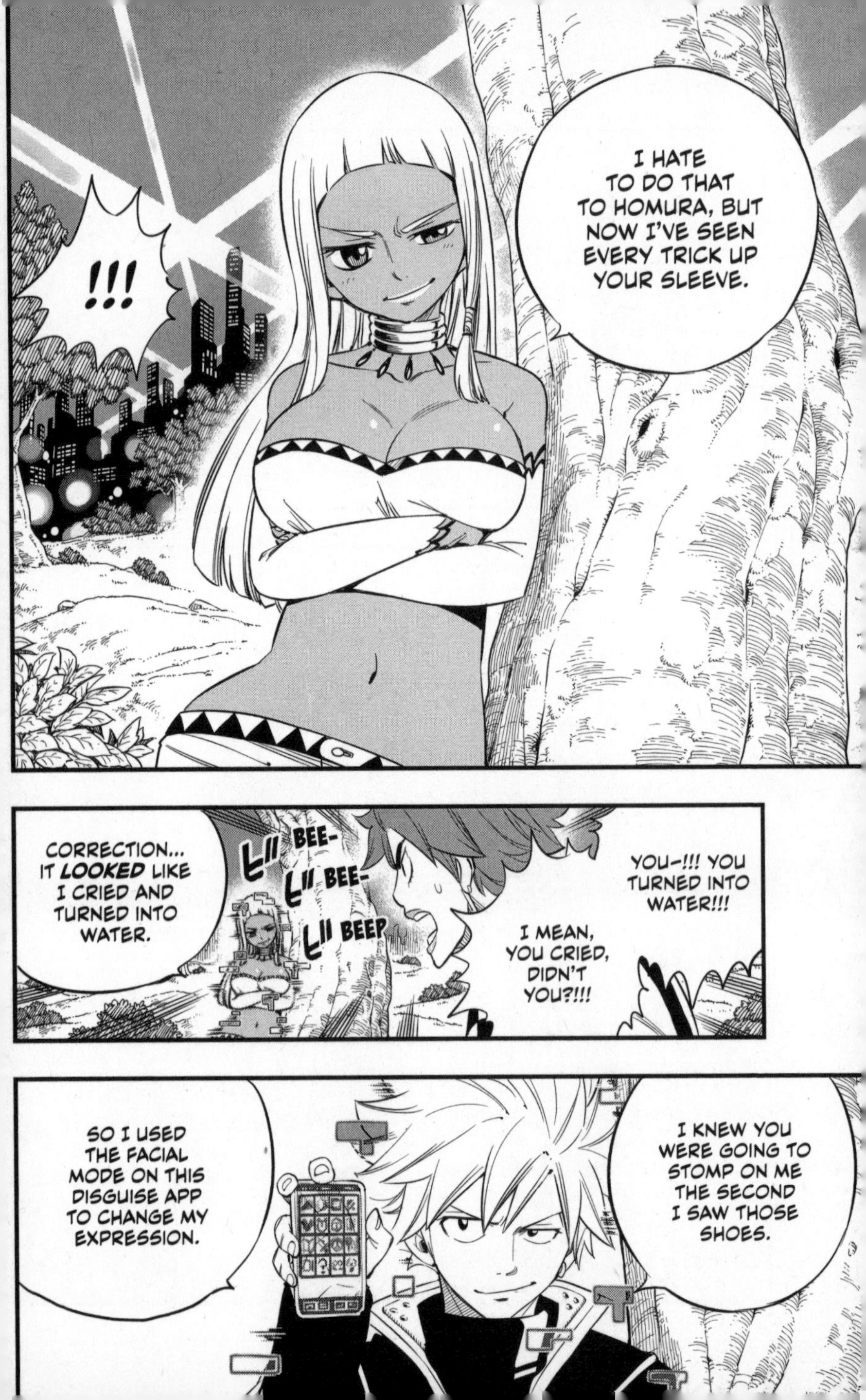
I HATE TO DO THAT TO HOMURA, BUT NOW I'VE SEEN EVERY TRICK UP YOUR SLEEVE.
!!!
YOU-!!! YOU TURNED INTO WATER!!!
I MEAN, YOU CRIED, DIDN'T YOU?!!!
BEE-
BEE-
BEEP
CORRECTION... IT LOOKED LIKE I CRIED AND TURNED INTO WATER.
I KNEW YOU WERE GOING TO STOMP ON ME THE SECOND I SAW THOSE SHOES.
SO I USED THE FACIAL MODE ON THIS DISGUISE APP TO CHANGE MY EXPRESSION.

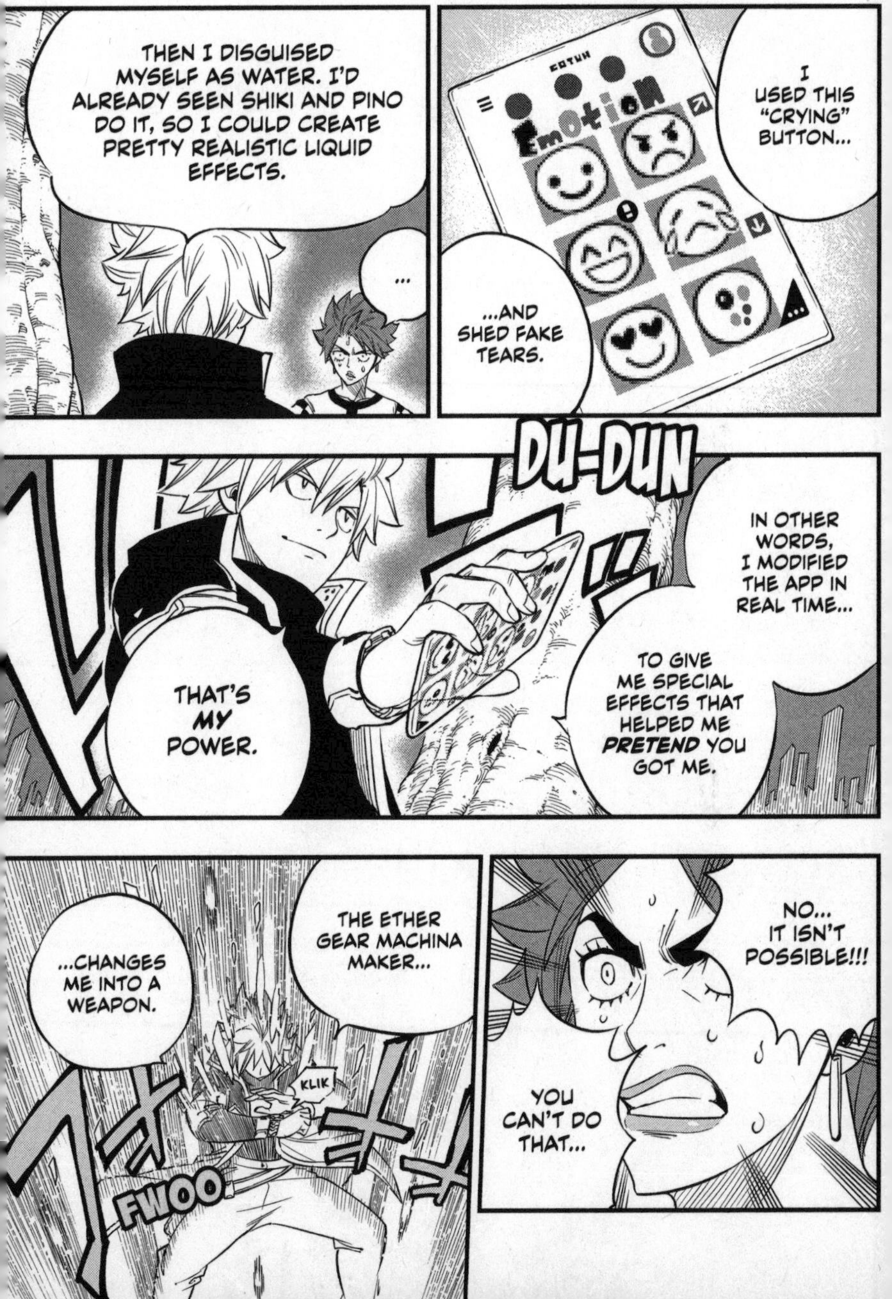
I USED THIS "CRYING" BUTTON...
...AND SHED FAKE TEARS.
THEN I DISGUISED MYSELF AS WATER. I'D ALREADY SEEN SHIKI AND PINO DO IT, SO I COULD CREATE PRETTY REALISTIC LIQUID EFFECTS.
...
DU-DUN
IN OTHER WORDS, I MODIFIED THE APP IN REAL TIME...
TO GIVE ME SPECIAL EFFECTS THAT HELPED ME PRETEND YOU GOT ME.
THAT'S MY POWER.
NO... IT ISN'T POSSIBLE!!!
YOU CAN'T DO THAT...
THE ETHER GEAR MACHINA MAKER...
...CHANGES ME INTO A WEAPON.
KLIK
FWOO

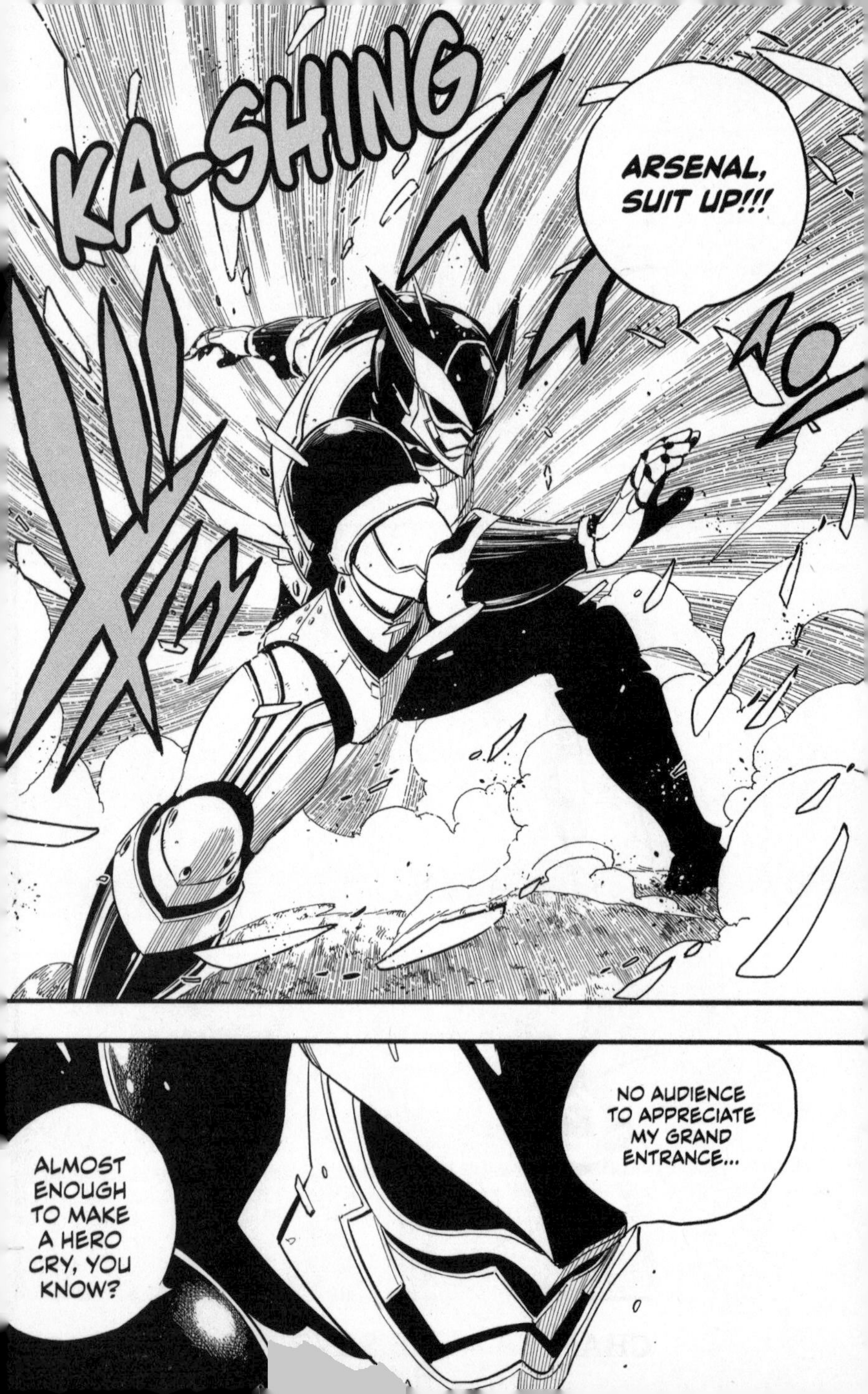
KA-SHING
ARSENAL, SUIT UP!!!
NO AUDIENCE TO APPRECIATE MY GRAND ENTRANCE...
ALMOST ENOUGH TO MAKE A HERO CRY, YOU KNOW?

EDENS ZERO

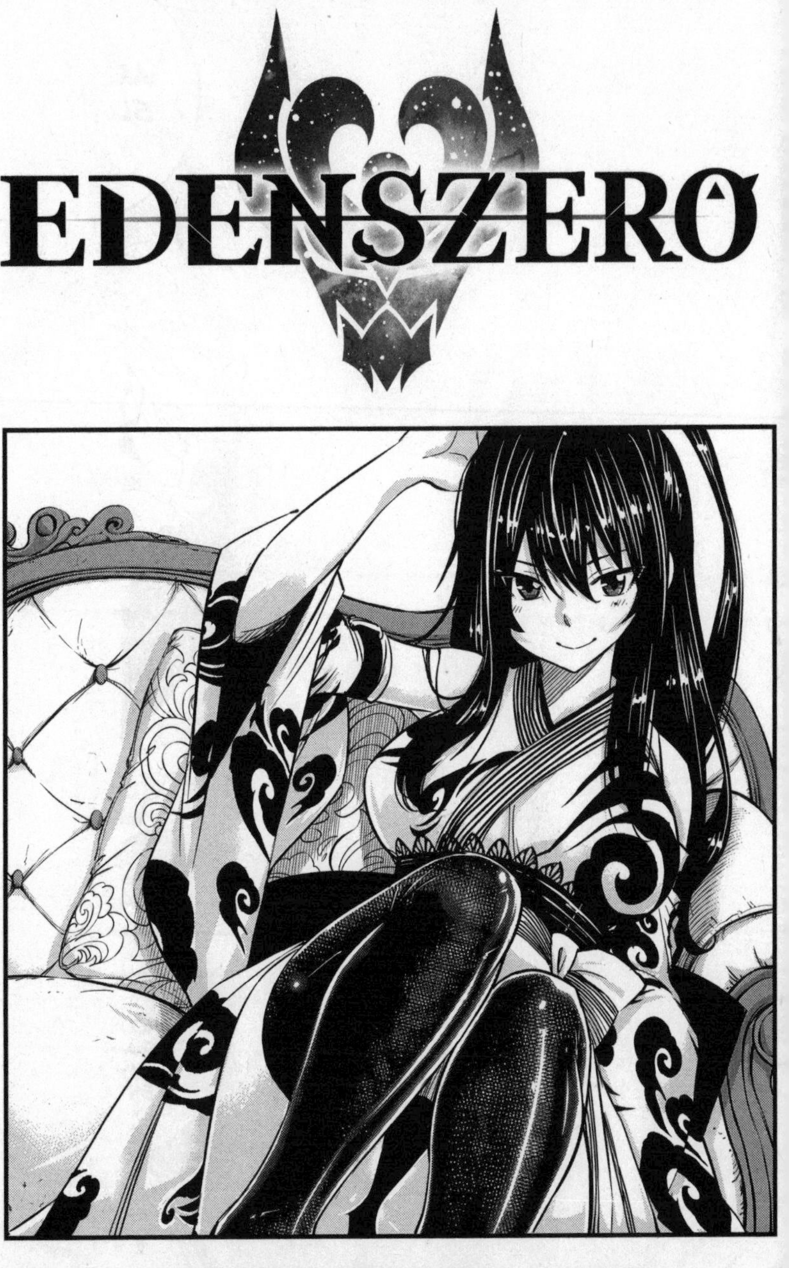

CHAPTER 74: WEISZ VS. LAGUNA

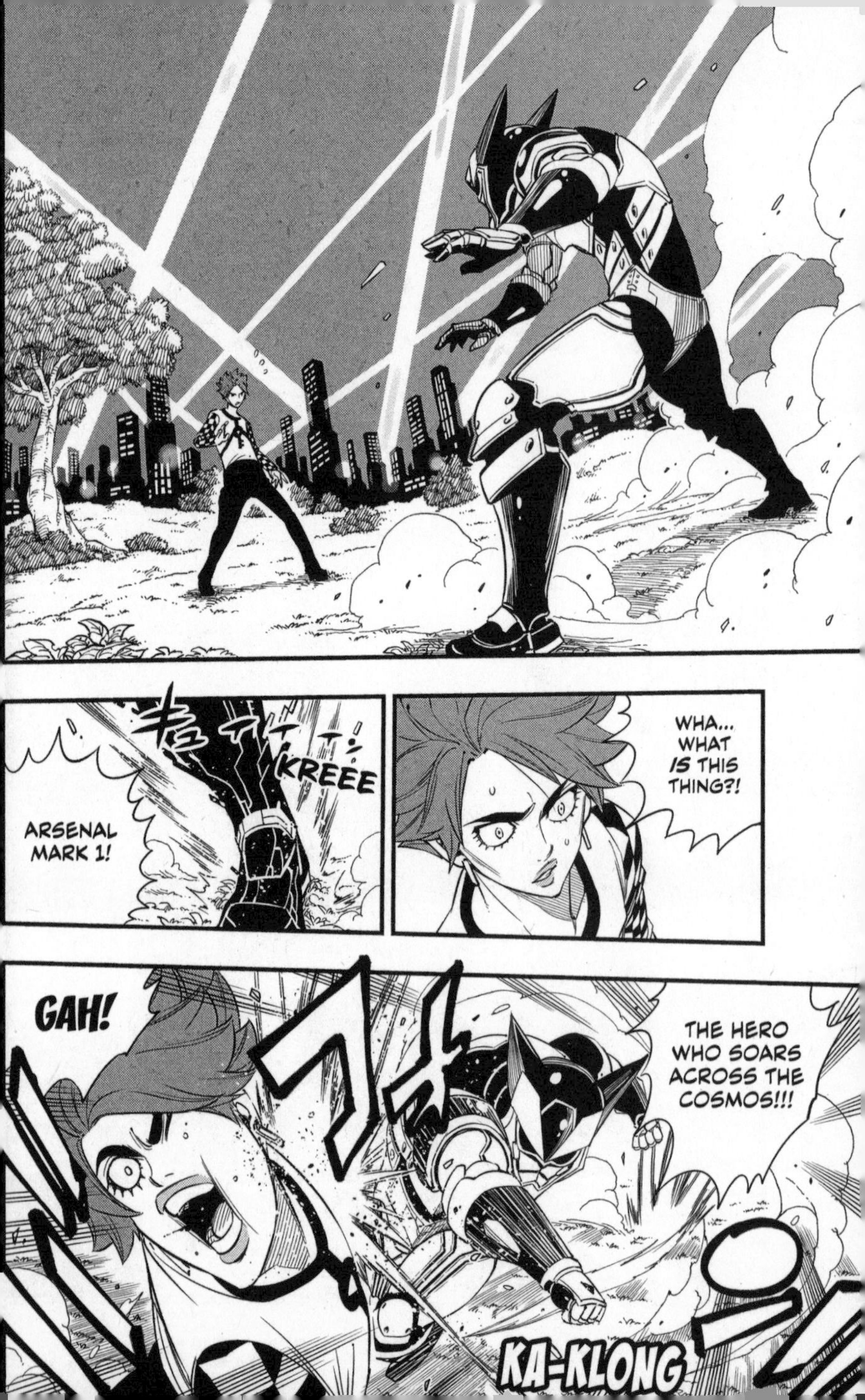
WHA... WHAT IS THIS THING?!
KREEE
ARSENAL MARK 1!
THE HERO WHO SOARS ACROSS THE COSMOS!!!
GAH!
KA-KLONG

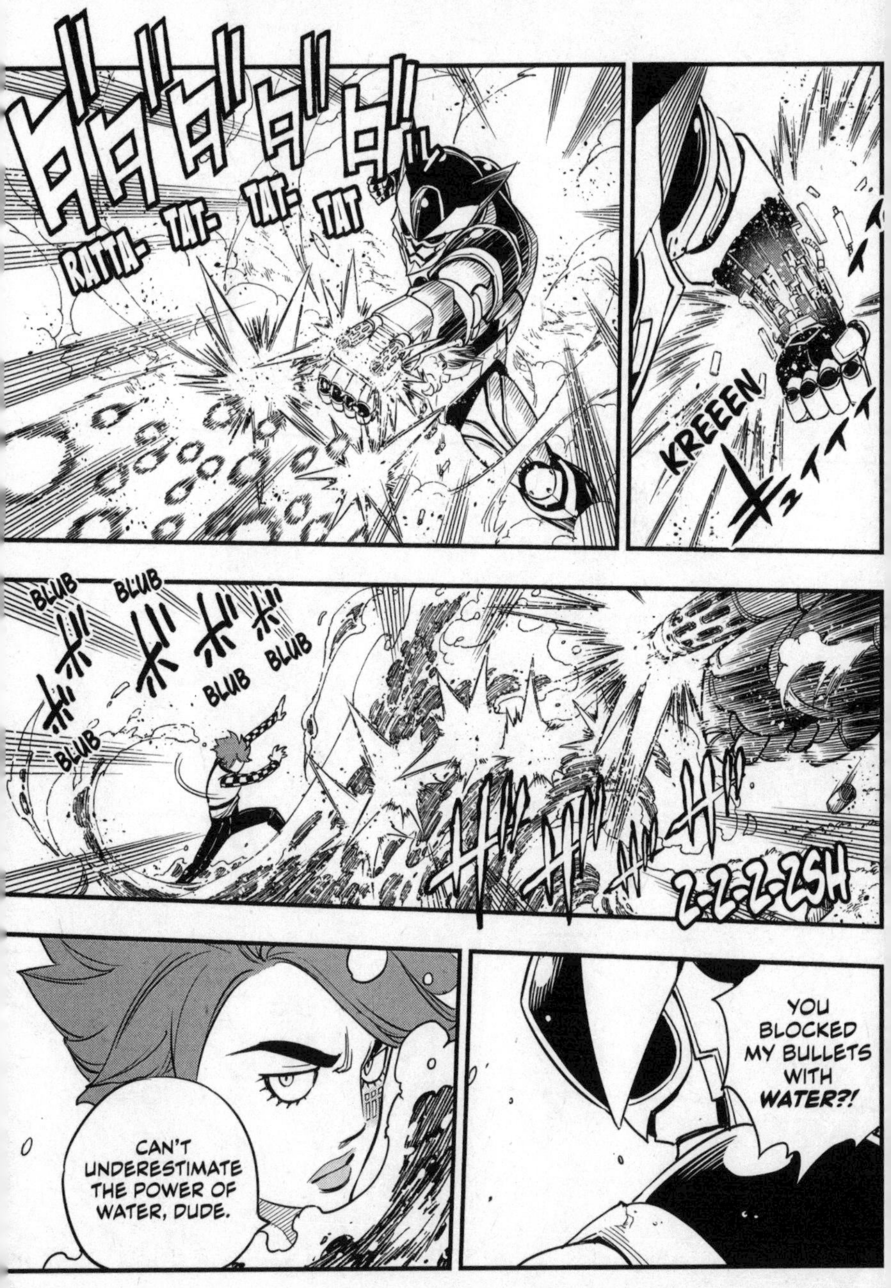
KREEEN
RATTA- TAT- TAT- TAT
BLUB
BLUB
BLUB
BLUB
BLUB
BLUB
Z-Z-Z-ZSH
YOU BLOCKED MY BULLETS WITH *WATER?!*
CAN'T UNDERESTIMATE THE POWER OF WATER, DUDE.

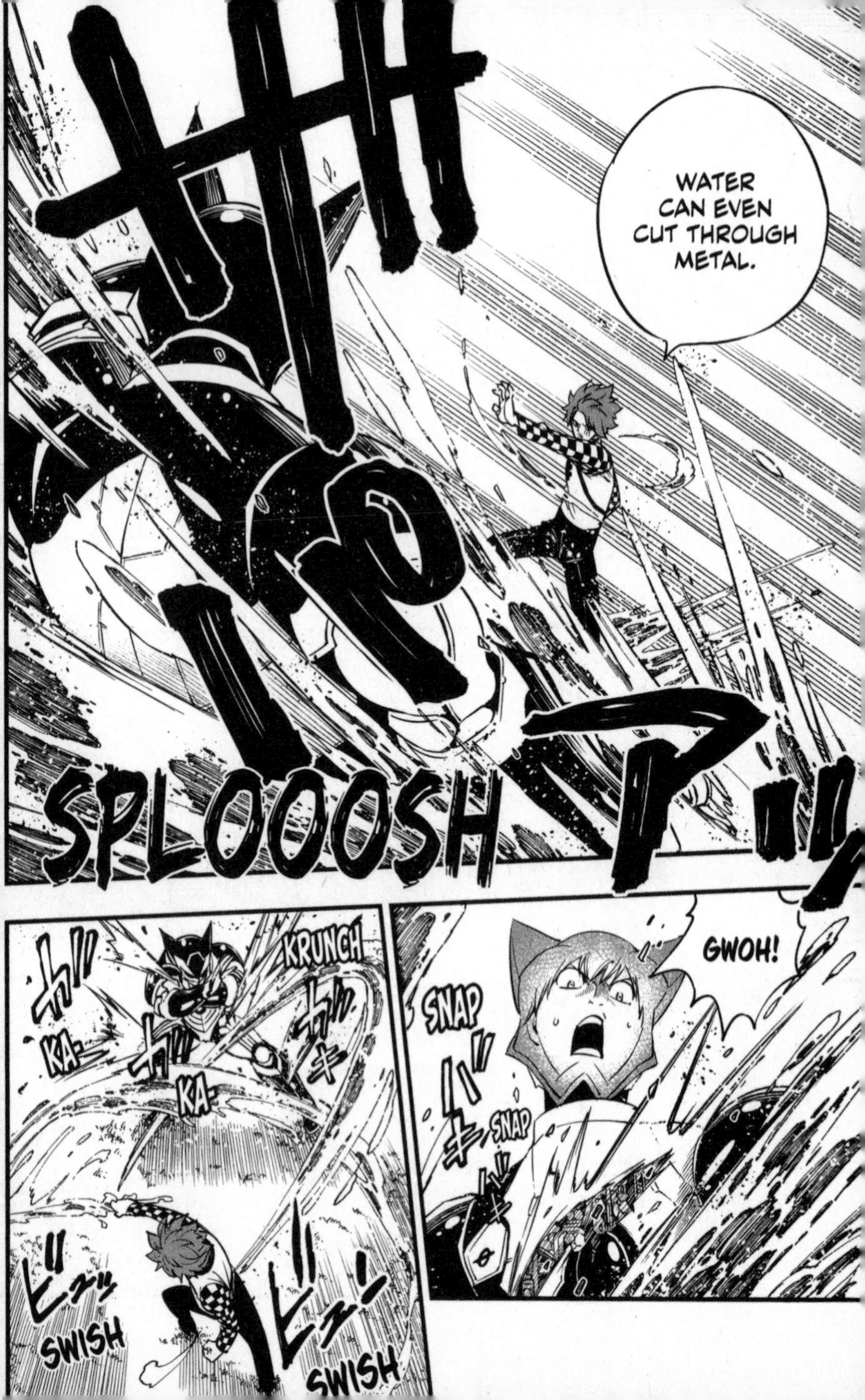
WATER CAN EVEN CUT THROUGH METAL.
SPLOOOSH
GWOH!
SNAP
SNAP
KRUNCH
KA-
KA
SWISH
SWISH

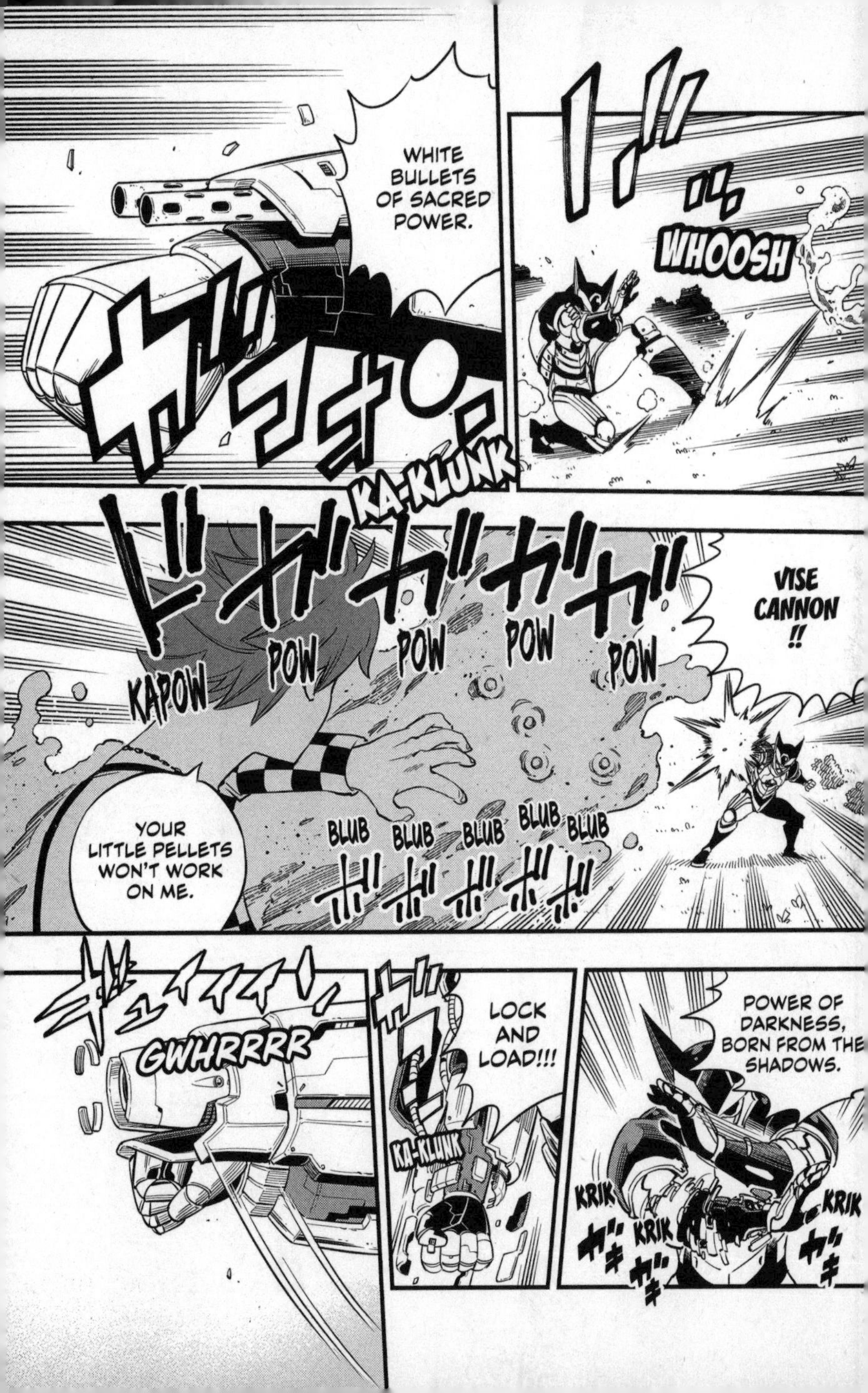
WHOOSH
WHITE BULLETS OF SACRED POWER.
KA-KLUNK
VISE CANNON!!
POW
POW
POW
POW
KAPOW
BLUB
BLUB
BLUB
BLUB
BLUB
YOUR LITTLE PELLETS WON'T WORK ON ME.
POWER OF DARKNESS, BORN FROM THE SHADOWS.
KRIK
KRIK
KRIK
LOCK AND LOAD!!!
KA-KLUNK
GWHRRRR

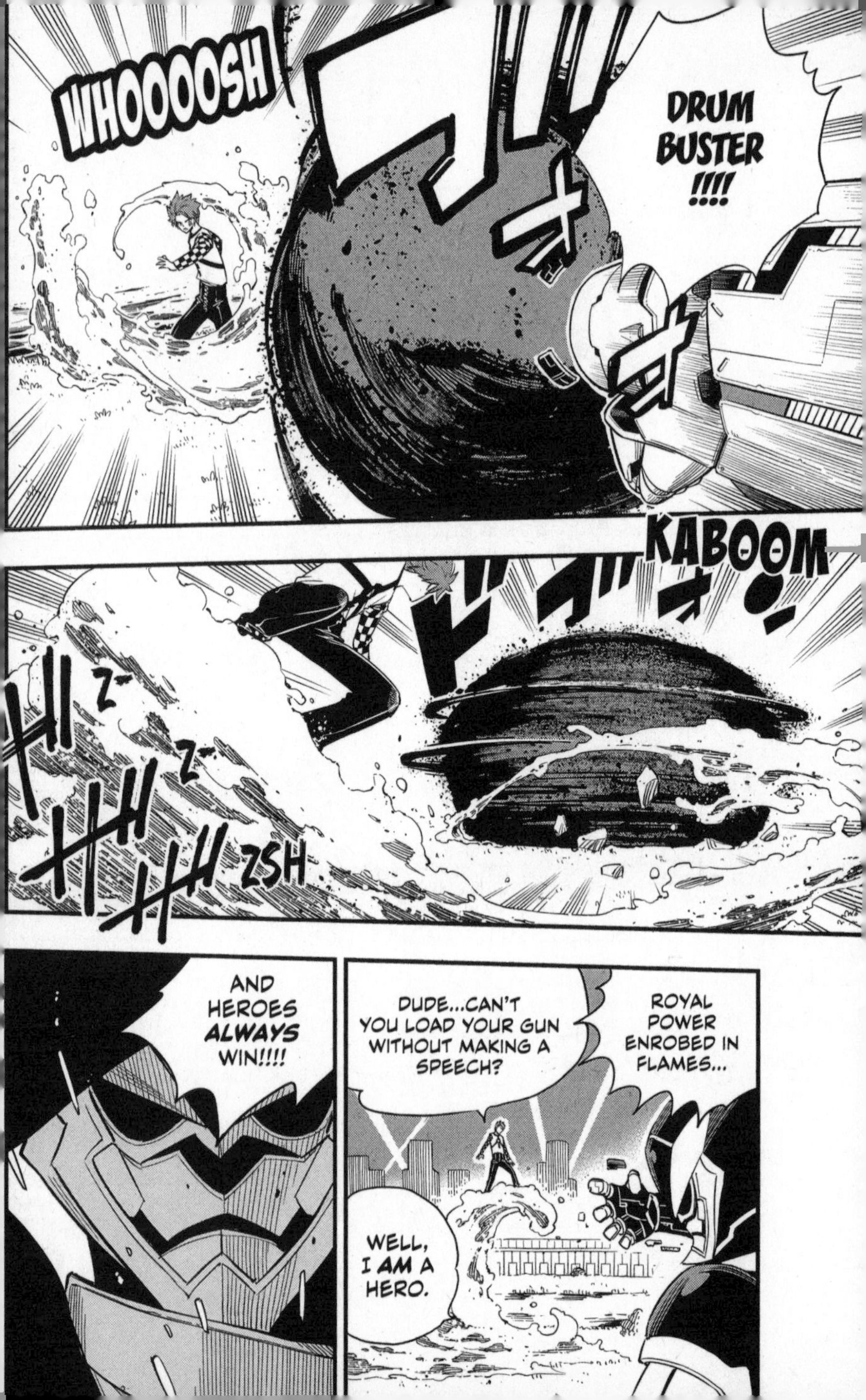
DRUM BUSTER!!!!
WHOOOOSH
KABOOM
Z
Z
ZSH
ROYAL POWER ENROBED IN FLAMES...
DUDE...CAN'T YOU LOAD YOUR GUN WITHOUT MAKING A SPEECH?
WELL, I AM A HERO.
AND HEROES ALWAYS WIN!!!!

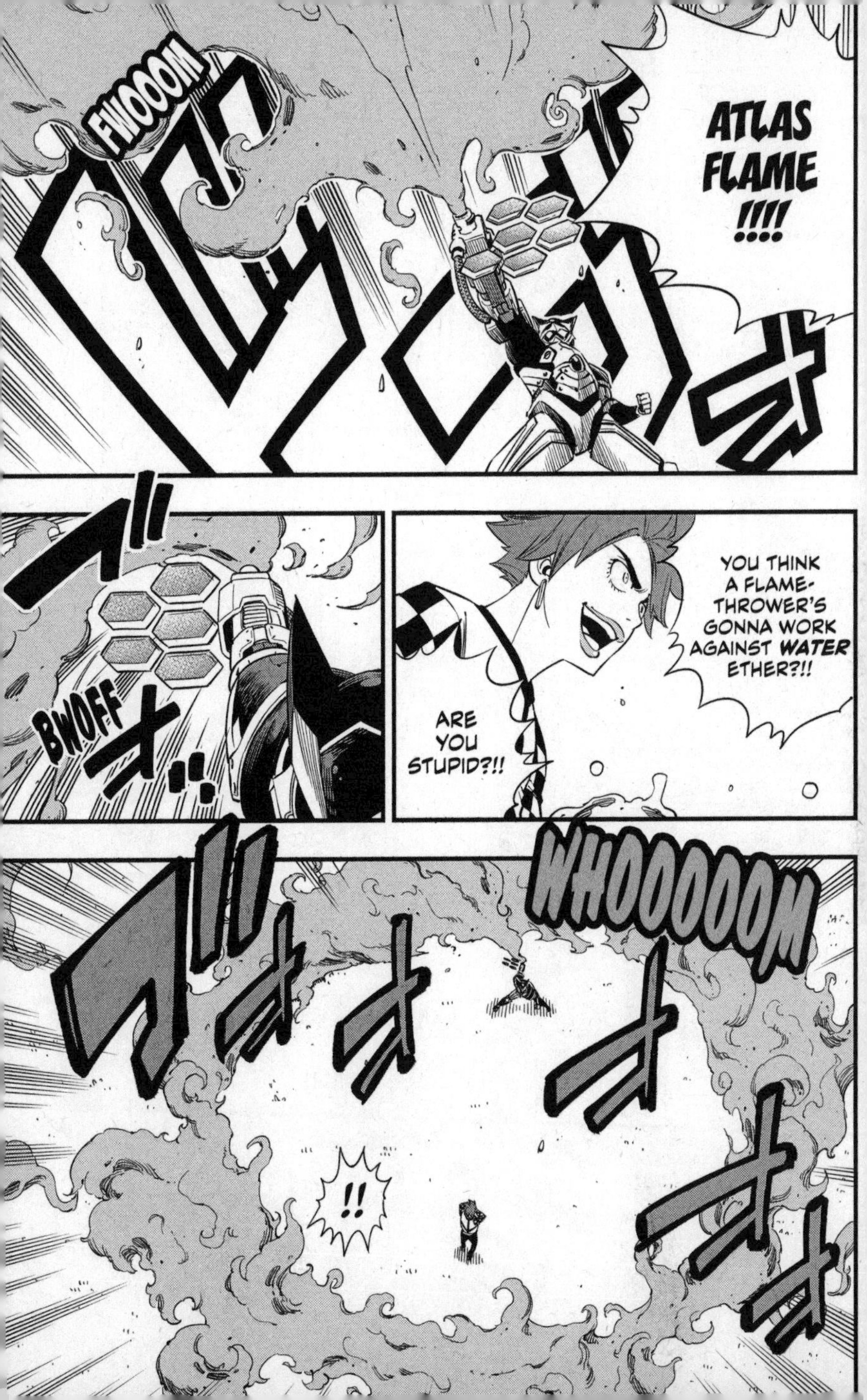
ATLAS FLAME!!!!
FWOOOM
YOU THINK A FLAME-THROWER'S GONNA WORK AGAINST WATER ETHER?!!
ARE YOU STUPID?!!
BWOFF
WHOOOOOOM
!!

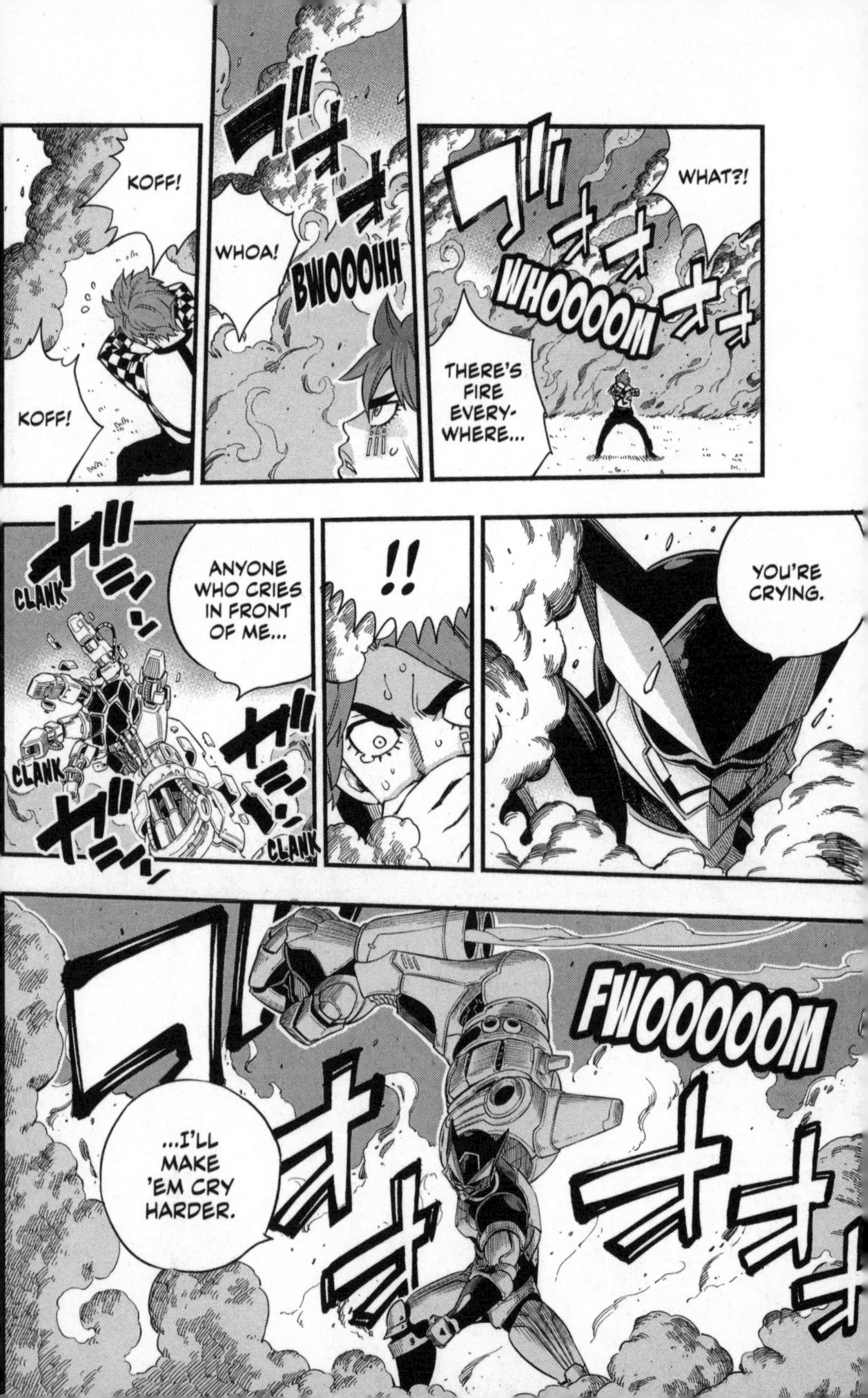
WHAT?!
WHOOOOM
THERE'S FIRE EVERY-WHERE...
WHOA!
BWOOOHH
KOFF!
KOFF!
YOU'RE CRYING.
!!
ANYONE WHO CRIES IN FRONT OF ME...
CLANK
CLANK
CLANK
FWOOOOOM
...I'LL MAKE 'EM CRY HARDER.

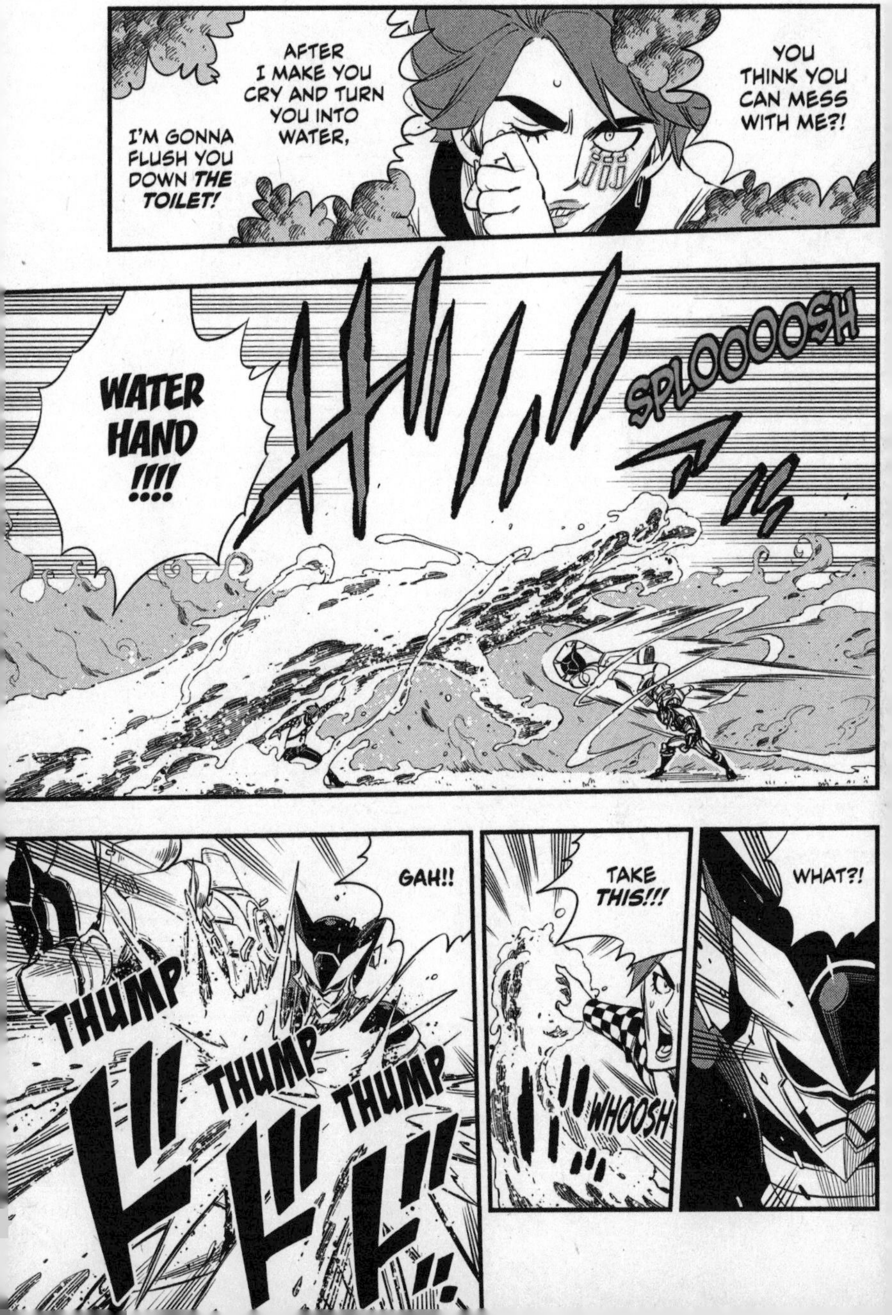
YOU THINK YOU CAN MESS WITH ME?!
AFTER I MAKE YOU CRY AND TURN YOU INTO WATER,
I'M GONNA FLUSH YOU DOWN ***THE TOILET!***
SPLOOOOSH
WATER HAND!!!!
WHAT?!
TAKE ***THIS!!!***
WHOOSH
GAH!!
THUMP
THUMP
THUMP

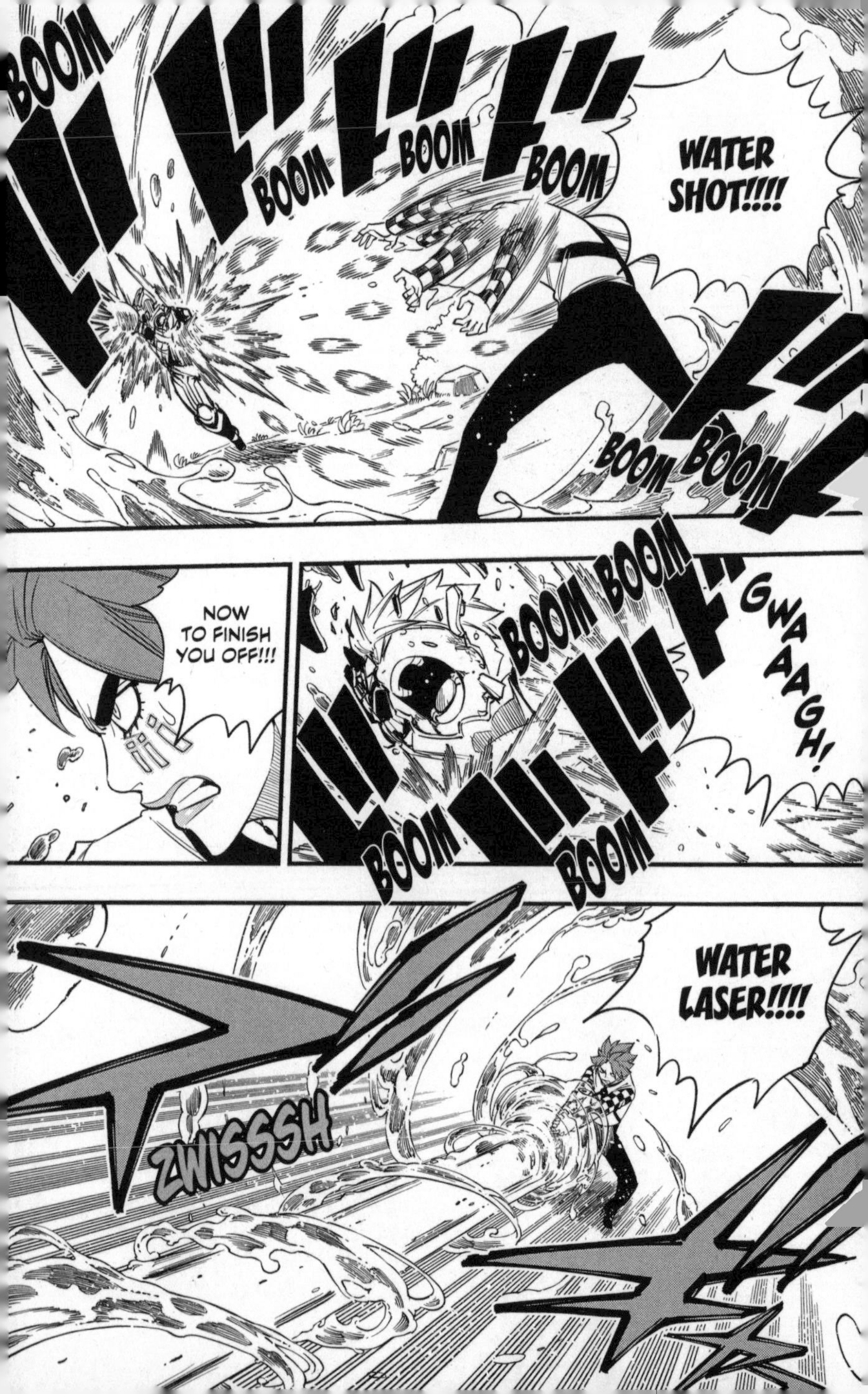
WATER SHOT!!!!
BOOM
BOOM
BOOM
BOOM
BOOM
BOOM
GWAAAAGH!
BOOM BOOM
BOOM
BOOM
NOW TO FINISH YOU OFF!!!
WATER LASER!!!!
ZWISSSH

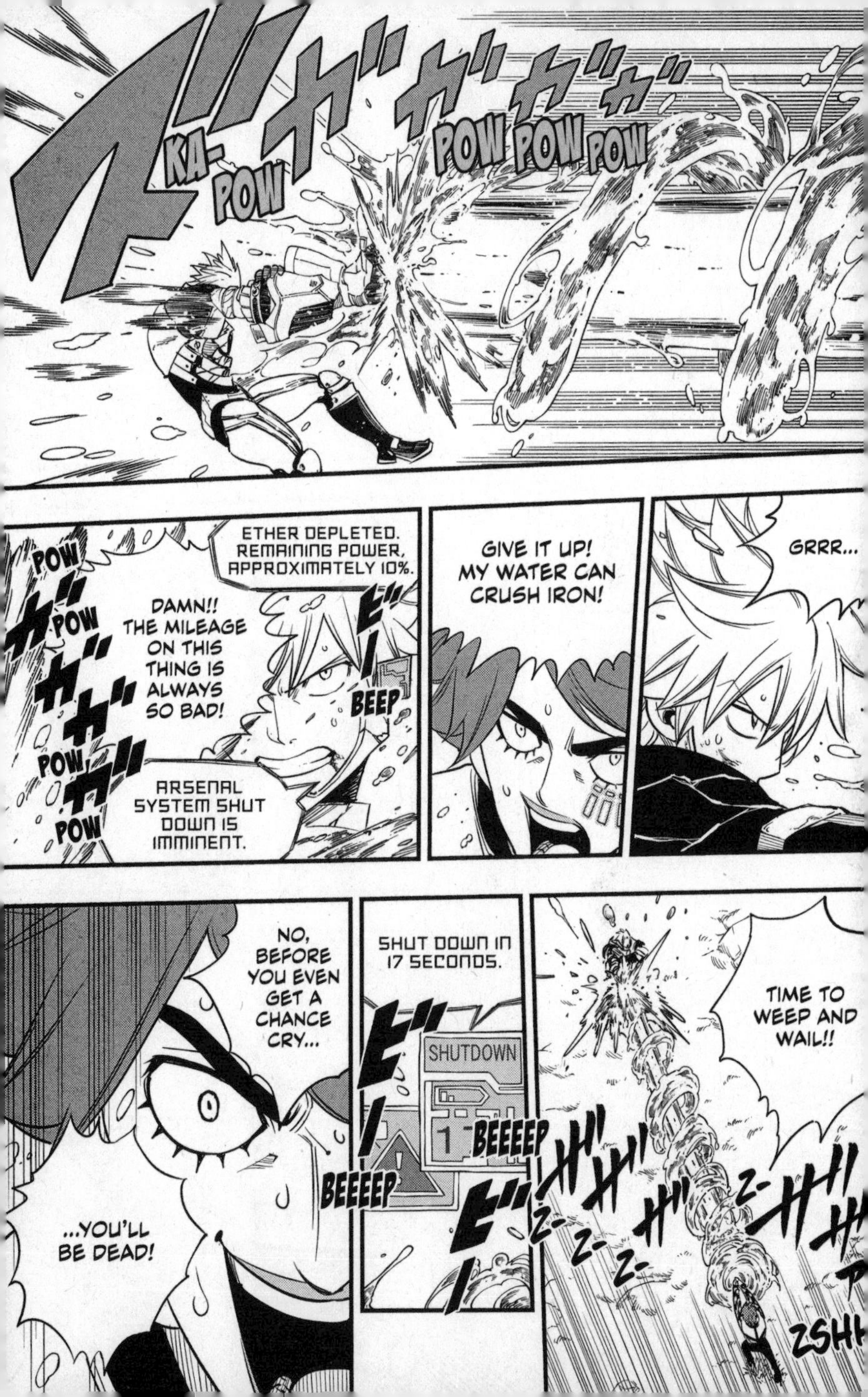
KA-POW
POW POW POW
GRRR...
GIVE IT UP! MY WATER CAN CRUSH IRON!
ETHER DEPLETED. REMAINING POWER, APPROXIMATELY 10%.
BEEP
DAMN!! THE MILEAGE ON THIS THING IS ALWAYS SO BAD!
POW POW POW POW
ARSENAL SYSTEM SHUT DOWN IS IMMINENT.
TIME TO WEEP AND WAIL!!
Z- Z- Z- Z-
ZSH
SHUT DOWN IN 17 SECONDS.
SHUTDOWN
BEEEEP
BEEEEP
NO, BEFORE YOU EVEN GET A CHANCE CRY...
...YOU'LL BE DEAD!

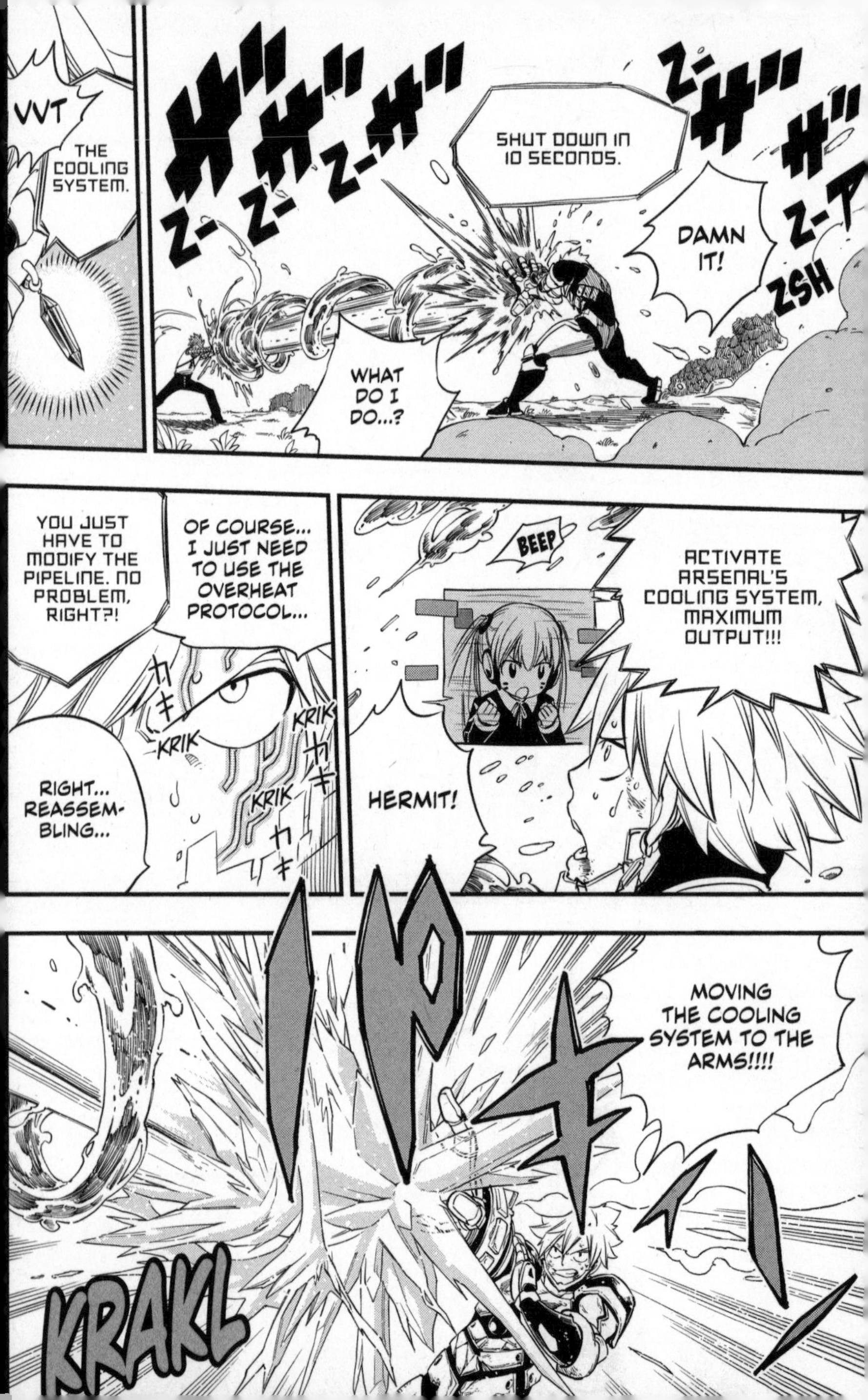
Z-
ZSH
SHUT DOWN IN 10 SECONDS.
DAMN IT!
Z-
Z-
Z-
WHAT DO I DO...?
VVT
THE COOLING SYSTEM.
BEEP
ACTIVATE ARSENAL'S COOLING SYSTEM, MAXIMUM OUTPUT!!!
HERMIT!
OF COURSE... I JUST NEED TO USE THE OVERHEAT PROTOCOL...
YOU JUST HAVE TO MODIFY THE PIPELINE. NO PROBLEM, RIGHT?!
KRIK
KRIK
KRIK
RIGHT... REASSEMBLING...
MOVING THE COOLING SYSTEM TO THE ARMS!!!!
KRAKL

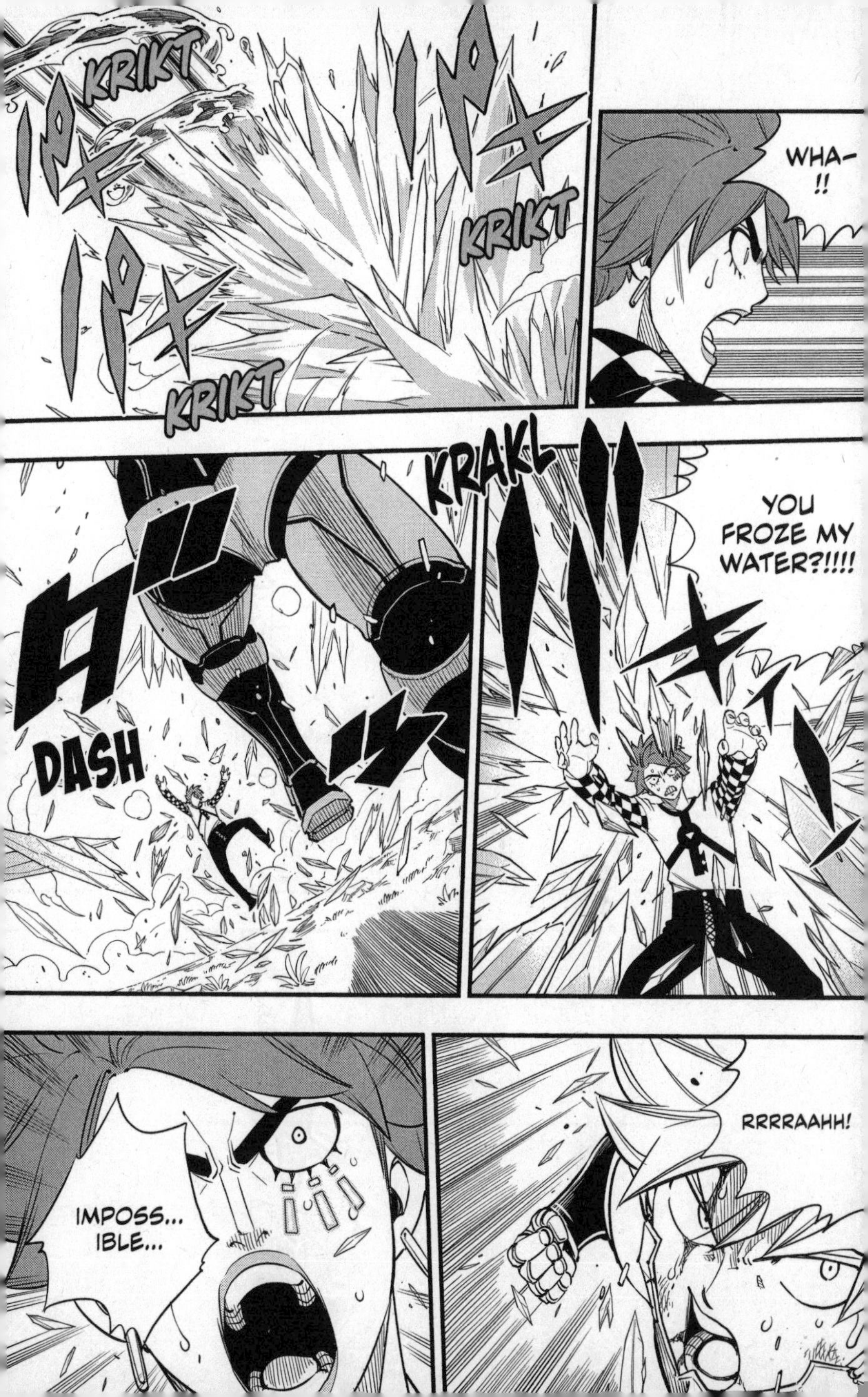
WHA-!!
KRIKT
KRIKT
KRIKT
KRAKL
YOU FROZE MY WATER?!!!!
DASH
RRRRAAHH!
IMPOSS... IBLE...

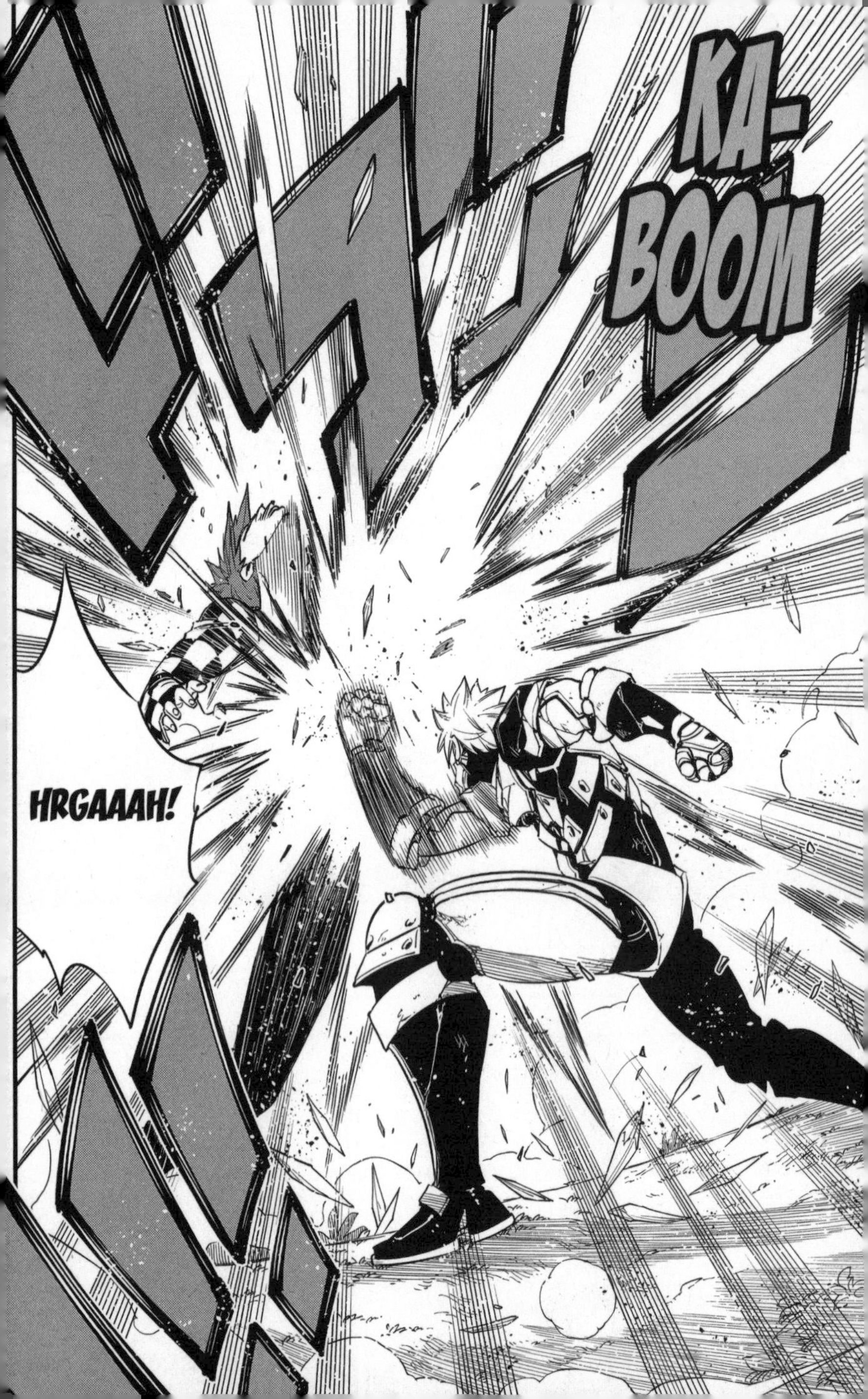
KA-
BOOM
HRGAAAH!

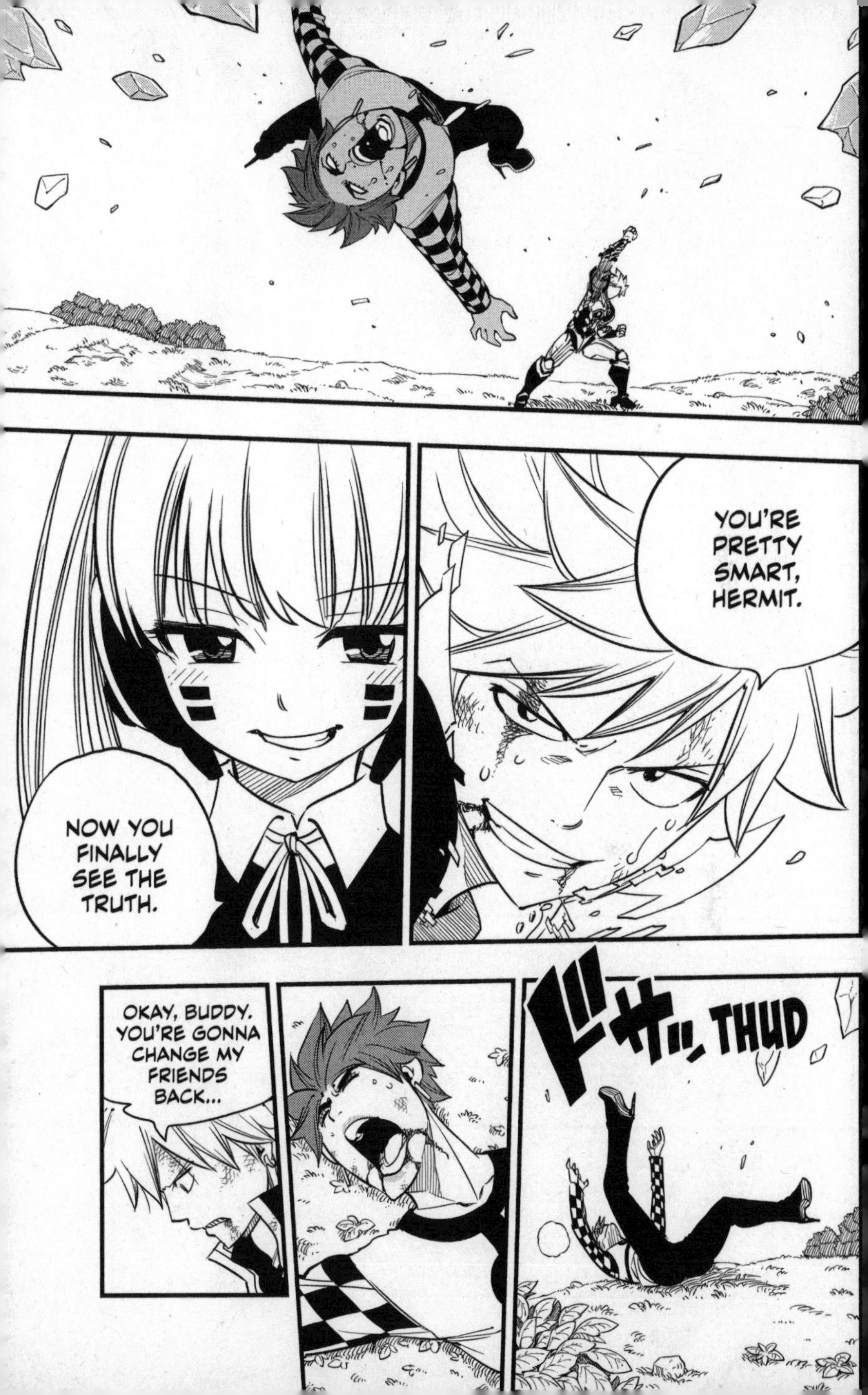
YOU'RE PRETTY SMART, HERMIT.
NOW YOU FINALLY SEE THE TRUTH.
THUD
OKAY, BUDDY. YOU'RE GONNA CHANGE MY FRIENDS BACK...

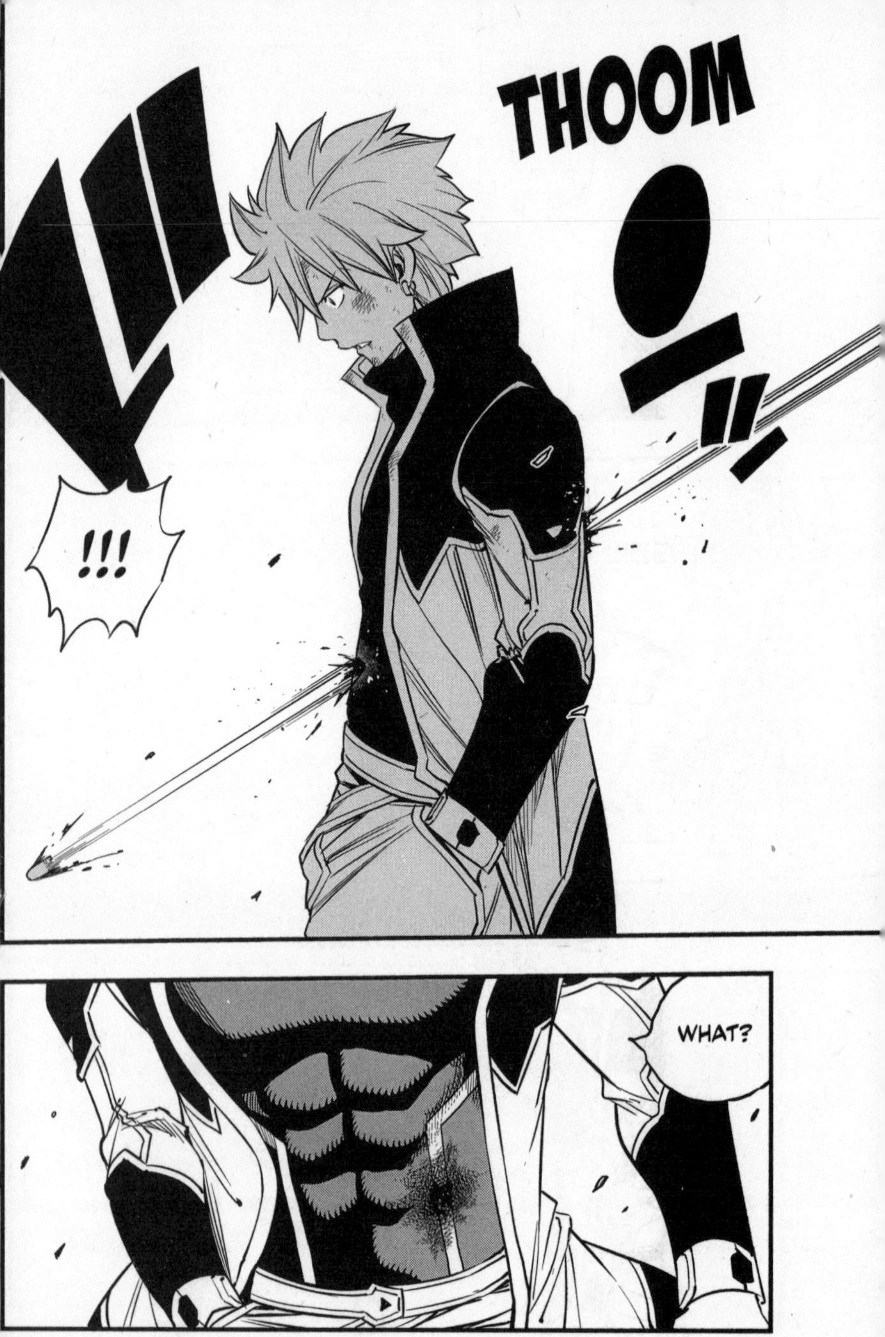
THOOM
!!!
WHAT?

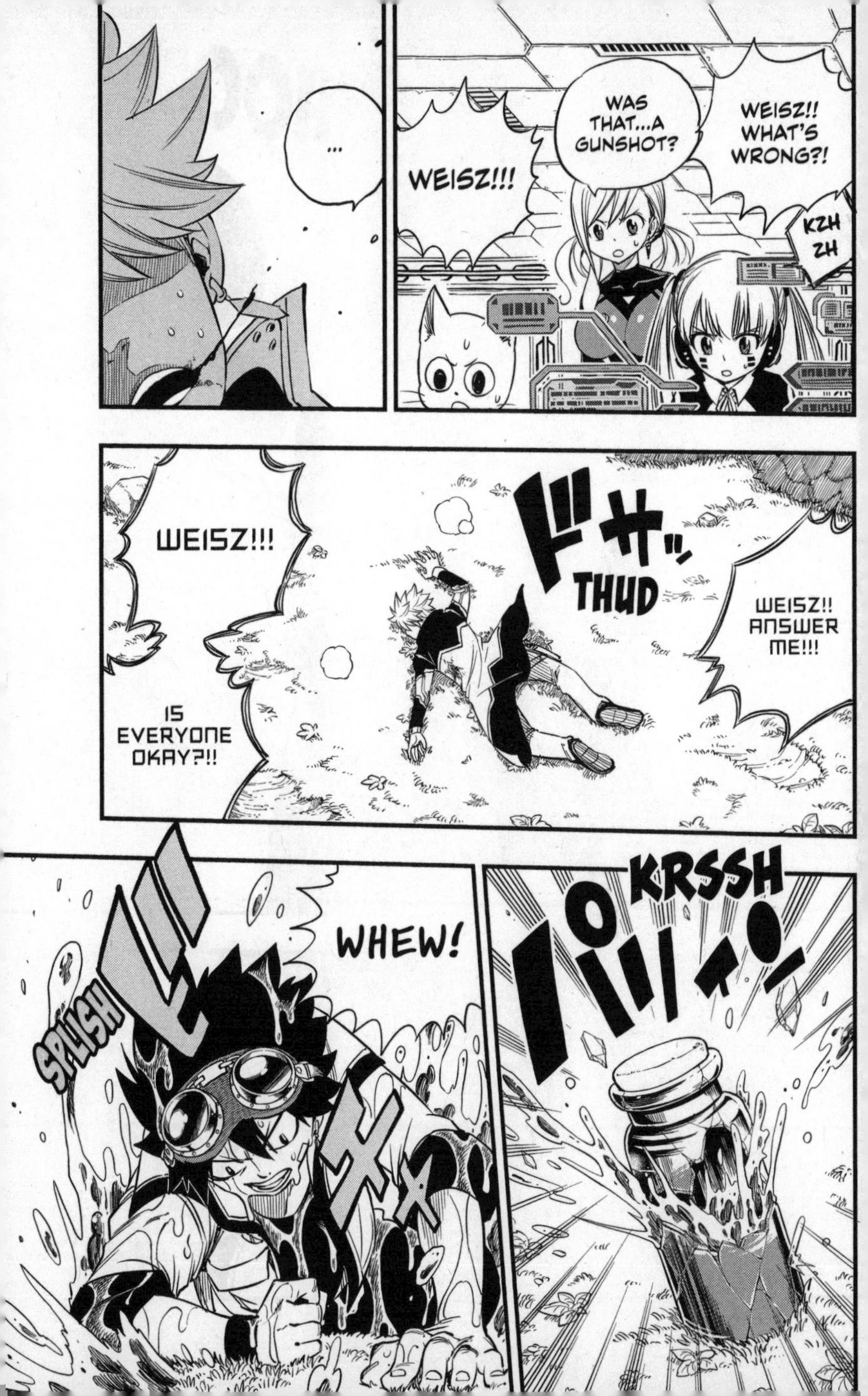
WEISZ!! WHAT'S WRONG?!
WAS THAT...A GUNSHOT?
KZH ZH
WEISZ!!!
...
WEISZ!! ANSWER ME!!!
THUD
WEISZ!!!
IS EVERYONE OKAY?!!
KRSSH
WHEW!
SPLISH

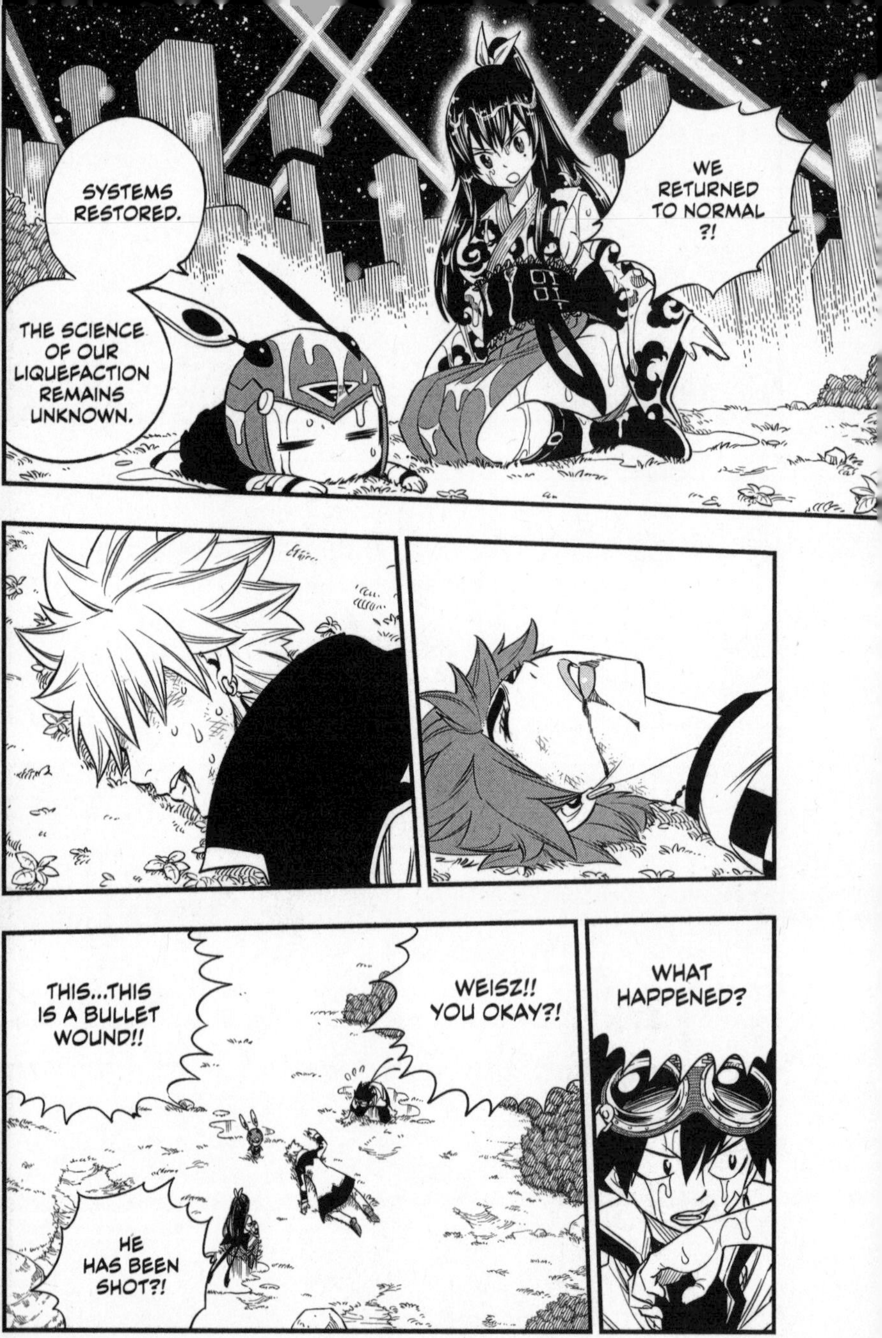
WE RETURNED TO NORMAL ?!
SYSTEMS RESTORED.
THE SCIENCE OF OUR LIQUEFACTION REMAINS UNKNOWN.
WHAT HAPPENED?
WEISZ!! YOU OKAY?!
THIS...THIS IS A BULLET WOUND!!
HE HAS BEEN SHOT?!

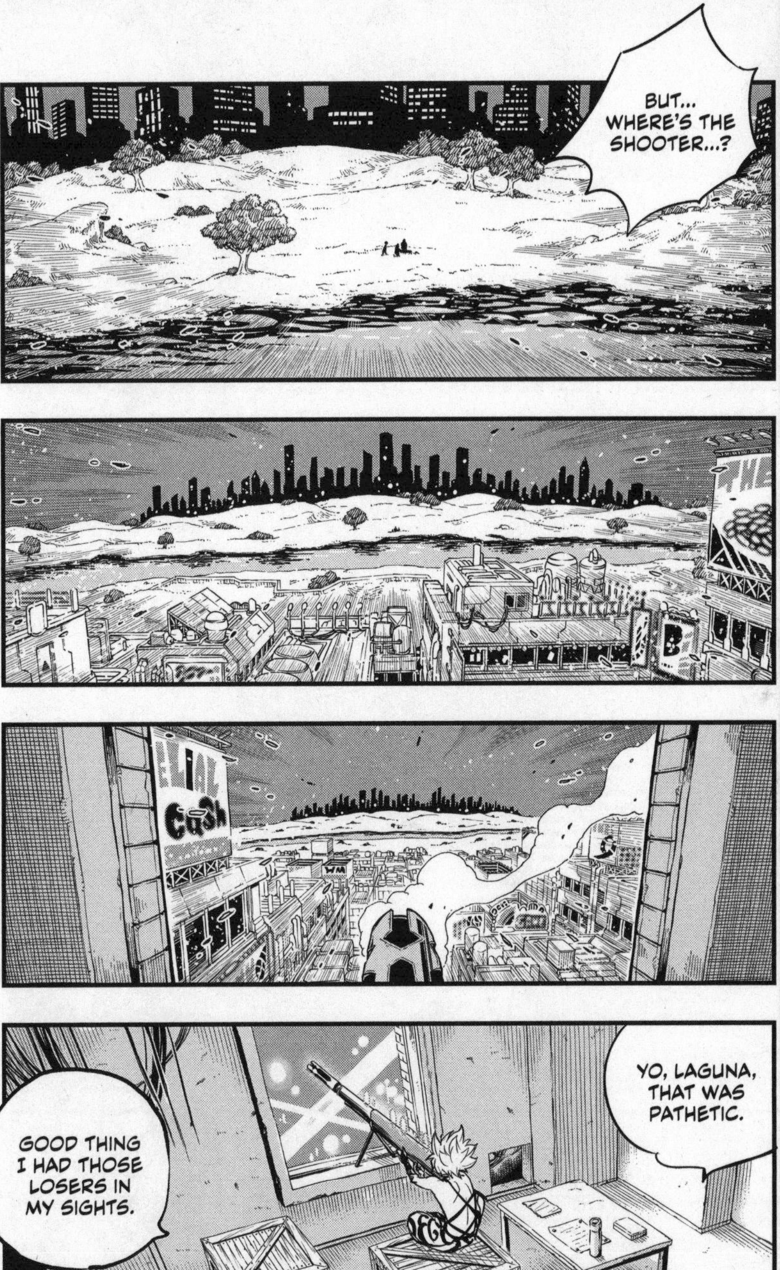
BUT... WHERE'S THE SHOOTER...?
YO, LAGUNA, THAT WAS PATHETIC.
GOOD THING I HAD THOSE LOSERS IN MY SIGHTS.

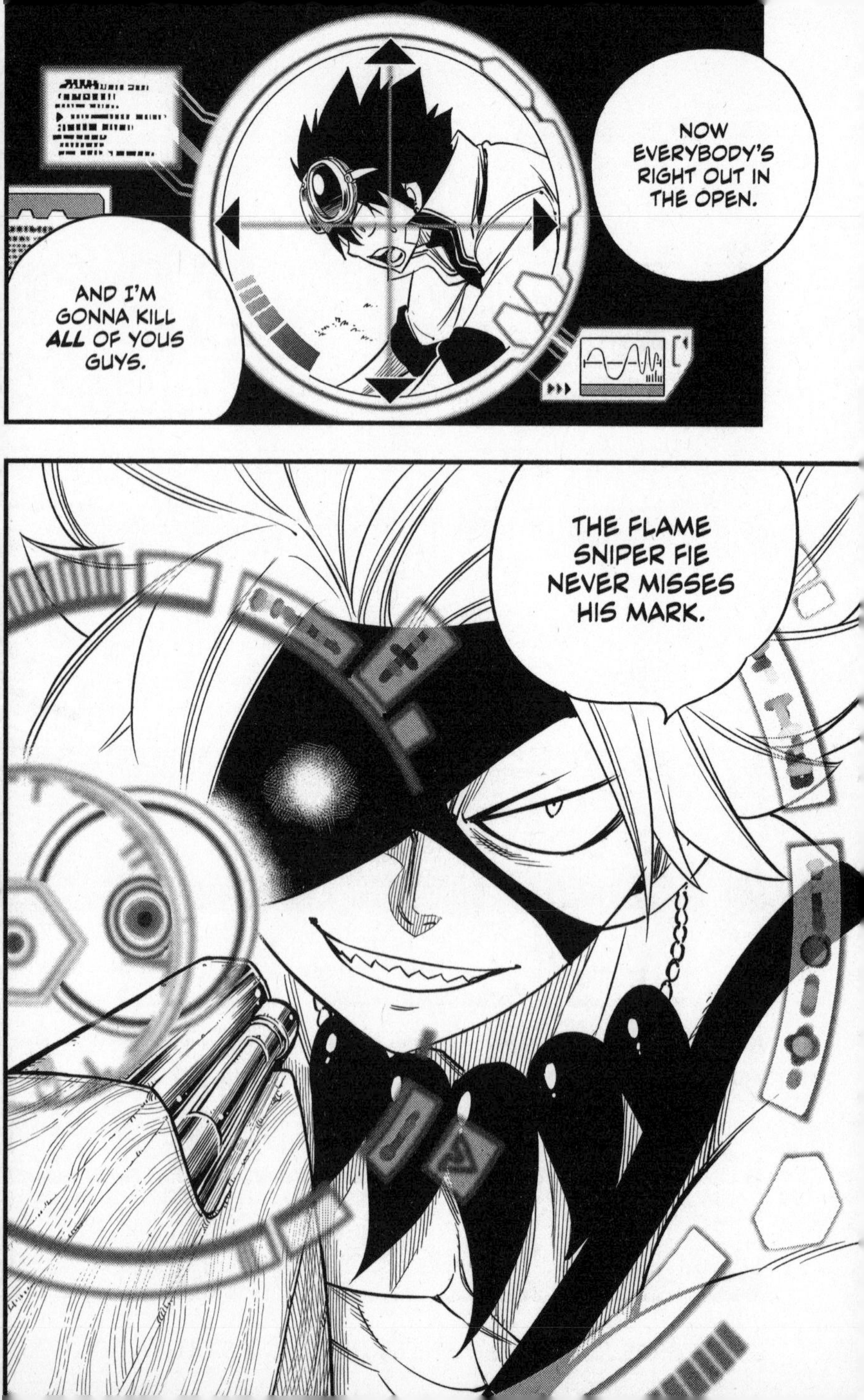
NOW EVERYBODY'S RIGHT OUT IN THE OPEN.
AND I'M GONNA KILL ALL OF YOUS GUYS.
THE FLAME SNIPER FIE NEVER MISSES HIS MARK.

EDENS ZERO

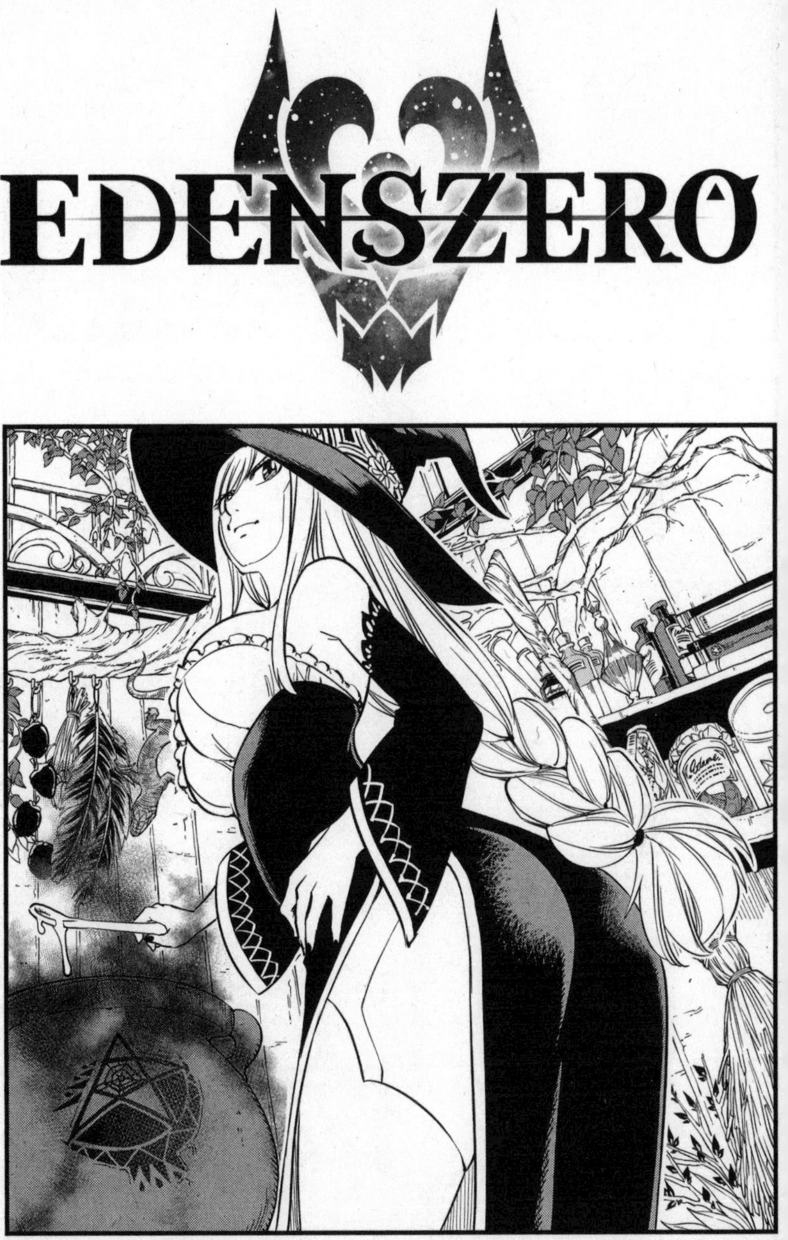

CHAPTER 75: A WIND BLOWS THROUGH THE SAKURA COSMOS

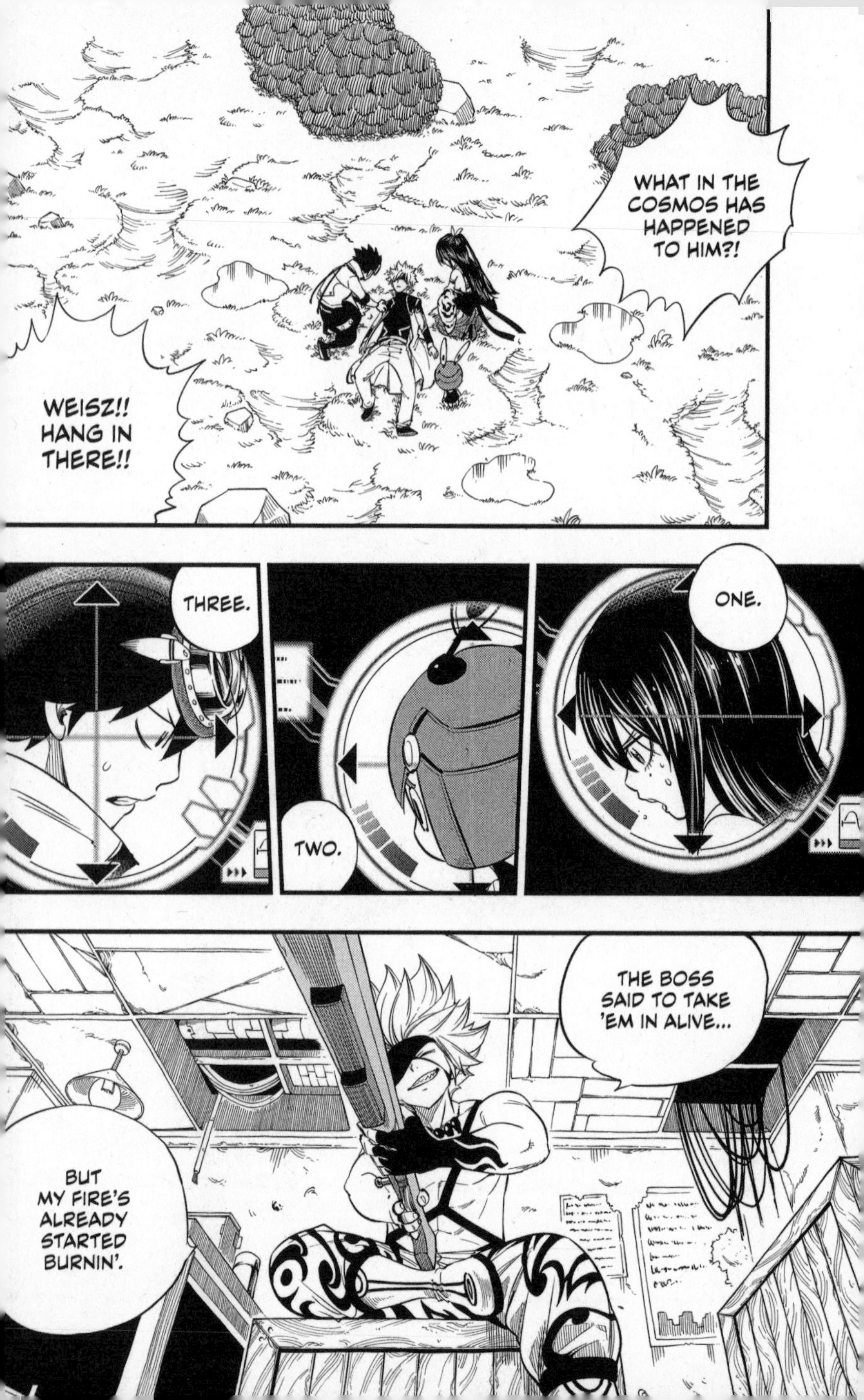
WHAT IN THE COSMOS HAS HAPPENED TO HIM?!
WEISZ!! HANG IN THERE!!
ONE.
TWO.
THREE.
THE BOSS SAID TO TAKE 'EM IN ALIVE...
BUT MY FIRE'S ALREADY STARTED BURNIN'.

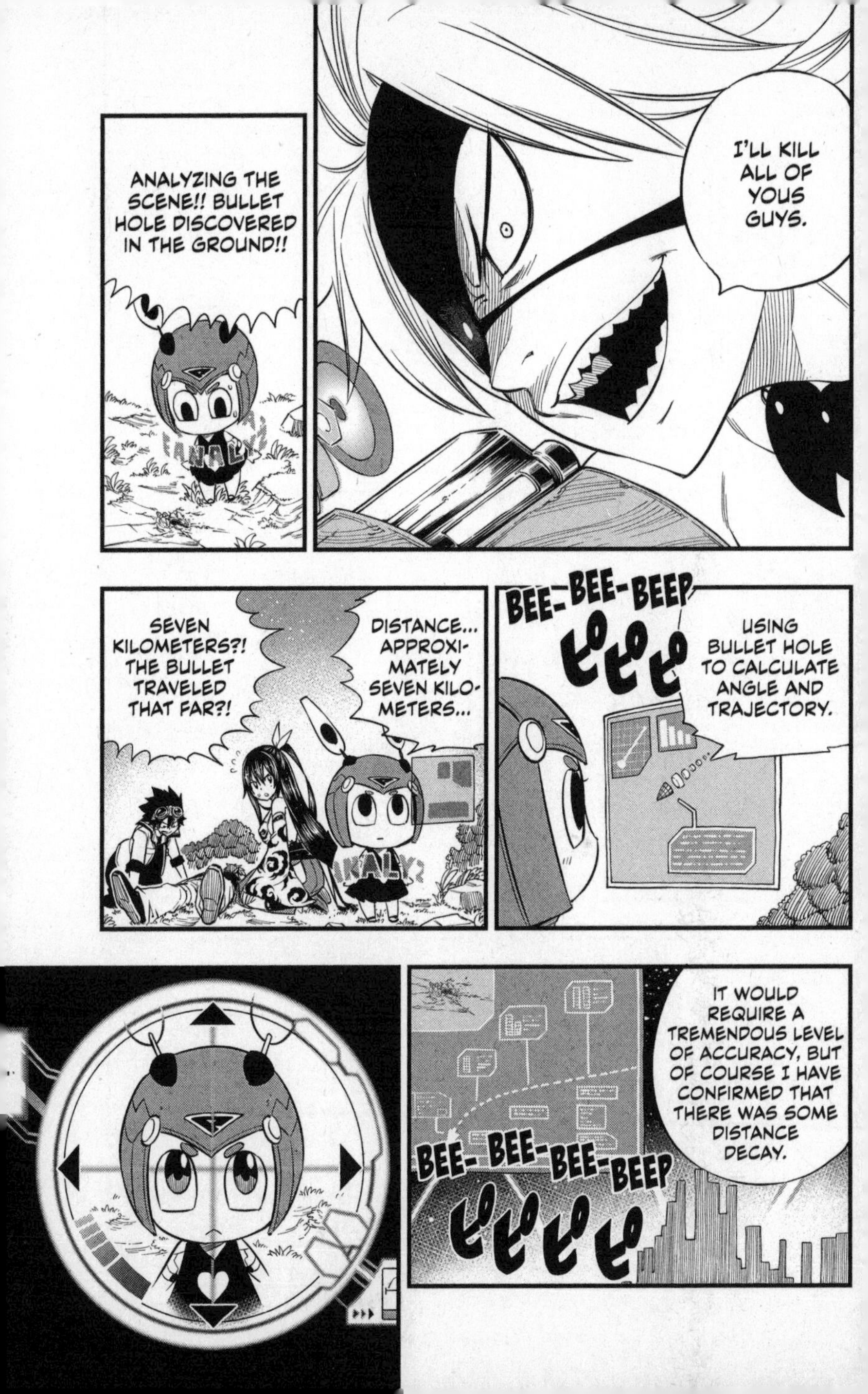
I'LL KILL ALL OF YOUS GUYS.
ANALYZING THE SCENE!! BULLET HOLE DISCOVERED IN THE GROUND!!
ANALYZ
USING BULLET HOLE TO CALCULATE ANGLE AND TRAJECTORY.
BEE-BEE-BEEP
ピピピ
DISTANCE... APPROXI-MATELY SEVEN KILO-METERS...
SEVEN KILOMETERS?! THE BULLET TRAVELED THAT FAR?!
ANALYZ
IT WOULD REQUIRE A TREMENDOUS LEVEL OF ACCURACY, BUT OF COURSE I HAVE CONFIRMED THAT THERE WAS SOME DISTANCE DECAY.
BEE-BEE-BEE-BEEP
ピピピピ

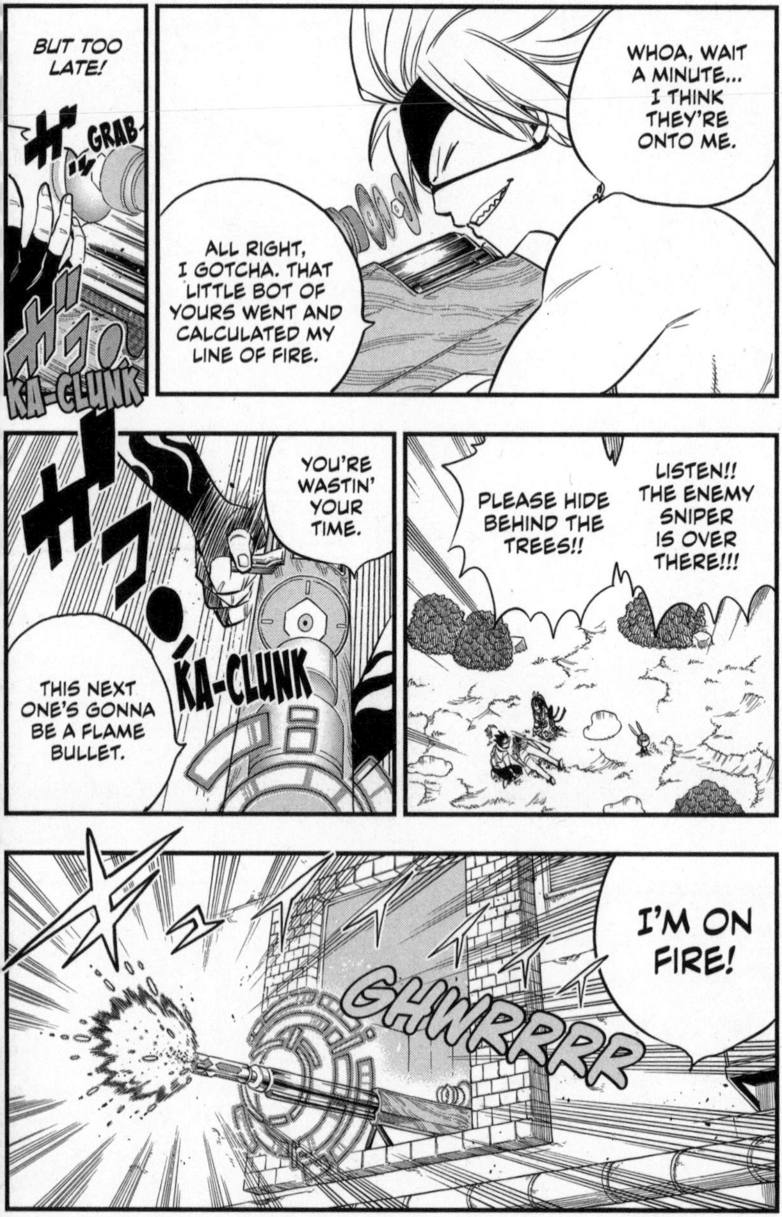
WHOA, WAIT A MINUTE... I THINK THEY'RE ONTO ME.
ALL RIGHT, I GOTCHA. THAT LITTLE BOT OF YOURS WENT AND CALCULATED MY LINE OF FIRE.
BUT TOO LATE!
GRAB
KA-CLUNK
LISTEN!! THE ENEMY SNIPER IS OVER THERE!!!
PLEASE HIDE BEHIND THE TREES!!
YOU'RE WASTIN' YOUR TIME.
KA-CLUNK
THIS NEXT ONE'S GONNA BE A FLAME BULLET.
I'M ON FIRE!
GHWRRRR

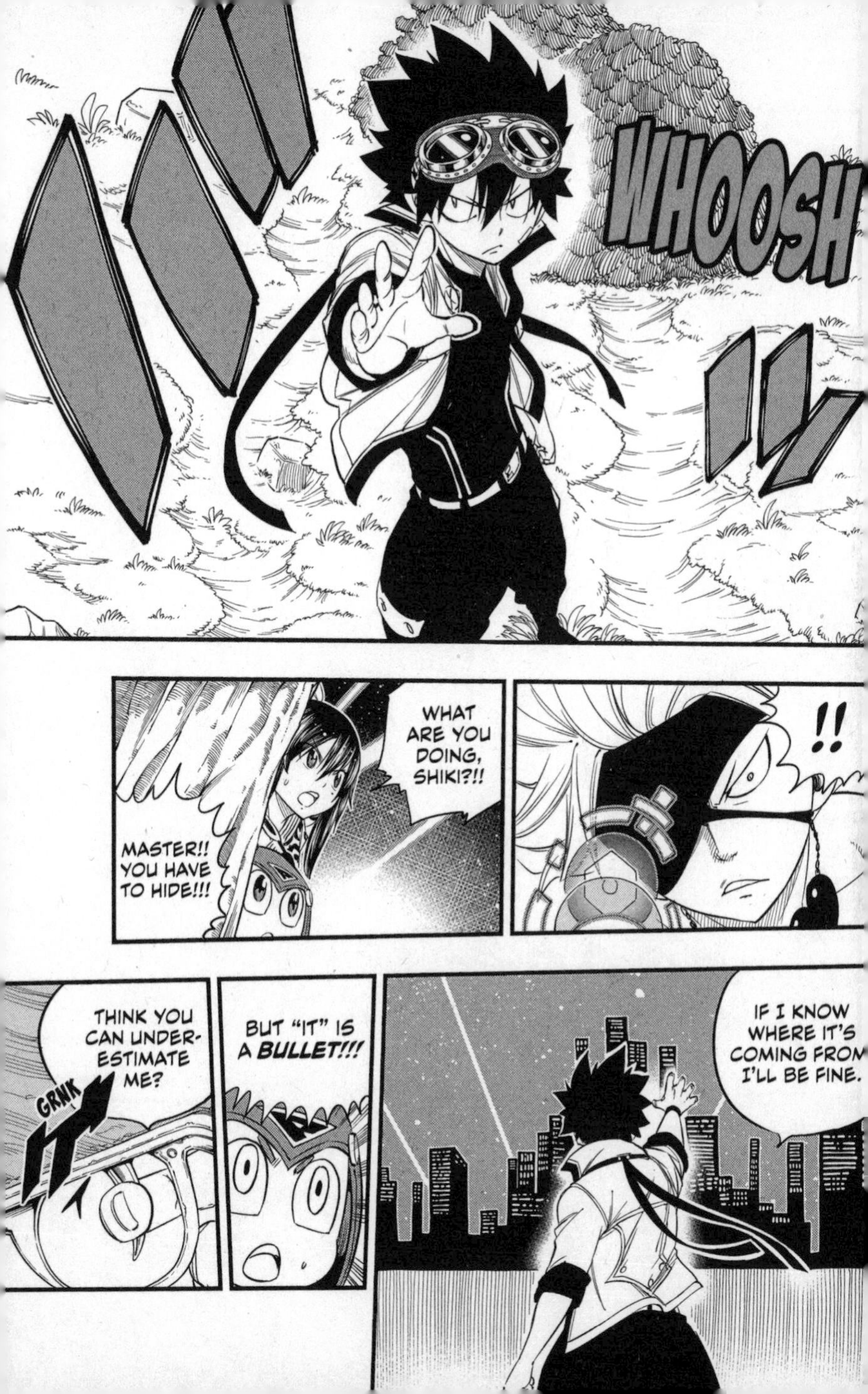
WHOOSH
!!
WHAT ARE YOU DOING, SHIKI?!!
MASTER!! YOU HAVE TO HIDE!!!
IF I KNOW WHERE IT'S COMING FROM I'LL BE FINE.
BUT "IT" IS A BULLET!!!
THINK YOU CAN UNDER-ESTIMATE ME?
GRNK

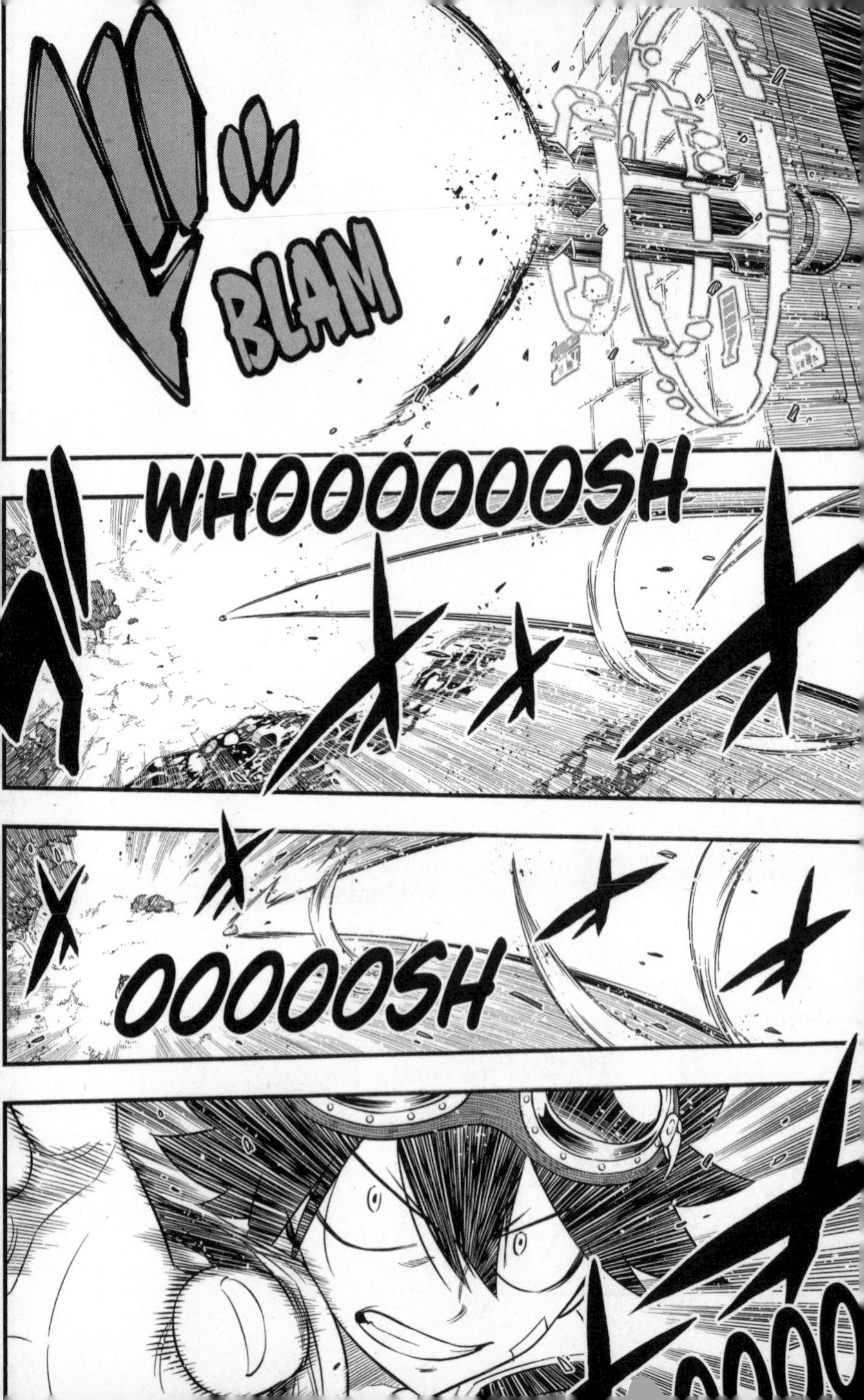
BLAM
WHOOOOOOOSH
OOOOOSH
OOOO

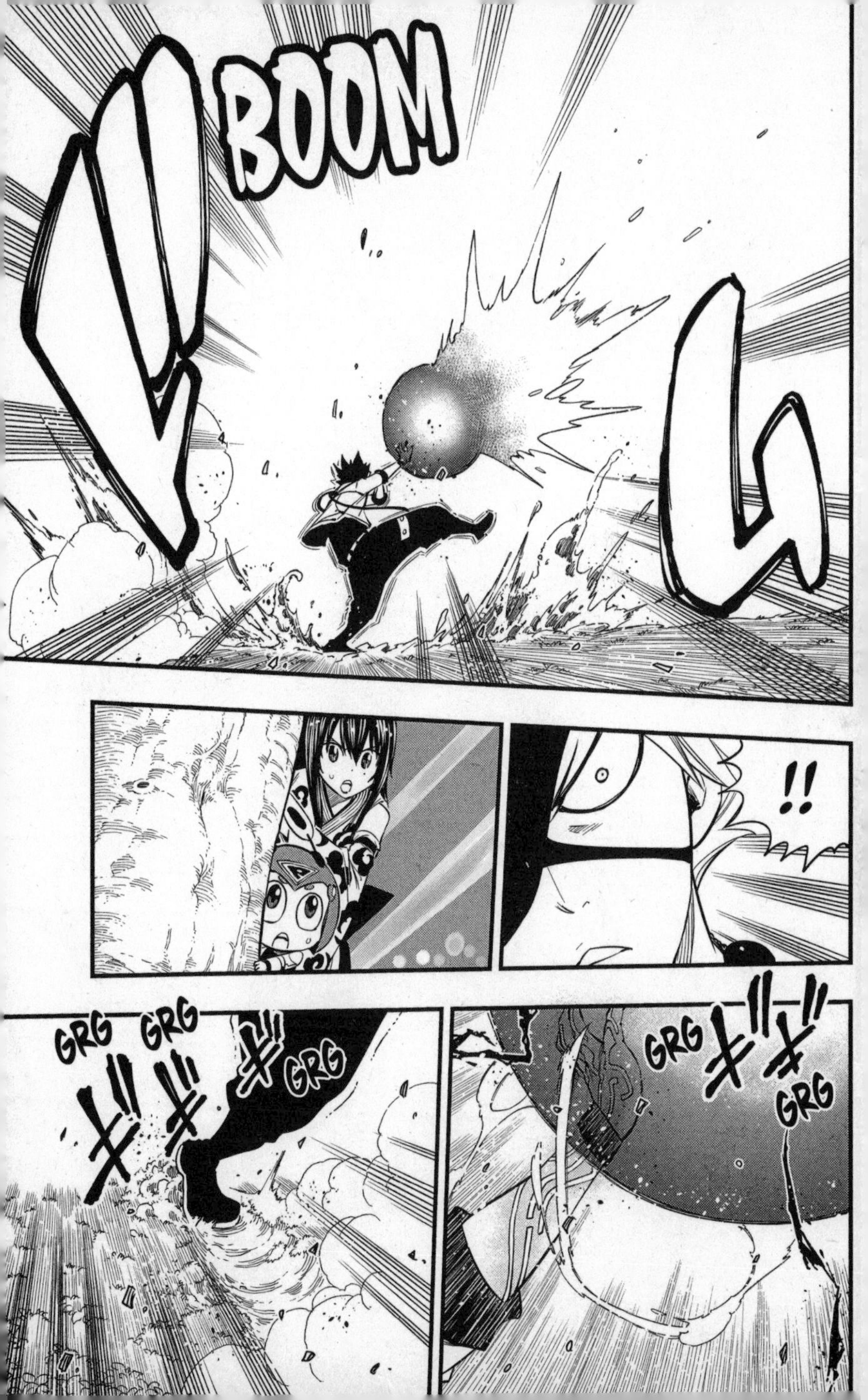
BOOM
!!
GRG
GRG
GRG
GRG
GRG

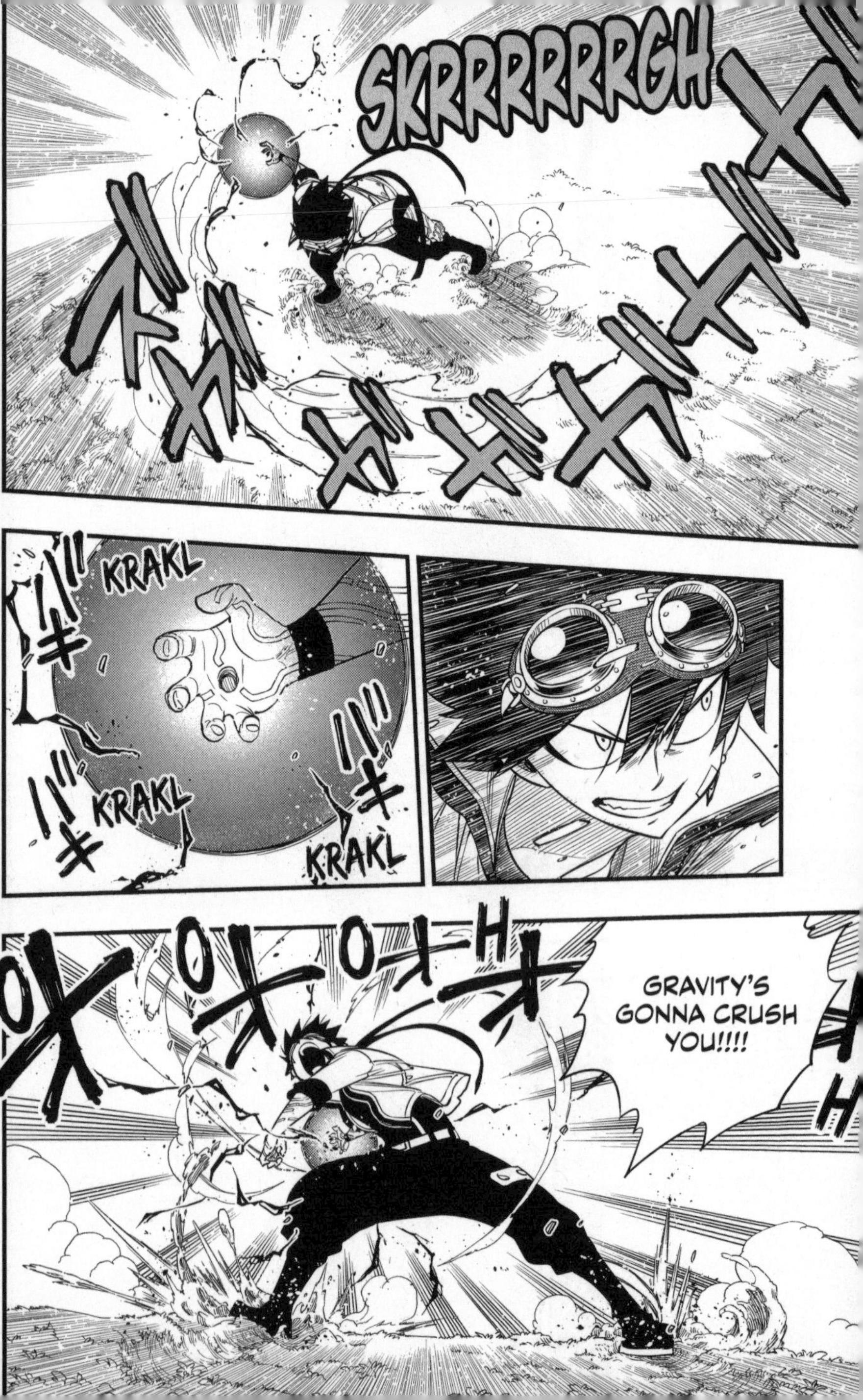
SKRRRRRRGH
KRAKL
KRAKL
KRAKL
GRAVITY'S GONNA CRUSH YOU!!!!

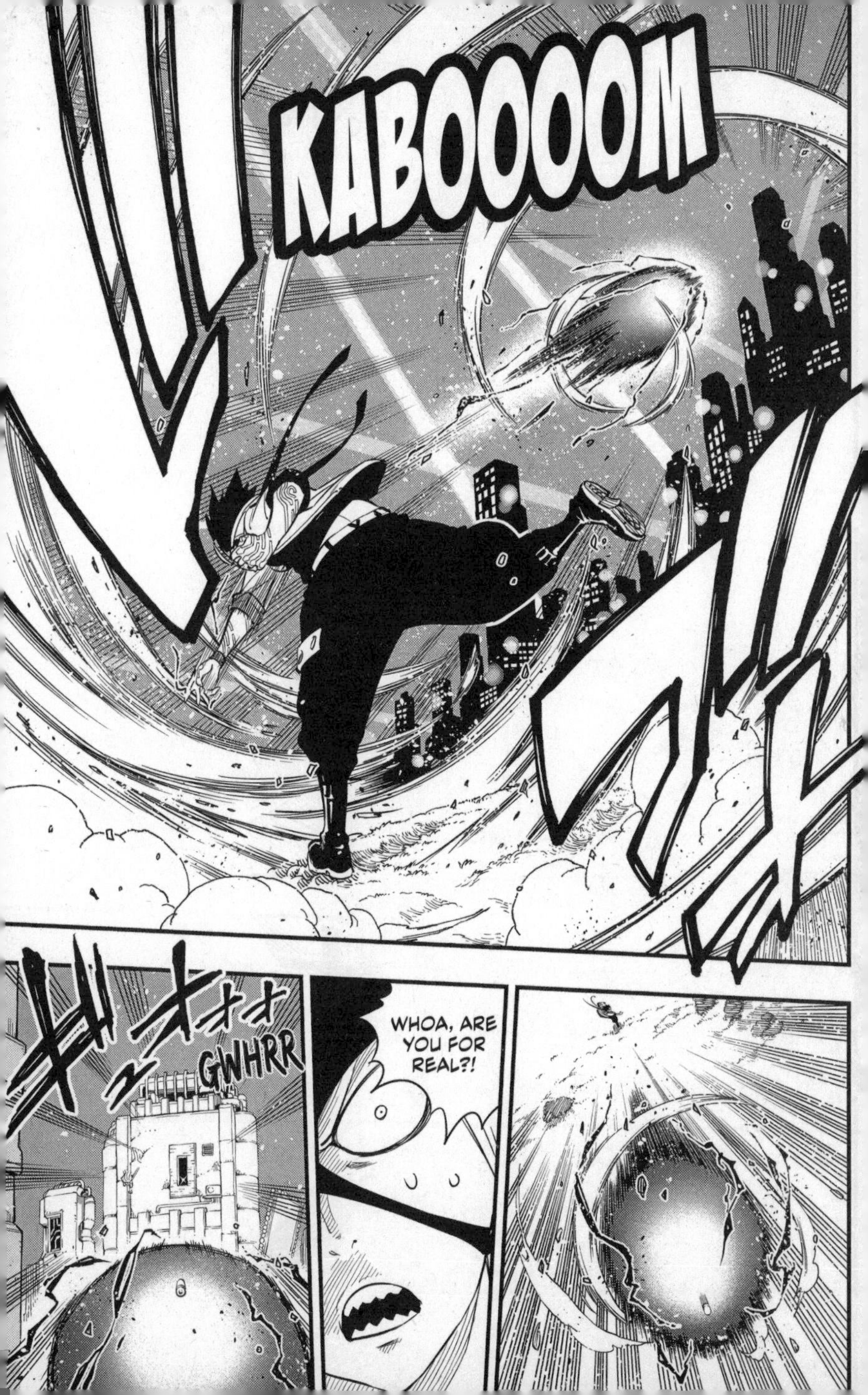
KABOOOOM
WHOA, ARE YOU FOR REAL?!
GWHRR

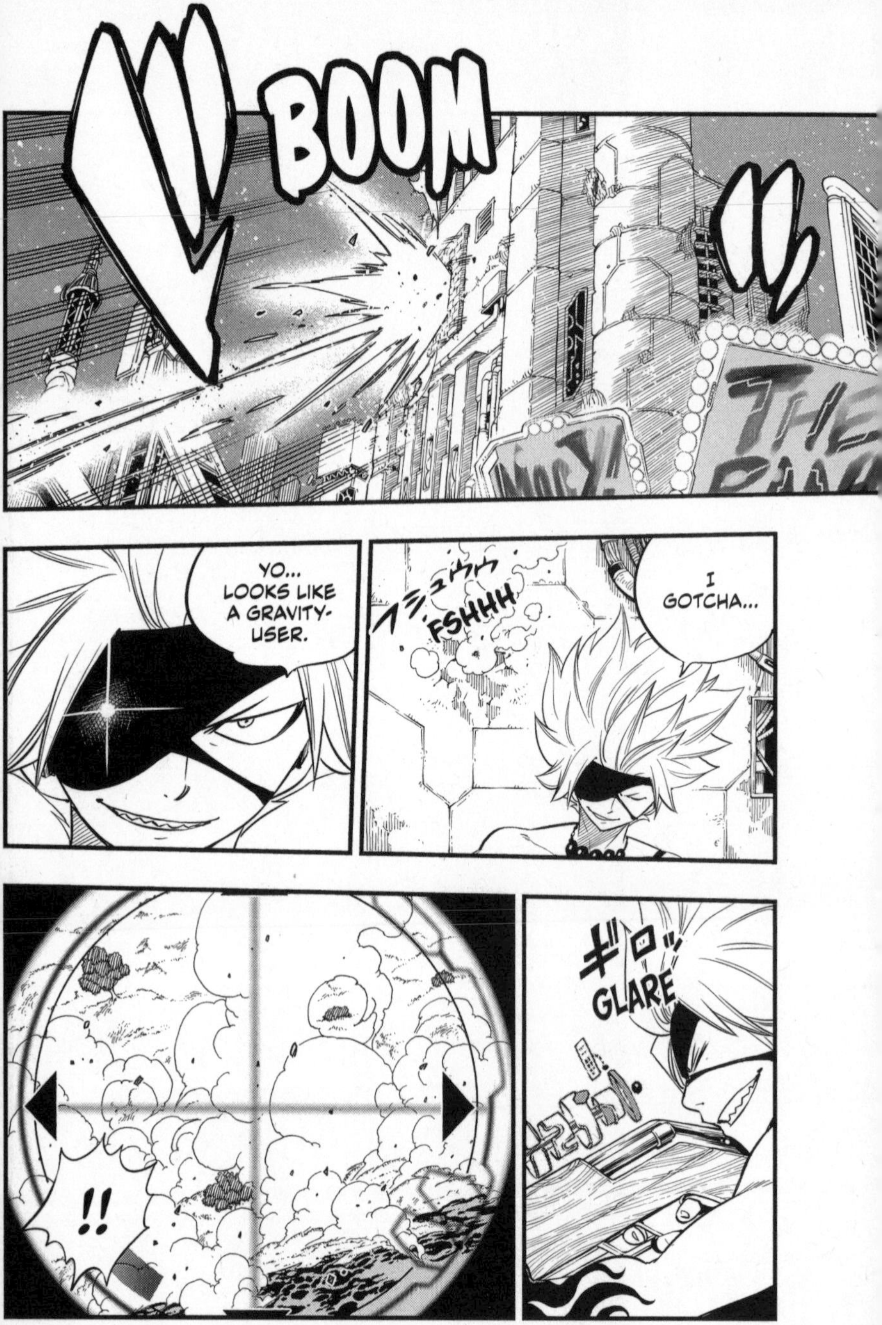
BOOM
フシュウウ
FSHHH
I GOTCHA...
YO... LOOKS LIKE A GRAVITY-USER.
ギロッ
GLARE
!!

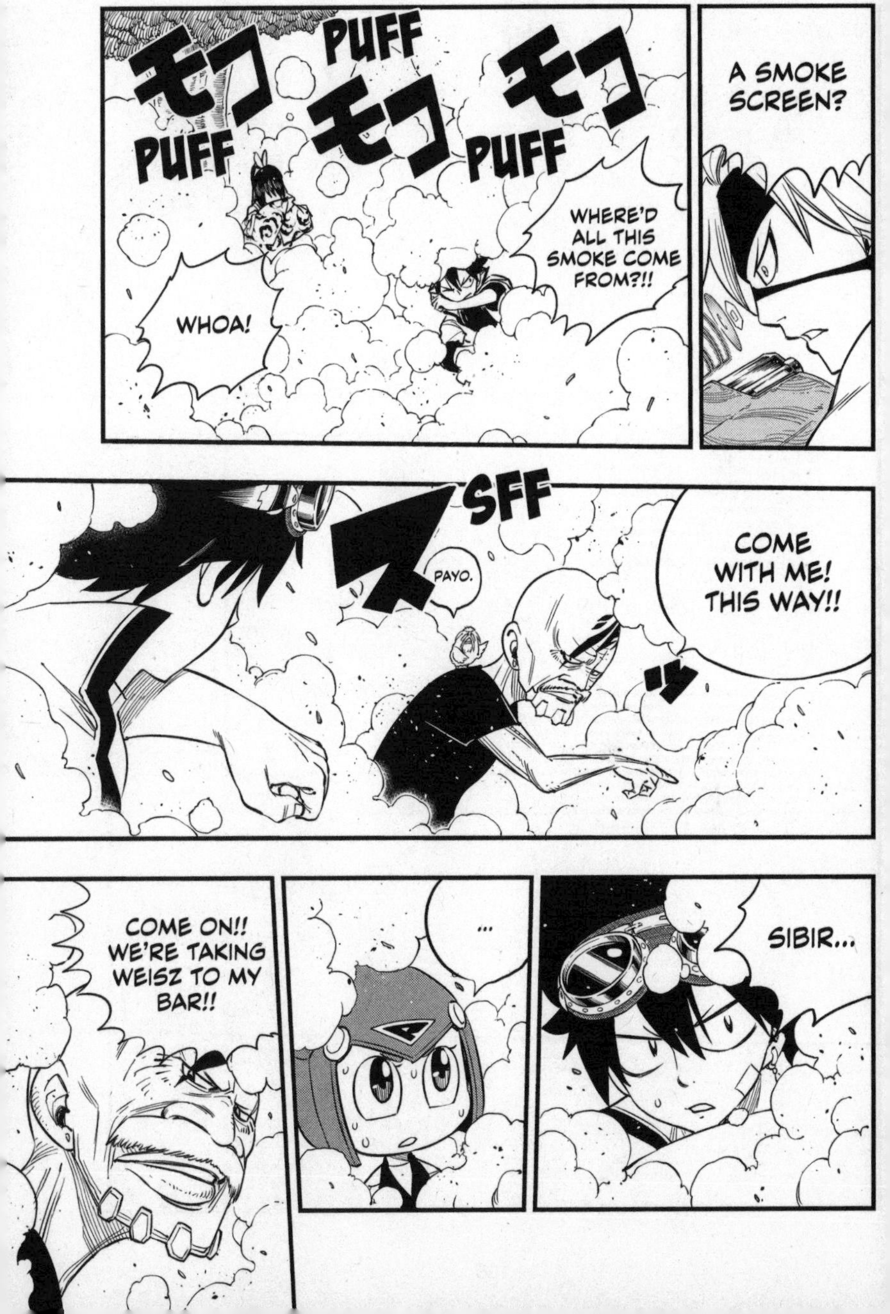
A SMOKE SCREEN?
モフ
PUFF
WHERE'D ALL THIS SMOKE COME FROM?!!
PUFF
モフ
PUFF
モフ
PUFF
WHOA!
COME WITH ME! THIS WAY!!
SFF
PAYO.
SIBIR...
...
COME ON!! WE'RE TAKING WEISZ TO MY BAR!!

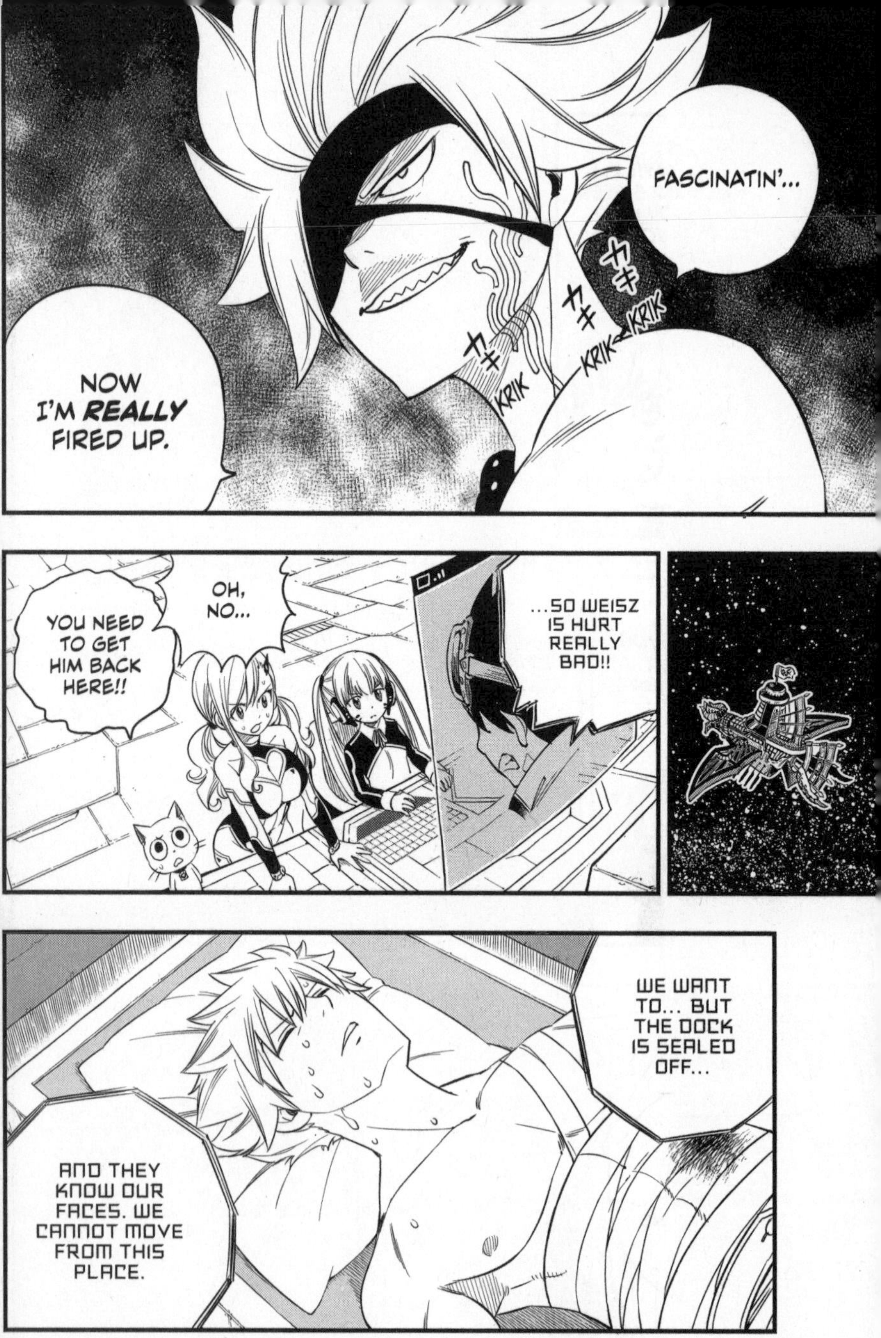
FASCINATIN'...
KRIK KRIK KRIK
NOW I'M ***REALLY*** FIRED UP.
...SO WEISZ IS HURT REALLY BAD!!
OH, NO...
YOU NEED TO GET HIM BACK HERE!!
WE WANT TO... BUT THE DOCK IS SEALED OFF...
AND THEY KNOW OUR FACES. WE CANNOT MOVE FROM THIS PLACE.

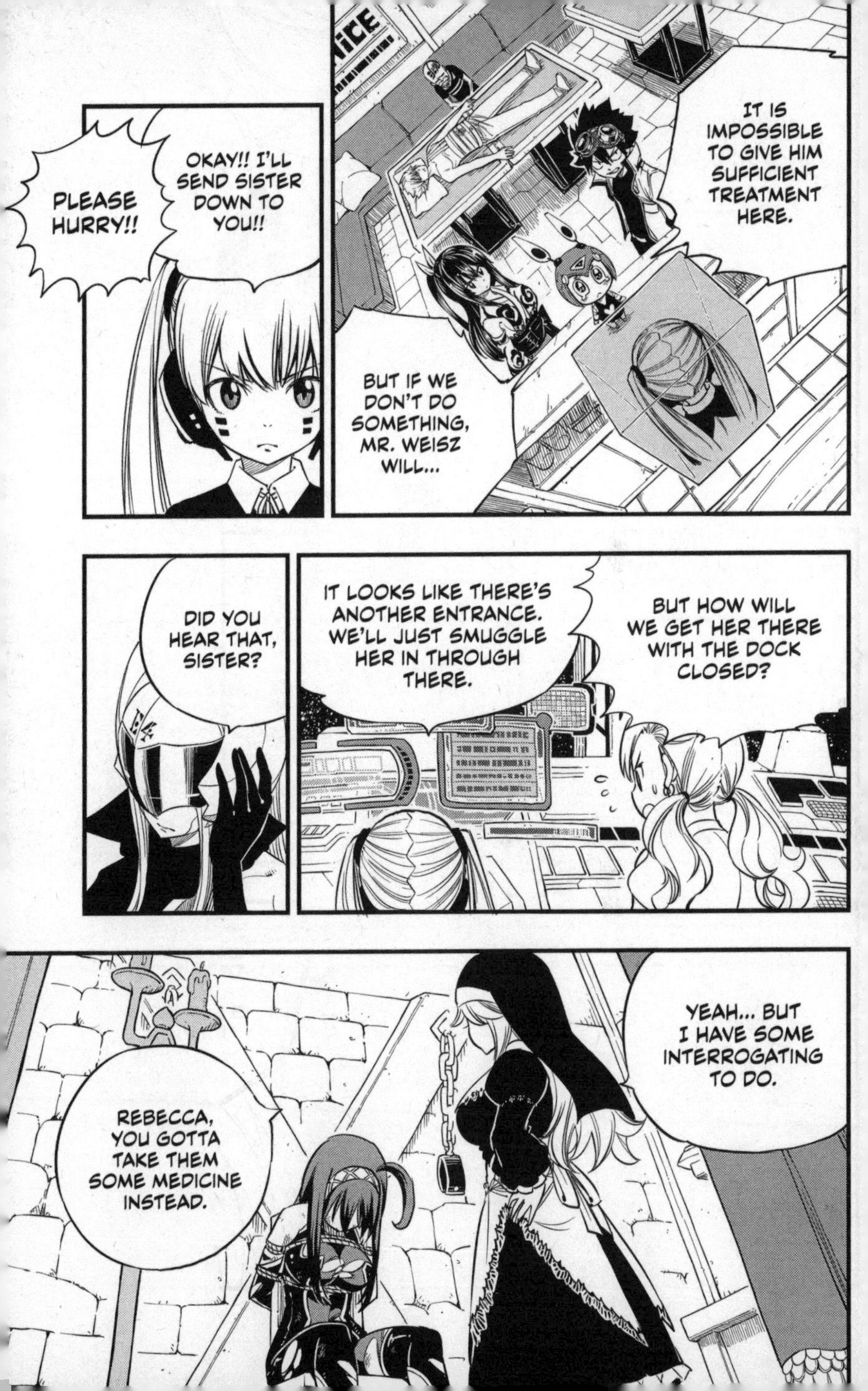

IT IS IMPOSSIBLE TO GIVE HIM SUFFICIENT TREATMENT HERE.
BUT IF WE DON'T DO SOMETHING, MR. WEISZ WILL...
OKAY!! I'LL SEND SISTER DOWN TO YOU!!
PLEASE HURRY!!
BUT HOW WILL WE GET HER THERE WITH THE DOCK CLOSED?
IT LOOKS LIKE THERE'S ANOTHER ENTRANCE. WE'LL JUST SMUGGLE HER IN THROUGH THERE.
DID YOU HEAR THAT, SISTER?
YEAH... BUT I HAVE SOME INTERROGATING TO DO.
REBECCA, YOU GOTTA TAKE THEM SOME MEDICINE INSTEAD.

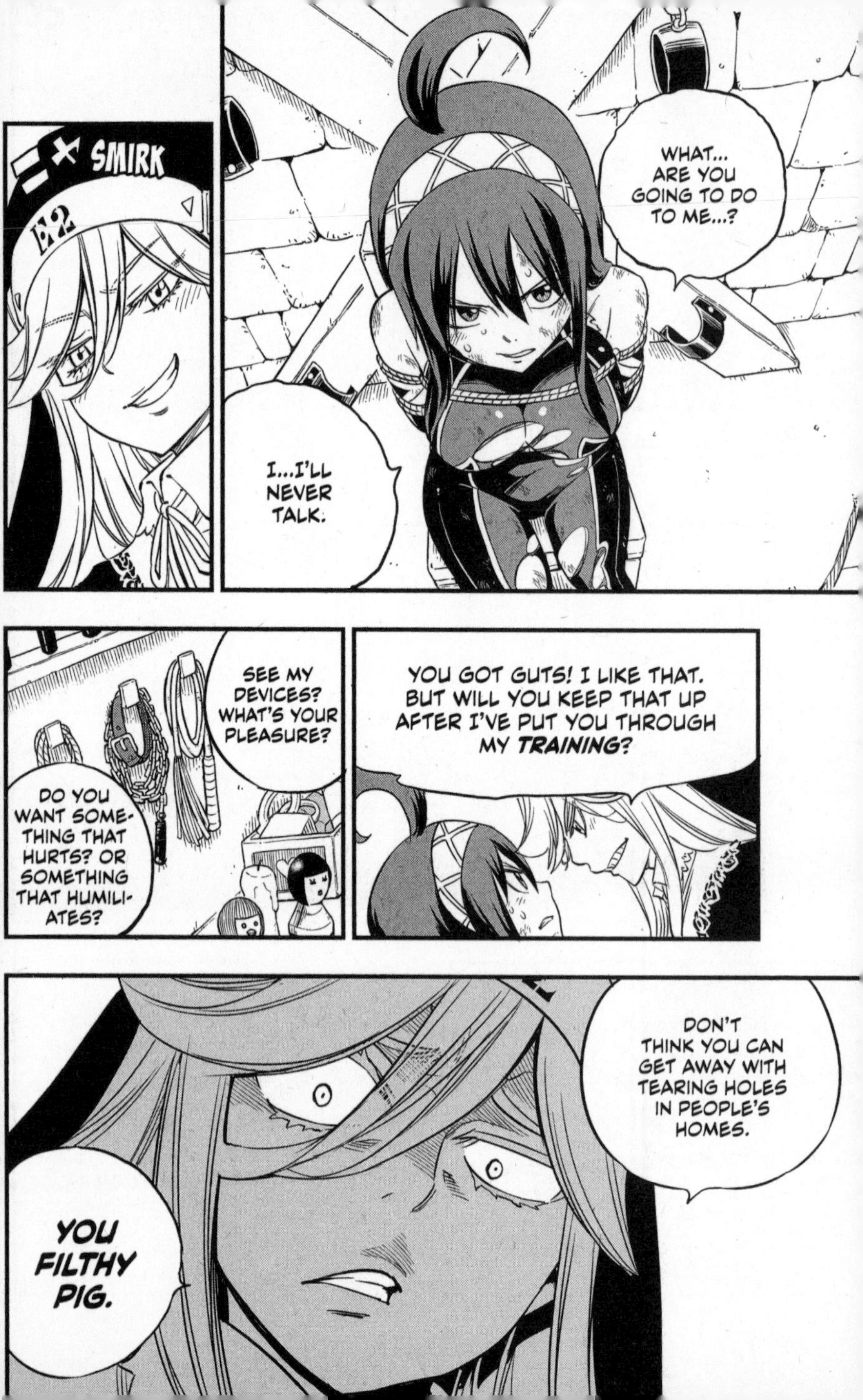
WHAT... ARE YOU GOING TO DO TO ME...?
I...I'LL NEVER TALK.
SMIRK
YOU GOT GUTS! I LIKE THAT. BUT WILL YOU KEEP THAT UP AFTER I'VE PUT YOU THROUGH MY *TRAINING*?
SEE MY DEVICES? WHAT'S YOUR PLEASURE?
DO YOU WANT SOMETHING THAT HURTS? OR SOMETHING THAT HUMILIATES?
DON'T THINK YOU CAN GET AWAY WITH TEARING HOLES IN PEOPLE'S HOMES.
YOU FILTHY PIG.

GSH

DON'T!

STAY AWAY...!! DON'T TOUCH ME!

CLATTER

EEP!

FLICK

JUST KIDDING.

OW!

STOP!!!

...

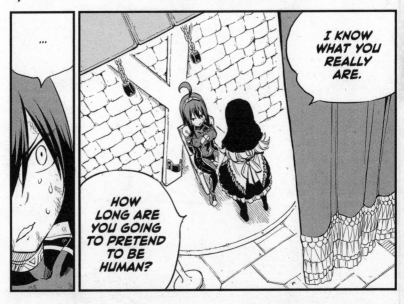

I KNOW WHAT YOU REALLY ARE.

HOW LONG ARE YOU GOING TO PRETEND TO BE HUMAN?

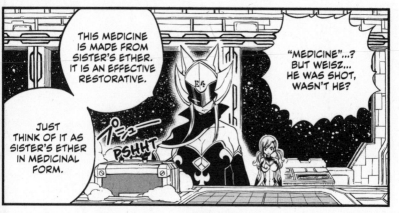

"MEDICINE"...? BUT WEISZ... HE WAS SHOT, WASN'T HE?
THIS MEDICINE IS MADE FROM SISTER'S ETHER. IT IS AN EFFECTIVE RESTORATIVE.
PSHHT
JUST THINK OF IT AS SISTER'S ETHER IN MEDICINAL FORM.
SISTER ENERGY.
SISTER ENERGY
TA-DAH!
LOOKS LIKE AN ENERGY DRINK.
IT WORKS ON HUMANS AND BOTS.
TAK
TAK
TAK
HURRY, REBECCA!!
I'M ON MY WAY!!!
DASH

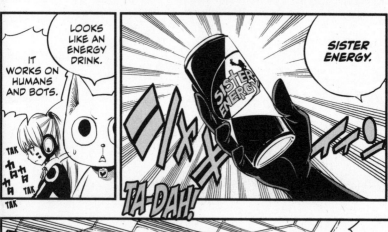

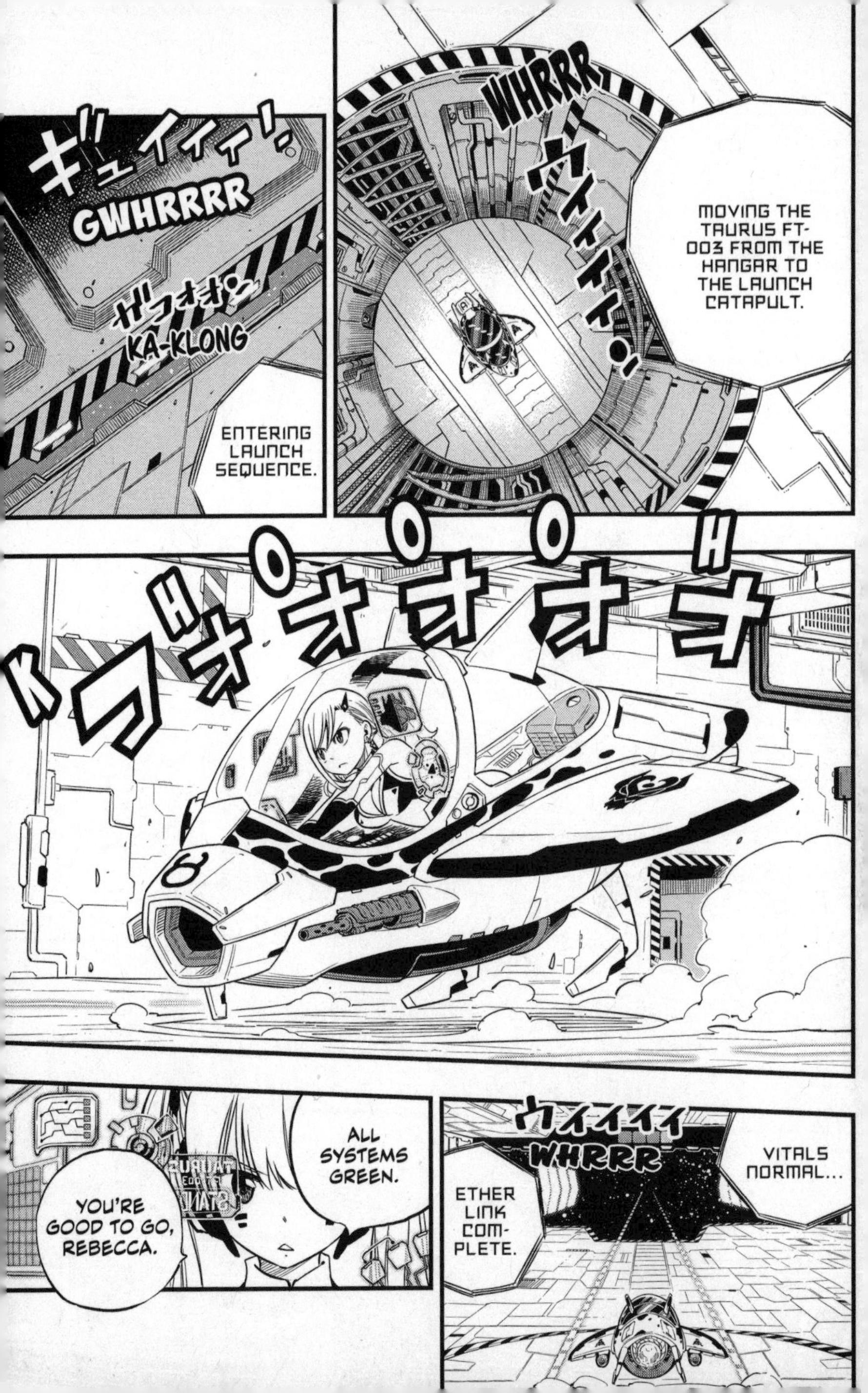
WHRRR
MOVING THE TAURUS FT-003 FROM THE HANGAR TO THE LAUNCH CATAPULT.
GWHRRRR
KA-KLONG
ENTERING LAUNCH SEQUENCE.
WHRRR
VITALS NORMAL...
ETHER LINK COMPLETE.
ALL SYSTEMS GREEN.
YOU'RE GOOD TO GO, REBECCA.

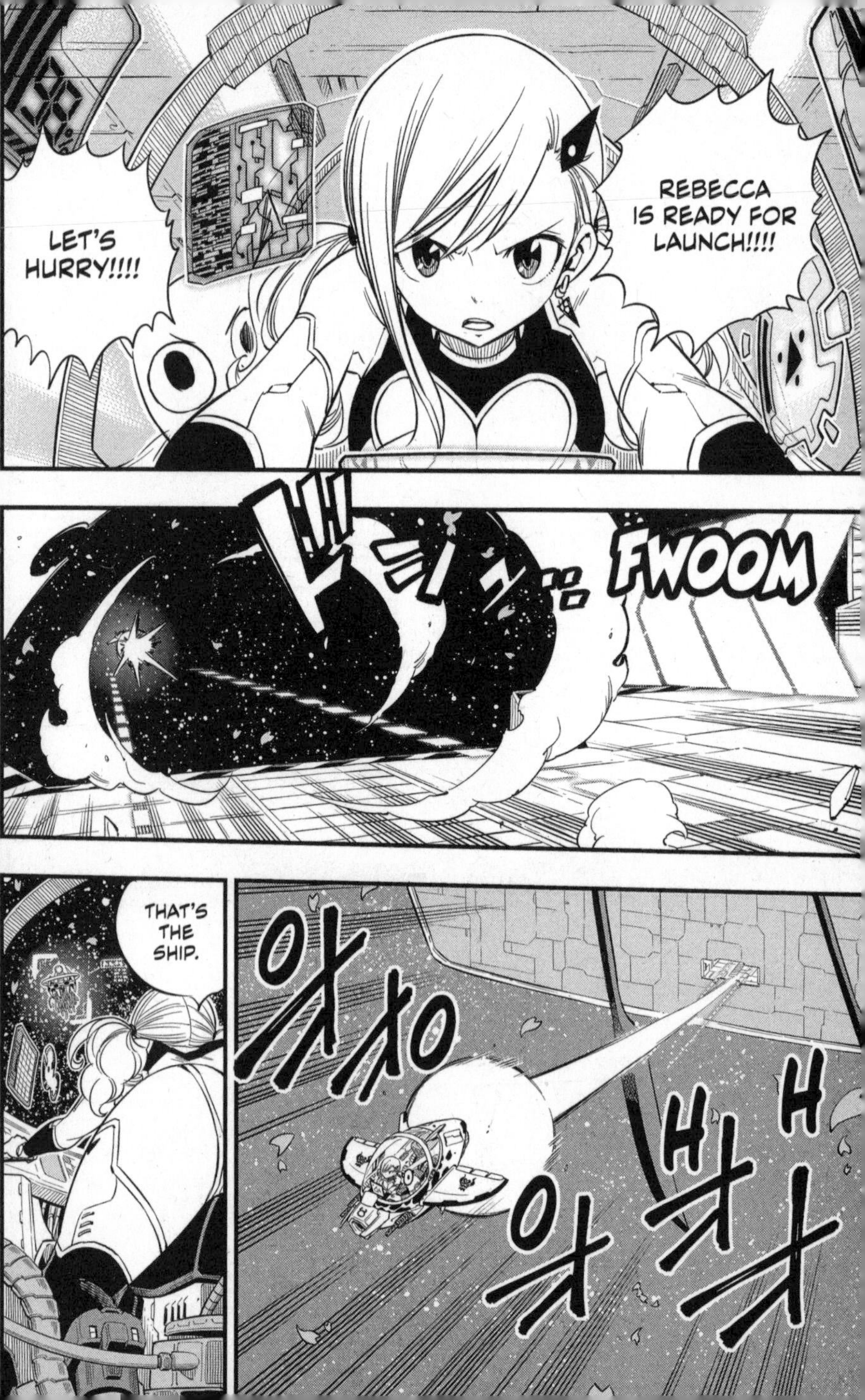
REBECCA IS READY FOR LAUNCH!!!!
LET'S HURRY!!!!
FWOOM
THAT'S THE SHIP.

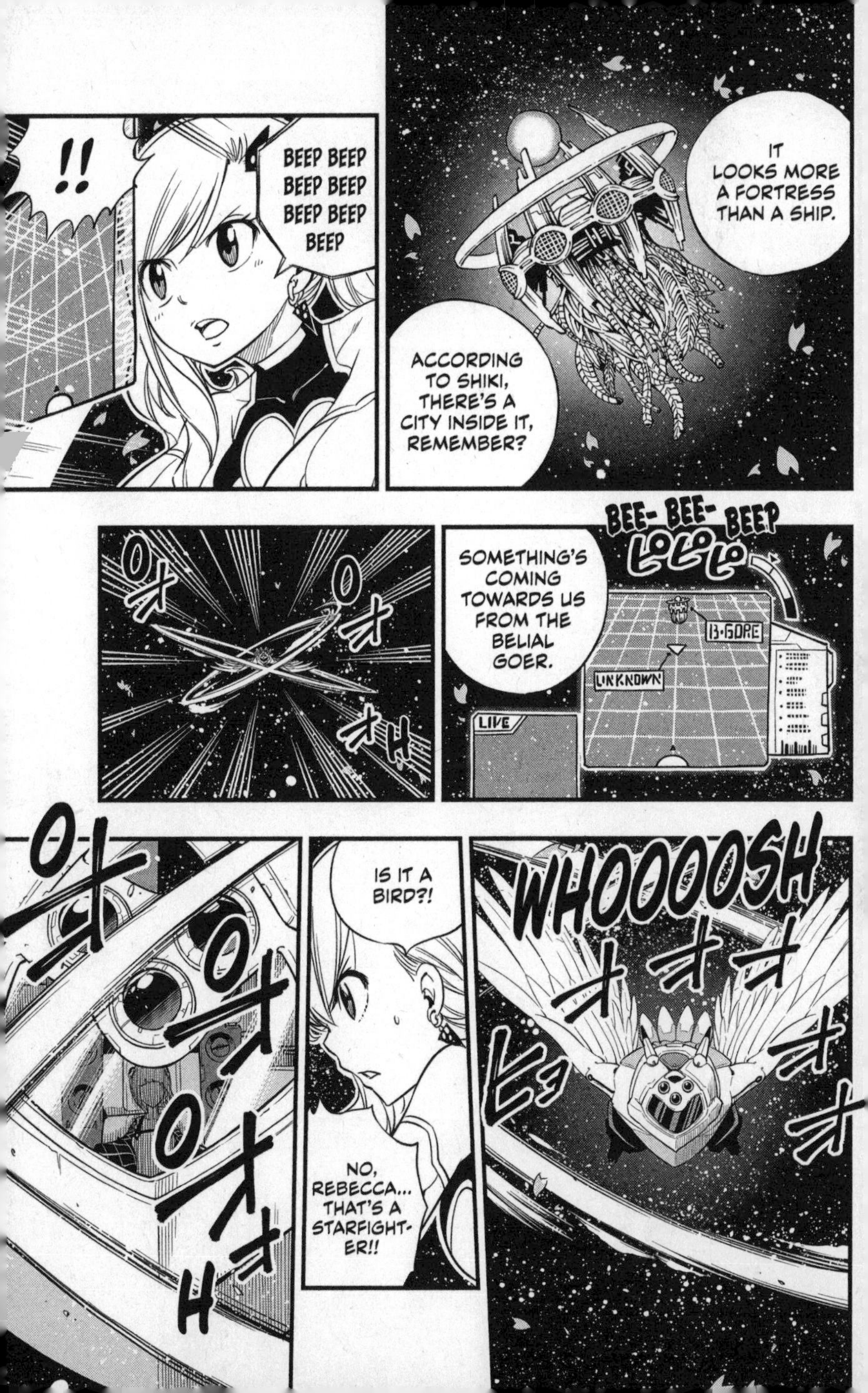
IT LOOKS MORE A FORTRESS THAN A SHIP.
ACCORDING TO SHIKI, THERE'S A CITY INSIDE IT, REMEMBER?
!!
BEEP BEEP BEEP BEEP BEEP BEEP BEEP
BEE- BEE- BEEP
SOMETHING'S COMING TOWARDS US FROM THE BELIAL GOER.
B-GORE
UNKNOWN
LIVE
WHOOOOSH
IS IT A BIRD?!
NO, REBECCA... THAT'S A STARFIGHTER!!

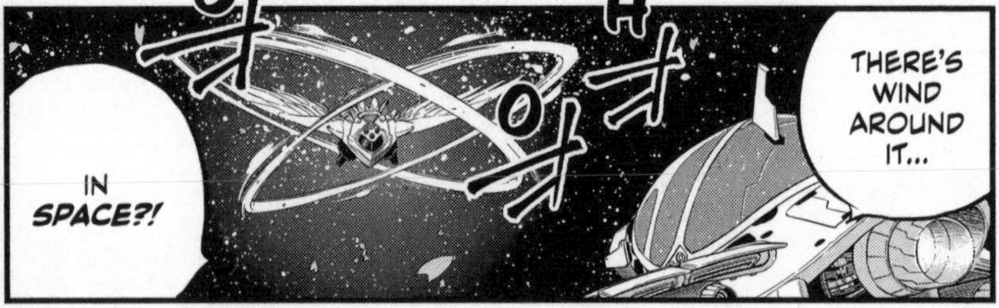
THERE'S WIND AROUND IT...
IN SPACE?!
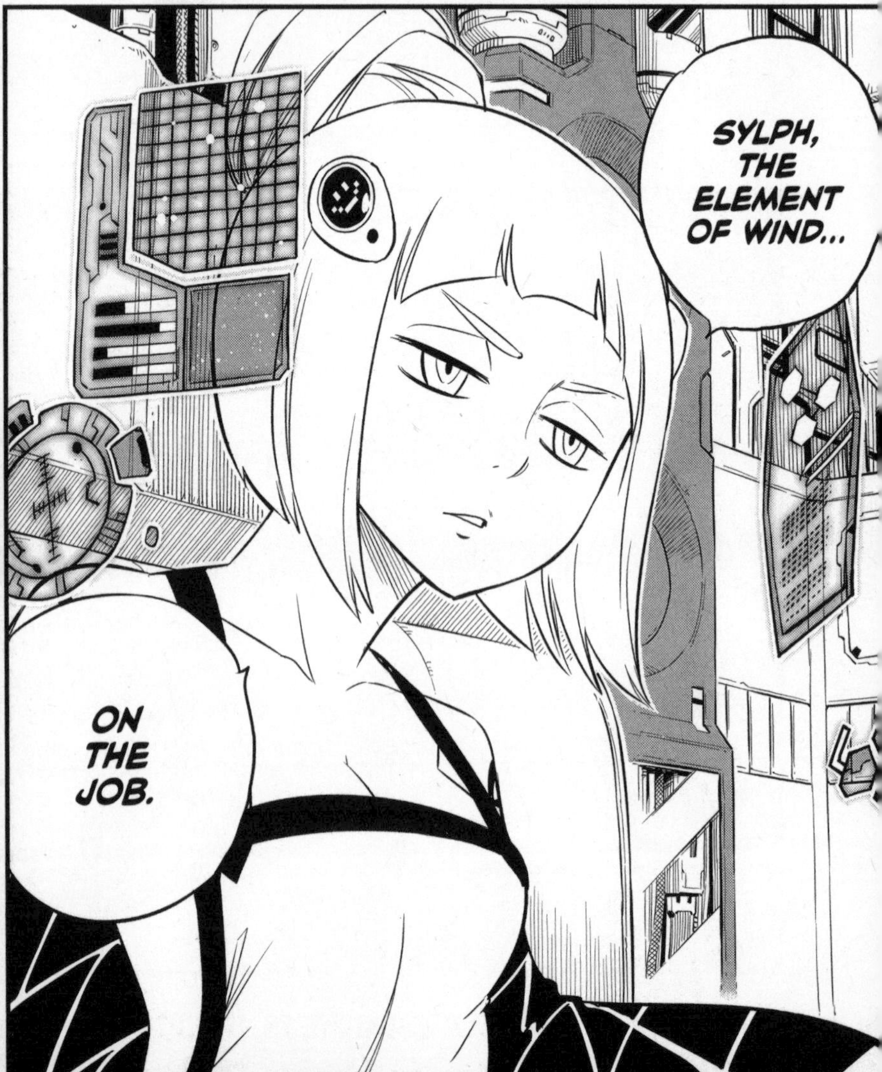
SYLPH, THE ELEMENT OF WIND...
ON THE JOB.

EDENS ZERO

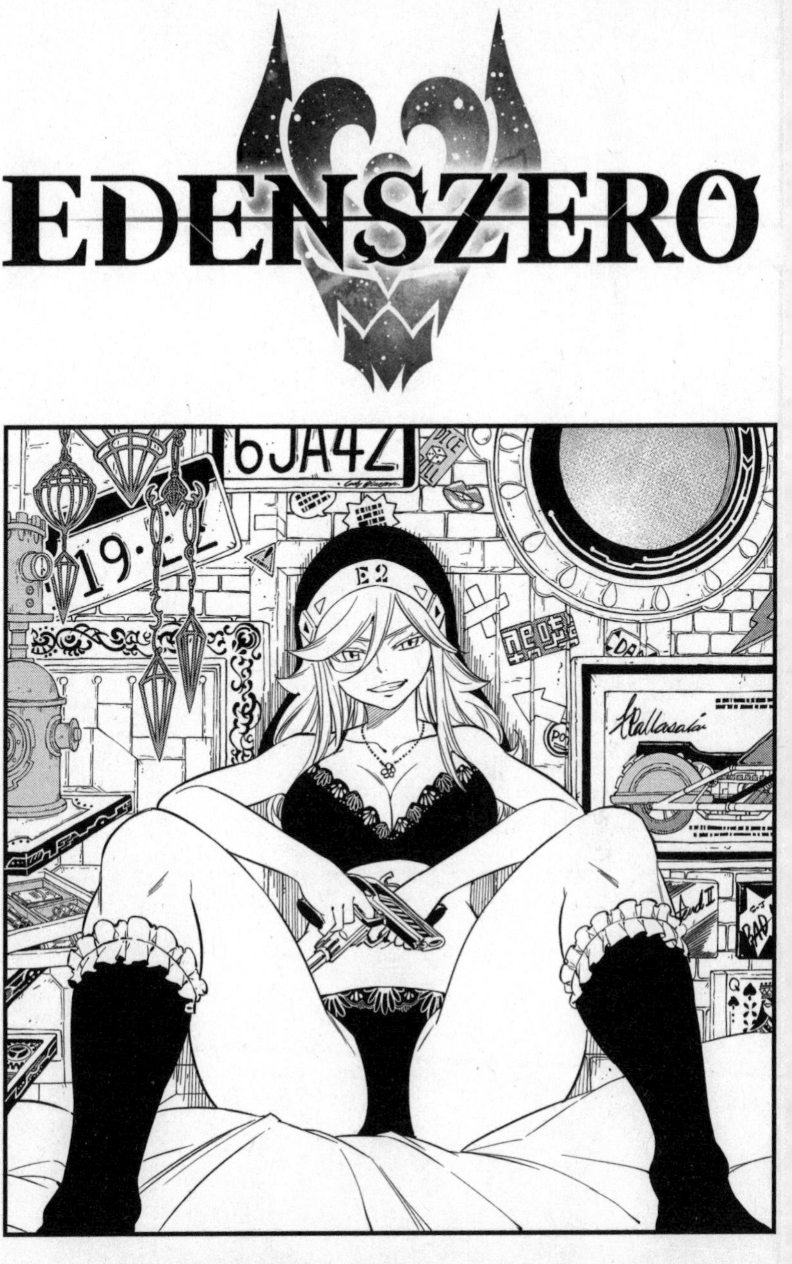
6JA42
E2

CHAPTER 76: REBECCA VS. SYLPH

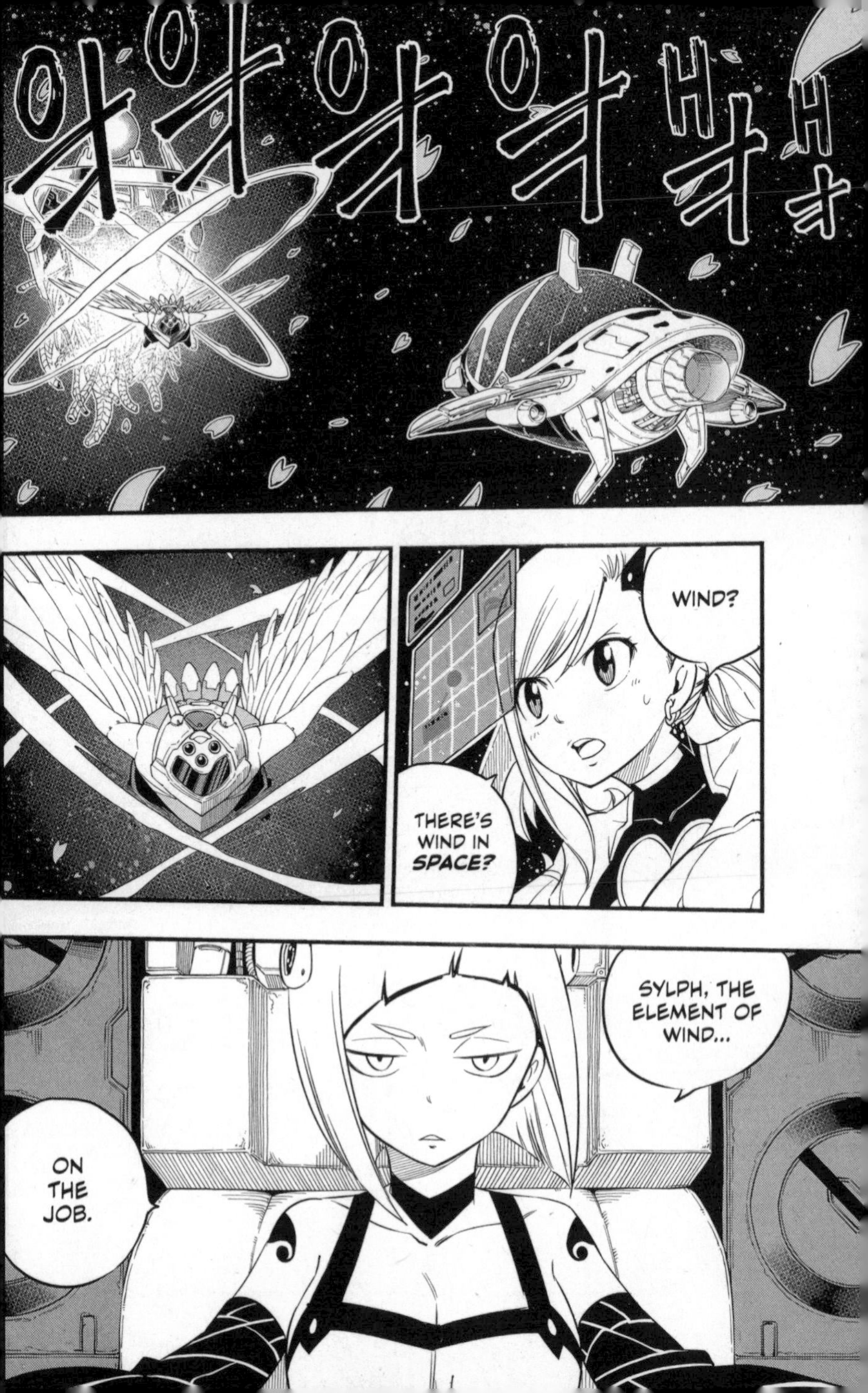
OOOOHH
WIND?
THERE'S WIND IN SPACE?
SYLPH, THE ELEMENT OF WIND...
ON THE JOB.

WHOOSH

REBECCA!! ABOVE YOU!!

BEEP BEEP BEEP BEEP BEEP BEEP BEEP BEEP

!

A SWARM OF DRONES!!

GZ4NNNG

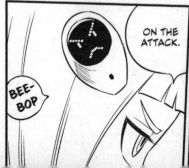

BEE-BOP

ON THE ATTACK.

WHERE DID THEY COME FROM?!!

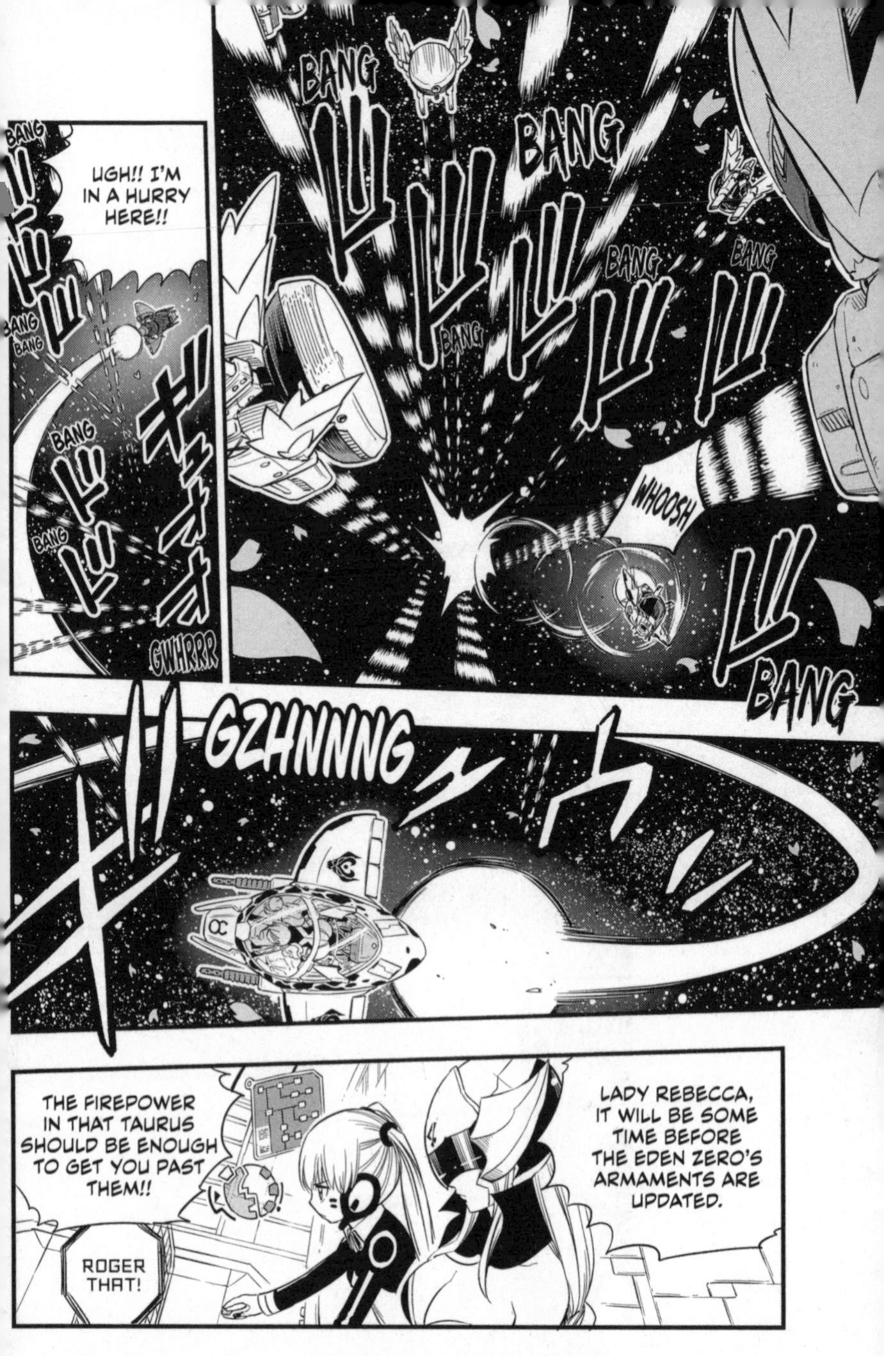
BANG
BANG
BANG
BANG
BANG
WHOOSH
BANG
BANG
UGH!! I'M IN A HURRY HERE!!
BANG
BANG
BANG
BANG
GWHRRR
GZHNNNG
LADY REBECCA, IT WILL BE SOME TIME BEFORE THE EDEN ZERO'S ARMAMENTS ARE UPDATED.
THE FIREPOWER IN THAT TAURUS SHOULD BE ENOUGH TO GET YOU PAST THEM!!
ROGER THAT!

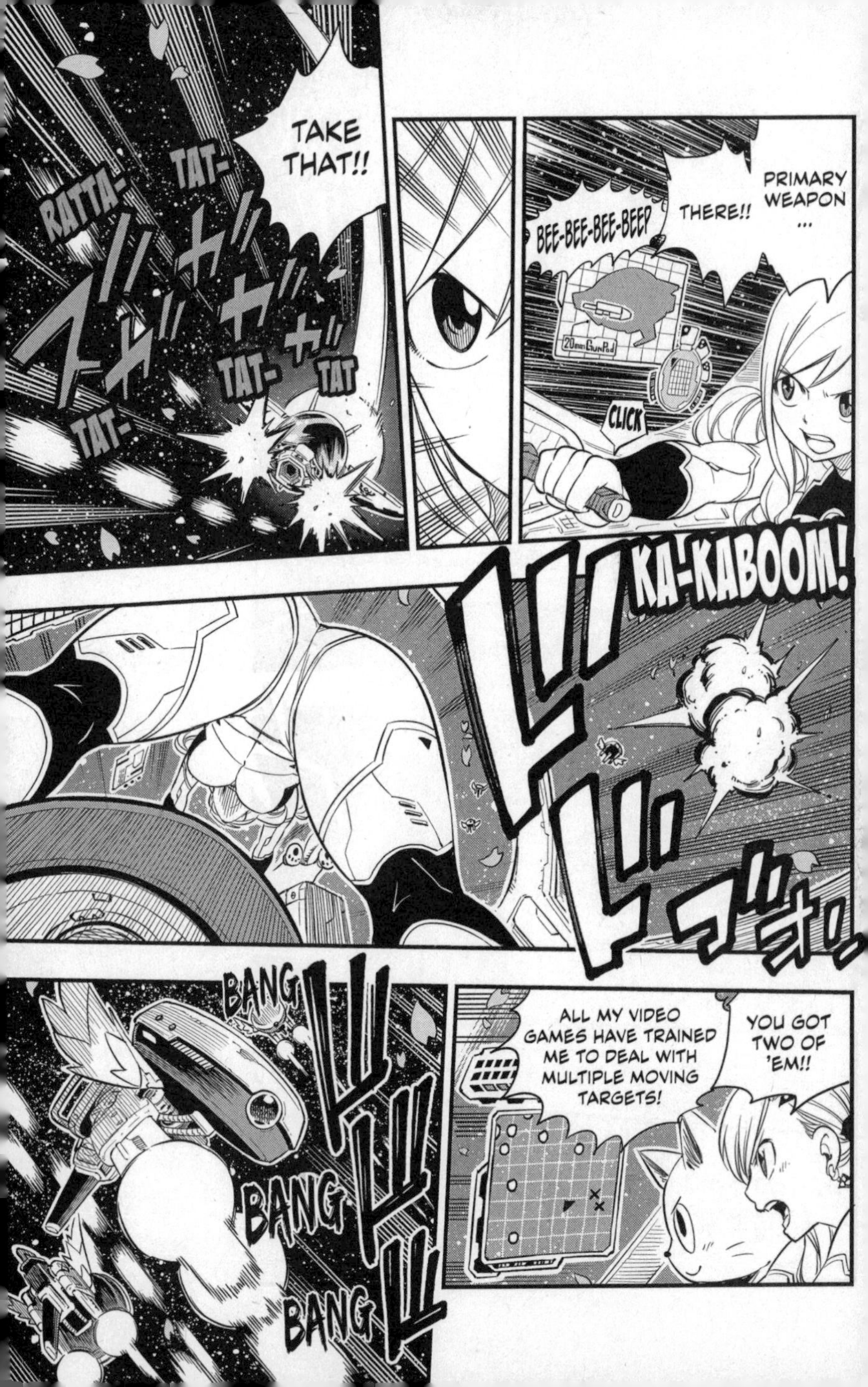

PRIMARY WEAPON ...
THERE!!
BEE-BEE-BEE-BEEP
20mm GunPod
CLICK
TAKE THAT!!
RATTA-
TAT-
TAT-
TAT-
TAT
KA-KABOOM!
YOU GOT TWO OF 'EM!!
ALL MY VIDEO GAMES HAVE TRAINED ME TO DEAL WITH MULTIPLE MOVING TARGETS!
BANG
BANG
BANG

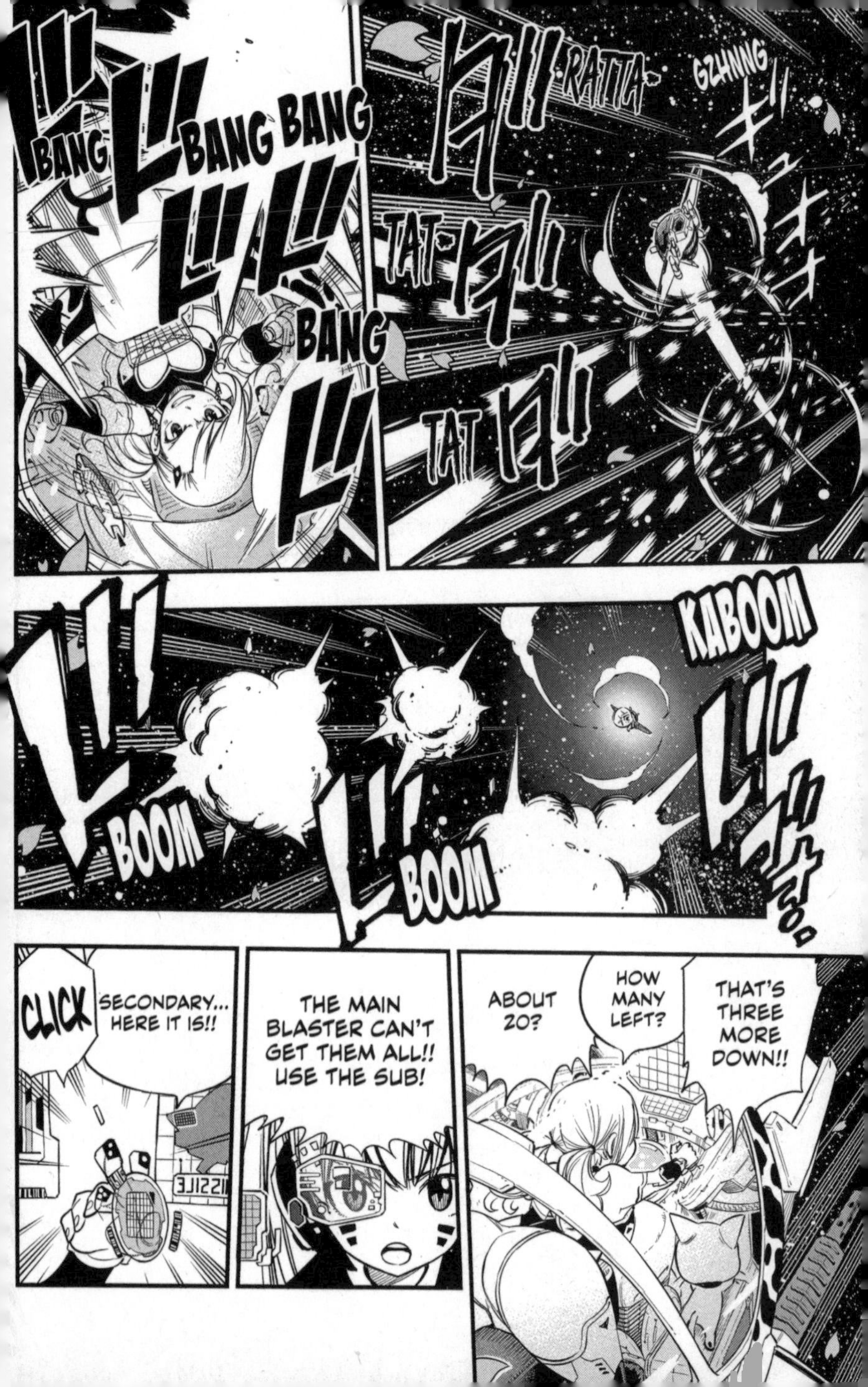
GZHNNG
RATTA-
TAT-
TAT
BANG BANG
BANG
BANG
KABOOM
BOOM
BOOM
THAT'S THREE MORE DOWN!!
HOW MANY LEFT?
ABOUT 20?
THE MAIN BLASTER CAN'T GET THEM ALL!! USE THE SUB!
SECONDARY... HERE IT IS!!
CLICK

HOMING MULTI-MISSILES!!

Always works in the anime!

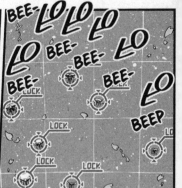

BEE- LO LO LO
LO BEE- LO
BEE- BEE- LO
BEE- LOCK BEE-
LOCK LO
BEEP
LOCK LO
LOCK LOCK

FIRE!!!!

BLAM BLAM BLAM BLAM
BLAM BLAM BLAM

BLAM BLAM BLAM BLAM BLAM BLAM
BLAM BLAM BLAM

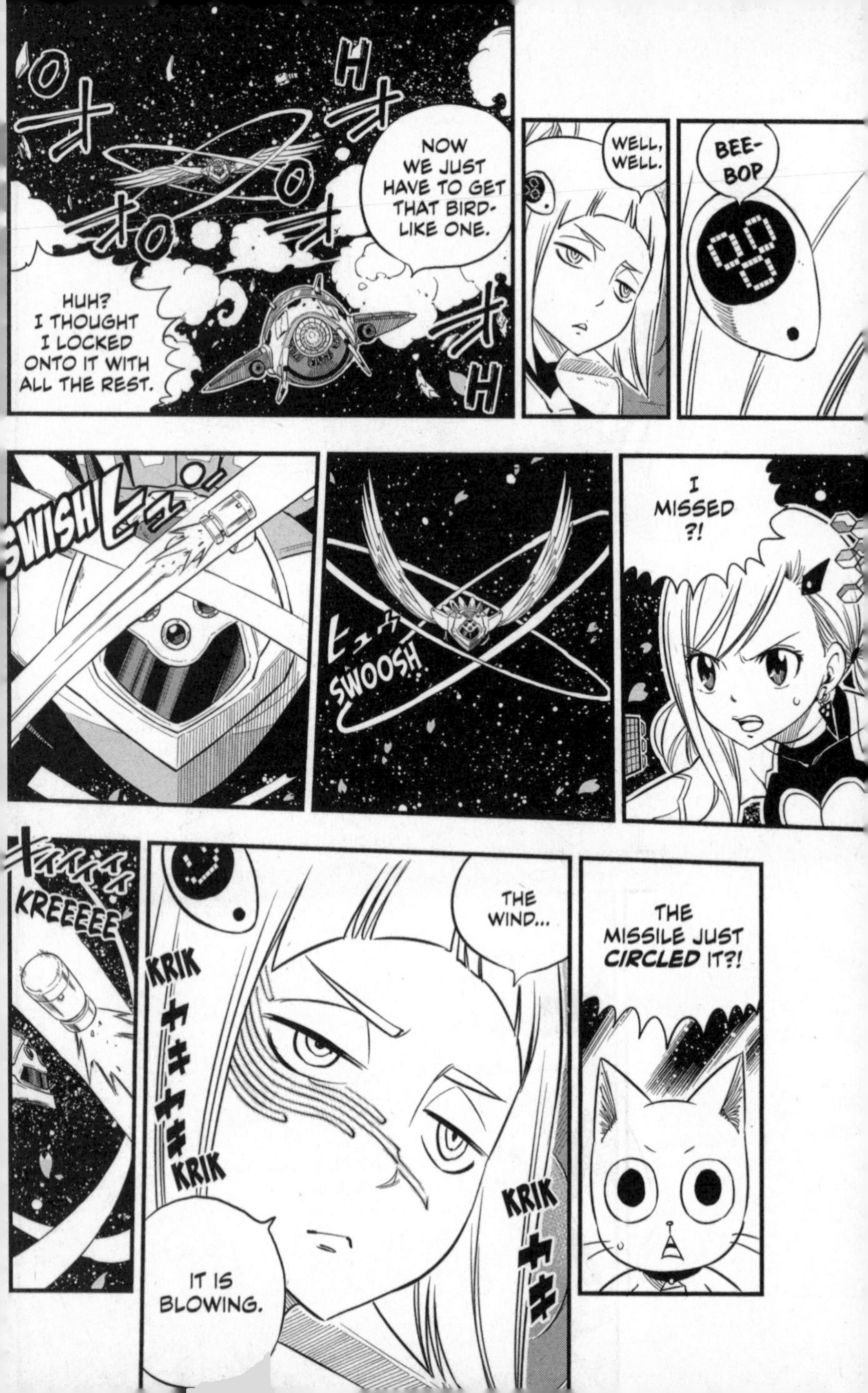
BEE-BOP
WELL, WELL.
NOW WE JUST HAVE TO GET THAT BIRD-LIKE ONE.
HUH? I THOUGHT I LOCKED ONTO IT WITH ALL THE REST.
I MISSED?!
SWOOSH
SWISH
THE MISSILE JUST CIRCLED IT?!
THE WIND...
KRIK
KRIK
KRIK
IT IS BLOWING.
KREEEEE

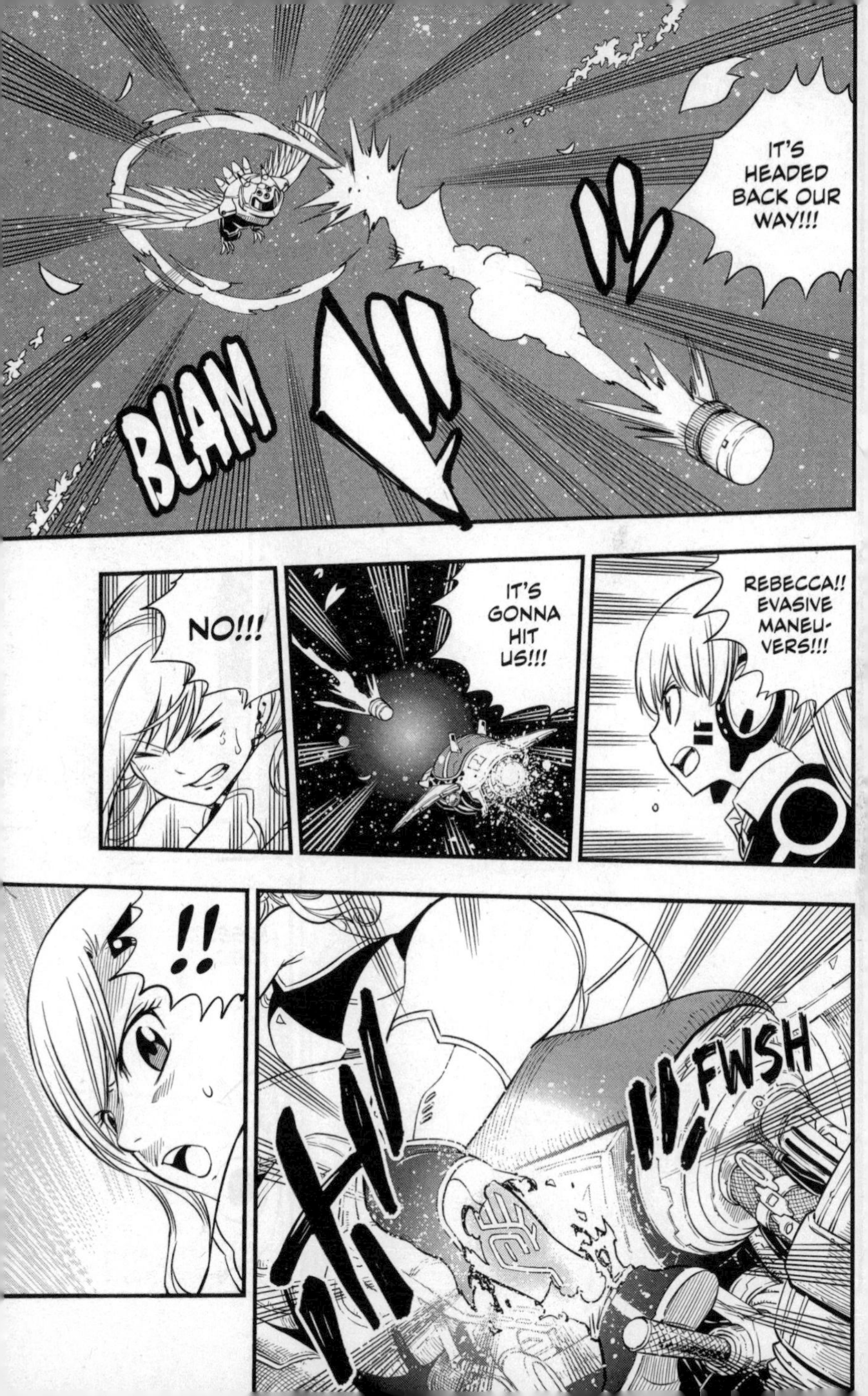
IT'S HEADED BACK OUR WAY!!!
BLAM
REBECCA!! EVASIVE MANEU-VERS!!!
IT'S GONNA HIT US!!!
NO!!!
FWSH
!!

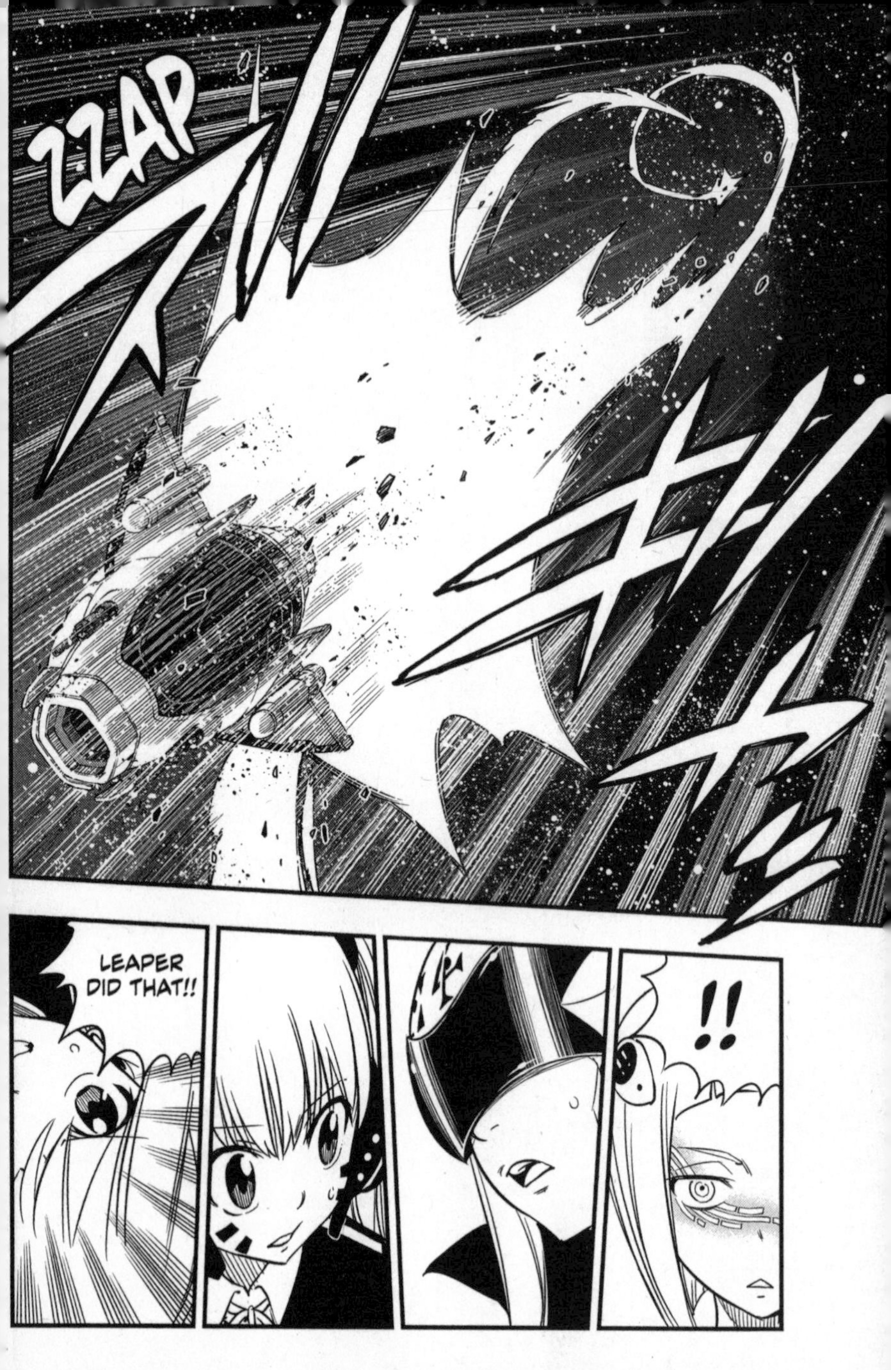
ZZAP
!!
LEAPER DID THAT!!

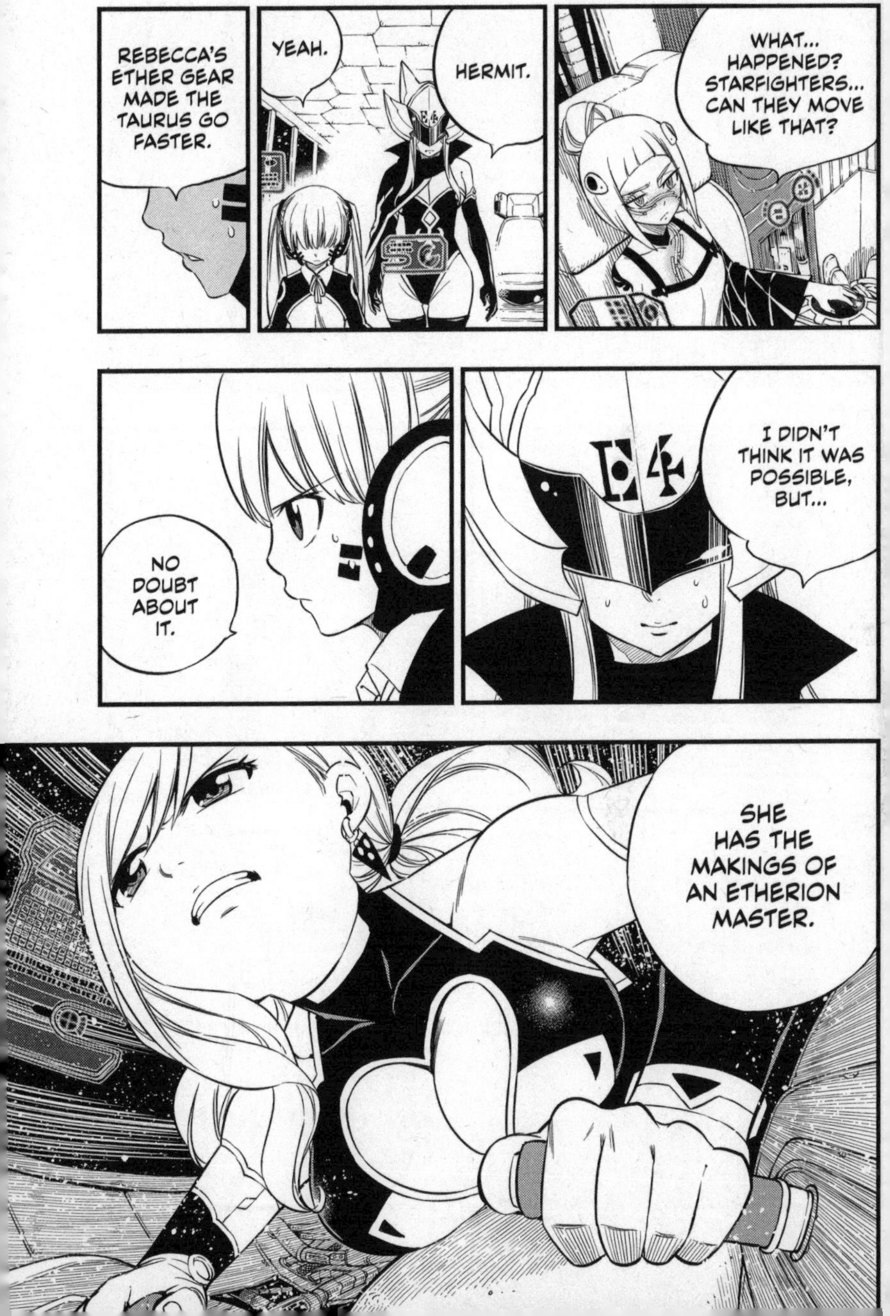
WHAT... HAPPENED? STARFIGHTERS... CAN THEY MOVE LIKE THAT?
HERMIT.
YEAH.
REBECCA'S ETHER GEAR MADE THE TAURUS GO FASTER.
I DIDN'T THINK IT WAS POSSIBLE, BUT...
NO DOUBT ABOUT IT.
SHE HAS THE MAKINGS OF AN ETHERION MASTER.

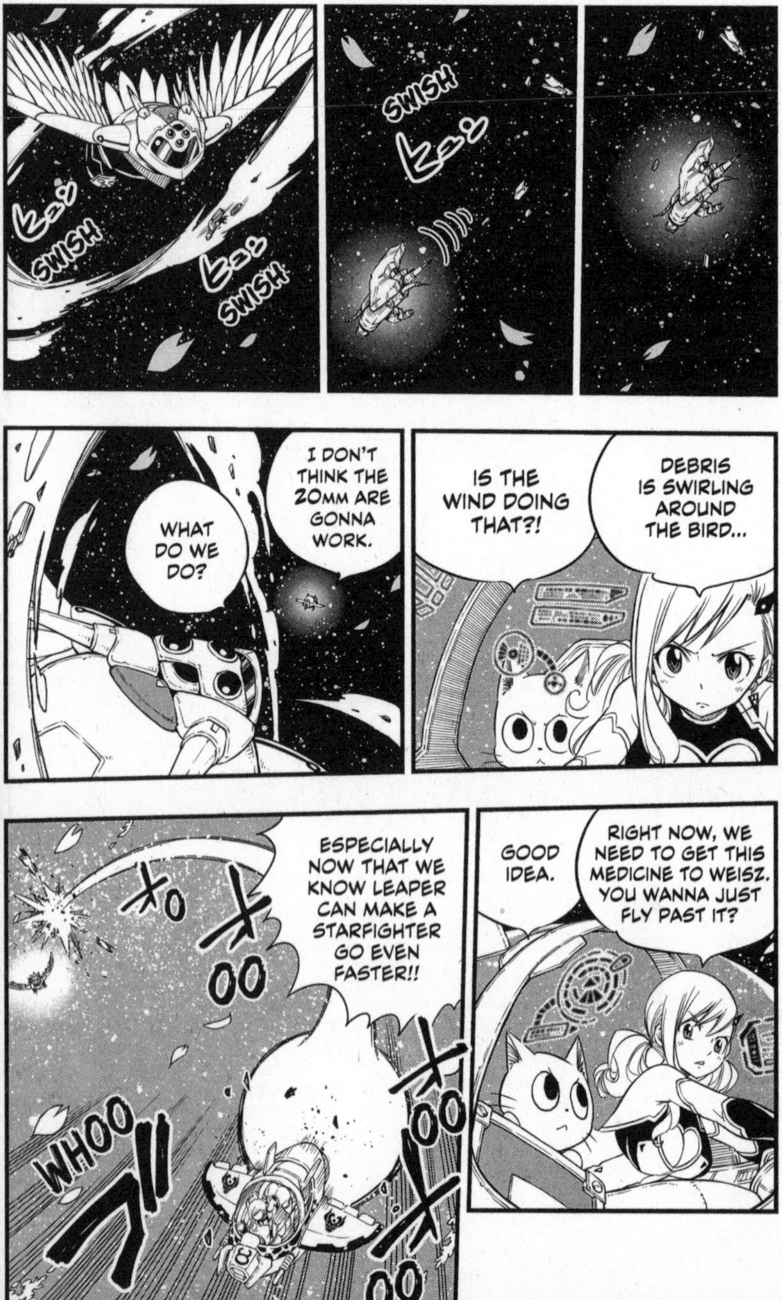
SWISH
SWISH
SWISH
DEBRIS IS SWIRLING AROUND THE BIRD...
IS THE WIND DOING THAT?!
I DON'T THINK THE 20MM ARE GONNA WORK.
WHAT DO WE DO?
RIGHT NOW, WE NEED TO GET THIS MEDICINE TO WEISZ. YOU WANNA JUST FLY PAST IT?
GOOD IDEA.
ESPECIALLY NOW THAT WE KNOW LEAPER CAN MAKE A STARFIGHTER GO EVEN FASTER!!
WHOO

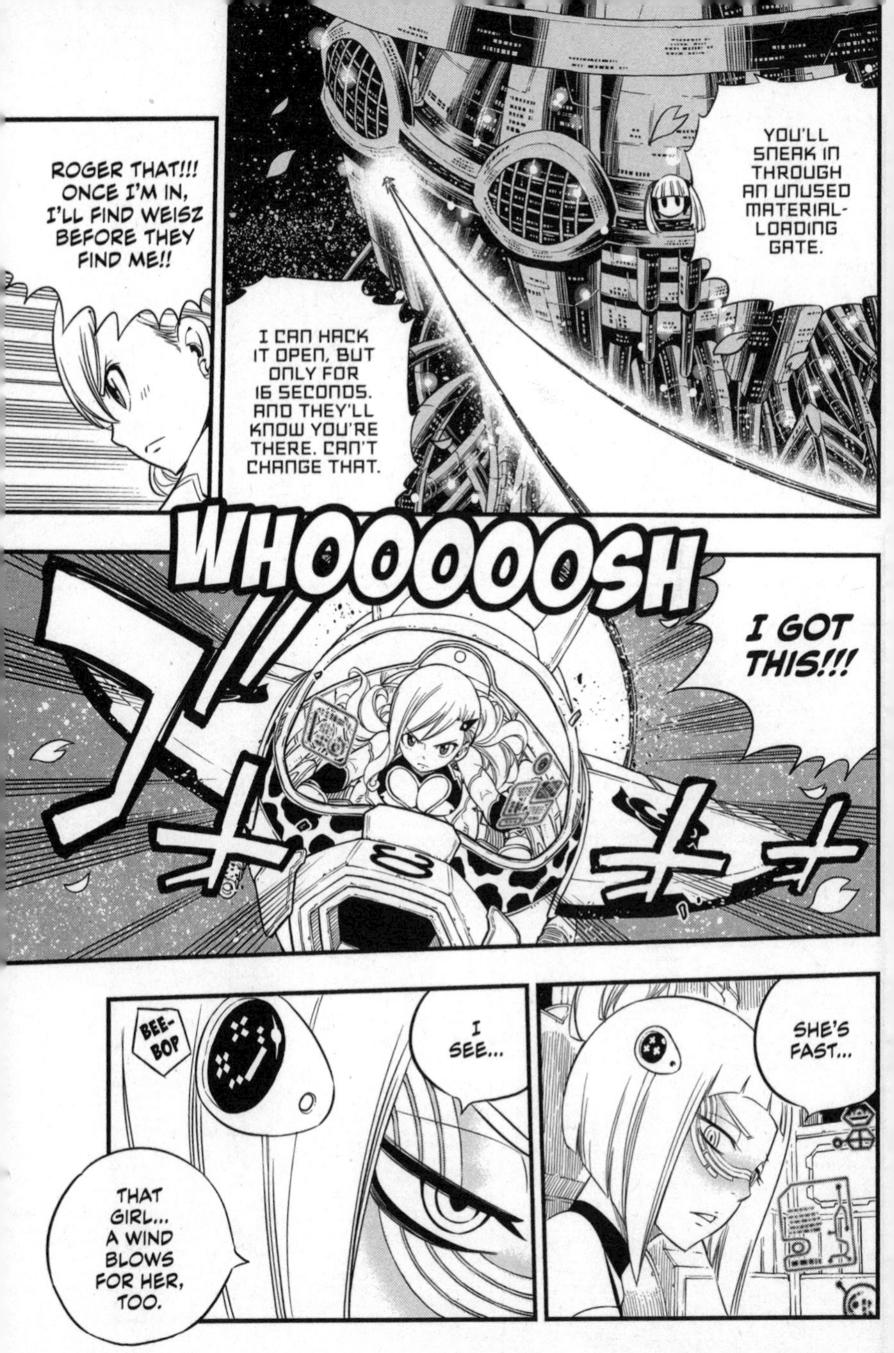
YOU'LL SNEAK IN THROUGH AN UNUSED MATERIAL-LOADING GATE.
I CAN HACK IT OPEN, BUT ONLY FOR 16 SECONDS. AND THEY'LL KNOW YOU'RE THERE. CAN'T CHANGE THAT.
ROGER THAT!!! ONCE I'M IN, I'LL FIND WEISZ BEFORE THEY FIND ME!!
WHOOOOOOSH
I GOT THIS!!!
SHE'S FAST...
BEE-BOP
I SEE...
THAT GIRL... A WIND BLOWS FOR HER, TOO.

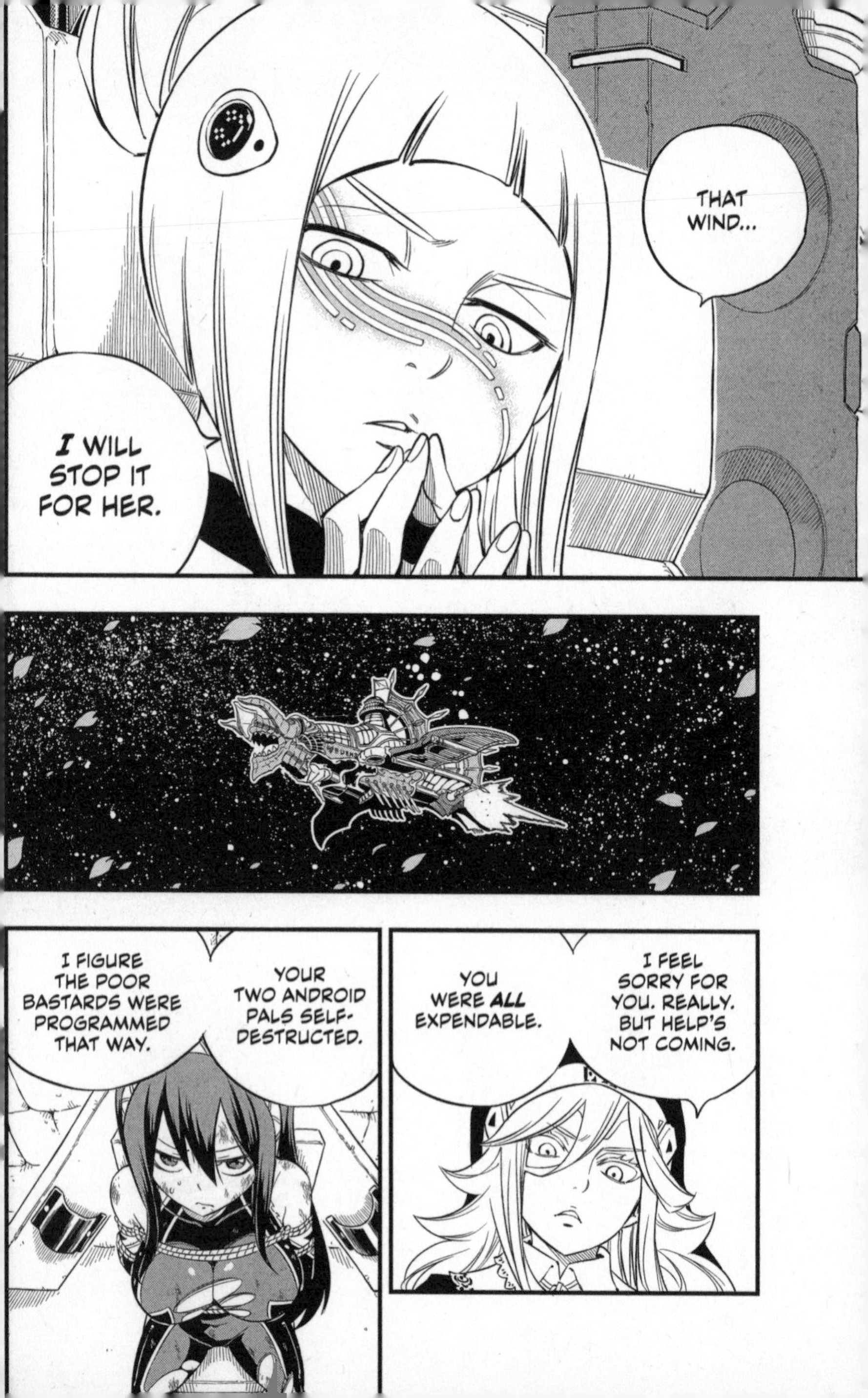
THAT WIND...
I WILL STOP IT FOR HER.
I FEEL SORRY FOR YOU. REALLY. BUT HELP'S NOT COMING.
YOU WERE ALL EXPENDABLE.
YOUR TWO ANDROID PALS SELF-DESTRUCTED.
I FIGURE THE POOR BASTARDS WERE PROGRAMMED THAT WAY.

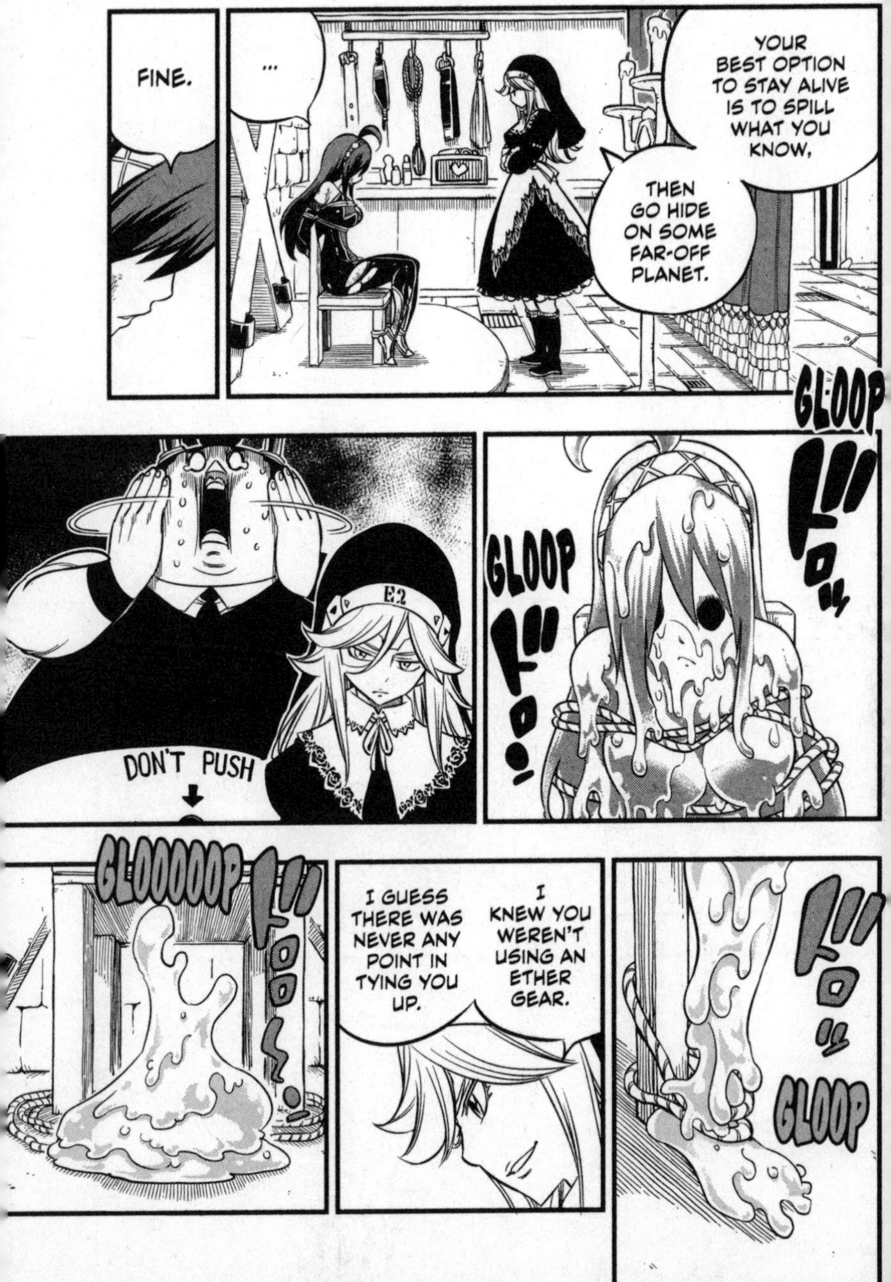
YOUR BEST OPTION TO STAY ALIVE IS TO SPILL WHAT YOU KNOW,
THEN GO HIDE ON SOME FAR-OFF PLANET.
...
FINE.
GLOOP
GLOOP
DON'T PUSH
GLOOP
I KNEW YOU WEREN'T USING AN ETHER GEAR.
I GUESS THERE WAS NEVER ANY POINT IN TYING YOU UP.
GLOOOOOP

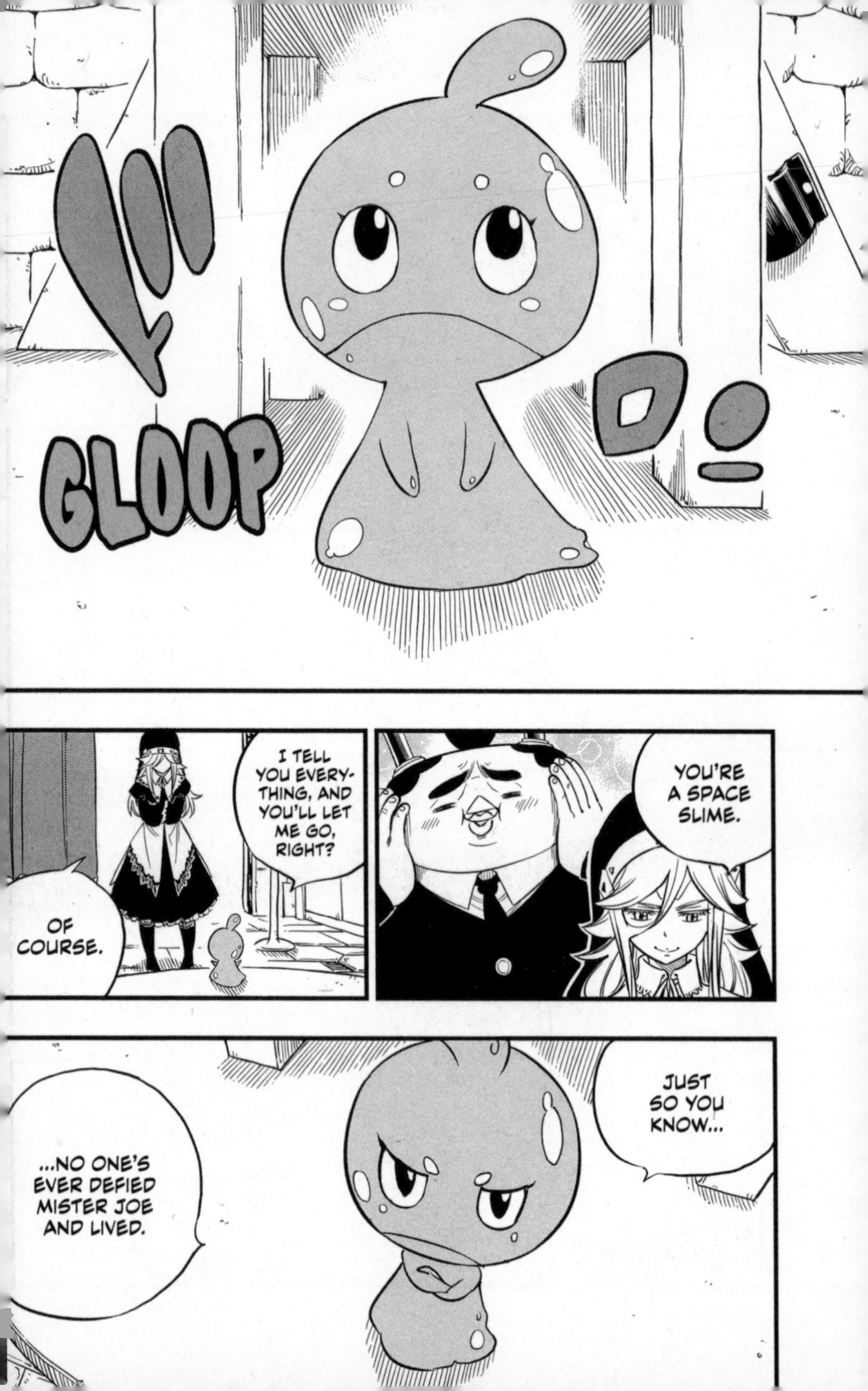
GLOOP
YOU'RE A SPACE SLIME.
I TELL YOU EVERY-THING, AND YOU'LL LET ME GO, RIGHT?
OF COURSE.
JUST SO YOU KNOW...
...NO ONE'S EVER DEFIED MISTER JOE AND LIVED.

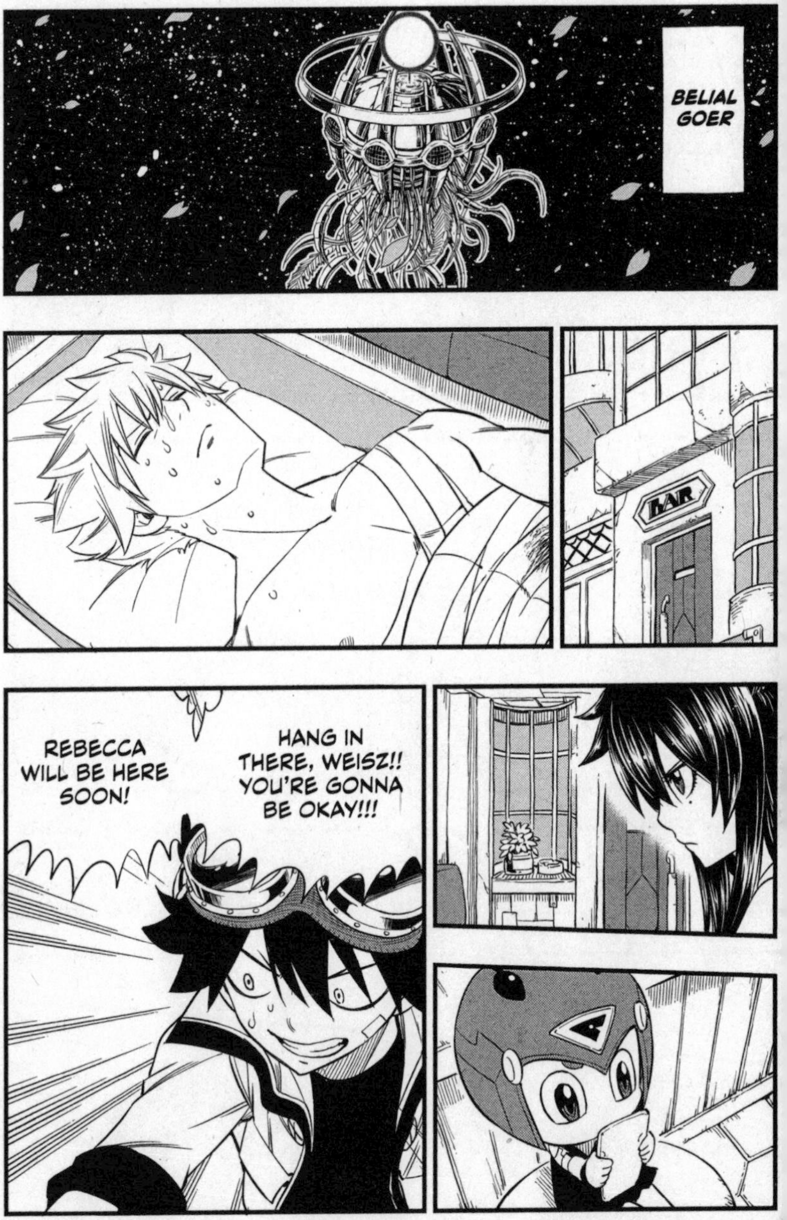
BELIAL GOER
BAR
HANG IN THERE, WEISZ!! YOU'RE GONNA BE OKAY!!!
REBECCA WILL BE HERE SOON!

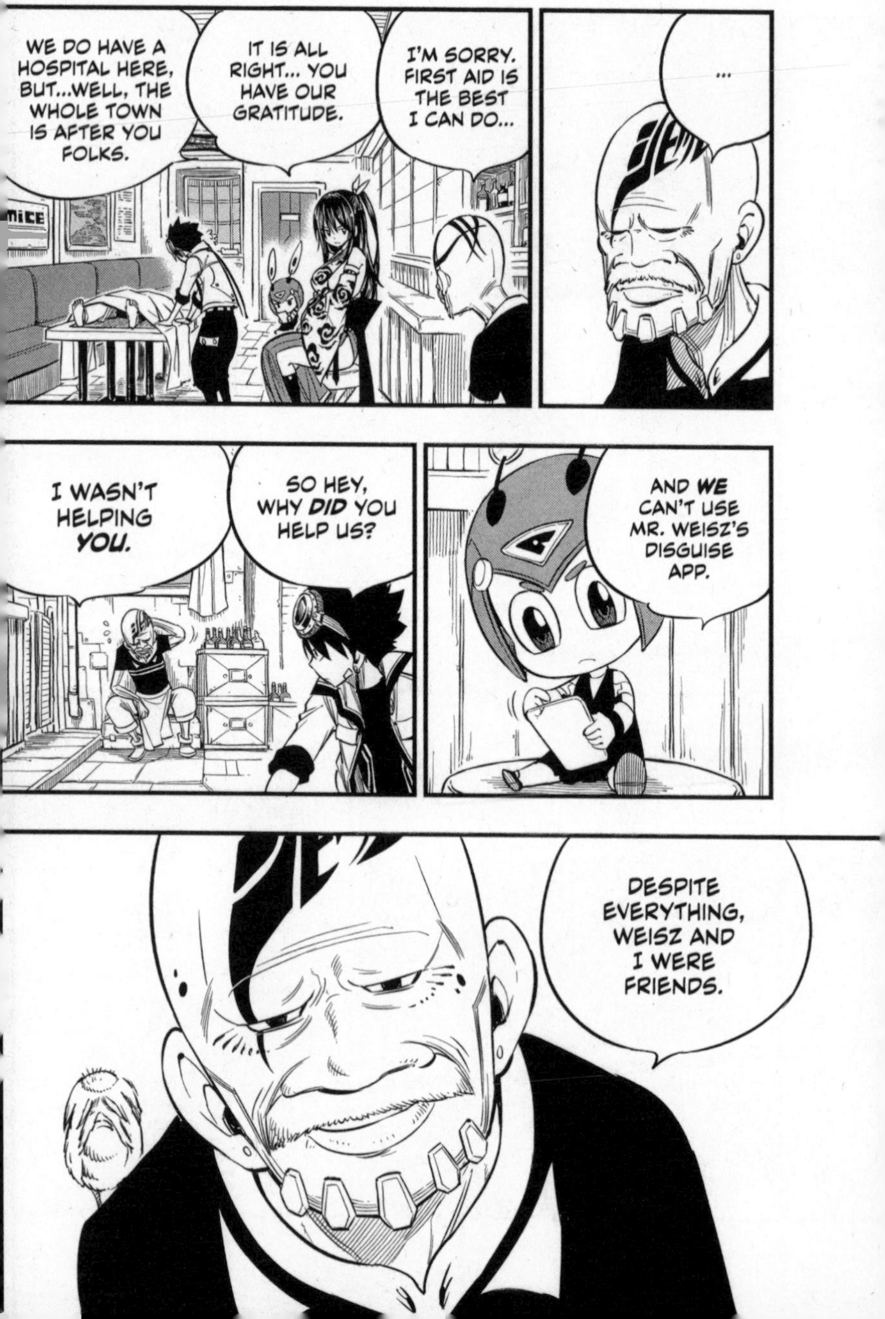
...
I'M SORRY. FIRST AID IS THE BEST I CAN DO...
IT IS ALL RIGHT... YOU HAVE OUR GRATITUDE.
WE DO HAVE A HOSPITAL HERE, BUT...WELL, THE WHOLE TOWN IS AFTER YOU FOLKS.
AND WE CAN'T USE MR. WEISZ'S DISGUISE APP.
SO HEY, WHY DID YOU HELP US?
I WASN'T HELPING YOU.
DESPITE EVERYTHING, WEISZ AND I WERE FRIENDS.

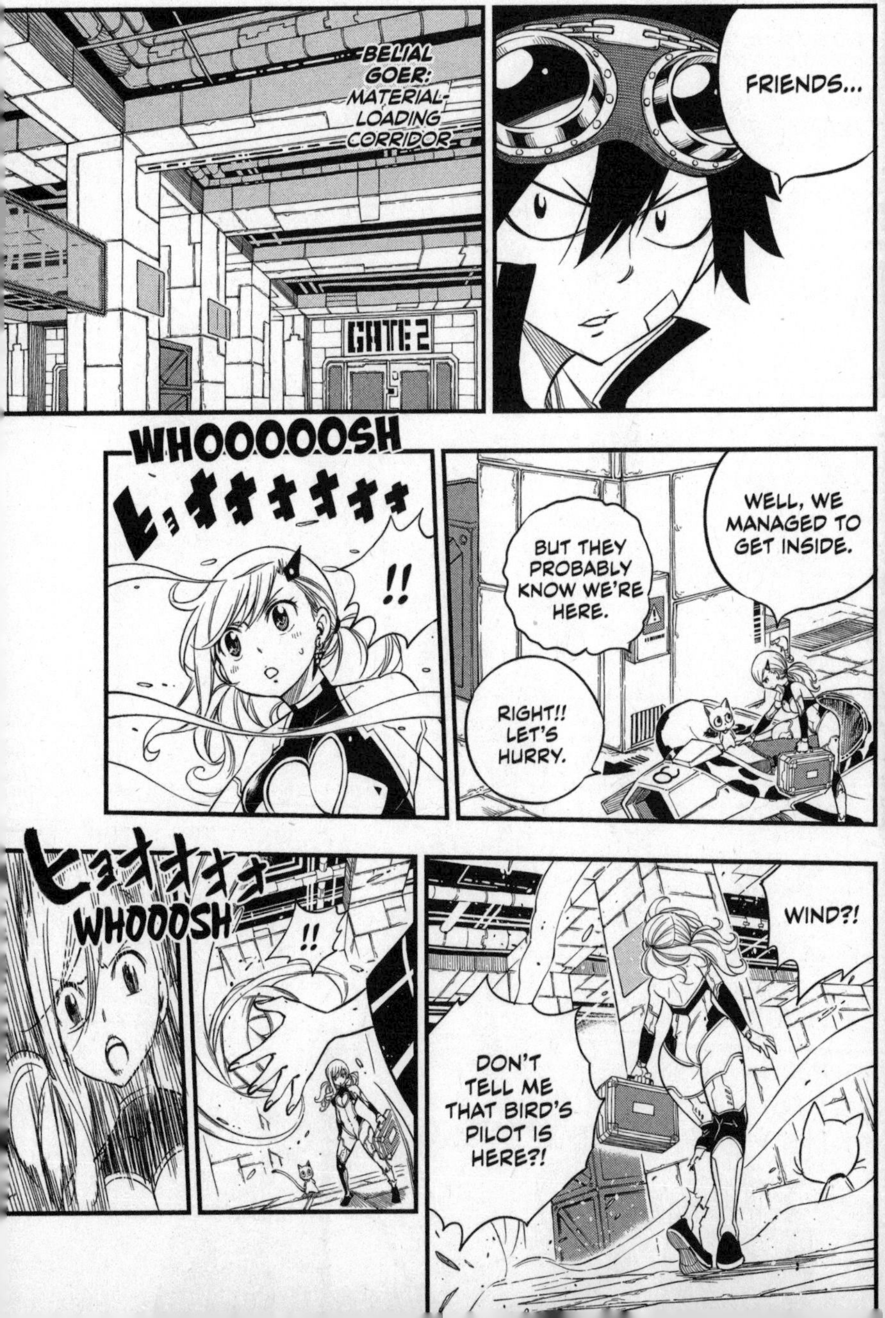
FRIENDS...
BELIAL GOER: MATERIAL-LOADING CORRIDOR
GATE 2
WELL, WE MANAGED TO GET INSIDE.
BUT THEY PROBABLY KNOW WE'RE HERE.
RIGHT!! LET'S HURRY.
WHOOOOOSH
!!
WIND?!
DON'T TELL ME THAT BIRD'S PILOT IS HERE?!
!!
WHOOOSH

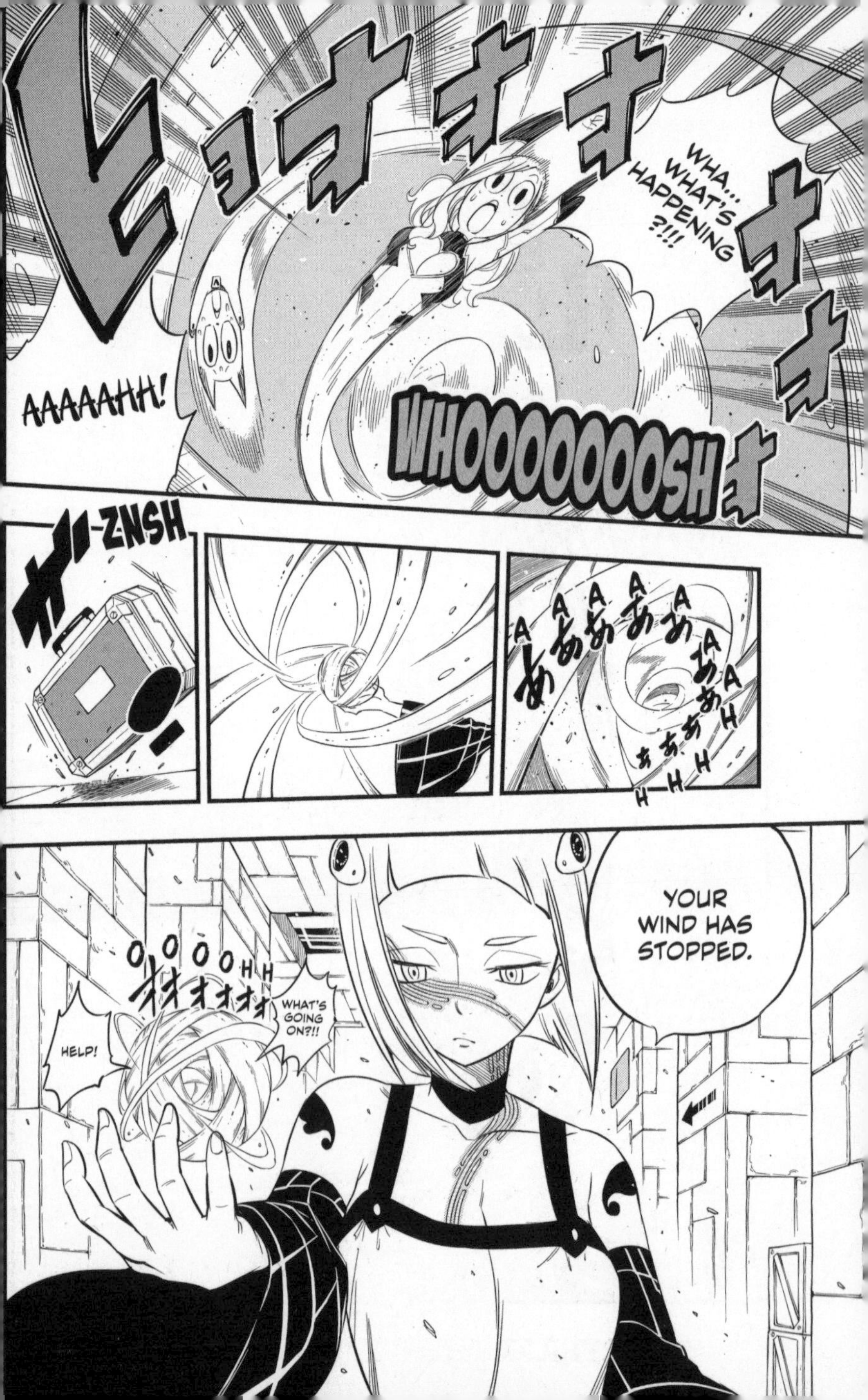
WHA... WHAT'S HAPPENING ?!!!
AAAAAHH!
WHOOOOOOOOSH
AAAAAAAAAAHHHHH
ZNSH
YOUR WIND HAS STOPPED.
WHAT'S GOING ON?!!
OOOOOHH
HELP!

EDENS ZERO

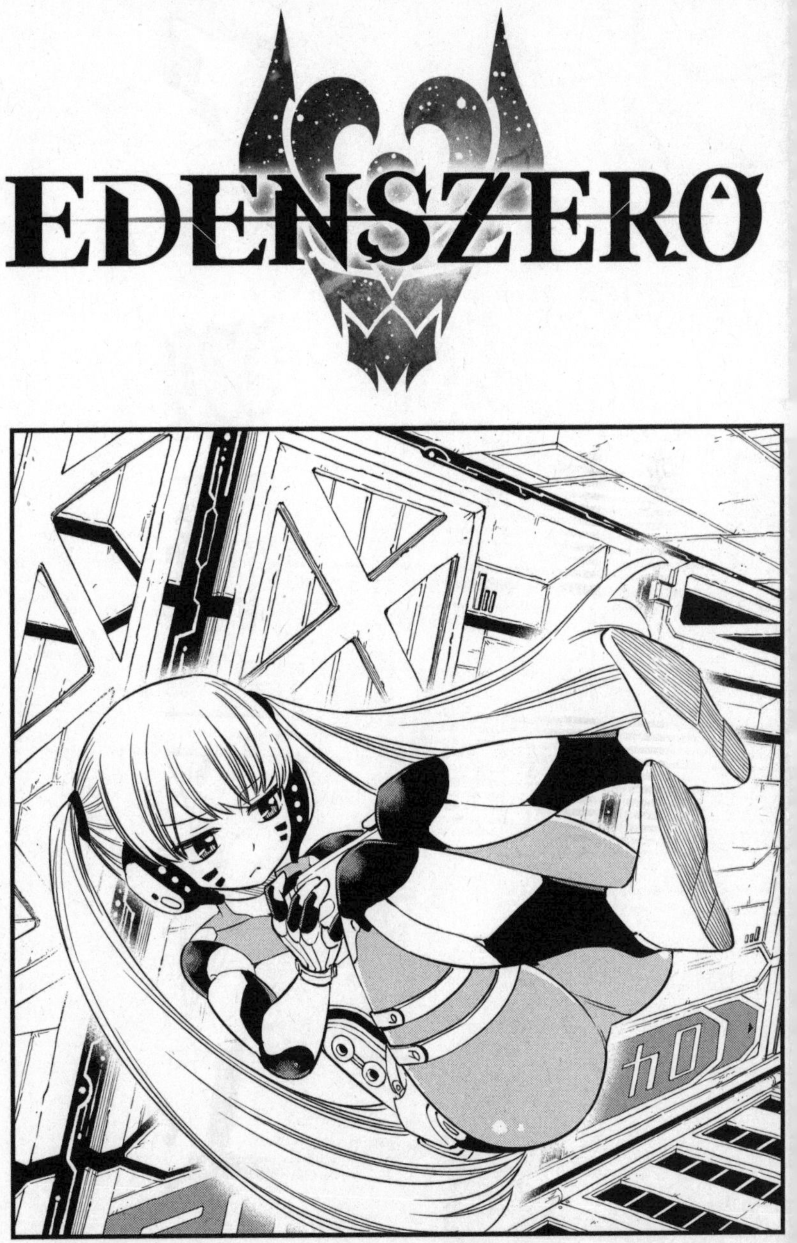

CHAPTER 77: THE WINDS THAT BIND

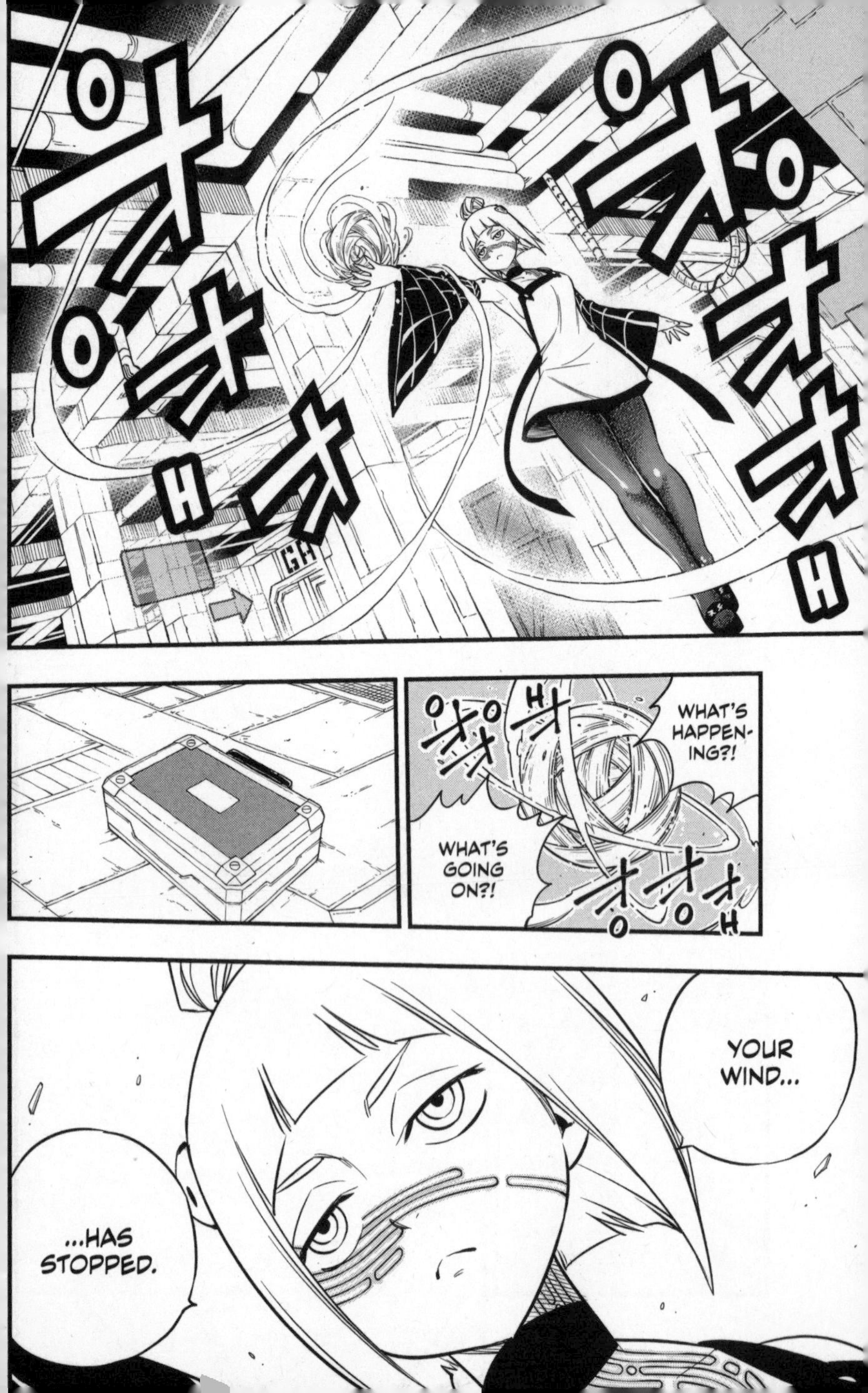
ポオオォH
ポオオォH
WHAT'S HAPPENING?!
WHAT'S GOING ON?!
YOUR WIND...
...HAS STOPPED.

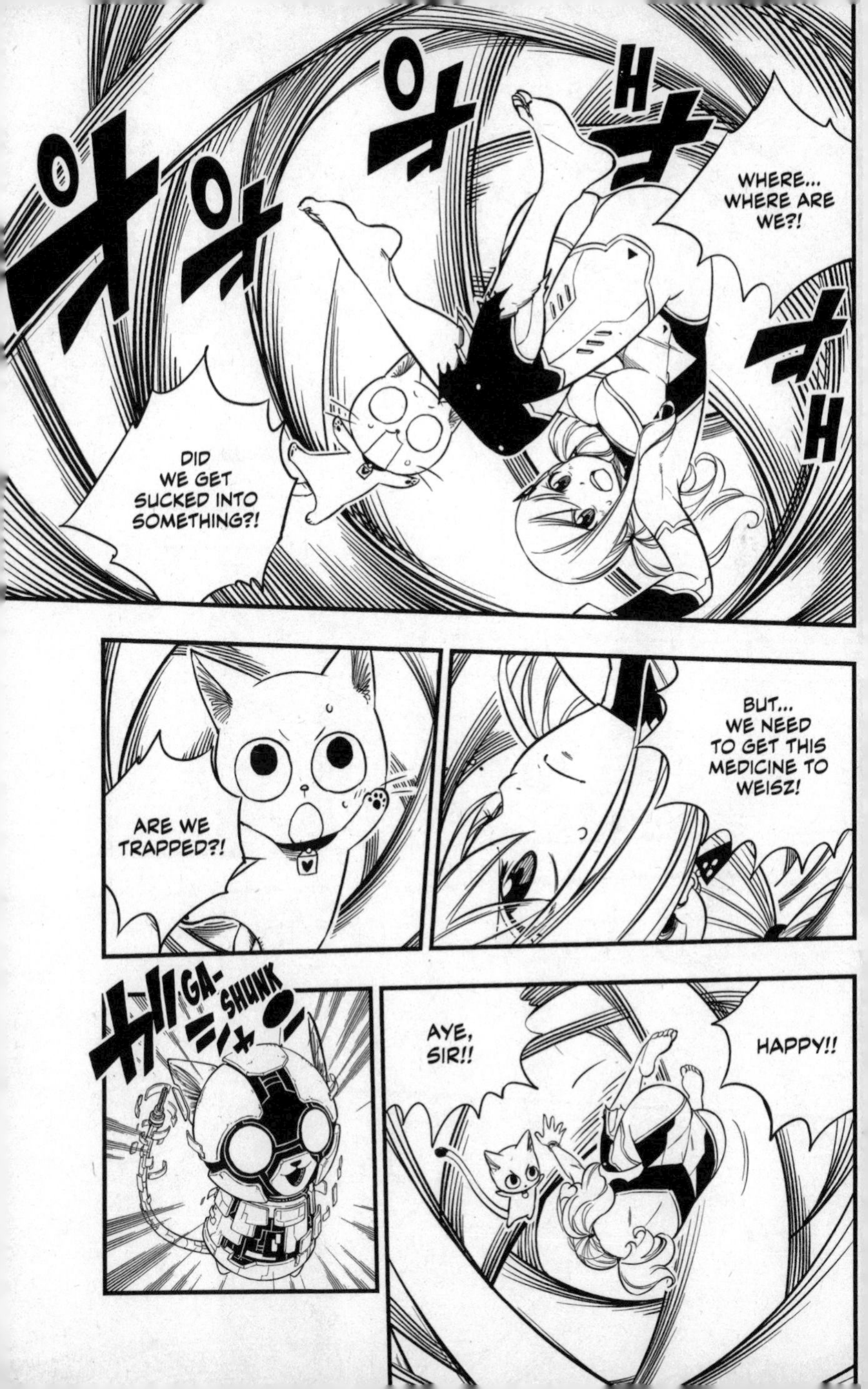
WHERE... WHERE ARE WE?!
H
H
DID WE GET SUCKED INTO SOMETHING?!
BUT... WE NEED TO GET THIS MEDICINE TO WEISZ!
ARE WE TRAPPED?!
HAPPY!!
AYE, SIR!!
GA-SHUNK

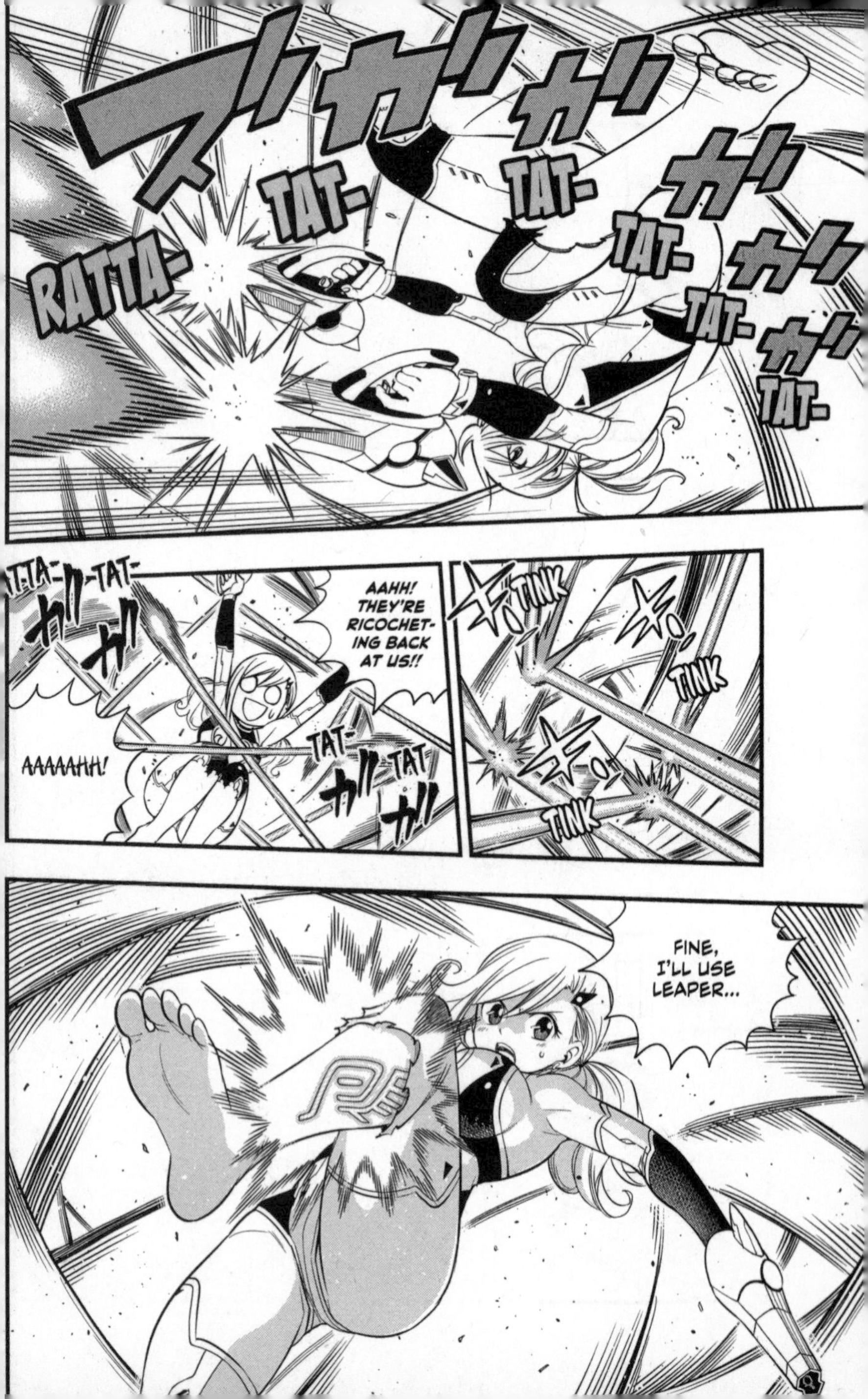
TAT-
TAT-
TAT-
TAT-
TAT-
TAT-
RATTA-
TINK
TINK
TINK
RATTA-TAT-TAT-
AAHH! THEY'RE RICOCHETING BACK AT US!!
TAT-
TAT
AAAAAHH!
FINE, I'LL USE LEAPER...

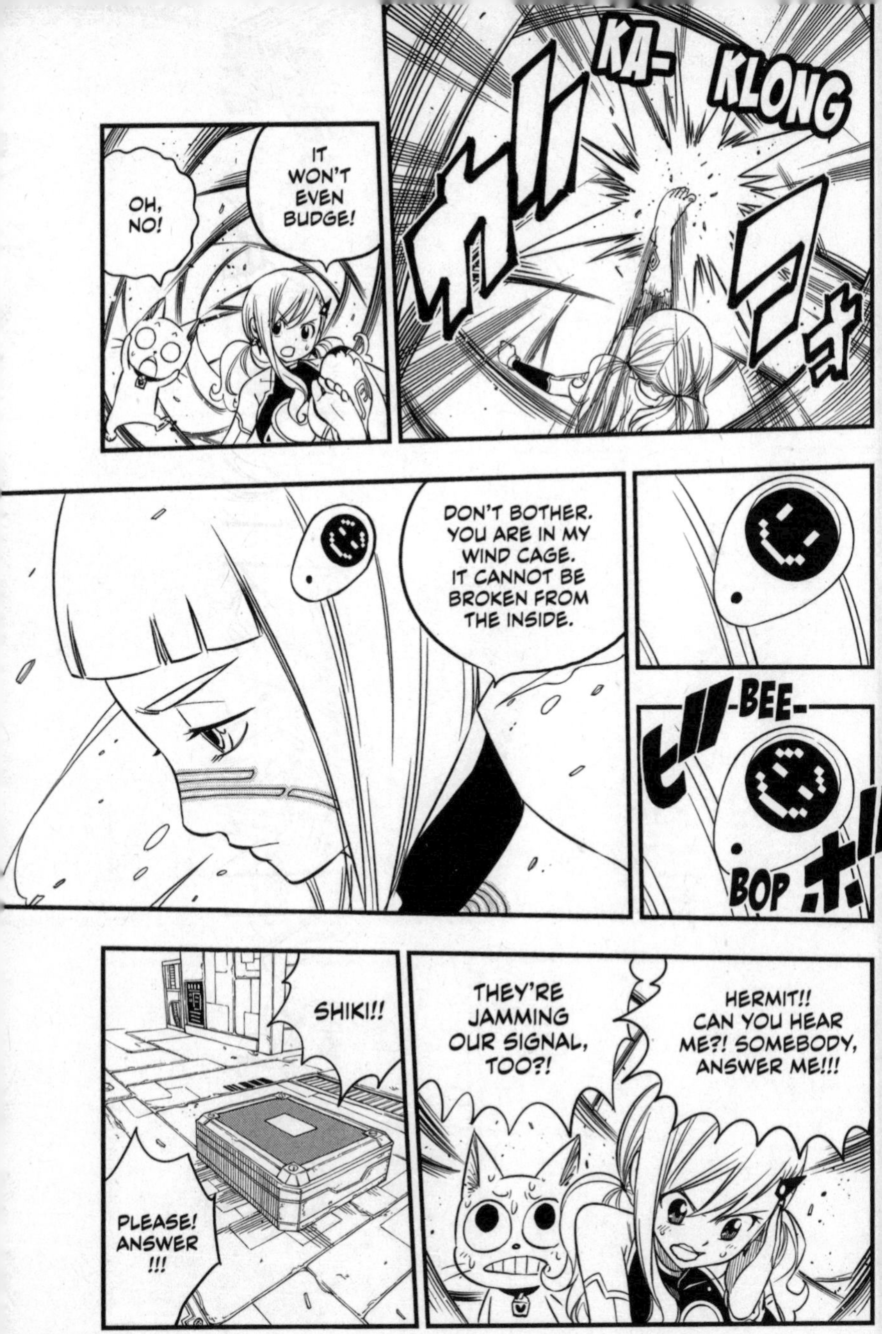
KA- KLONG
IT WON'T EVEN BUDGE!
OH, NO!
-BEE-
BOP
DON'T BOTHER. YOU ARE IN MY WIND CAGE. IT CANNOT BE BROKEN FROM THE INSIDE.
HERMIT!! CAN YOU HEAR ME?! SOMEBODY, ANSWER ME!!!
THEY'RE JAMMING OUR SIGNAL, TOO?!
SHIKI!!!
PLEASE! ANSWER !!!

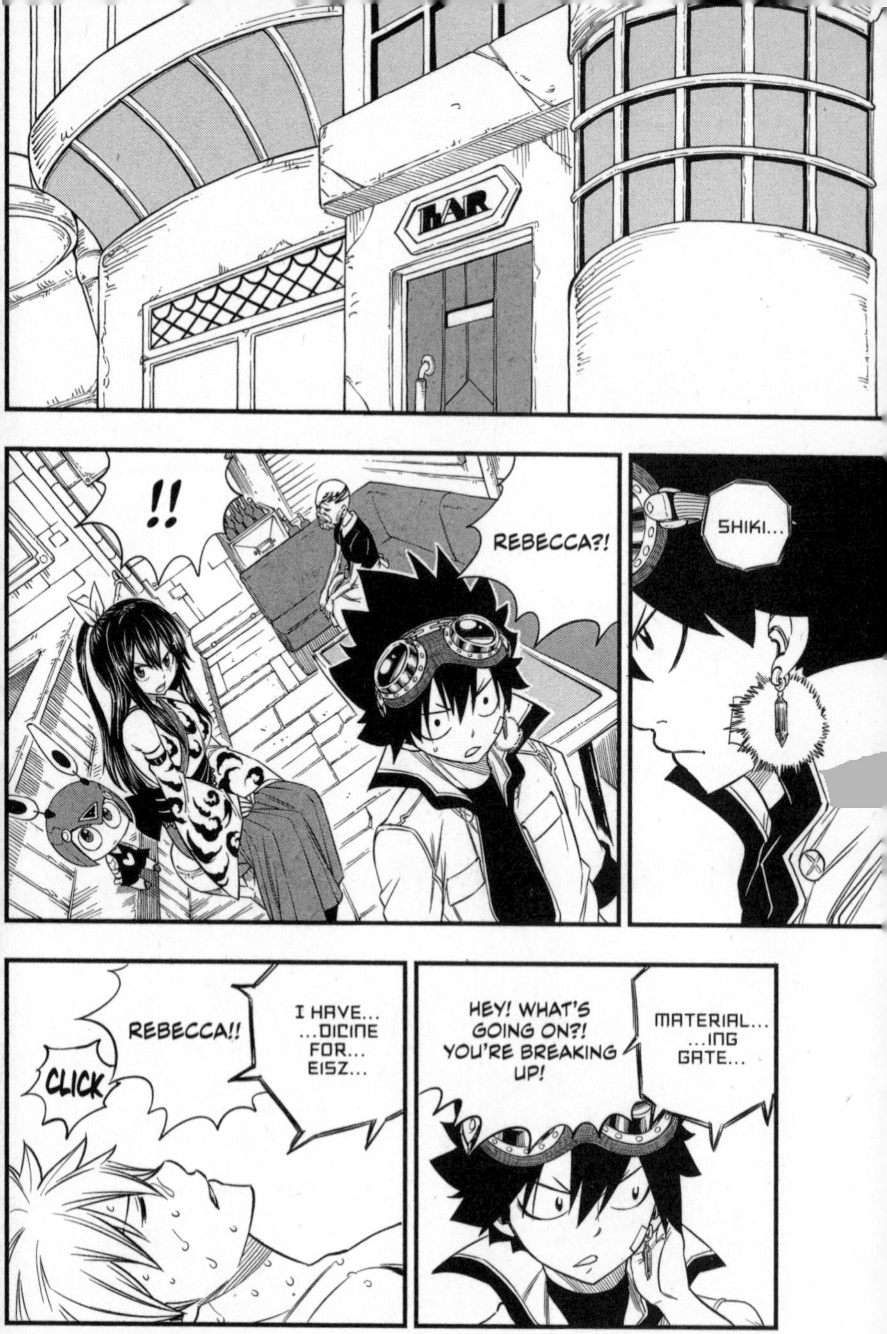
BAR
SHIKI...
REBECCA?!
!!
MATERIAL... ...ING GATE...
HEY! WHAT'S GOING ON?! YOU'RE BREAKING UP!
I HAVE... ...DICINE FOR... EISZ...
REBECCA!!
CLICK

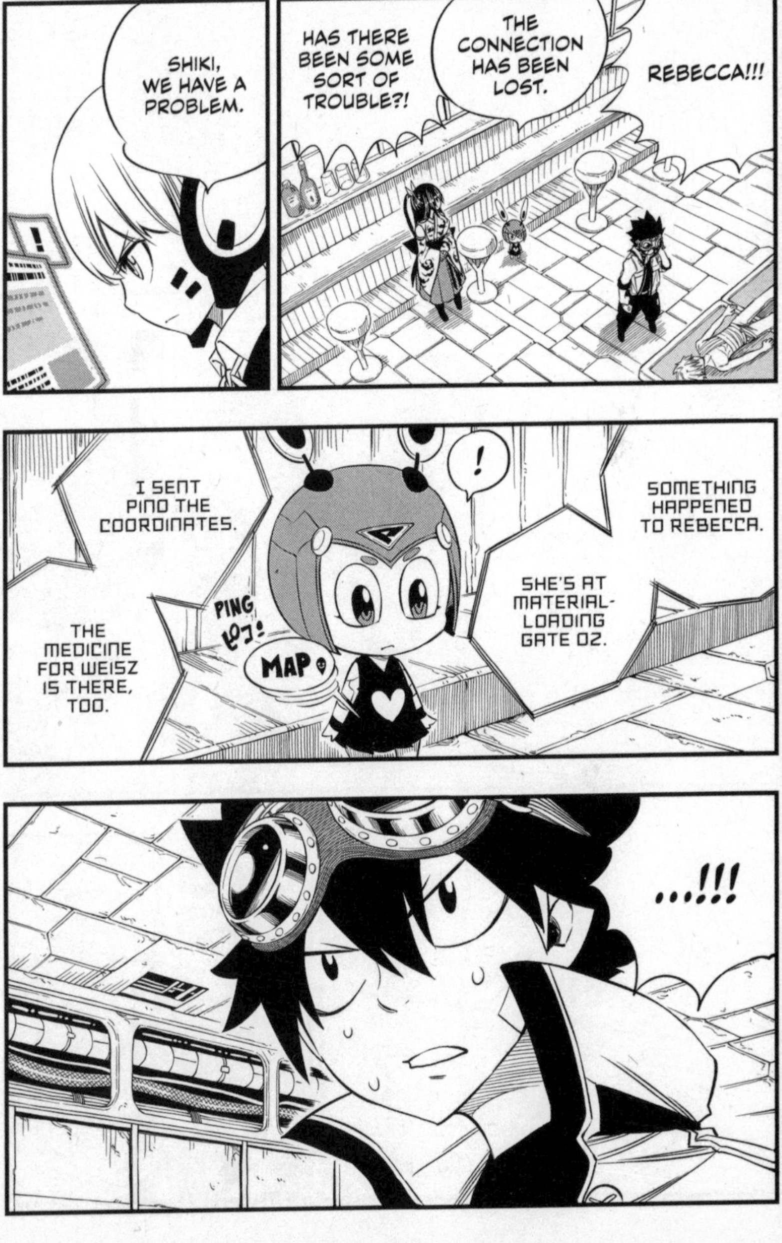
REBECCA!!!
THE CONNECTION HAS BEEN LOST.
HAS THERE BEEN SOME SORT OF TROUBLE?!
SHIKI, WE HAVE A PROBLEM.
!
SOMETHING HAPPENED TO REBECCA.
SHE'S AT MATERIAL-LOADING GATE 02.
I SENT PINO THE COORDINATES.
PING
MAP
THE MEDICINE FOR WEISZ IS THERE, TOO.
...!!!

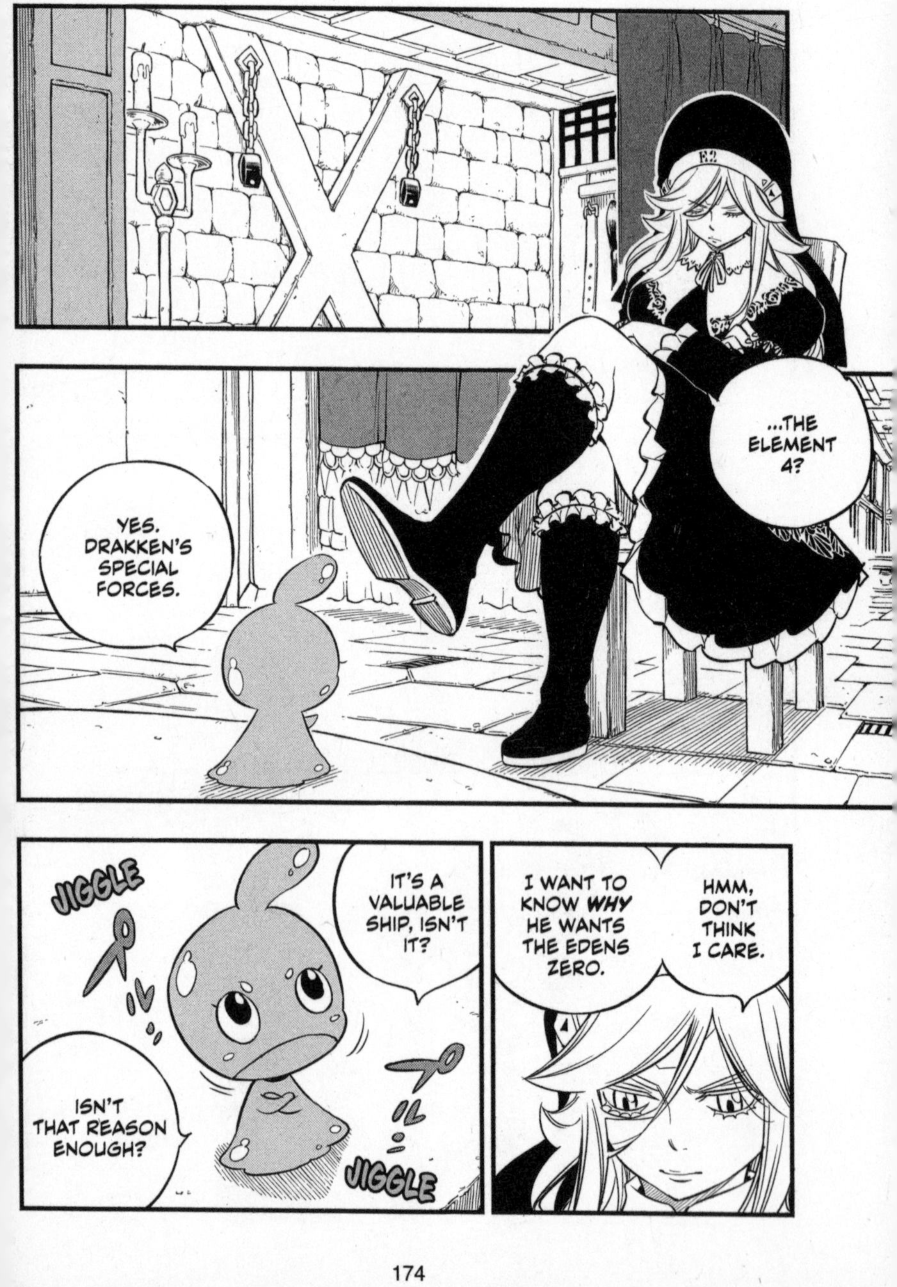
...THE ELEMENT 4?
YES. DRAKKEN'S SPECIAL FORCES.
HMM, DON'T THINK I CARE.
I WANT TO KNOW *WHY* HE WANTS THE EDENS ZERO.
IT'S A VALUABLE SHIP, ISN'T IT?
JIGGLE
ISN'T THAT REASON ENOUGH?
JIGGLE

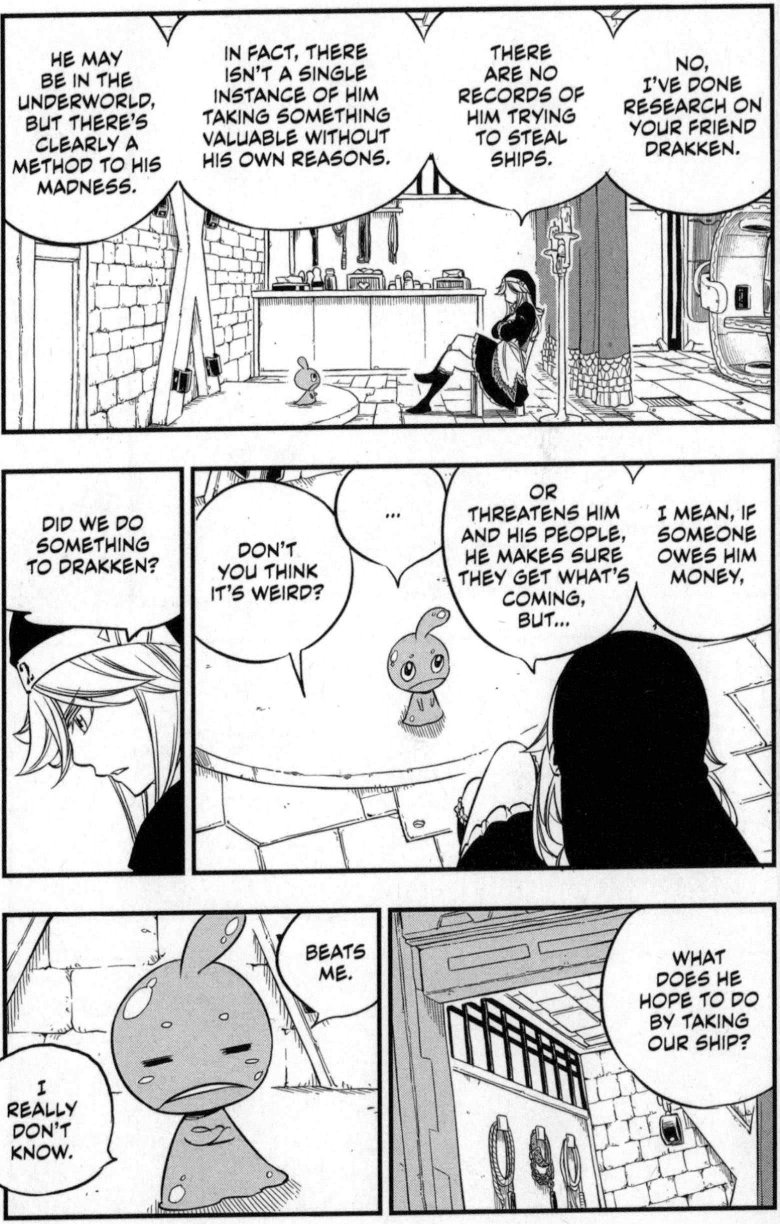
NO, I'VE DONE RESEARCH ON YOUR FRIEND DRAKKEN.
THERE ARE NO RECORDS OF HIM TRYING TO STEAL SHIPS.
IN FACT, THERE ISN'T A SINGLE INSTANCE OF HIM TAKING SOMETHING VALUABLE WITHOUT HIS OWN REASONS.
HE MAY BE IN THE UNDERWORLD, BUT THERE'S CLEARLY A METHOD TO HIS MADNESS.
I MEAN, IF SOMEONE OWES HIM MONEY,
OR THREATENS HIM AND HIS PEOPLE, HE MAKES SURE THEY GET WHAT'S COMING, BUT...
...
DON'T YOU THINK IT'S WEIRD?
DID WE DO SOMETHING TO DRAKKEN?
WHAT DOES HE HOPE TO DO BY TAKING OUR SHIP?
BEATS ME.
I REALLY DON'T KNOW.

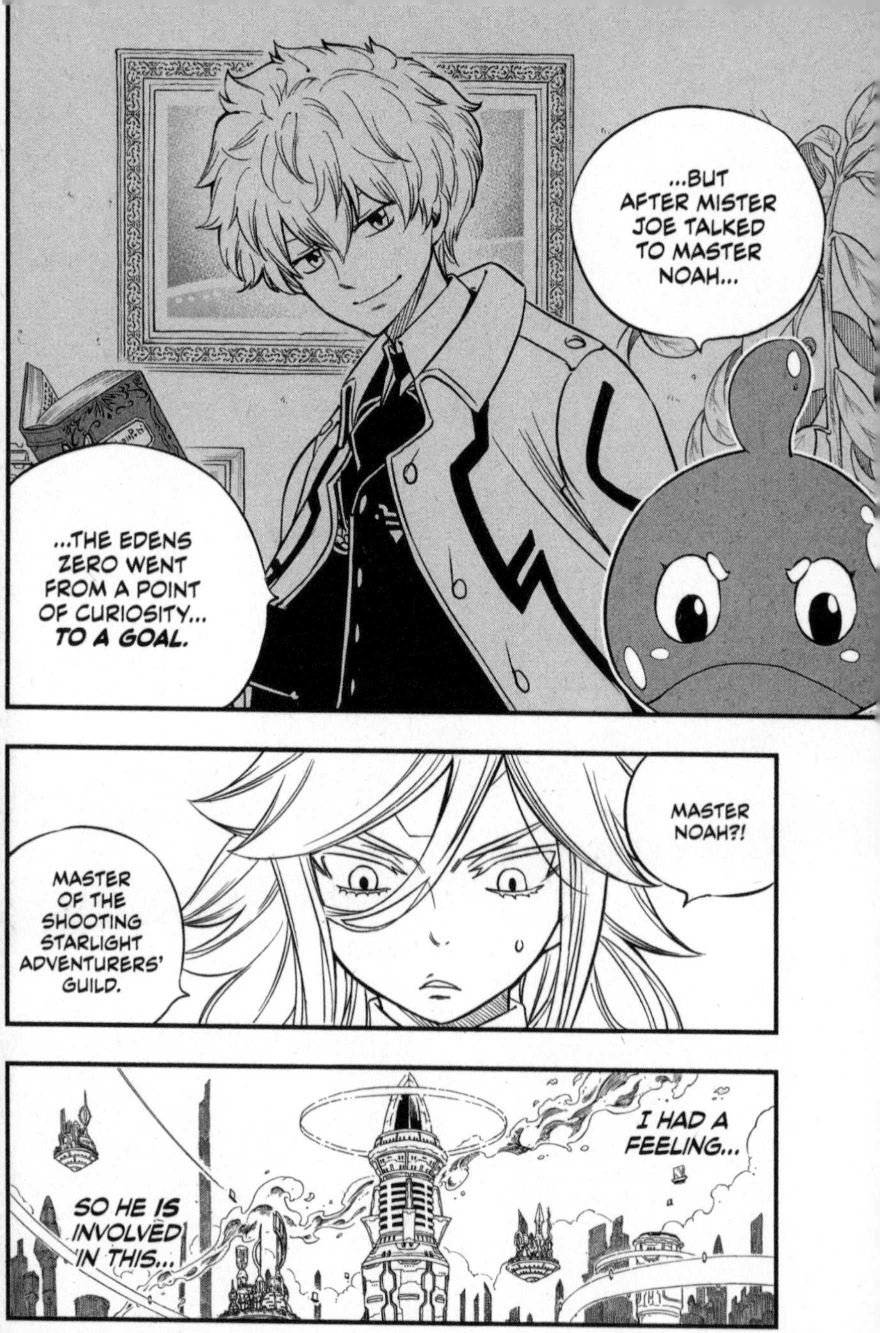
...BUT AFTER MISTER JOE TALKED TO MASTER NOAH...
...THE EDENS ZERO WENT FROM A POINT OF CURIOSITY... ***TO A GOAL.***
MASTER NOAH?!
MASTER OF THE SHOOTING STARLIGHT ADVENTURERS' GUILD.
I HAD A FEELING...
SO HE IS INVOLVED IN THIS...

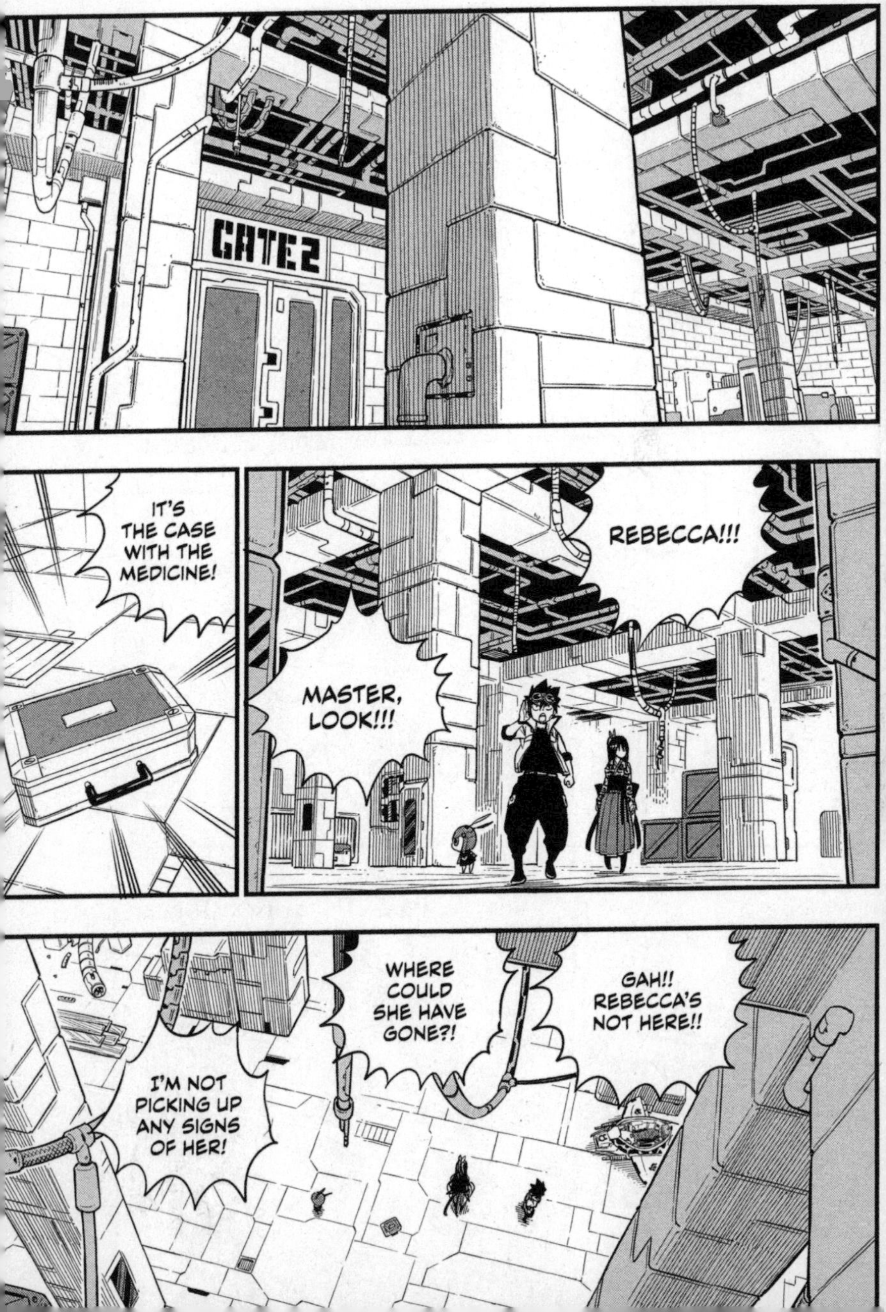
GATE 2
REBECCA!!!
MASTER, LOOK!!!
IT'S THE CASE WITH THE MEDICINE!
GAH!! REBECCA'S NOT HERE!!
WHERE COULD SHE HAVE GONE?!
I'M NOT PICKING UP ANY SIGNS OF HER!

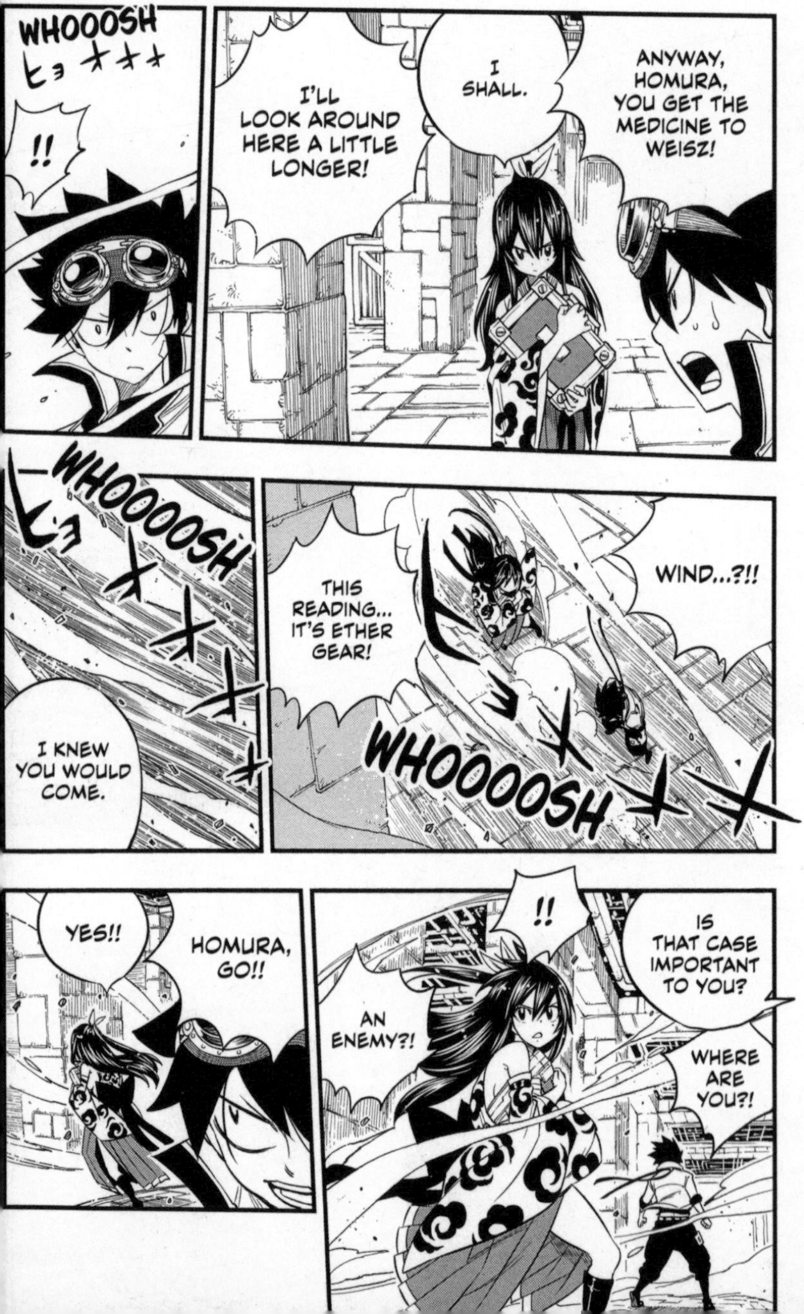
ANYWAY, HOMURA, YOU GET THE MEDICINE TO WEISZ!
I SHALL.
I'LL LOOK AROUND HERE A LITTLE LONGER!
WHOOOSH
ヒョオオオ
!!
WIND...?!!
THIS READING... IT'S ETHER GEAR!
WHOOOOSH
WHOOOOSH
I KNEW YOU WOULD COME.
IS THAT CASE IMPORTANT TO YOU?
!!
WHERE ARE YOU?!
AN ENEMY?!
HOMURA, GO!!
YES!!

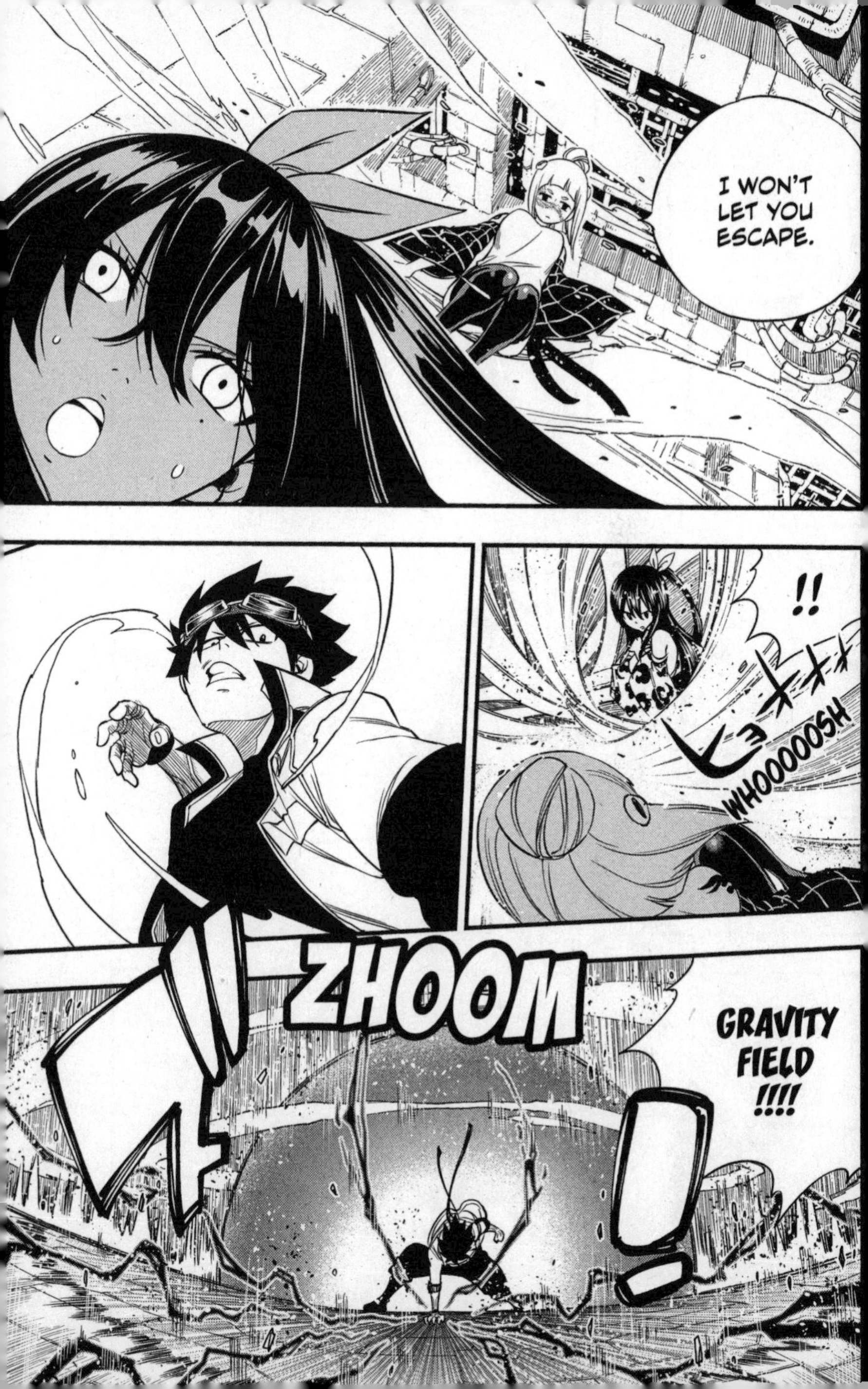
I WON'T LET YOU ESCAPE.
!!
WHOOOOOSH
GRAVITY FIELD !!!!
ZHOOM
!

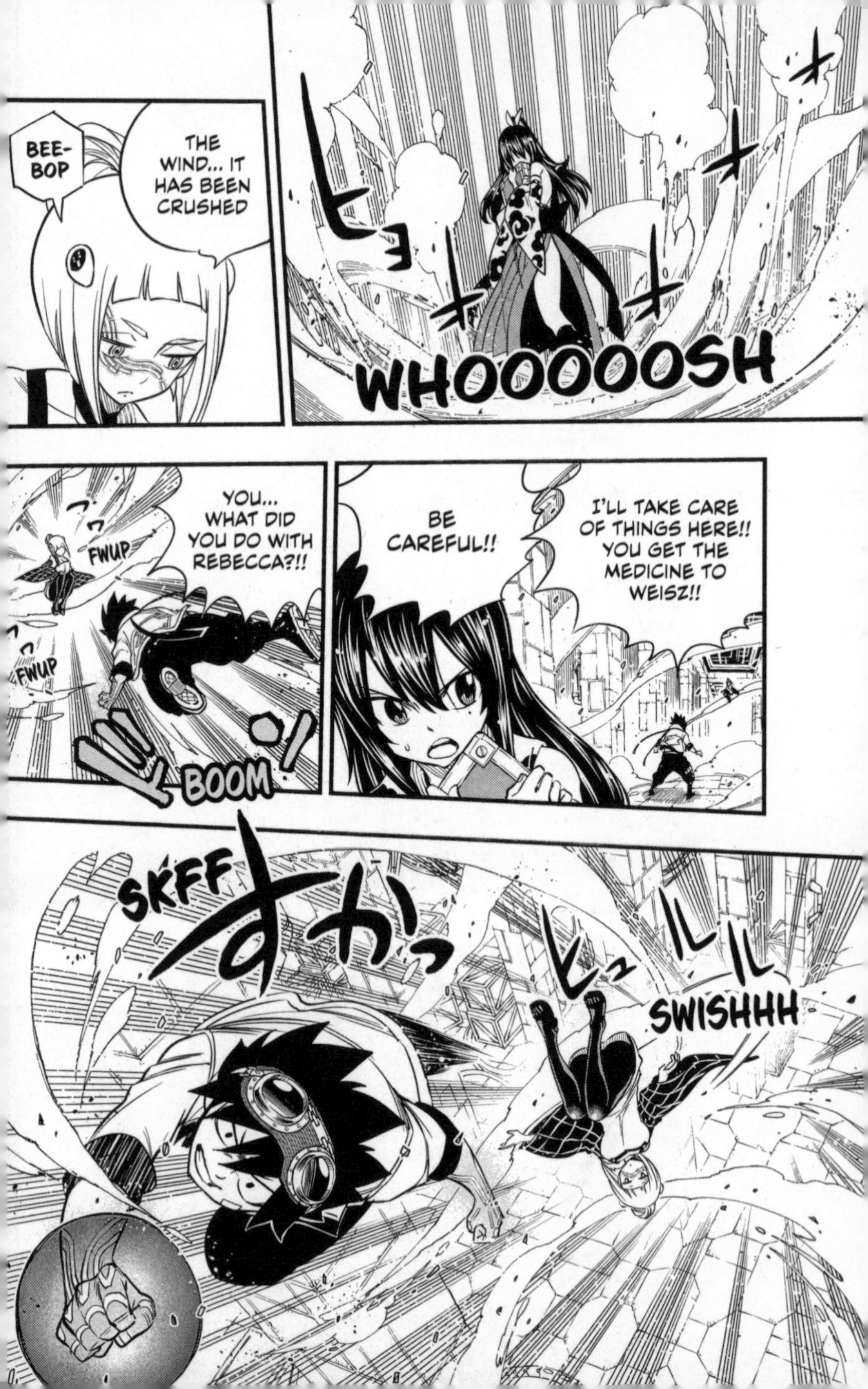
WHOOOOOSH
THE WIND... IT HAS BEEN CRUSHED
BEE-BOP
I'LL TAKE CARE OF THINGS HERE!! YOU GET THE MEDICINE TO WEISZ!!
BE CAREFUL!!
YOU... WHAT DID YOU DO WITH REBECCA?!!
FWUP
FWUP
BOOM
SWISHHH
SKFF

BEE-BOP

SWISHHH

HE IS JUST AS YOU DESCRIBED HIM, BROTHER.

THMP

FWUP

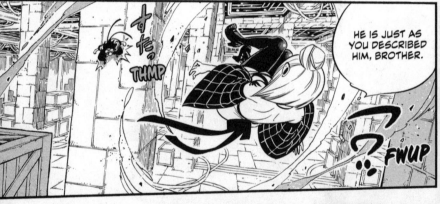

YOU'RE-!!!

!!!

WHOOSH

HUH?

I HAVEN'T SEEN YOU SINCE GUILST.

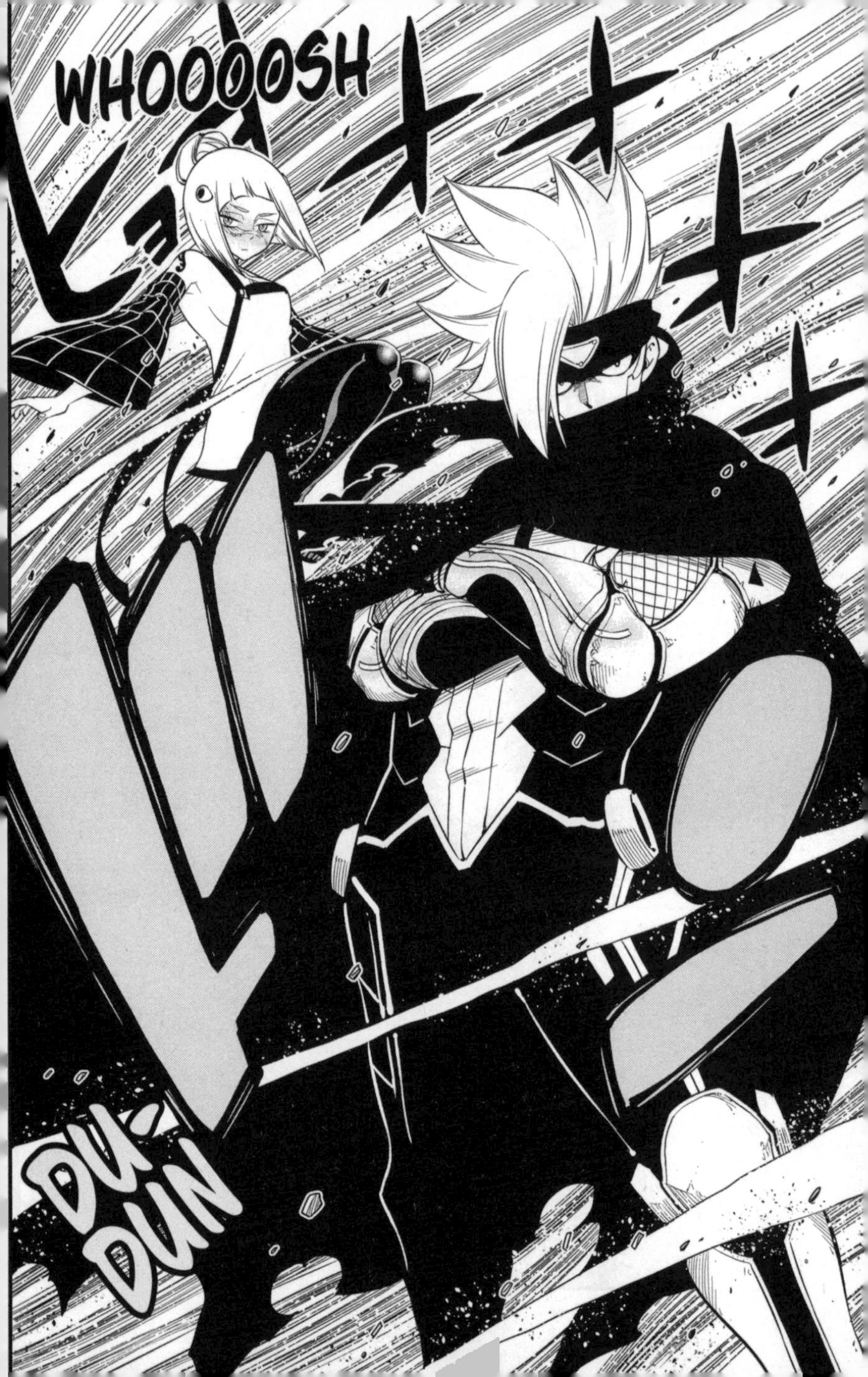
WHOOOOSH
DU-DUN

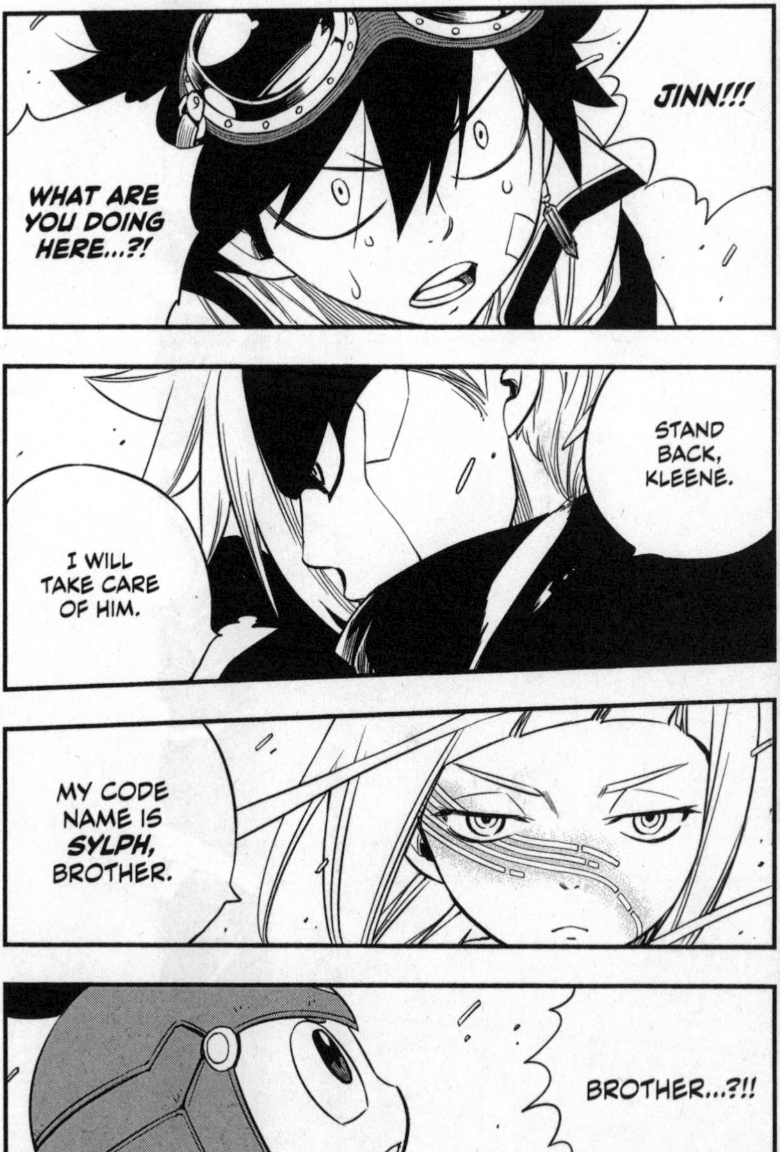
JINN!!!
WHAT ARE YOU DOING HERE...?!
STAND BACK, KLEENE.
I WILL TAKE CARE OF HIM.
MY CODE NAME IS *SYLPH*, BROTHER.
BROTHER...?!!

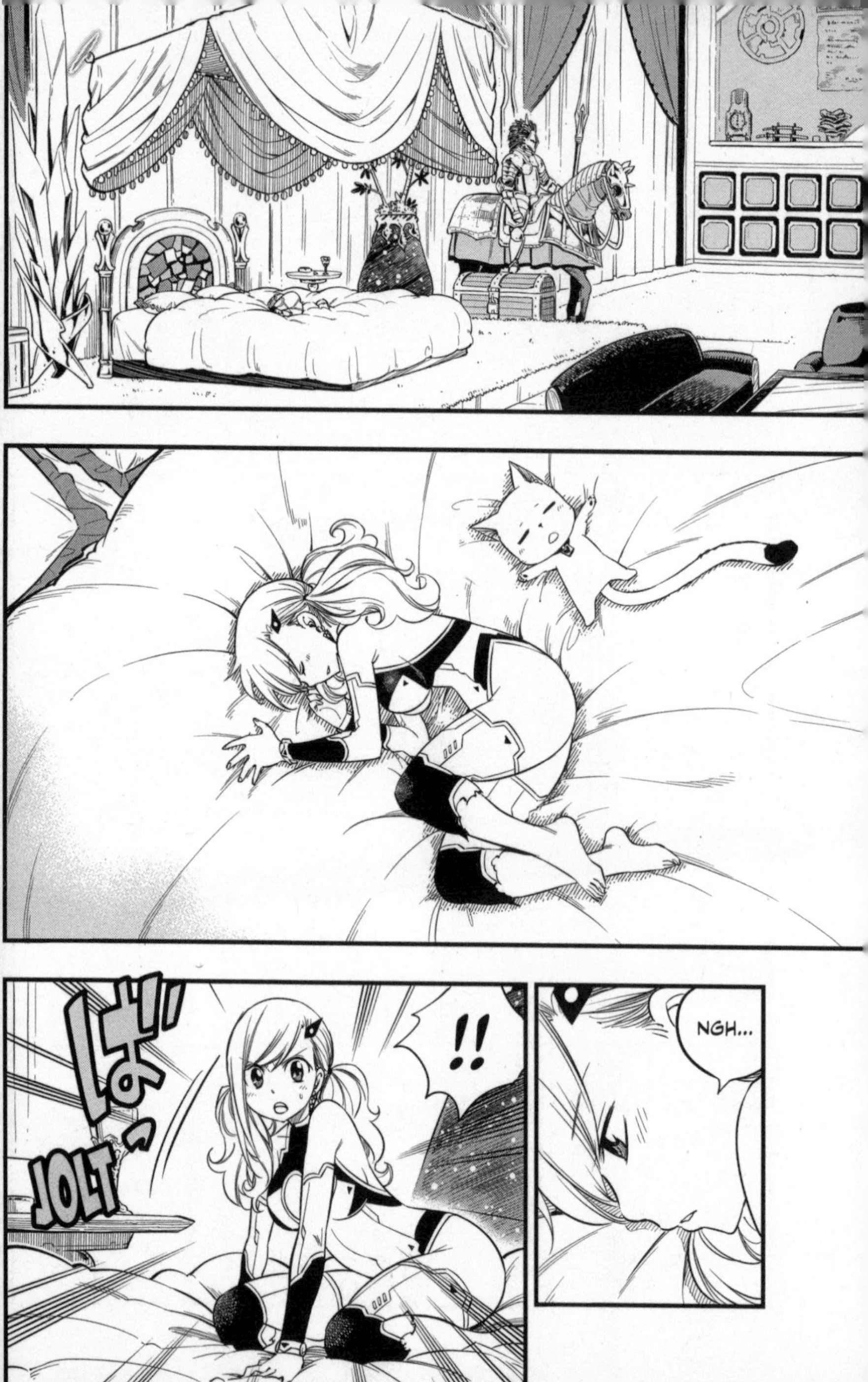
NGH...
!!
ばっ
JOLT

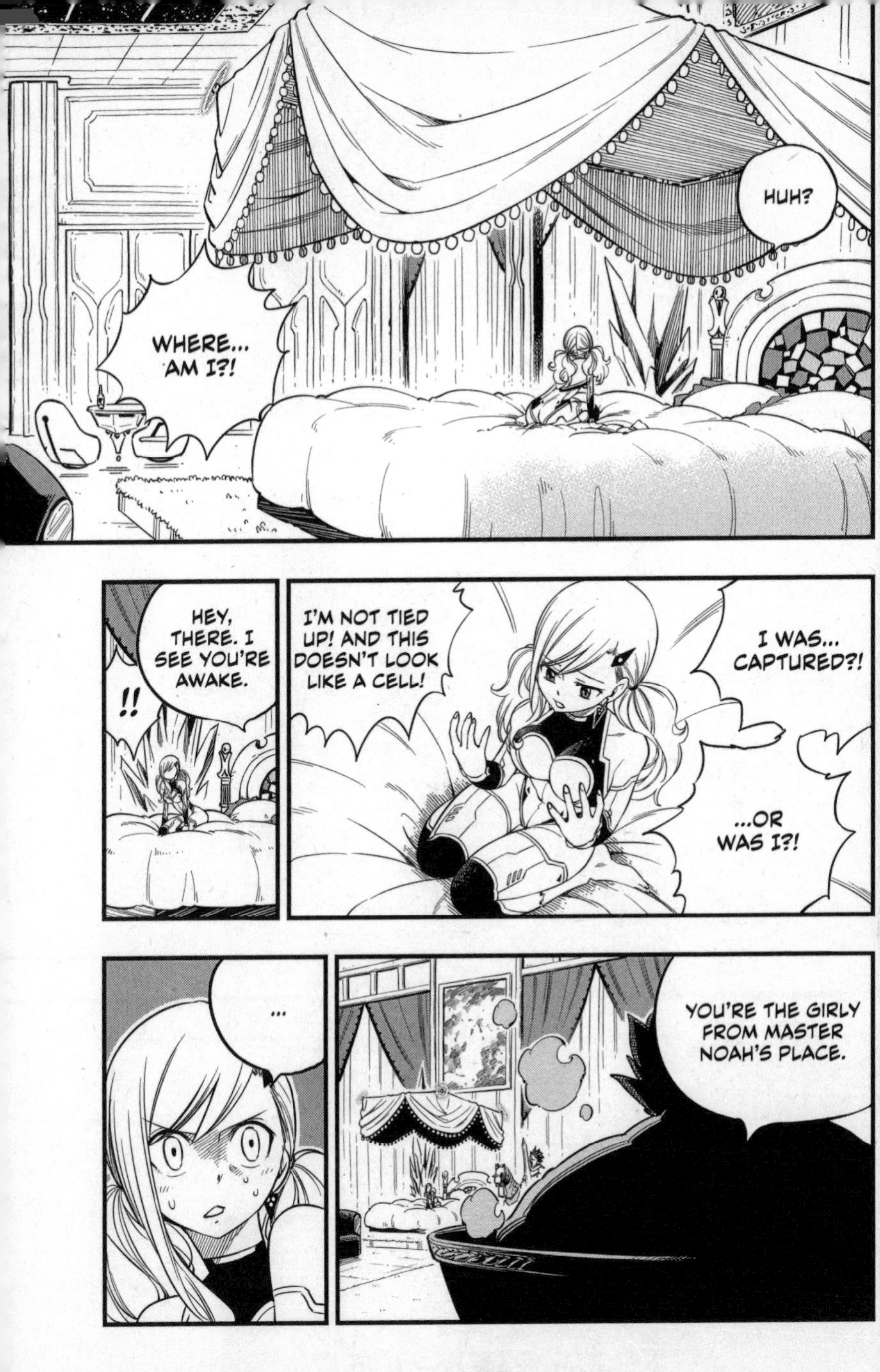
HUH?
WHERE... AM I?!
I WAS... CAPTURED?!
...OR WAS I?!
I'M NOT TIED UP! AND THIS DOESN'T LOOK LIKE A CELL!
HEY, THERE. I SEE YOU'RE AWAKE.
!!
YOU'RE THE GIRLY FROM MASTER NOAH'S PLACE.
...

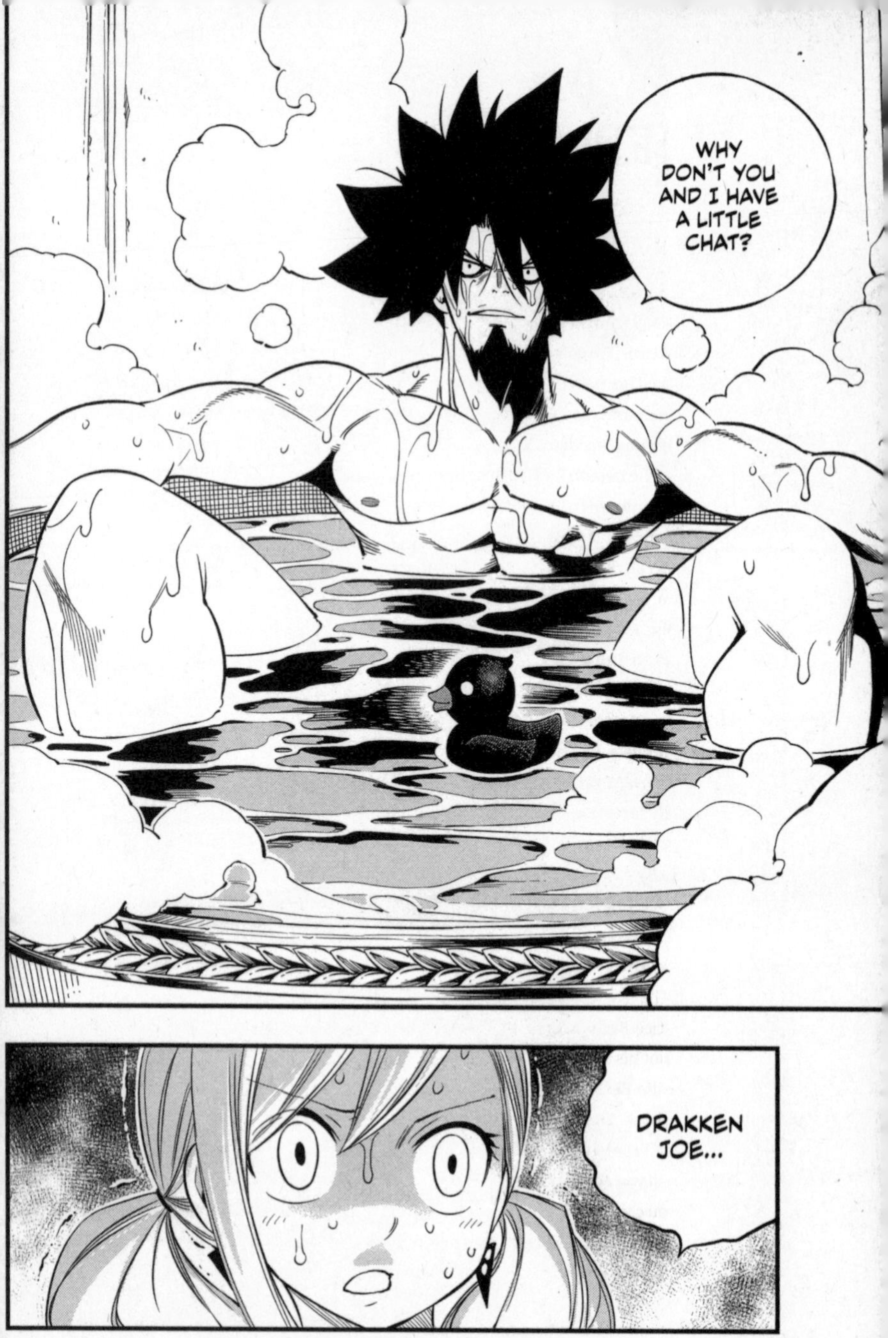
WHY DON'T YOU AND I HAVE A LITTLE CHAT?
DRAKKEN JOE...

TO BE CONTINUED...

AFTERWORD

The Sakura Cosmos arc has finally reached its climax. The story's going to get a little heavy from here on, but I'm sure Mosco will heal our wounded souls.

This time, I'm going to talk about where the characters' names came from.

· Shiki: The main characters in a lot of my works are named after seasons, so this time, partly as a way to put them all together, I went with Shiki, which means "four seasons." Incidentally, my early drafts had him as Ziggy. This would later become the Demon King's name, and it comes from David Bowie's "Ziggy Stardust." That's the album I'm always listening to when creating this story. You might like to try listening to it while you read EDENS ZERO.

· Rebecca: Shiki is always going on about "friends, friends," so I thought of Rebecca, the rock band, whose most famous song is "Friends."

· Weisz: I think I named him "wise," because it means smart, or something.

· Pino: I asked myself, "How can I make EMP sound cute?" and this is what I got.

· Homura: I gave her a name meaning "flame" because I wanted the name to make people think of red and fire.

· Sister Ivry: Just because. I liked the sound of it.

· Valkyrie Yuna: I wanted to make her a darker-skinned character with a clasically Japanese name.

Witch and Hermit have names, too. You'll see those in the main series eventually.

· Mosco: He had his mysterious catchphrase of "Moscoy" first, and the name came from that.

· Elsie: There was a character named Erza in my last series, and I tweaked her name. The "-sie" also sounds like the "sea," because she's a pirate.

· Justice: Because he has a strong sense of justice. Incidentally, this is a code name, not his real name.

· Labilia: Because it sounds kind of like "lovely."

· Drakken: From a retro video game.

· Jinn: From a wind spirit.

I'll tell you about the other characters some other time.

As you can see, my naming sense is pretty haphazard, and is mostly based on what I'm feeling at the time. That's caused me a lot of regret, but I always have so many characters so if I'm honest, it stems from me not wanting to sweat it!

WELCOME TO THE NEXT INSTALLMENT OF...

(YOUSEI-SAN, OSAKA)

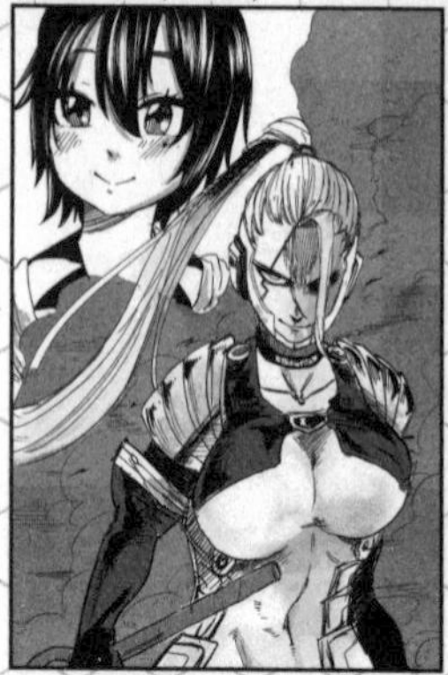

▲ SHE INHERITED HER MENTOR'S SWORD AND LEGACY. MASTER-AND-APPRENTICE AS WELL AS PARENT-AND-CHILD, THEY ARE THE MOST POWERFUL DUO.

(SUZUNE AOKI-SAN, SAITAMA)

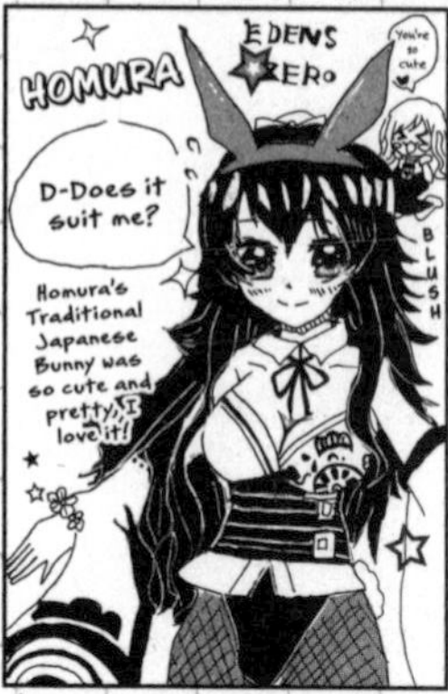
HOMURA
EDENS ZERO
You're so cute
D-Does it suit me?
BLUSH
Homura's Traditional Japanese Bunny was so cute and pretty, I love it!

▲ HOMURA, TOO, IS DELIGHTED TO WEAR WEISZ'S ULTIMATE CREATION, THE YAMATO BUNNY.

(KAGAMI MOCHI-SAN, AICHI)

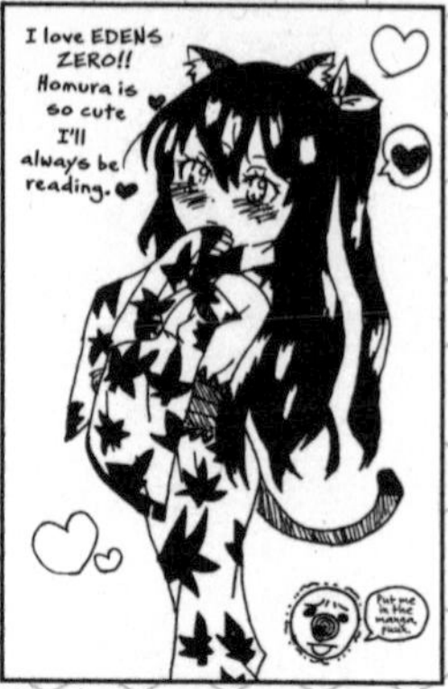
I love EDENS ZERO!! Homura is so cute I'll always be reading.

▲ HOMURA WITH CAT EARS AND TAIL. THE BASHFUL LOOK ON HER FACE IS ADORABLE.

MASHIMA'S ONE-HIT KO

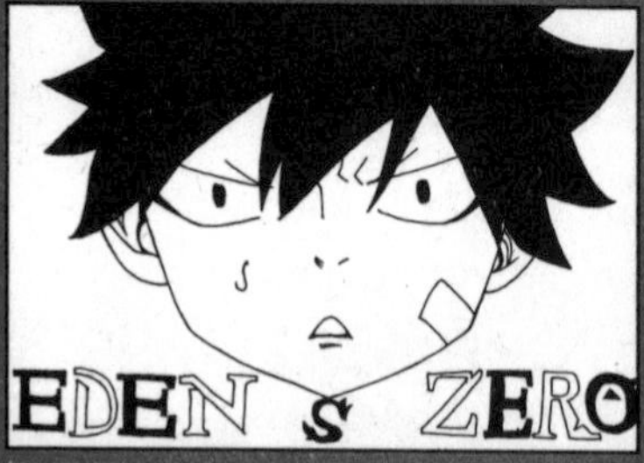
EDEN S ZERO

(KIMINA IGARASHI-SAN, NIIGATA)

▼ I WONDER WHY.... I LOOK AT CONFUSED SHIKI, AND I GET CONFUSED, TOO.

(TART-SAN, YAMANASHI)

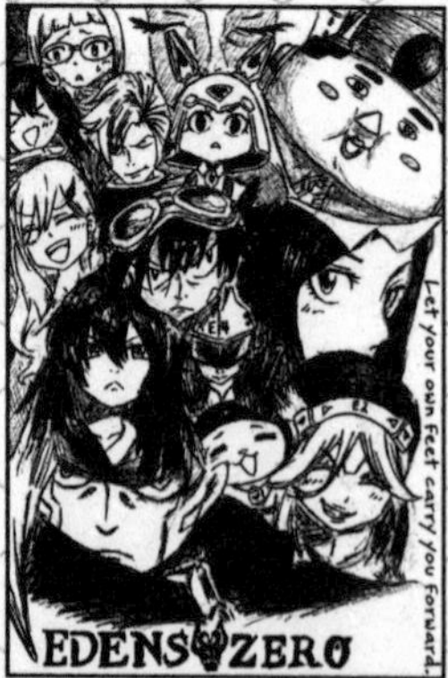
Let your own feet carry you forward.
EDENS ZERO

▼ AN AMAZING MASTERPIECE, CHOCK-FULL OF CHARACTERS! THANK YOU!!!

EDITOR'S NOTE: DRAWING SUBMISSIONS LIMITED TO JAPAN

E2 DRAWING

(FORGETFUL-SAN, FUKUSHIMA)

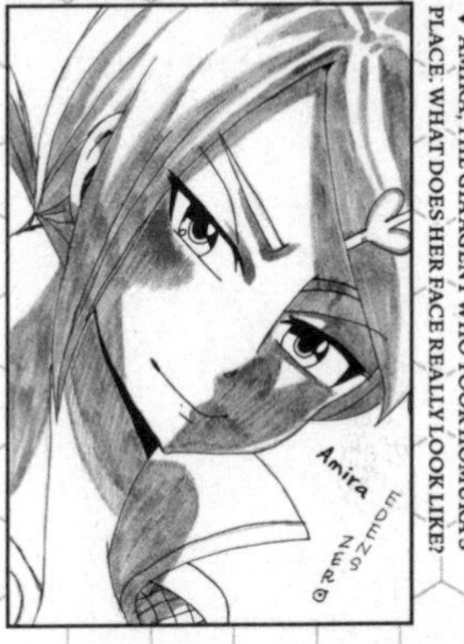
Amira
EDENS ZERO

▼ AMIRA, THE GIA AGENT WHO TOOK HOMURA'S PLACE: WHAT DOES HER FACE REALLY LOOK LIKE?

(RIKAKO NAGAI-SAN, SHIZUOKA)

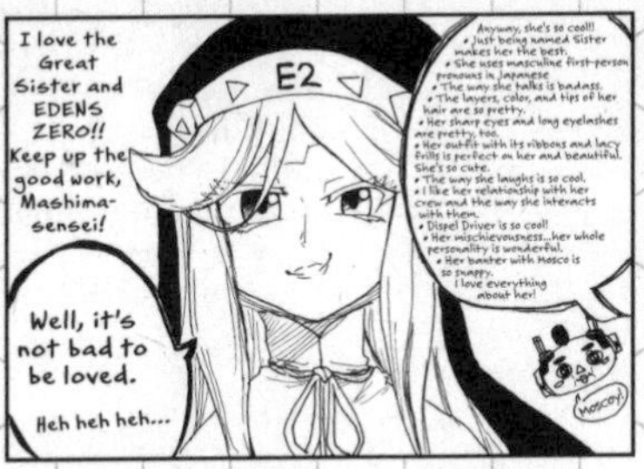
Anyway, she's so cool!!
• Just being named Sister makes her the best.
• She uses masculine first-person pronouns in Japanese
• The way she talks is badass.
• The layers, color, and tips of her hair are so pretty.
• Her sharp eyes and long eyelashes are pretty, too.
• Her outfit with its ribbons and lacy frills is perfect on her and beautiful. She's so cute.
• The way she laughs is so cool.
• I like her relationship with her crew and the way she interacts with them.
• Dispel Driver is so cool!
• Her mischievousness...her whole personality is wonderful.
• Her banter with Mosco is so snappy.
I love everything about her!
Mosco!
E2
I love the Great Sister and EDENS ZERO!! Keep up the good work, Mashima-sensei!
Well, it's not bad to be loved.
Heh heh heh...

▼ SISTER'S FOUL MOUTH IS UNMATCHED. BUT ONCE YOU GET USED TO IT, DOES IT INFECT YOU...?!

(PUPERIPE-SAN, FUKUOKA)

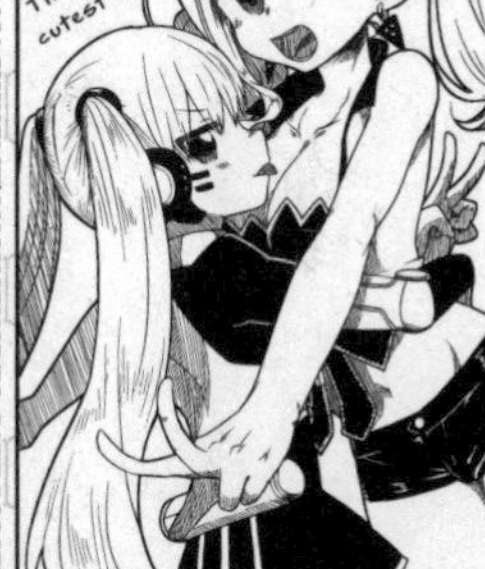
EDENS ZERO
They're the cutest duo!!

▼ HUMAN? MACHINE? IT'S NONSENSE TO CATEGORIZE PEOPLE THAT WAY. IF THEIR HEARTS ARE CONNECTED, THEY'RE THE BEST OF FRIENDS!

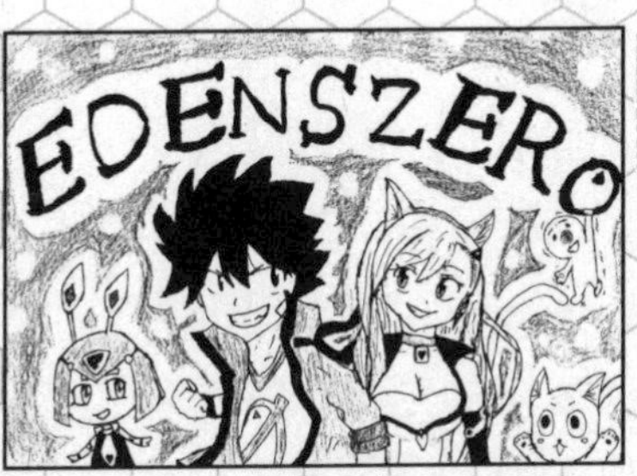
EDENSZERO

▼ SHIKI AND REBECCA ARE GETTING MORE IN SYNC. I LIKE THE LOOKS IN THEIR EYES.

(YŌKO ŌEDA-SAN, FUKUSHIMA)

(HONAYA-SAN, AICHI)

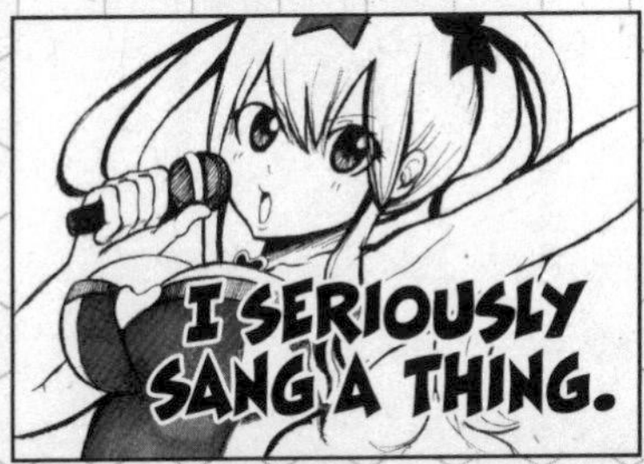
I SERIOUSLY SANG A THING.

▼ ANIME WILL SAVE THE UNIVERSE BUT WILL HER SINGING VOICE RULE THE GALAXY? ♪

The adorable new odd-couple cat comedy manga from the creator of the beloved *Chi's Sweet Home*, in full color!

Sue & Tai-chan

Konami Kanata

Sue is an aging housecat who's looking forward to living out her life in peace... but her plans change when the mischievous black tomcat Tai-chan enters the picture! Hey! Sue never signed up to be a catsitter! *Sue & Tai-chan* is the latest from the reigning meow-narch of cute kitty comics, Konami Kanata.

SAINT ☆ YOUNG MEN

A LONG AWAITED ARRIVAL IN PREMIUM 2-IN-1 HARDCOVER

After centuries of hard work, Jesus and Buddha take a break from their heavenly duties to relax among the people of Japan, and their adventures in this lighthearted buddy comedy are sure to bring mirth and merriment to all!

"Brilliant…the physical comedy and facial expressions will make you literally LOL."
—Sam Humphries (host of *DC Daily*; writer, *Green Lanterns*, *Legendary Star-Lord*)

A Kodansha Comics Trade Paperback Original
EDENS ZERO 9 copyright © 2020 Hiro Mashima
English translation copyright © 2020 Hiro Mashima

All rights reserved.

Published in the United States by Kodansha Comics, an imprint of Kodansha USA Publishing, LLC, New York.

Publication rights for this English edition arranged through Kodansha Ltd., Tokyo.

First published in Japan in 2020 by Kodansha Ltd., Tokyo.

ISBN 978-1-63236-983-3

Original cover design by Narumi Miura (G x complex).

Printed in the United States of America.

www.kodanshacomics.com

9 8 7 6 5 4 3 2 1
Translation: Alethea Nibley & Athena Nibley
Lettering: AndWorld Design
Editing: Haruko Hashimoto
Kodansha Comics edition cover design by Phil Balsman

Publisher: Kiichiro Sugawara

Director of publishing services: Ben Applegate
Associate director of operations: Stephen Pakula
Publishing services managing editor: Noelle Webster
Assistant production manager: Emi Lotto, Angela Zurlo